FROMMER'S
EasyGuide

TO   W9-AFU-476

Santa Fe, Taos & Albuquerque

By
Don and Barbara Laine

Easy Guides are   ✦ Quick To Read   ✦ Light To Carry
✦ For Expert Advice   ✦ In All Price Ranges

FrommerMedia LLC

Published by
FROMMER MEDIA LLC

Copyright © 2016 by Frommer Media LLC. All rights reserved. No part of this publication may be repro-
duced, stored in a retrieval system, or transmitted in any form or by any means, electronic, mechanical,
photocopying, recording, scanning or otherwise, except as permitted under Sections 107 or 108 of the
1976 United States Copyright Act, without the prior written permission of the Publisher. Requests to the
Publisher for permission should be addressed to customer_service@FrommerMedia.com.

Frommer's is a registered trademark of Arthur Frommer. Frommer Media LLC is not associated with any
product or vendor mentioned in this book.

ISBN 978-1-62887-244-6 (paper), 978-1-62887-245-3 (e-book)

Editorial Director: Pauline Frommer
Development Editor: Holly Hughes
Production Editor: Lynn Northrup
Cartographer: Roberta Stockwell
Indexer: Maro Riofrancos

For information on our other products or services, see www.frommers.com.

Frommer Media LLC also publishes its books in a variety of electronic formats. Some content that
appears in print may not be available in electronic formats.

Manufactured in the United States of America

5 4 3 2 1

FROMMER'S STAR RATINGS SYSTEM

Every hotel, restaurant, and attraction listed in this guide has been ranked for quality and value. Here's
what the stars mean:

★ Recommended
★★ Highly Recommended
★★★ A must! Don't miss!

AN IMPORTANT NOTE

The world is a dynamic place. Hotels change ownership, restaurants hike their prices, museums
alter their opening hours, and buses and trains change their routings. And all of this can occur
in the several months after our authors have visited, inspected, and written about these hotels,
restaurants, museums and transportation services. Though we have made valiant efforts to keep
all our information fresh and up-to-date, some few changes can inevitably occur in the periods
before a revised edition of this guidebook is published. So please bear with us if a tiny number
of the details in this book have changed. Please also note that we have no responsibility or liabil-
ity for any inaccuracy or errors or omissions, or for inconvenience, loss, damage, or expenses suf-
fered by anyone as a result of assertions in this guide.

CONTENTS

ABOUT THE AUTHORS

Residents of northern New Mexico for more than 40 years, **Don and Barbara Laine** have traveled extensively throughout New Mexico, the Rocky Mountains, and the Southwest, exploring the mountains, deserts, cities, and towns in search of unique outdoor adventures, hidden historic gems, and the perfect green chile cheeseburger. The Laines have authored or contributed to a number of Frommer's travel guides, including *Frommer's EasyGuide to National Parks of the American West*, and have also written *Little-Known Southwest, New Mexico & Arizona State Parks*, and *Best Short Hikes in Arizona* for The Mountaineers Books.

ABOUT THE FROMMER'S TRAVEL GUIDES

For most of the past 50 years, Frommer's has been the leading series of travel guides in North America, accounting for as many as 24% of all guidebooks sold. I think I know why.

Though we hope our books are entertaining, we nevertheless deal with travel in a serious fashion. Our guidebooks have never looked on such journeys as a mere recreation, but as a far more important human function, a time of learning and introspection, an essential part of a civilized life. We stress the culture, lifestyle, history, and beliefs of the destinations we cover, and urge our readers to seek out people and new ideas as the chief rewards of travel.

We have never shied from controversy. We have, from the beginning, encouraged our authors to be intensely judgmental, critical—both pro and con—in their comments, and wholly independent. Our only clients are our readers, and we have triggered the ire of count- less prominent sorts, from a tourist newspaper we called "practically worthless" (it unsuc- cessfully sued us) to the many rip-offs we've condemned.

And because we believe that travel should be available to everyone regardless of their incomes, we have always been cost-conscious at every level of expenditure. Though we have broadened our recommendations beyond the budget category, we insist that every lodging we include be sensibly priced. We use every form of media to assist our readers, and are particularly proud of our feisty daily website, the award-winning Frommers.com.

I have high hopes for the future of Frommer's. May these guidebooks, in all the years ahead, continue to reflect the joy of travel and the freedom that travel represents. May they always pursue a cost-conscious path, so that people of all incomes can enjoy the rewards of travel. And may they create, for both the traveler and the persons among whom we travel, a community of friends, where all human beings live in harmony and peace.

Arthur Frommer

THE BEST OF NORTHERN NEW MEXICO

Northern New Mexico is a land of contrasts and contradictions, and extremes in climate and cultures. One day you're hiking among prickly pear cactus and sagebrush, hoping you brought enough drinking water to get you back to the trail head. Next day you're speeding down a mountainside on skis as the falling snow fills the tracks you leave behind. Here you'll find American Indians living much like their ancestors did hundreds of years ago, practically alongside the nuclear scientists who design the weapons of tomorrow and try to find solutions for the problems of today. There are refined chamber music concerts, wild Texas two-steppin' bars, and practically everything in between.

As you explore northern New Mexico, you'll see the magical beauty in both land and spirit that has captured the hearts of so many artists, writers, and thinkers. And we hope you'll also experience some of that magic yourself, and take a little bit of it back home when you leave.

THE best NORTHERN NEW MEXICO EXPERIENCES

- **Taos Pueblo,** Veterans Highway, Taos Pueblo (www.taospueblo. com; © **575/758-1028**): If you see only one American Indian site in your northern New Mexico visit, this should be it. This awe-inspiring structure, where 200 residents still live much as their ancestors did more than 700 years ago, is bold and imposing, with mud-built rooms poetically stacked to echo the shape of Taos Mountain behind them. You can visit resident artists' studios, munch on bread baked in a *horno* (a beehive-shaped oven),

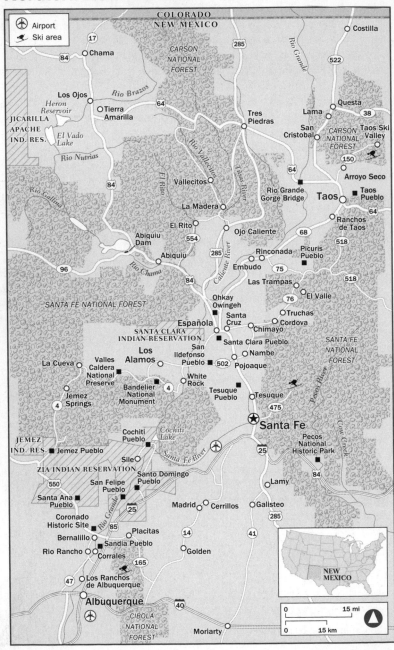

and wander past the fascinating ruins of the old church and cemetery. See p. 146.

o **High Road to Taos:** This spectacular 80-mile route into the mountains between Santa Fe and Taos takes you through red-painted deserts, villages bordered by apple and peach orchards, and the foothills of 13,000-foot peaks. You can stop in Cordova, known for its woodcarvers, or Chimayo, known for its weavers—even rub some "healing dust" between your fingers at the fabled **Santuario de Chimayo.** See p. 117.

o **Santa Fe Opera:** One of the finest opera companies in the United States has called Santa Fe home for more than a half-century. Performances are held during the summer months in a hilltop, open-air (but mostly under-roof) amphitheater. See p. 101.

o **Albuquerque International Balloon Fiesta:** The desert skies fill with color as the world's largest balloon rally assembles some 600 hot-air balloons. Highlights are the mass ascension at sunrise and the special shapes rodeo, in which balloons in all sorts of whimsical forms, from liquor bottles to cows, rise into the sky. See p. 209.

o **Northern New Mexican Enchiladas:** There are few things more New Mexican than the enchilada. Order red or green chiles, or "Christmas" chiles (half red, half green), covered with rich sauces seasoned with garlic and oregano. New Mexican cuisine doesn't overdo on the cheese and sour cream, so the flavors of the chiles, corn, and meats can be savored. See p. 30.

THE best MUSEUMS

o **Georgia O'Keeffe Museum:** Renowned modernist artist Georgia O'Keeffe fell in love with the deserts of the Southwest in the 1930s and moved to the isolated northern New Mexico community of Abiquiu in 1949, which inspired her best-known works—striking paintings of flowers, animal skulls, and stark landscapes. See p. 72.

o **Museum of International Folk Art:** Santa Fe's perpetually expanding collection of folk art is the largest in the world, with thousands of objects from more than 100 countries. You'll find an amazing array of imaginative works, ranging from Hispanic folk art *santos* (carved saints) to Indonesian textiles and African sculptures. See p. 76.

o **Harwood Museum of Art:** If you're going to see just one art museum in northern New Mexico, make it this small but stunning showcase for the art that made Taos famous. See p. 143.

o **Millicent Rogers Museum:** This Taos museum features among the best collections anywhere of turquoise and silver American Indian jewelry, Navajo rugs, Pueblo pottery, and other southwestern arts and crafts, born out of the personal collection of Standard Oil heiress Millicent Rogers. See p. 145.

o **New Mexico Museum of Natural History and Science:** Here you'll stroll through 12 billion years of natural history, from the very beginnings to the age of dinosaurs and beyond, with interactive exhibits, a planetarium, and a huge-screen theater. This Albuquerque science museum is actually fun, and (we'll say this quietly so the kids don't hear) educational. See p. 205.

o **Unser Racing Museum:** You don't have to be a fan of auto racing to appreciate this Albuquerque museum dedicated to the Unsers, New Mexico's first family of auto racing. There are the racecars that won the Indy 500, some fascinating cars and motorcycles from the early days of motorized racing, and a fun simulator that conveys what it's like to race in an Indianapolis 500. See p. 199.

THE best SPLURGE HOTELS

o **Inn of the Five Graces:** Just a few blocks from Santa Fe Plaza, this Relais & Chateaux inn spoils guests unmercifully with elaborately decorated suites with *kilim* rugs and ornately carved beds and floral-decked courtyards. The name comes from the Eastern concept of the five senses: sight, sound, touch, smell, and taste, all of which are stimulated here. See p. 52.

o **Rosewood Inn of the Anasazi:** Just steps from the Santa Fe Plaza, this posh sandstone hotel offers a taste of ancestral Puebloan architecture, with all the historic charm but none of the hardships these ancient peoples endured, thanks to excellent amenities and stellar service. See p. 53.

o **El Monte Sagrado:** With guest rooms, suites, and casitas set around a grassy "Sacred Circle," this eco-resort in Taos is the quintessence of luxury. Every detail, from the waterfalls and chemical-free pool and hot tubs to the authentic theme decor in the rooms, has been created with conscious care. See p. 124.

o **La Fonda:** Settle into old Santa Fe at this historic hotel that combines all the modern conveniences you expect in a splurge hotel with enough historic ambience to knock your socks off. Head to the Bell Tower Bar for a drink with a spectacular sunset view. See p. 52.

THE best MODERATELY PRICED HOTELS

o **El Rey Inn:** For historic charm and relatively reasonable rates (for Santa Fe), head to El Rey Inn. Built in the 1930s and added on to and upgraded over the years, the inn offers a variety of room types, all different but nicely appointed, with a Route 66 ambience and nicely landscaped grounds. See p. 54.

o **Santa Fe Motel and Inn:** Rooms at this inn, located six blocks from the Santa Fe Plaza, smartly combine the ambience of the Southwest—bold colors and some handmade furniture—with a standard motel price tag. See p. 53.

- **Sagebrush Inn & Suites:** This sprawling property about 3 miles south of Taos can please almost any taste, from old adobe rooms with kiva fireplaces to modern executive suites with all the 21st-century amenities. Set back from the highway with lovely landscaped grounds, Sagebrush Inn is a pleasant oasis to escape to at the end of a busy sightseeing day. The huge lobby bar is also a hotspot for country music and dancing. See p. 127.

- **Old Taos Guesthouse:** Surrounded by acres of countryside, this hacienda-style B&B provides a lovely rural stay at one of the best moderately priced accommodations in Taos. All rooms have private entrances, some have fireplaces, and both the views and the breakfasts are great. See p. 131.

- **Hotel Albuquerque at Old Town:** Just steps from Albuquerque's Old Town, this reasonably priced hotel has artfully decorated rooms with southwestern decor, good views of the Sandia Mountains, and excellent service. See p. 180.

THE best SPECIAL OCCASION RESTAURANTS

- **Bouche French Bistro:** Why fly to Paris to celebrate that special occasion when you could find the same atmosphere (and delectable cuisine) in this 75-year old nondescript building off the beaten path in Santa Fe? Chef Charles Dale prepares a variety of French specialties, ranging from coq au vin to pumpkin ravioli with duck confit—and of course, steak au poivre with pommes frites. See p. 60.

- **The Bull Ring:** Steak lovers unite—this is your restaurant. For years a hangout for politicos and other New Mexico bigwigs when it was located next to Santa Fe's state Capital Building, in 1995 it moved to its present location with a promise of serving the best beef available. And it has lived up to that promise. You can't go wrong with any of the beef, from the half-pound Bull Burger to the 14-ounce New York strip; other options include grilled salmon and lamb chops. Portions are generous and service is top-notch. See p. 62.

- **The Compound:** This Santa Fe classic serves daring contemporary American food, combining traditional regional ingredients with Mediterranean influences. You'll likely enjoy the organic Scottish salmon or the braised lamb shank. Even lunch entrees are a step above, such as the house-cured pastrami sandwich. See p. 62.

- **Shohko Café:** Who in the world would come to a place 1,000 miles from the nearest ocean to eat raw fish in a former brothel? Lots of people, and if you're a fan of sushi, you should, too. Santa Fe's Shohko Café isn't just the top sushi restaurant in northern New Mexico, it's as good as anything in the coastal cities. Combine East and West with the shrimp-stuffed green chile tempura. See p. 64.

o **De La Tierra:** Great food in wonderful Taos surroundings—what more could you ask for? Seasonal and local organic ingredients are used when available, and the dinner entrees, such as chipotle barbecued pork ribs, filet mignon, and grilled trout tacos, are truly special. See p. 135.

o **Doc Martin's:** Historic ambience, an inviting patio away from the traffic, and consistently excellent food are what make Doc Martin's a long-time favorite of Taos locals. The menu is fairly short, specializing in American and New Mexican dishes, and there's a good weekend brunch. We recommend the pan-seared trout and chile relleno, and what we consider the best green chile cheeseburger in New Mexico. See p. 135.

THE best EVERYDAY RESTAURANTS

o **Plaza Café Southside:** Hidden off busy Cerrillos Road next to a movie theater, this sister restaurant to Santa Fe's downtown Plaza Cafe is worth seeking out. There's a 1950's diner look, with some northern New Mexico touches, and the menu features basic American and New Mexican offerings. The chile is hot, breakfasts are excellent, and baked goods are prepared in-house. See p. 70.

o **The Shed:** A Santa Fe luncheon institution since 1953, The Shed occupies several rooms in a rambling hacienda built in 1692. It specializes in genuine northern New Mexico dishes, which are sometimes a bit "hot" (that's New Mexico-speak for tongue-roasting spicy). Favorites include the enchiladas and the green chile stew. See p. 67.

o **Orlando's New Mexican Café:** This family-run restaurant a few miles north of Taos is where locals bring out-of-town visitors to experience real northern New Mexico cuisine. Nothing flashy, just basic dishes done well, from carne adovada to enchiladas to burritos. See p. 142.

o **Chama River Brewing Company:** This busy Albuquerque brewpub does a good job with all the usual pub favorites—fish and chips, burgers—but excels at prime rib and blackened salmon, as well as some interesting specialties such as red chile–braised duck legs and goat cheese–stuffed zucchini. See p. 188.

o **Mario's Pizzeria & Ristorante:** Started (and still owned by) a Sicilian family that emigrated to America more than 50 years ago, this Italian favorite was transplanted to Albuquerque from Queens, New York, in 1972. The lasagna and pizza are especially good. See p. 191.

o **Rex's Hamburgers:** Okay, it's just a fast-food hamburger joint, but this Albuquerque spot is a really, really good fast-food hamburger joint. The burgers are juicy and tasty, there are fish and steak sandwiches or full dinners, and the menu also includes burritos and tacos. The malts alone are worth the trip. See p. 192.

THE best THINGS TO DO FOR FREE

○ **The Galleries Along Canyon Road:** Originally a Pueblo Indian route over the mountains and later an artists' community, Santa Fe's Canyon Road is now gallery central—the arts capital of the Southwest. The narrow one-way street is lined with more than 100 galleries, in addition to restaurants and private residences, where artwork ranges from the beautiful to the bizarre, from offbeat to world-class. See p. 95.

○ **Pueblo Dances:** These Indian dances, related to the changing cycles of the earth, offer a unique chance to see how an indigenous culture worships and celebrates. Throughout the year, the Pueblo people participate in ceremonies ranging from harvest and deer dances to those commemorating the feast days of their particular saints—all in the mystical light of the northern New Mexico sun. See p. 196.

○ **Hiking Rio Grande Gorge:** You'll first see it as you come over a rise heading toward Taos, a colossal slice in the earth formed 130 million years ago. Drive about 35 miles north of Taos, near the village of Cerro, to the Wild Rivers Recreation Area, where you can hike down through millions of years of geologic history to dip your toes in the fabled *rio*. See p. 156.

○ **Old Town:** Albuquerque's commercial center until about 1880, Old Town still gives a remarkable sense of what life was once like in a southwestern village. Meander down crooked streets and narrow alleys, rest in the cottonwood-shaded plaza, and browse the jewelry, pottery, and weavings sold by American Indians under a portal on the plaza. See p. 197.

THE best OUTDOOR ACTIVITIES

○ **Taos Ski Valley:** World-renowned for its challenging runs and spectacular powder snow, Taos Ski Valley has long been a pilgrimage site for extreme skiers. Newer bowls now accommodate intermediate and beginning skiers; a massive multiyear upgrading of the entire ski area is underway. See p. 152.

○ **Sandia Peak Tramway:** The world's longest tramway ferries passengers 2¾ miles, from Albuquerque's city limits to the summit of the 10,378-foot Sandia Peak. On the way, you may see rare Rocky Mountain bighorn sheep and circling birds of prey. Go in the evening to watch the sun set, and then enjoy the glimmering city lights on your way down. See p. 198.

○ **Bandelier National Monument:** These ruins provide a spectacular peek into the lives of the ancestral Puebloan culture, which reached its peak in this area around A.D. 1100. Less than 15 miles south of Los Alamos, the ruins spread across a peaceful canyon populated by deer and rabbits. Make your way through the canyon to the most dramatic site, a kiva and dwelling in a cave 140 feet above the canyon floor. See p. 114.

o **White-Water Rafting on the Rio Grande:** In spring and early summer, the region's most notorious white-water trip, the Taos Box, takes rafters on an 18-mile jaunt through the Rio Grande Gorge. Less extreme types can enjoy a trip down the river from Pilar and still get plenty wet. See p. 157.

o **Llama Trekking:** Also in the Taos area, llama outfitters take hikers on unique day or multiday trips: You get to enjoy the scenery while the stout and docile creatures do the heavy lifting. The trips come with gourmet food. See p. 157.

o **Hot-Air Ballooning:** One of the biggest treats about being in Albuquerque or Taos is waking each day and seeing colorful globes floating serenely on the horizon. The experience of riding in one, however, is indescribable. You're literally floating, being carried along by nothing but the wind. Try it! See p. 208 or 154.

o **Bosque del Apache National Wildlife Refuge:** About 80 miles south of Albuquerque lies one of the nation's finest wildlife refuges. In early December, the refuge may harbor as many as 45,000 snow geese, 60,000 ducks of various species, and close to 20,000 sandhill cranes. Seeing them "fly out" to the fields in search of food in the morning or "fly in" to the lakes in the evening is a life-altering experience. See p. 221.

THE best THINGS TO DO WITH KIDS

o **The Museum of International Folk Art:** Toys, toys, and more toys fill the Girard Wing of this world-class museum in Santa Fe. It's the center of a collection of over 100,000 dolls, masks, dioramas, animals, and other objects gathered from over 100 countries. There's a play area and hands-on craft section for itchy fingers, as well as a gift shop that's almost over-whelming in its colorful selection. You may have to drag the kids out. See p. 76.

o **The Santa Fe Children's Museum:** Interactive exhibits and hands-on activities here will keep the kids happy and busy. Older kids will love the 16-foot climbing wall that, outfitted with helmets and harnesses, they can scale, and a 1-acre southwestern horticulture garden, complete with animals, wetlands, and a greenhouse. See p. 86.

o **Taos Ski Valley:** New Mexico's best and most famous ski area is known primarily for its wonderful expert terrain, but Taos Ski Valley is also a good family destination. It welcomes snowboarders and has an excellent children's ski school. Taos' 18,000-square-foot children's center offers many services, from children's equipment rental to babysitting. See p. 152.

o **Riding the Cumbres & Toltec Scenic Railroad:** Step back to the days of the Wild West and get some cinders in your hair aboard this steam-powered train, a handy day trip from Santa Fe. Kids will have fun watching as the train chugs up the mountains, and especially enjoy the open gondola car. See p. 172.

○ **The Anderson-Abruzzo Albuquerque International Balloon Museum:** Fun and fascinating, entertaining and educational, this Albuquerque museum is a favorite of kids because of its many hands-on children's activities, multimedia technology, and the balloon flight simulator. See p. 196.

○ **Explora:** Part science center, part children's museum, part Grandma's attic and Grandpa's garage, and part laboratory, Albuquerque's Explora is a favorite with children because it provides real hands-on experiences with small spaces of mostly tabletop exhibits with hand-sized parts made for manipulating. Younger children love the arts and crafts workshop, where they can make something to take home. See p. 205.

○ **BioPark Zoo:** Hey, kids, want to see a dragon? Along with about 1,000 other animals, this zoo has two dragons—Sunny, a 10-foot-long, 155-pound Komodo dragon, and his girlfriend Nancy. There are also polar bears, giraffes, sea lions (with underwater viewing), big cats, elephants, and apes. And there's a kid-size train to haul everyone around the grounds. See p. 200.

THE best OFFBEAT EXPERIENCES

○ **Watching Zozobra Burn:** Part of the annual early-September Las Fiestas de Santa Fe, this ritual draws crowds to the core of the city to cheer as "Old Man Gloom," a giant marionette, moans and struggles as he burns. The Fiestas also include Masses, parades, dances, food, and arts. See p. 231.

○ **Theater Grottesco:** This Santa Fe theater troupe likes to shock, confuse, confound, and tickle its audience's funny bones. Their original works combine adept movement with sound, story, and, well . . . brilliance. See p. 102.

○ **D. H. Lawrence Ranch:** On a remote ranch north of Taos, this memorial—really more of a shrine—offers a look into the oddly touching devotion of his widow for this controversial author, who lived and wrote in the area in the early 1920s. See p. 147.

○ **American International Rattlesnake Museum:** A natural fit for a desert capital like Albuquerque, this small museum displays living specimens of common, uncommon, and very rare rattlesnakes of North, Central, and South America, in naturally landscaped habitats. Some 30 species are included, along with oddities such as albino and patternless rattlesnakes. See p. 206.

NORTHERN NEW MEXICO IN DEPTH

Although Santa Fe has claimed the title of "The City Different," all of northern New Mexico really qualifies as being different from mainstream America. When you wake up in Santa Fe, Taos, or even Albuquerque (probably the closest New Mexico gets to a "normal" community), you know you're not in Chicago, or Long Island, or even Los Angeles. The only similar example we can think of is the French Quarter of New Orleans, but even that's nothing like New Mexico.

In many ways, visiting northern New Mexico is like visiting a foreign country. The landscape is rugged and unforgiving, the weather unpredictable, and the customs, at least to some, are strange. Maybe that's why so many people love it.

From the moment you set foot in this 121,666-square-mile state, you're met with wildly varied terrain, temperature, and temperament. On a single day, you might experience temperatures from 25° to 75°F (-4° to 24°C). From the vast heat and dryness of White Sands in the summer to the subzero, snow-encrusted Wheeler Peak in the winter, New Mexico's beauty is carved by extremes.

Culturally, this is also the case. Pueblo, Navajo, and Apache tribes occupy much of the state's lands, many of them still speaking their native languages and observing the traditions of their people. Some even live without running water and electricity. Meanwhile, the local Hispanics tend to remain deeply linked to their Spanish roots, practicing a devout Catholicism and speaking a centuries-old Spanish dialect; some still live by subsistence farming in tiny mountain villages.

New Mexico has its very own sense of time and its own social mores. People rarely arrive on time for appointments, and businesses don't always hold to their posted hours. In most cases, people wear whatever they want here: You'll see men dressed for formal occasions in a buttoned collar with a bolo tie and neatly pressed jeans, and women in cowboy boots and broomstick skirts.

And yes, ladies, it's perfectly acceptable here to wear pearls with your blue jeans.

All this leads to a certain lost-and-not-caring-to-be-found spell that the place casts on visitors. We find ourselves standing amid the dust or sparkling light, within the extreme heat or cold, not sure whether to speak Spanish or English. That's when we let go completely of mainstream society's dictates. We slip into a kayak and let the river take us, or hike a peak and look at the world from a new perspective. Or we climb into a car and drive past ancient ruins, past ghost mining towns, under hot-air balloons, and around hand-smoothed adobe *santuarios*—all on the road to nowhere, New Mexico's best destination. At some point in your travels, you'll likely find yourself on this road, and you'll realize that there's no destination so fine.

NEW MEXICO TODAY

New Mexico is a cultural tapestry with many strands. First came the ancestral Puebloans (also called the Anasazi), an enigmatic people who inhabited this area from A.D. 1100 until the arrival of the Spanish conquistadors, around 1550. When the conquistadors arrived, they imposed a new, foreign order on the resident Americans and their land, changing most American Indian names, renaming the villages "pueblos," and forcefully converting Indian populations to Catholicism. With the opening of the Santa Fe Trail in 1821, however, Anglos began to move into the territory, with the United States gaining possession in the 1840s during the Mexican War. Today, northern New Mexico is experiencing a reconquest of sorts, as the Anglo population soars and outside money and values again make their way in. The process continues to transform New Mexico's three distinct cultures and their unique ways of life, albeit in a less violent manner than during the Spanish conquest.

DATELINE

3000 B.C. First evidence of stable farming settlements in region.

A.D. 700 Earliest evidence of ancestral Puebloan presence.

1540 Francisco Vásquez de Coronado marches to Cíbola in search of a Native American "city of gold." When he leaves 2 years later, he declares his mission a failure.

1598 In what is considered the founding of New Mexico, Juan de Oñate establishes the first Spanish capital north of present-day Española. In **1608,** Oñate is removed as governor and sent to Mexico City to face charges of abuse of power and mistreatment of the American Indians.

1610 Immigration to New Mexico increases; Don Pedro de Peralta establishes Santa Fe as capital.

1680 Pueblo tribes revolt against Spanish, driving the colonists back to Mexico. The colonists will not recapture Santa Fe until **1692.**

1706 Albuquerque established.

1739 First French traders enter Santa Fe.

continues

Certainly, the Anglos—many of them from large cities—add a cosmopolitan flavor to life here. The variety of restaurants has greatly increased, as have entertainment options. For their relatively small sizes, the communities of Taos and Santa Fe offer a broad variety of restaurants and cultural events. Santa Fe has developed a strong dance and drama scene, with treats such as flamenco and opera, and Taos is where you want to go for chamber music. Albuquerque has an exciting nightlife scene downtown; you can walk from club to club and hear a wealth of jazz, rock, country, and alternative music.

> ### Impressions
>
> "Things which apply elsewhere often do not apply in New Mexico."
> —Lew Wallace, governor of New Mexico Territory (1878–81) and author of *Ben-Hur*

Unfortunately, many newcomers, attracted by the adobe houses and exotic feel of the place, often bring only a loose appreciation for the area and fail to even try to blend in. Some tend to romanticize the lifestyle of the other cultures and trivialize their beliefs. American Indian symbols, for example, are used in ever-popular southwestern decorative motifs; New Age groups appropriate valued rituals, such as sweats (in which believers sit encamped in a very hot, enclosed space to cleanse their spirits). The effects of cultural and economic change are even apparent throughout the countryside, where land is being developed at an alarming rate.

Transformation of the local way of life is also apparent in the number of new stores springing up. For some residents, these are a welcome relief from the ubiquitous western clothing stores and provincial dress shops, but the downside is that historic city plazas, which once provided goods and services for the resident communities, are now jammed with T-shirt shops and galleries

1779 Tabivo Naritgant, leader of rebellious Comanche tribes, falls to Spanish forces. The Comanches and Utes will finally sign a treaty with the Spanish in **1786.**	**1846** Mexican War breaks out; Gen. Stephen Kearny takes possession of New Mexico for United States. In **1847,** Governor Charles Bent is killed during a revolt in Taos against U.S. control. In **1848,** Mexico officially cedes New Mexico to United States.
1821 Mexico gains independence from Spain; Santa Fe Trail opened to international trade.	
1828 Kit Carson, the legendary frontiersman, arrives in Taos.	**1864** Navajos relocated to Bosque Redondo Reservation, at Fort Sumner in eastern New Mexico, by what is known as the infamous "Long Walk." They will return to their native homeland in **1868.**
1841 Soldiers from Texas invade New Mexico and claim all land east of the Rio Grande for Texas, but are driven out by New Mexico forces.	

aimed at tourists. Many locals now rarely visit their plazas except during special events such as fiestas.

Environmental threats are another regional reality. Nuclear-waste issues form part of an ongoing conflict affecting the entire Southwest, and a section of southern New Mexico has been designated a nuclear-waste site. Because much of the waste must pass through Santa Fe, the U.S. government, along with the New Mexico state government, constructed a bypass that directs some transit traffic around the west side of the city.

Still, population growth has also brought positive changes, and many locals have directly benefited from New Mexico's influx of wealthy newcomers and its popularity as a tourist destination. Businesses and industries large and small have come to the area, bringing money and jobs. Local artists and artisans have also benefited, and many craftspeople—furniture makers, tin workers, potters, and weavers—have expanded their businesses.

The influx of people and new ideas has broadened the sensibility of what would otherwise be a fairly provincial state. There is generally a live-and-let-live attitude here that is unusual in smaller communities, and the area has become a refuge for many gays and lesbians, as well as for political exiles, such as Tibetans. With them has developed a level of tolerance you would generally find only in very large cities.

Northern New Mexico's extreme popularity as a tourist destination has leveled out somewhat in the 21st century. Though some artists and many businesspeople lament the loss of the crowds we had back in the '80s, many residents are glad that the wave has subsided. It's good news for travelers, too; you no longer have to compete so heavily for restaurant seats or space when hiking through ruins. Though parts of northern New Mexico have lost some of the unique charm that attracted so many to the area, the overall feeling is still one of mystery and a cultural depth unmatched in the world.

1878–81 Lincoln County War erupts; epitomizes the lawlessness and violence of the Wild West.

1879 Atchison, Topeka, and Santa Fe Railroad routes main line through Las Vegas, Albuquerque, El Paso, and Deming, where connection is made with California's South Pacific Line.

1886 Apache chief Geronimo captured; signals end of New Mexico's Indian wars.

1898 Painters Ernest Blumenschein and Bert Phillips arrive in Taos. They will found the Taos Society of Artists in **1914.**

1912 New Mexico becomes the 47th state.

1924 American Indians granted full U.S. citizenship.

1943 Los Alamos National Laboratory built; "Manhattan Project" scientists spend 2 years in complete seclusion developing nuclear weapons. The first atomic bomb will be exploded at Trinity Site in **1945.**

continues

Preserving Cultural Identity

Faced with new challenges to their ways of life, both American Indians and Hispanics are marshaling forces to protect their cultural identities. A prime concern is language. Through the years, many Pueblo people have begun to speak more and more English, with their children getting little exposure to their native tongue. In a number of the pueblos, elders are working with schoolchildren in language classes. Some of the pueblos have even developed written dictionaries, the first time their languages have been presented in this form.

Some pueblos have introduced programs to conserve the environment, preserve ancient seed strains, and protect religious rites. Because their religion is tied closely to nature, a loss of natural resources would threaten the entire culture. Certain rituals have been closed to outsiders, the most notable being some of the rituals of Shalako at Zuni, a popular and elaborate series of year-end ceremonies.

Hispanics, through art and observance of cultural traditions, are also embracing their roots. In northern New Mexico, murals depicting important historic events, such as the Treaty of Guadalupe Hidalgo of 1848, adorn many walls. The **Spanish Market** in Santa Fe has expanded into a grand celebration of traditional arts—from tin working to *santo* (icon) carving. Public schools in the area have bilingual education programs, allowing students to embrace their Spanish-speaking roots.

Hispanics are also making their voices heard, insisting on more conscientious development of their neighborhoods and rising to positions of power in government. Former congressman Bill Richardson, Hispanic despite his Anglo surname, was appointed U.S. ambassador to the United Nations and then left that post to become energy secretary in President Clinton's cabinet,

1947 Reports of a flying saucer crash near Roswell make national headlines, despite U.S. Air Force's denials that it has occurred. Not until 1994 will the U.S. Air Force, under pressure from Congress, reopen its investigation. The final conclusion states that the debris found was likely from tests of a secret Cold War spy balloon. UFO believers allege a cover-up.

1948 American Indians granted the right to vote in state elections.

1972 Pioneer balloonist Sid Cutter establishes Albuquerque International Balloon Fiesta.

1984 New Mexico's last remaining section of famed Route 66, near San Jon, is abandoned.

1990 New Mexico's last uranium mine, near Grants, closes.

2010 Santa Fe celebrates 400-year anniversary.

TRADITIONAL bread baking

While visiting the pueblos in New Mexico, you'll probably notice adobe beehive-shaped outdoor ovens, known as *hornos*, which American Indians have used to bake bread for hundreds of years. Usually in the evening, the bread dough (made of white flour, lard, salt, yeast, and water) is made and kneaded, the loaves are shaped, set to rise, and in the morning placed in the oven heated by a wood fire. They bake for about an hour. If you would like to try a traditional loaf, you can buy one at the **Indian Pueblo Cultural Center** in Albuquerque (see p. 196) and at many of the pueblos.

and was later governor of New Mexico. The current governor of New Mexico is Susana Martinez, who is not only the state's first woman governor, but also the first Hispanic female governor in the U.S.

Gambling Wins & Losses

Gambling, a fact of life and source of much-needed revenue for American Indian tribes across the country, has been a center of controversy in northern New Mexico for a number of years. In 1994, Governor Gary Johnson signed a pact with tribes in New Mexico, ratified by the U.S. Department of the Interior, to allow full-scale gambling. **Tesuque Pueblo** was one of the first to begin a massive expansion, and many other pueblos followed suit.

Many New Mexicans are concerned about the tone gambling sets in their state. The casinos are for the most part large, neon-bedecked buildings that stand out sorely on some of New Mexico's most picturesque land, often managed by outsiders. Though most residents appreciate the boost that gambling brings to the Indian people—it does provide some with jobs—critics wonder where gambling profits actually go, and if the casinos are really a good thing for the tribes long-term. Another negative is that the low-cost meals offered by most casinos to get would-be gamblers in the doors have severely impacted the business of nearby restaurants, even driving some to close down.

Santa Fe Today

There's a magic in Santa Fe that's difficult to explain, but you'll sense it when you glimpse an old adobe building set against blue mountains and giant billowing thunderheads, or when you hear a ranchero song come from a lowrider's radio and you smell chicken and chile grilling at a roadside vending booth. Although it's quickening, the pace of life here is still a few steps slower than that in the rest of the country. We use the word *mañana* to describe the pace—which doesn't mean "tomorrow" exactly, it just means "not today." There's also a level of creativity here that you'll find in few other places in the world. Artists who have fled big-city jobs come here to follow their passions, alongside locals who grew up making crafts and continue to do so. Conversations often center on how to plan one's day to take advantage of the incredible outdoors while still making enough money to survive.

However, Santa Fe's precipitous growth and enduring tourist popularity have led to conflict and squabbling. Outsiders have bought up land in the hills around the city, building housing developments and sprawling single-family homes. The hills that local populations claimed for centuries as their own are being overrun, while property taxes for all have skyrocketed. Local outcry has prompted the city to implement zoning restrictions on where and how development can proceed. Some of the restrictions include banning building on ridge tops and on steep slopes and limiting the size of homes built.

Only in recent years have Santa Fe's politicians become conscientious about the city's growth. Former mayor Debbie Jaramillo was one of the first local politicians to take a strong stand against growth. A fiery native of Santa Fe, she came into office in the 1990s as a representative of *la gente* (the people) and set about discouraging tourism and rapid development. Subsequent mayors have taken a middle-of-the-road approach to the issue, which has resulted in a calmer community and an increase in tourism and development.

Taos Today

A funky town in the middle of a beautiful, sage-covered valley, Taos is full of narrow streets dotted with galleries and shops, and locals are determined to keep it that way. Perhaps more so than other major northern New Mexico tourist centers—okay, we'll say it, tourist traps—Taos has a vocal and active contingent of residents who consistently work to block heavy development in the area. Several times since the 1980s they have stalled plans to expand their airport, a battle that continues today; in the 1990s, they blocked plans for a $40-million golf course and housing development; and in 2003, they prevented a Super Wal-Mart from opening. It's hard to say where Taos gets its rebellious strength; the roots may lie in the hippie community that settled here in the '60s, or possibly the Pueblo community around which the city formed. After all, Taos Pueblo was at the center of the 17th-century Pueblo revolt.

Still, changes occur, even in Taos. The blinking light that for years residents used as a reference point has given way to a real traffic light. You'll also see the main route through town becoming more and more like Cerrillos Road in Santa Fe, as fast-food restaurants and service businesses set up shop. Though the town is working on alternate routes to channel through-traffic around downtown, there's no feasible way of widening the main drag because the street—which started out as a wagon trail—is bordered closely by historic buildings.

Albuquerque Today

The largest city in New Mexico, Albuquerque is more like a suburb without a city. Sure, there are some relatively tall buildings and there is an old town surrounding a plaza, but it doesn't feel like a metropolis. It's an easy city to get around in, has shopping centers dotted among residential areas, and plenty of parking. Many New Mexicans from outside Albuquerque consider it primarily a destination for seeing medical specialists and doing some serious shopping. This is where you'll find Costco, Sam's Club, and the state's major furniture and appliance stores.

Of course, growth has had its effect. The city, which old-timers remember as being little more than a big town, now sprawls more than 20 miles, from the lava-crested mesas on the west side of the Rio Grande to the steep alluvial slopes of the Sandia Mountains on the east, and north and south through the Rio Grande Valley. New subdivisions seem to sprout up almost daily.

Despite the growth, though, Albuquerque is prized by New Mexicans for its genuineness. You'll find none of the self-conscious artsy atmosphere of Santa Fe here. Instead, there's a traditional New Mexico feel that's evident when you spend some time in the downtown area, a place of shiny skyscrapers built around the original Route 66 that still maintains some of its 1950s charm.

The city's growing pains are symbolized by concerns over **Petroglyph National Monument** on the west side. The area is characterized by five extinct volcanoes. Adjacent lava flows became a hunting and gathering place for prehistoric Indians, who left a chronicle of their beliefs etched in the dark basalt boulders; more than 25,000 petroglyphs have been found in the preserve. Still, it's difficult to ponder what life was like here for the peoples who carved these images, when you're bombarded with the sound of traffic whizzing by and the sight of a trailer park nearby.

NEW MEXICO THROUGH TIME

The Pueblo tribes of the upper Rio Grande Valley are descendants of the people we used to call Anasazi, but are now better known as ancestral Puebloans. From the mid-9th to the 13th centuries, these people lived in the Four Corners Region, where the states of New Mexico, Arizona, Colorado, and Utah now meet. On rock faces throughout northern New Mexico, you'll see the petroglyphs they left behind, circular symbols carved in sandstone—the wavy mark of Avanu, the river serpent; or the ubiquitous Kokopelli playing his magic flute. The ancestral Puebloans built spectacular structures—you get an idea of their scale and intricacy at the ruins at **Chaco Canyon** and **Mesa Verde.** It isn't known exactly why they abandoned their homes; some archaeologists believe it was due to drought, others claim it was social unrest, but most now believe it was likely a combination of both. Most theories suggest that they moved from these sites to such areas as Frijoles Canyon (**Bandelier National Monument**) and **Puye,** where they built villages resembling the ones they had left. Then several hundred years later, for reasons not yet understood, they moved down from the canyons onto the flat plain next to the Rio Grande. By the time the Spaniards arrived in the 1500s, the Pueblo culture was well established throughout what would become northern and western New Mexico.

Architectural style was a unifying mark of the otherwise diverse ancestral Puebloan and today's Pueblo cultures. Both built condominium-style communities of stone and mud adobe bricks, three and four stories high (five stories at Taos). Grouped around central plazas, the villages incorporated circular spiritual chambers called *kivas.* As farmers, the ancestral Puebloan and Pueblo peoples used the waters of the Rio Grande and its tributaries to

Historic Trails & Sites

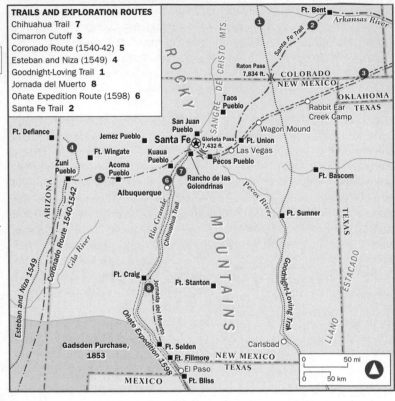

TRAILS AND EXPLORATION ROUTES
Chihuahua Trail **7**
Cimarron Cutoff **3**
Coronado Route (1540-42) **5**
Esteban and Niza (1549) **4**
Goodnight-Loving Trail **1**
Jornada del Muerto **8**
Oñate Expedition Route (1598) **6**
Santa Fe Trail **2**

irrigate fields of corn, beans, and squash. They also hunted deer, rabbits, and whatever else was in the area, and created elaborate pottery.

The Spanish Occupation

After conquering Mexico's Aztecs from 1519 to 1521, the Spanish ventured into the upper Rio Grande area. In 1540, Francisco Vásquez de Coronado led an expedition in search of the fabled Seven Cities of Cíbola, coincidentally introducing horses and sheep to the region. Neither Coronado nor a succession of fortune-seeking conquistadors could locate the legendary cities of gold, so the Spanish concentrated their efforts on exploiting the people already here.

Franciscan priests attempted to turn the Pueblo people into model peasants. Their churches became the focal points of every pueblo, with Catholic schools an essential adjunct. By 1625, there were approximately 50 churches in the Rio Grande Valley. (Two of the Pueblo missions, at Isleta and Acoma, are still in use today.) The Pueblos, however, weren't enthused about doing "God's work" for the Spanish—building new adobe missions, tilling fields, and weaving garments for export to Mexico—so Spanish soldiers came north to back the padres in extracting labor. In effect, the Pueblo people were forced into slavery.

Santa Fe was founded in 1610 as the seat of Spanish government in the upper Rio Grande. Governor Don Pedro de Peralta named the settlement La Villa Real de la Santa Fe de San Francisco de Asis (The Royal City of the Holy Faith of St. Francis of Assisi). The **Palace of the Governors** has been used continuously as a public building ever since—by the Spanish, Pueblos (1680–92), Mexicans, and Americans. Today it stands as the flagship of the state museum system.

Decades of oppression by the Spanish colonials led to Pueblo unrest. Uprisings in the 1630s at Taos and Jemez left village priests dead and triggered even more repression. In 1680, a unified Pueblo rebellion, orchestrated from Taos, succeeded in driving the Spaniards from the upper Rio Grande Valley. The leaders of the revolt defiled or destroyed the churches, just as the Spanish had destroyed the religious symbols of the native people. Revolutionaries took the Palace of the Governors, where they burned archives and prayer books, and converted the chapel into a kiva. They also burned much of the property in Santa Fe that had been built by the Europeans and laid siege to Spanish settlements up and down the Rio Grande Valley. Forced to retreat to Mexico, the colonists were not able to retake Santa Fe until 12 years later. Bloody battles raged for the next several years, but by the beginning of the 18th century, Nuevo Mexico was again firmly in Spanish hands.

In the mid-1700s, the Franciscans priests departed, exasperated by their failure to wipe out all vestiges of traditional Pueblo religion. Throughout the Spanish occupation, eight generations of Pueblos had clung tenaciously to their way of life. However, by the 1750s, the number of Pueblo villages had shrunk by half.

The Arrival of the Anglos

The first Anglos to spend time in the upper Rio Grande Valley were mountain men: itinerant hunters, trappers, and traders. Trailblazers of the U.S. westward expansion, they began settling in New Mexico in the first decade of the 19th century. Many married into Pueblo or Hispanic families.

Perhaps the best known was **Kit Carson,** a sometime federal agent, sometime scout, whose legend is inextricably interwoven with that of early Taos. Though he seldom stayed in one place for long, he considered the Taos area his home. It is believed he was married three times, to women in the Arapaho and Cheyenne tribes, and finally to Josepha Jaramillo, the Hispanic daughter of a leading Taos citizen. Later he became a prime force in the final subjugation of the Navajos, leading what was called the "Long Walk." The Taos home where he lived off and on for 40 years, until his death in 1868, is now a museum.

Wagon trains and eastern merchants followed Carson and the other early settlers. Santa Fe, Taos, and Albuquerque, already major trading and commercial centers at the end of the **Chihuahua Trail** (the Camino Real from Veracruz, Mexico, 1,000 miles south), became the western terminals of the new **Santa Fe Trail** (from Independence, Missouri, 800 miles east).

After Mexico gained its independence from Spain in 1821, the newly independent Mexico granted the Pueblo people full citizenship and abandoned restrictive trade laws instituted by their former Spanish rulers. Nevertheless, over the subsequent 25 years of direct rule from Mexico City, things were still not peaceful in the upper Rio Grande. Instead, they were marked by ongoing rebellion against severe taxation, especially in Taos. Neither did things quiet down when the United States assumed control of the territory during the U.S.–Mexican War. Shortly after General Stephen Kearney occupied Santa Fe (in a bloodless takeover) on orders of President James Polk in 1846, a revolt in Taos, in 1847, led to the slaying of Charles Bent, the new governor of New Mexico. In 1848, the Treaty of Guadalupe Hidalgo officially transferred title of New Mexico, along with Texas, Arizona, and California, to the United States.

Aside from Kit Carson, perhaps the two most notable personalities of 19th-century New Mexico were priests. **Father José Martínez** (1793–1867) was one of the first native-born priests to serve his people. Ordained in Durango, Mexico, he jolted the Catholic church after assuming control of the Taos parish. Martínez abolished the obligatory church tithe because it was a hardship on poor parishioners, published the first newspaper in the territory (in 1835), and fought large land acquisitions by Anglos after the United States annexed the territory.

On all these issues, Martínez was at loggerheads with **Bishop Jean-Baptiste Lamy** (1814–88), a Frenchman appointed in 1851 to supervise the affairs of the first independent New Mexican diocese. Lamy, upon whose life Willa Cather based her novel *Death Comes for the Archbishop,* served the diocese for 37 years. Lamy didn't take kindly to Martínez's independent streak and, after repeated conflicts, excommunicated the maverick priest in 1857. But Martínez was steadfast in his preaching. He established an independent church and continued as northern New Mexico's spiritual leader until his death.

Lamy made many positive contributions to New Mexico, especially in the fields of education and architecture. Santa Fe's Romanesque **Cathedral of St. Francis** and the nearby Gothic-style **Loretto Chapel,** for instance, were constructed under his aegis. But he was adamant about adhering to strict Catholic religious tenets. Martínez, on the other hand, embraced the folk tradition, including the craft of *santero* (religious icon) carving, and tolerated the Penitentes, a flagellant sect that had flourished since the Franciscans' departure.

Impressions

"In New Mexico he always awoke a young man; not until he rose and began to shave did he realize that he was growing older."

—Archbishop Latour in Willa Cather's *Death Comes for the Archbishop,* 1927

The Railroad Boom & the 20th Century

With the advent of the **Atchison, Topeka & Santa Fe Railway** in 1879, New Mexico began to boom. Albuquerque in particular blossomed in the wake of a series of major gold strikes in the Madrid Valley, close to ancient turquoise mines. By the time the gold lodes began to shrink in the 1890s, cattle and sheep ranching had become well entrenched. The territory's growth culminated in statehood in 1912.

Territorial governor **Lew Wallace,** who served from 1878 to 1881, was instrumental in promoting interest in the arts, which today flourish in northern New Mexico. While occupying the Palace of the Governors, Wallace penned the great biblical novel *Ben-Hur.* In the 1890s, Ernest Blumenschein, Bert Phillips, and Joseph Sharp launched the Taos art colony; it boomed in the decade following World War I when Mabel Dodge Luhan, D. H. Lawrence, Georgia O'Keeffe, Willa Cather, and many others visited or established residence in the area.

> ### Impressions
>
> "I am become death, the shatterer of worlds."
> —J. Robert Oppenheimer, quoting from ancient Hindu texts, shortly after the successful detonation of the first atomic bomb

During World War II, the federal government purchased an isolated boys' camp west of Santa Fe and turned it into the **Los Alamos National Laboratory,** where the Manhattan Project and other top-secret atomic experiments were developed and perfected. The science and military legacies continue today; Albuquerque is among the nation's leaders in attracting defense contracts and high technology. The relatively unsettled desert landscape here has attracted such projects as the Very Large Array, the world's most powerful radio telescope, which began operations in 1981, and the Waste Isolation Pilot Project, the nation's first deep-geologic repository for permanent disposal of radioactive waste, which began storage operations in 1998. Holloman Air Force Base, near White Sands National Monument, served as the landing space for the U.S. space shuttle *Columbia* in 1982, and Spaceport America, the world's first purpose-built base for commercial outer-space transport, began development in 2006 in the desert 45 miles north of Las Cruces.

ART & ARCHITECTURE

Land of Art

It's all in the light—or at least that's why many artists say they were drawn to northern New Mexico. In truth, the light is only part of the attraction: Nature in this part of the country, with its awe-inspiring thunderheads, endless expanse of blue skies, and rugged desert, is itself a canvas. To record the wonders of earth and sky, the ancestral Puebloans imprinted images—in the form of **petroglyphs** and **pictographs**—on the sides of caves and on stones, as well as on the sides of pots shaped from clay dug in the hills. Today's Pueblo tribes carry on that legacy, and other more recent arrivals copy those motifs.

Life in northern New Mexico is shaped by the arts. Everywhere you turn, you see pottery, paintings, jewelry, and weavings. You're liable to meet an artist whether you're having coffee in a Taos cafe or walking along Canyon Road in Santa Fe. Oh, and be careful driving along the dirt back roads—you wouldn't want to run over a painter at his easel or a photographer hovered over her tripod.

Each Indian pueblo has a trademark design, such as Santa Clara's and San Ildefonso's black pottery and Zuni's needlepoint silver work. Bear in mind that the images used often have deep symbolic meaning. When purchasing art or an artifact, you may want to talk to its maker about what the symbols mean. Hispanic villages are also distinguished by their artistic identities. Chimayó has become a center for Hispanic weaving, while the village of Cordova is known for its *santo* (icon) carving. *Santos, retablos* (paintings), and *bultos* (sculptures), as well as works in tin, are traditional devotional arts tied to the Roman Catholic faith. Often, these works are sold out of artists' homes, an opportunity for you to glimpse the lives of the artists and the surroundings that inspire them.

Many non-native artists have also flocked here, particularly during the 20th and 21st centuries, and established important art societies. One of the most notable is the **Taos Society of Artists.** Its founders, artists **Bert Phillips** and **Ernest L. Blumenschein,** were traveling through the area from Colorado on a mission to sketch the Southwest when their wagon broke down north of Taos. The scenery so impressed them that they abandoned their journey and stayed. Joseph Sharp joined them, and still later came Oscar Berninghaus, Walter Ufer, Herbert Dunton, and others. You can see a brilliant collection of some of their romantically lit portraits and landscapes at the **Taos Art Museum.** Another major player in Taos' artistic development was writer and arts patron **Mabel Dodge Luhan,** who in the 1920s held court for many notables, including Georgia O'Keeffe, Willa Cather, and D. H. Lawrence. All of these elements explain why Taos—a town of just under 6,000 inhabitants—has so many arts-and-crafts galleries, as well as numerous resident painters, sculptors, photographers, and writers.

Santa Fe's own art society was begun in the 1920s by a nucleus of five painters who became known as **Los Cinco Pintores.** Jozef Bakos, Fremont Ellis, Walter Mruk, Willard Nash, and Will Shuster lived in the area of dusty Canyon Road (now the de facto arts center of Santa Fe). Despite its relatively small size, Santa Fe today is considered one of the top three art markets in the United States.

Perhaps the most celebrated artist associated with northern New Mexico is **Georgia O'Keeffe** (1887–1986), a painter who worked and lived most of her later years in the region. O'Keeffe's first sojourn to New Mexico in 1929 inspired her sensuous paintings of the area's desert landscape and bleached animal skulls. She lived in the small picturesque community of Abiquiu, about 42 miles northwest of Santa Fe on US 84. The **Georgia O'Keeffe Museum,** the only museum in the United States dedicated entirely to an internationally renowned woman artist, opened in Santa Fe in 1997.

Santa Fe is also home to the **Institute of American Indian Arts,** where many of today's leading American Indian artists have studied, including the Apache sculptor Allan Houser (whose works you can see near the State Capitol building and in other public areas in Santa Fe). Possibly the best-known

American Indian painter is the late R. C. Gorman, an Arizona Navajo who made his home in Taos for more than two decades and became known for his bright, somewhat surrealistic depictions of Navajo women. Also in the spotlight is Dan Namingha, a Hopi artist who weaves images of native symbols into contemporary designs. Other notable local artists include Tammy Garcia, a young Taos potter who for years swept the awards at Indian Market with her intricately shaped and carved pots; Cippy Crazyhorse, a Cochiti who has acquired a steady following for his silver jewelry; and noted muralist and Santa Fe native Frederico Vigil, whose frescoes are all around the area.

Art is for sale everywhere, from small shows at the pueblos to major markets such as the Spanish Market and Indian Market in Santa Fe. Under the portals along the Santa Fe and Albuquerque plazas, you'll find a variety of works in silver, stone, and pottery for sale; you'll also find city streets lined with galleries, some very slick, some more modest. If you're interested in buying art, however, some caution should be exercised; there's a lot of schlock out there, targeting the tourist trade. It seems that every year brings news reports of another arrest for selling counterfeit American Indian jewelry and pottery, usually manufactured overseas. Yet if you persist, you're likely to find much inspiring work as well. Be sure to buy at established shops, museum stores, or directly from the artisans themselves.

A Rich Architectural Melting Pot

Northern New Mexico's distinctive architecture reflects the diversity of cultures that have left their imprint on the region. The first people in the area, the ancestral Puebloans, built stone and mud homes at the bottom of canyons and inside caves. **Pueblo-style adobe architecture** evolved and became the basis for traditional New Mexican homes: sun-dried clay bricks mixed with grass for strength, mud-mortared, and covered with additional protective layers of mud. Roofs are supported by a network of *vigas*—long beams whose ends protrude through the outer facades—and *latillas,* smaller stripped branches layered over the vigas. Other adapted Pueblo architectural elements include plastered adobe-brick kiva fireplaces, *bancos* (adobe benches that protrude from walls), and *nichos* (small indentations within a wall in which religious icons are placed). These adobe homes are characterized by flat roofs and soft, rounded contours.

Spaniards wedded many elements to Pueblo style, such as portals (porches held up with posts, often running the length of a home) and enclosed patios, as well as the simple, dramatic sculptural shapes of Spanish mission arches and bell towers. They also brought elements from the Moorish architecture found in southern Spain: heavy wooden doors and elaborate *corbels*—carved wooden supports for the vertical posts.

With the opening of the Santa Fe Trail in 1821, and later the 1860s gold boom, more Anglo settlers arrived, launching the next wave of building. They contributed architectural elements such as the neo-Grecian and Victorian influences popular in the United States at the time. What came to be known as **Territorial-style** architecture introduced one significant new feature: pitched rather than flat roofs. Territorial style also included brick facades and cornices as well as porches, often placed on the second story; you'll also note millwork on doors, wood trim around windows and doorways, double-hung windows, and Victorian bric-a-brac. In **Santa Fe Plaza,** you can see these two architectural styles converge: On the west side is a Territorial-style balcony, while the Palace of the Governors is marked by Pueblo-style vigas and over-size Spanish/Moorish doors.

In Santa Fe, many other styles flourish: Compare the Romanesque architecture of the **St. Francis Cathedral** to the Gothic-style **Loretto Chapel,** brought by Archbishop Lamy from France, as well as the railroad station built in the **Spanish Mission style** popular in the early part of the 20th century. Since 1957, however, strict city building codes have required that all new structures within the circumference of the Paseo de Peralta conform to one of two revival styles: Pueblo or Territorial. The regulation also limits the height of the buildings and restricts the types of signs permitted, and it requires buildings to be topped by flat roofs.

Albuquerque also has a broad array of styles, most evident in a visit to **Old Town.** There, you'll find the large Italianate brick house known as the **Herman Blueher home,** built in 1898; throughout Old Town you'll find little *placitas,* homes, and haciendas built around courtyards, a strategy developed not only for defense purposes, but also as a way to accommodate several generations of the same family in different wings of a single dwelling. **The Church of San Felipe de Neri** at the center of Old Town is situated between two folk Gothic towers. This building was begun in a cruciform plan in 1793; subsequent architectural changes resulted in an interesting mixture of styles.

The most notable architecture in Taos is the **Taos Pueblo,** the site of two structures emulated in homes and business buildings throughout the Southwest. Built to resemble Taos Mountain, which stands behind it, the two structures are pyramidal in form, with the different levels reached by ladders. Also quite prevalent is architecture echoing colonial hacienda style, such as the **Martinez Hacienda,** an example of a hacienda stronghold. Built without windows facing outward, it originally had 20 small rooms, many with doors opening out to the courtyard. One of the few refurbished examples of colonial New Mexico architecture, the hacienda is on the National Historic Registry. You can also wander through artist **Ernest Blumenschein's home,** built in 1797 and restored by Blumenschein in 1919. It represents another New Mexico architectural phenomenon: homes that were added onto year after year. Doorways are typically low, and floors rise and fall at the whim of the earth beneath them.

As you head into villages in the north, you'll see steep-pitched roofs on most homes. This is because the common flat-roof style doesn't shed snow; the water builds up and causes roof problems. In just about any town in northern New Mexico, you may detect the strong smell of tar, a sure sign that another resident is laying out thousands to fix his enchanting but frustratingly flat roof.

Today, especially in Santa Fe and Albuquerque, few new homes are actually built of adobe. Instead, most are constructed with wood frames and plasterboard, and then stuccoed over to look like adobe. A keen eye can see the difference: True adobe buildings have rounded corners—what locals call feminine lines—while fake adobe buildings have more sharp and clear-cut lines.

A number of northern New Mexico architects and builders today are employing innovative architectural designs to create a Pueblo-style feel. They incorporate straw bails, pumice-crete, rammed earth, old tires, and even aluminum cans in the construction of homes. Most of these elements are used in the same way bricks are used, stacked and layered, and then covered over with plaster and made to look like adobe. West of Taos, a number of "earthships" have been built. Many of these homes are constructed with alternative materials, most bermed into the sides of hills, utilizing the earth as insulation. Many are off-the-grid, relying on the sun and wind for power.

A visitor could spend an entire trip to northern New Mexico focusing on the architecture, and some do. As well as relishing the wealth of architectural styles, you'll find more subtle elements everywhere. You may encounter an ox-blood floor, for example. An old Spanish tradition, ox blood is spread in layers and left to dry, hardening into a glossy finish that's known to last centuries. You're also likely to see coyote fences—narrow cedar posts lined up side by side, a system early settlers devised to keep their animals safe. Winding around homes and buildings you'll see *acequias,* ancient irrigation canals still maintained by locals for watering crops and trees. And throughout the area you'll notice that old walls are whimsically bowed, and windows and floors are often crooked, constant reminders of the effects time has had on even these stalwart structures.

THE sun worshippers OF NEW MEXICO

One of the simplest yet most easily recognized state flags in the U.S., New Mexico's official flag got its start in the 1920s with a flag-designing contest organized by the Daughters of the American Revolution. The winning design, officially proclaimed in 1925, turned out to be a red sun symbol, called a Zia, with a yellow background.

The design of the Zia is an interpretation of a sun image found on a late-19th-century water jar from Zia Pueblo. The image is a circle from which four points radiate, and each of the four points is made up of four themes: the four seasons of the year (spring, summer, autumn, winter); the four directions of earth (north, south, east, west); the four times of day (sunrise, noon, evening, night); and the four stages of life (childhood, youth, adulthood, old age), all tied together in the circle of life.

ANTHROPOLOGY 101: BELIEFS & RITUALS

Religion has always been a defining element in the life of the Pueblo people. Within the cosmos, which they view as a single whole, all living creatures are mutually dependent. Thus, every relationship a human being may have, whether with a person, an animal, or a plant, has spiritual significance. A hunter prays before killing a deer, asking the creature to sacrifice itself to the tribe. A slain deer is treated as a guest of honor, and the hunter performs a ritual in which he sends the animal's soul back to its community, so that it may be reborn. Even the harvesting of plants requires prayer, thanks, and ritual.

The Pueblo people believe that their ancestors originally lived under the ground, which, as the place from which plants spring, is the source of all life. According to their beliefs, the original Pueblos, encouraged by burrowing animals, entered the world of humans—the so-called "fourth" world— through a hole, a *sipapu.* The ways in which this came about and the deities that the Pueblo people worship vary from tribe to tribe. Most, however, believe this world is enclosed by four sacred mountains, where four sacred colors—coral, black, turquoise, and yellow or white—predominate.

There is no single great spirit ruling over this world; instead, it is watched over by a number of spiritual elements. Most common are Mother Earth and Father Sun. In this desert land, the sun is an element of both life and death. The tribes watch the skies closely, tracking solstices and planetary movements, to determine the optimal time for crop planting.

Ritualistic dances are occasions of great symbolic importance. Usually held in conjunction with the feast days of Catholic saints (including Christmas Eve), Pueblo ceremonies demonstrate how Christian elements were absorbed without surrendering traditional beliefs. To this day, communities enact medicine dances, fertility rites, and prayers for rain and for good harvests. The spring and summer corn, or *tablita,* dances are among the most impressive. Most ceremonies begin with an early-morning Mass and procession to the plaza; the image of the saint is honored at the forefront. The rest of the day is devoted to song, dance, and feasting, with performers masked and clad as deer, buffalo, eagles, or other creatures.

Visitors are usually welcome to attend Pueblo dances, but they should respect the tribe's requests not to be photographed or recorded. It was exactly this lack of respect that led the Zunis to ban outsiders from attending many of their famous Shalako ceremonies.

Catholicism, imposed by the Spaniards, has infused northern New Mexico with another elaborate set of beliefs. This is a Catholicism heavy with iconography, expressed in carved *santos* (statues) and beautiful *retablos* (paintings) adorning the altars of many cathedrals. Catholic churches are the focal points of most northern New Mexico villages. If you take the high road to Taos, be sure to note the church in **Las Trampas,** as well as the one in **Ranchos de Taos;** both have 3- to 4-foot-thick walls sculpted from adobe and old-world interiors with beautiful *retablos* on the walls.

danse MACABRE

The **Dance of the Matachines,** a ritualistic dance performed at northern New Mexico pueblos and in many Hispanic communities, reveals the cultural miscegenation, identities, and conflicts that characterize northern New Mexico. It's a dark and vivid ritual in which a little girl, Malinche, is wedded to the church. The dance, depicting the taming of the native spirit, is difficult even for historians to decipher.

Brought to the New World by the Spaniards, the dance has its roots in the painful period during which the Moors were driven out of Spain. However, some symbols seem obvious: At one point, men bearing whips tame "El Toro," a small boy dressed as a bull who has been charging about rebelliously. The whip-men symbolically castrate him and then stroll through the crowd, pretending to display the dismembered body parts, as if to warn villagers of the consequences of disobedience. At another point, a hunched woman-figure births a small troll-like doll, perhaps representative of the union between Indian and Hispanic cultures.

The Dance of the Matachines ends when two *abuelo* (grandparent) figures dance across the dirt, holding up the just-born baby, while the Matachines, adorned with bishop-like headdresses, follow them away in a recessional march.

Many Hispanics in northern New Mexico maintain strong family and Catholic ties, and they continue to honor traditions associated with both. Communities plan elaborate celebrations such as the *quinceañera* for young girls reaching womanhood, and weddings with big feasts and dances in which well-wishers pin money to the bride's elaborately laced gown.

If you happen to be in the area during a holiday, you may even get to see a religious procession or pilgrimage. Most notable is the **pilgrimage to the Santuario de Chimayo,** an hour's drive north of Santa Fe. Constructed in 1816, the sanctuary has long been a pilgrimage site for Roman Catholics who attribute miraculous healing powers to the earth found in the chapel's anteroom. Several days before Easter, fervent believers begin walking the highway headed north or south to Chimayo, some carrying large crosses, others carrying nothing but small bottles of water.

In recent years, New Mexico has also become known (and in some circles, ridiculed) for **New Age pilgrims and celebrations.** The roots of the local movement are hard to trace. It may have something to do with northern New Mexico's centuries-old reputation as a place where rebel thinkers come to enjoy freedom of beliefs, or maybe it's a relic of the hippie invasion of the 1960s. Pueblo spirituality and a deeply felt connection to the land have also drawn New Agers. At any rate, there's a thriving New Age network here with alternative churches, healing centers, and healing schools. You'll find all sorts of alternative medicine and fringe practices, from aromatherapy to rolfing (a form of massage that realigns the muscles and bones in the body), and chelation therapy (in which an IV drips ethylene diamine tetra-acetic acid into the blood to remove heavy metals).

These New Age practices are often the butt of local humor. One pointed joke asks: "How many New Agers does it take to change a light bulb?" Answer: "None. They just form a support group and learn to live in the dark." For many, however, there's much good to be found in the movement. The Dalai Lama visited Santa Fe because the city is seen as a healing center and has become a refuge for Tibetans. Notable speakers such as Ram Dass and Thomas Moore have also come to the area. Many spiritual seekers find exactly what they are looking for in the receptive northern New Mexico desert and mountains.

BOOKS, FILMS & MUSIC

Books

Many well-known writers made their homes in New Mexico in the 20th century. In the 1920s, the most celebrated were **D. H. Lawrence** and **Willa Cather,** both short-term Taos residents. Lawrence, the controversial English novelist, spent time here between 1922 and 1925; he reflected on his sojourn in *Mornings in Mexico* and *Etruscan Places.* Lawrence's Taos period is also described in *Lorenzo in Taos,* written by his patron, Mabel Dodge Luhan. Cather, a Pulitzer-Prize winner famous for her depictions of the pioneer spirit, was inspired to write *Death Comes for the Archbishop*—a fictionalized account of 19th-century Santa Fe bishop Jean-Baptiste Lamy—by her stay in the region. Frank Waters (1902–95), a part-time resident from the 1930s on, gives a strong sense of Pueblo tradition in his classics *People of the Valley* and *The Man Who Killed the Deer.*

Many contemporary authors also live in and write about New Mexico. John Nichols, of Taos, whose *Milagro Beanfield War* was made into a Robert Redford movie in 1987, writes insightfully about the problems of poor Hispanic farming communities. The late Tony Hillerman of Albuquerque for decades wove mysteries around Navajo tribal police in books such as *Listening Woman* and *A Thief of Time.* More recently, Sarah Lovett has followed in his footsteps with a series of gripping mysteries, most notably *Dangerous Attachments.*

The Hispanic novelist Rudolfo Anaya's *Bless Me, Ultima* (1972) and Pueblo writer Leslie Marmon Silko's *Ceremony* (1977) capture the lifestyles of their respective peoples. A coming-of-age story, Richard Bradford's *Red Sky at Morning* (1968) juxtaposes the various cultures of New Mexico. Edward Abbey wrote of the desert environment and politics; his *Fire on the Mountain* (1962), set in New Mexico, was one of his most powerful works.

For general histories of the state, try Myra Ellen Jenkins and Albert H. Schroeder's *A Brief History of New Mexico* (University of New Mexico Press, 1974) and Marc Simmons's *New Mexico: An Interpretive History* (University of New Mexico Press, 1988).

Films

Over the years, so many movies have been filmed in New Mexico that we can't list them all, but here's a sampling: *Silverado* (1985), a lighthearted western; the heartfelt miniseries *Lonesome Dove* (1989), based on a Larry

McMurtry novel; Billy Bob Thornton's film adaptation (2000) of the novel *All the Pretty Horses;* Ron Howard's film version of *The Missing* (2003); and Billy Crystal in *City Slickers* (1991).

Favorite classics include *Butch Cassidy and the Sundance Kid* (1969), filmed in Taos and Chama; *The Cowboys* (1972), with John Wayne; Clint Eastwood's *Every Which Way But Loose* (1978); and Dennis Hopper and Peter Fonda in the 1960s classic *Easy Rider* (1969).

For a comprehensive list of movies and TV shows filmed at least partly in New Mexico, see **www.nmfilm.com**, then under "Public Interest," click on "Filmography." You'll get a list and then can click on a title for all sorts of information, including where in the state the filming took place.

Music

Such musical legends as Bo Diddley, Buddy Holly, Roy Orbison, and the Fireballs basked in New Mexico's light for parts of their careers. More recent musicians whose music really reflects the state include Mansanares, two brothers who grew up in Abiquiu, known for their Spanish guitar and soulful vocals. Look for their album *Nuevo Latino*. Master flute player Robert Mirabal's music is informed by the ceremonial music he grew up with at Taos Pueblo. Check out his 2006 Grammy Award–winning album *Sacred Ground*. Using New Mexico as his creative retreat since the 1980s, Michael Martin Murphey often plays live in Red River, north of Taos, where fans always cheer for his most notable song, "Wildfire." *The Best of Michael Martin Murphey* gives a good taste of his music. Country music superstar Randy Travis calls Santa Fe home. His newest release, *Around the Bend,* is a treasure, as are his classics.

EATING & DRINKING IN NORTHERN NEW MEXICO

You know you're in a food-conscious place when the local newspaper uses chile peppers (and onions) to rate movies, as does Santa Fe's *New Mexican.* A large part of that city's cachet as a chic destination derives from its famous cuisine, while Taos and Albuquerque are developing tasty reputations themselves. Competition among restaurants is fierce, giving visitors plenty of options from which to choose. Aside from establishments serving regional New Mexican cuisine, there are also French, Italian, Asian, and Indian restaurants, as well as interesting hybrids of those. And not all restaurants are high-end; several hidden gems satisfy your taste buds without emptying your wallet.

Dinner reservations are always recommended at the higher-end restaurants and are essential during peak seasons. Most restaurants are casual, so almost any attire is fine, though for the more expensive ones you'll probably feel more comfortable being at least a little dressed up. Only a few restaurants serve late—try to plan dinner before 8pm. If you arrive late and are starving, Albuquerque and Santa Fe have 24-hour Denny's fast-food restaurants, but get into Taos late and you're simply out of luck.

YOU SAY chili, WE SAY chile

You'll never see "chili" on a menu in New Mexico. Or you shouldn't. Real New Mexicans are adamant that *chile,* the Spanish spelling of the word, is the only way to spell it—no matter what your dictionary may say.

Virtually anything you order in a restaurant is likely to be topped with a chile sauce. Chile forms the base for the red and green sauces that top most New Mexico dishes such as enchiladas and burritos. One is not necessarily hotter than the other; spiciness depends on the type, and where and during what kind of season (dry or wet) the chiles were grown. Some of the best come from the tiny community of Hatch, along I-25 toward the state's southern border; many restaurants make a point of bragging that they use Hatch chile.

If you're not accustomed to spicy foods, certain varieties will make your eyes water, your sinuses drain, and your palate feel as if it's on fire. **Warning:** No amount of water or beer will alleviate the sting, it just spreads it. Dairy products work best. Drink milk or add grated cheese or sour cream to your food. A *sopaipilla* drizzled with honey is also helpful.

But don't let these words of caution scare you away from genuine New Mexico chiles. The pleasure of eating them far outweighs the pain. Start slowly, with salsas and chile sauces first, perhaps *rellenos* (stuffed peppers) next. You can also ask your servers how "hot" the chile is today, and in some cases you can have it served on the side and add it gradually.

In 1999, the New Mexico State Legislature passed a memorial adopting "Red or Green?" as the official state question, and if you order practically any genuine New Mexico food you'll most likely be asked. The correct answer is "Red," "Green," or "Christmas," which means to mix them.

New Mexican regional cuisine isn't the same as Mexican cuisine or even those American variations, Tex-Mex and Cal-Mex. New Mexican cooking is a product of southwestern history. American Indians taught the Spanish conquerors about corn—how to roast it and how to make corn pudding, stewed corn, cornbread, cornmeal, and *posole* (hominy)—and they also taught the Spanish how to use chile peppers, a crop indigenous to the New World, having been first harvested in the Andean highlands as early as 4000 B.C. Meanwhile, the Spaniards brought the practice of eating beef to the area. Later newcomers introduced other elements: From Mexico, for instance, came an interest in seafood. Regional New Mexican cuisine blends elements such as sauces from Mexico's Yucatán Peninsula or Central American dishes such as fried bananas served with beans.

The basic ingredients of New Mexico cooking are three indispensable, locally grown foods: **chile, beans,** and **corn.** Of these, perhaps the most crucial is the **chile,** whether brilliant red or green and with various levels of spicy bite. (See the box above.) Spotted or painted **pinto beans** with a nutty taste are simmered with garlic, onion, cumin, and red chile powder and served as a side dish. When mashed and refried in oil, they become *frijoles refritos.* **Corn** supplies the vital dough, called *masa,* for tortillas and tamales. New Mexican corn comes in six colors, of which yellow, white, and blue are the most common.

Even if you're familiar with Mexican cooking, the dishes you know are likely to be prepared differently here, and even here every restaurant has its own little twists on our regional standards. The following is a rundown of some regional dishes, a number of which aren't widely known outside the Southwest.

BISCOCHITO A cookie made with anise and lard, especially popular at Christmastime. (If you get an anise cookie that doesn't contain lard, it's not a biscochito.)

BREAKFAST BURRITO Scrambled eggs, potatoes, some kind of meat (usually bacon or sausage) wrapped in a flour tortilla with red or green chile sauce and melted cheese. You can choose to eat your breakfast burrito either hand-held, with the chile inside, or "smothered" on a plate and covered with chile sauce.

CARNE ADOVADA Tender pork marinated in red chile sauce, herbs, and spices, and then baked.

CHILE RELLENOS Chile peppers, often breaded, then stuffed with cheese, deep-fried, and sometimes covered with green chile sauce.

EMPANADA A fried pie with nuts and currants.

ENCHILADAS Tortillas either rolled or layered with chicken, beef, and/or cheese, topped with chile sauce.

GREEN CHILE CHEESEBURGER Practically every restaurant in the state claims to offer the world's best green chile cheeseburger. Lately, some fancy Santa Fe restaurants have been adding items to their green chile cheeseburgers, such as aioli mayonnaise, avocado, caramelized onions, or pineapple and shrimp. Don't buy it! A green chile cheeseburger is just that—a good-quality burger with cheddar cheese, topped with green chile (usually chopped but sometimes whole), and served on a bun. A strip or two of bacon, maybe, but that's it.

GREEN CHILE STEW Green chiles cooked in a stew with chunks of meat, beans, and potatoes. Usually served with a tortilla on the side to mop up the goop.

HUEVOS RANCHEROS Fried eggs on corn tortillas, topped with cheese and red or green chile, served with pinto beans.

PAN DULCE A sweet American Indian bread.

POSOLE A corn soup or stew (called hominy in parts of the South), sometimes prepared with pork and chile.

SOPAIPILLA A lightly fried puff pastry served with honey, or better yet, a honey-butter mixture, served as a dessert, or stuffed with meat and vegetables as a main dish.

TACOS Spiced chicken or beef, served either in soft tortillas or crispy shells, with cheese and chile. If you see fish tacos on the menu, you're in a Mexican, not New Mexican, restaurant.

TAMALES A dish made from cornmeal mush, wrapped in husks and steamed. (It tastes a lot better than this description makes it sound!)

SUGGESTED NORTHERN NEW MEXICO ITINERARIES

3

You may already have an idea of how you want to spend your time in New Mexico—power shopping, perhaps, or time-traveling through ancient cultures. Once you're here, however, you just might realize that there's more to this magical place than you expected. To make sure you don't miss the essentials, here are three possible driving itineraries, each starting in Albuquerque.

Northern New Mexico offers an amazing range of museums, some excellent opportunities to enjoy a live music or theater performance, plus other indoor activities. But to really experience it, you need to get out and see the people, observe some of the customs and traditions, breathe the pristine air of the mountains, and watch the sun drop below the distant horizon. With this in mind, these itineraries combine scenic drives with city stays. Take your time—linger at a cafe, take a short hike, or wander a plaza. You might be surprised at how easily northern New Mexico seeps into your psyche.

NORTHERN NEW MEXICO IN A WEEK

A week in northern New Mexico isn't quite long enough to do justice to the area's rich and varied landscape, but if that's all the time you have, you can certainly hit some of the highlights. Gaze at ancient drawings etched into stone at Petroglyph National Monument, browse the shops around Santa Fe's Plaza, and marvel at the play of light on the Rio Grande Gorge in Taos. See map on p. 33.

Days 1 & 2: Albuquerque

If it's early enough and you have some energy left after arriving, head to **Old Town** (p. 197), where you can wander the

Northern New Mexico in a Week

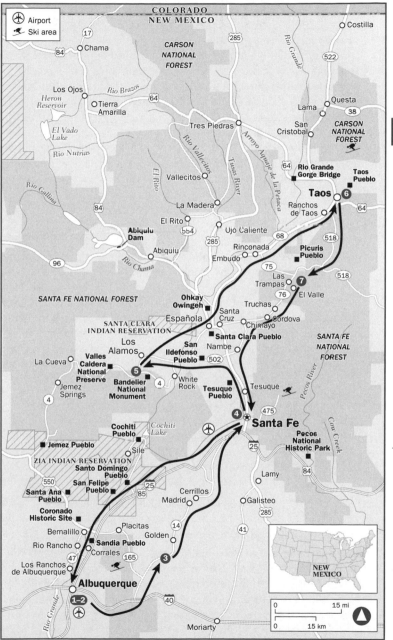

plaza and peruse the shops. Be sure to duck into some of the back alleyways and little nooks—you'll uncover some of the city's most innovative shops in these areas. Or, head over to the **Indian Pueblo Cultural Center** (p. 196) for an historical view of the Pueblo world and a look at the art and craftsmanship they are producing today.

On Day 2, start out at **ABQ BioPark** (p. 199) in the vicinity of **Old Town Plaza.** You can easily spend a couple of hours here exploring the Aquarium and strolling the Botanic Gardens. And if you like zoos as much as we do, hop on the Park's **Rio Line** for an easy and fun ride over to the BioPark Zoo (p. 200). Next, head west of town to **Petroglyph National Monument** (p. 204). (If you visit in summer, head here first, before the day heats up.) If the weather's really lousy (unusual here in the Land of Enchantment, but it does happen) or you're more of a history or art buff, visit the **Albuquerque Museum** (p. 194) for a unique look at how art and history intersect. In the late afternoon, find your way to Central Avenue, just south of Old Town, and drive east on **Historic Route 66.** It takes you straight through downtown and the Nob Hill district, eventually reaching the foothills of the Sandia Mountains. Finish your day with a ride up the **Sandia Peak Tramway** (p. 198). Once on top, you might hike along the crest, though this isn't safe for young kids. Ideally, you should ride up in daylight, watch the sunset, and then ride back down for a dazzling view of the city lights. You may even want to dine up on the peak at **High Finance Restaurant and Tavern** (p. 186)—practically every table has a great view out its many windows.

Day 3: The Turquoise Trail & Santa Fe

For a prettier and more relaxing drive than you'll get on the interstate, strike out for the ghost towns and other sights along the **Turquoise Trail** (p. 219) on your way to Santa Fe. Stop in **Madrid** (p. 220) and browse through a few of the galleries, and when you reach **Cerrillos** (p. 220), take a short side trip to Cerrillos State Park. This will put you in Santa Fe in time to do a little shopping and sightseeing. Head straight to the **plaza** and take our walking tour (p. 87). While browsing the wares for sale by the American Indians under the Palace portal, you might inquire about the significance of symbols on pottery or in the jewelry design. Eat dinner at the **Bull Ring** (p. 62).

Day 4: Santa Fe Arts

In the morning, take a stroll and do some shopping on **Canyon Road** (p. 95), with its top-notch assortment of art galleries. For lunch, head to **Cowgirl BBQ** (p. 64) for fun surroundings and good chow. Time now to head up to Museum Hill, where you can take your pick from four unique museums: the **Museum of International Folk Art** (p. 76), the **Museum of Indian Arts and Culture** (p. 76), the **Wheelwright Museum of the American Indian** (p. 77), and the **Museum of Spanish Colonial Art**

(p. 76). At sunset during the warmer months, a smart option is to enjoy a cocktail at the bell tower of the historic **La Fonda** hotel (p. 52).

Day 5: Bandelier National Monument & North to Taos

Head north out of town to **Bandelier National Monument** (p. 114). Linger among the ruins, and be sure to climb the ladders to see the kiva set high above the canyon floor. Then continue north to Taos. As you make the final climb out of the canyon, pull over into the parking area on your right for a dramatic view of the Rio Grande Gorge in the late afternoon shadows, and the magnificent Sangre de Cristo Mountains with Taos spread at their feet. On your way through Ranchos de Taos, stop for a look at **San Francisco de Asis church** (p. 146), then head to **La Cocina de Taos** (p. 138) for dinner.

Day 6: Taos

Start the day exploring **Taos Pueblo** (p. 146) when the sun strikes the face of the four- and five-story adobe. Then head out to the **Millicent Rogers Museum** (p. 145), and if time permits, make a quick trip to see—and walk out on—the **Rio Grande Gorge Bridge** (p. 149). You can then ditch your car for the afternoon and step out on foot. Wander **Taos Plaza,** do some shopping, check out the **Ernest L. Blumenschein Home & Museum** (p. 143), the **Harwood Museum of Art** (p. 143), or the **Taos Firehouse Collection** (p. 150). At cocktail time, head to the **Adobe Bar** (p. 135), and follow that up with dinner at **Doc Martin's** (p. 135), both in the **Historic Taos Inn** (p. 126).

Day 7: The High Road

On your last day, enjoy a real Taos breakfast at **Michael's Kitchen** (p. 142) and then head south on the **High Road to Taos** (p. 117). Be sure to spend some time at the lovely **Santuario de Chimayo** (p. 117) to hear about its miraculous healing dirt, and stop for lunch at **Rancho de Chimayo** (p. 117). Depending on your flight time the next morning, stay the night in Santa Fe or Albuquerque.

NORTHERN NEW MEXICO IN 2 WEEKS

If you have 2 weeks to spend exploring the region, consider yourself fortunate. In addition to hitting the highlights, you'll be able to spend time getting to know such places as Los Alamos and ride an historic narrow gauge steam train. See map on p. 37.

Days 1–4: Albuquerque & Santa Fe

For days 1 to 4, follow the previous itinerary, "Northern New Mexico in a Week."

Day 5: Santa Fe

In the morning, browse around the Plaza area some more, spending a little extra time at the **Museum of Contemporary Native Arts** (p. 77) and the **Loretto Chapel** (p. 81). Have lunch at **La Cantina at the Coyote Cafe** (p. 66), enjoying the colorfully painted rooftop terrace. In the afternoon, make your way over to the **Georgia O'Keeffe Museum** (p. 72), finishing off with a visit to the "Roundhouse," **New Mexico's State Capitol** (p. 84) and the only round capitol building in the United States. For an excellent steak dinner, you can't miss at the **Rio Chama Steakhouse** (p. 64).

Day 6: High Road to Taos

On Day 6, travel the **High Road to Taos** (see p. 117), stopping to visit the **Santuario de Chimayo** (p. 117) and hear about its miraculous healing dirt, and maybe sampling real northern New Mexico cuisine for lunch at **Rancho de Chimayo** (p. 117). On the way into Taos, stop at the **San Francisco de Asis church** (p. 146) to gaze at the most-photographed back side of a church, with its huge buttresses, perhaps adding dinner across the street at **Old Martina's Hall** (p. 139).

Days 7 & 8: Taos

Begin by exploring **Taos Pueblo** (p. 146) when the sun strikes the face of the four- and five-story adobe. Then head to the **Millicent Rogers Museum** (p. 145), and if time permits, make a quick trip to see—and walk out on—the **Rio Grande Gorge Bridge** (p. 149). You can then ditch your car for the afternoon and step out on foot. Wander **Taos Plaza,** do some shopping, check out the **Ernest L. Blumenschein Home & Museum** (p. 143), the **Harwood Museum of Art** (p. 143), or the **Taos Firehouse Collection** (p. 150). At cocktail time, head to the **Adobe Bar** (p. 135), and follow that up with dinner at **Doc Martin's** (p. 135), both in the Historic Taos Inn.

Start Day 8 with a real Taos breakfast at **Michael's Kitchen** (p. 142) and then visit the **Taos Art Museum** (p. 146). The Fechin Home where the museum is housed is a work of art in itself. Take a stroll around the **Kit Carson Park and Cemetery** (p. 149), where the famed frontier scout is buried, then head to **La Hacienda de Los Martinez** (p. 145) for a look at how a well-to-do trader lived in the early 19th century.

Day 9: The Enchanted Circle

Take the 90-mile loop from Taos north through old Hispanic villages and mining towns to see some of the region's most picturesque landscapes. If you're a literary type, be sure to stop at the **D. H. Lawrence Ranch** (p. 147), and if you're a hiker, stretch your legs at the **Wild Rivers Recreation Area** (p. 169). You can lunch in either Red River or Eagle Nest.

Northern New Mexico in 2 Weeks

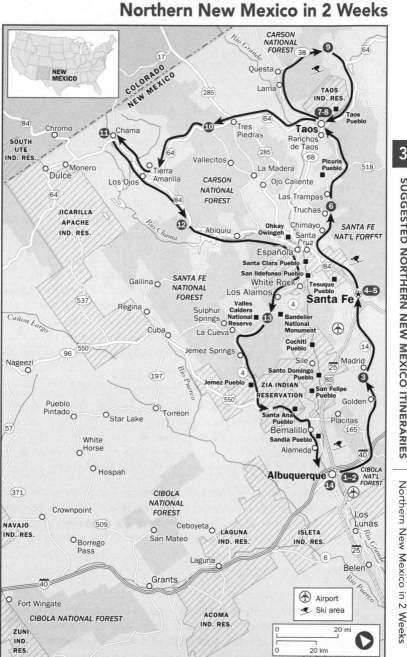

37

Day 10: West to Chama

If you're traveling in the spring, summer, or fall, take a scenic—not speedy—drive west through the mountains to **Chama.** Stop at one of the overlooks when you top out, stretch your legs, and gaze at the huge formation called the Brazos Box. Once in Chama, stroll around town and the depot to get a feel for the area's steam train history, and prepare for tomorrow's ride on the **Cumbres & Toltec Scenic Railroad** (p. 172). Volunteers are sometimes on hand to relate stories about the train and its history. Be sure to make your train reservations well in advance. As well as offering a great ride, the Cumbres & Toltec is a living train museum, so sit back and enjoy your ride into yesterday. Or, if you're not a train buff, take a whitewater raft trip through the exciting **Taos Box** (p. 157) or Pilar.

If it's wintertime, when the trains aren't running, here's an excellent high-desert option: Stay in Taos and head to **Taos Ski Valley** (p. 152) for a day of skiing.

Day 11: Cumbres & Toltec Scenic Railroad

Spend the day riding the **Cumbres & Toltec Scenic Railroad** (p. 172). You can ride the train to the luncheon stop at Osier Pass and turn around and come back, or continue on the train all the way to Antonito, Colorado, and return to Chama by bus. Spend the night in Chama. If you don't ride the train and have stayed in Taos, take a **llama trek** (p. 157), with a gourmet lunch, or (in winter) spend another day on the slopes at **Taos Ski Valley** (p. 152).

Day 12: Head South to Los Alamos

Drive south through stupendous scenery, passing through Georgia O'Keeffe country: Abiquiu and the crimson-and-white hills she painted (see p. 72). When you reach **Los Alamos** (p. 111), be aware that you've left ancient history behind and entered a town that didn't exist before World War II. But there's plenty to see before you bed down for the night.

Day 13: Bandelier National Monument

You might make a side trip to **Valles Caldera National Preserve** (p. 116), before driving to **Bandelier National Monument** (p. 114), where you'll hike among ancient ruins. Follow the Main Loop Trail through the ruins, making sure you stop to climb the ladders to the kiva perched high on the canyon wall. Finally, drive back to Albuquerque.

Day 14: Albuquerque

A great finale to your visit would be to take a **balloon ride** (p. 208) first thing in the morning. (Be sure to make your reservations well in advance.) Then head to the **Anderson-Abruzzo Albuquerque International Balloon Museum** (p. 196) to learn about ballooning's history. Finish the afternoon cooling off at your hotel pool, or if you're feeling energetic, visit the **National Hispanic Cultural Center** (p. 197). Have dinner at **Chama River Brewing Company** (p. 188) or **Trombino's Bistro Italiano** (p. 191).

AN ACTIVE TOUR OF NORTHERN NEW MEXICO

Anyone who skis, hikes, mountain bikes, or rafts knows that all of the Southwest is unsurpassed in its offerings for outdoor enthusiasts. New Mexico is no exception, and the highest concentration of these sports and outdoor activities lies in the north. You can ski world-class terrain at **Taos Ski Valley,** bike the edge of the **Rio Grande Gorge,** and hike the mountains among the ancestral Puebloan ruins at **Bandelier National Monument.** Be aware that the region is known for its mercurial weather conditions—always be prepared for extremes. Also, most of northern New Mexico is over 6,000 feet in elevation, so it may take you time to catch your breath. Be patient on the long upward hills. The sports you do will, of course, depend a lot on the season. For the full benefit of this trip, take it in late March or early April. With a little advance preparation, you might be able to ski and river raft on the same trip! See map on p. 40.

Days 1 & 2: Albuquerque

When you arrive in Albuquerque, you may want to get acclimated to the city by strolling through **Old Town** (p. 197) and visiting the **ABQ BioPark** (p. 199) to get a sense of the nature in the area. A visit to the **Indian Pueblo Cultural Center** (p. 196) will acquaint you with some of the culture you'll encounter as you head north. On Day 2, for a truly unique experience, you may want to schedule a **balloon ride** (p. 208) first thing in the morning. Just be sure to make advance reservations for this exhilarating activity. If you're a bike rider or hiker, head to **Petroglyph National Monument** (p. 204) to see thousands of symbols etched in stone. In the evening, ride the **Sandia Peak Tramway** (p. 198) and go hiking along the crest. If you like, you can have dinner at the **High Finance Restaurant and Tavern** (p. 186) and view the city lights as you come down.

Day 3: The Turquoise Trail to Santa Fe

For a prettier and more relaxing drive than you'll get on the interstate, strike out for the ghost towns and other sights along the **Turquoise Trail** (p. 219) on your way to Santa Fe. Stop in **Madrid** (p. 220) and browse through a few of the galleries, and when you reach **Cerrillos** (p. 220) take a short side trip to the Cerrillos State Park. This will put you in Santa Fe in time to do some sightseeing. Head straight to the **plaza** (p. 87), the **Palace of the Governors** (p. 74), and the **St. Francis Cathedral** (p. 82). While browsing the wares for sale by the American Indians under the

An Active Tour of Northern New Mexico

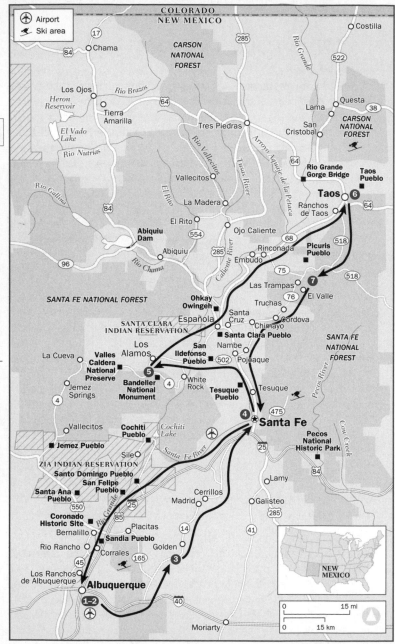

Palace portal, you might inquire about the significance of symbols on pottery or in the jewelry design. Eat dinner at **Bouche French Bistro** (p. 60).

Day 4: Santa Fe

Use your own bike or rent a cruiser in town to ride around the plaza and up **Canyon Road** (p. 91). Stop at the top of Canyon Road at the **Randall Davey Audubon Center** (p. 82) to do some bird-watching. Alternatively, you may want to head to the mountains to do some hiking on the **Borrego Trail** (p. 92) or, if it's winter, some skiing at **Ski Santa Fe** (p. 93). Finish your day at one of the fun restaurants or cafes near the **Plaza** (p. 87). In the evening, depending on the season, you may want to take in some of Santa Fe's excellent arts, such as the **Santa Fe Opera** (p. 101) or the **Santa Fe Chamber Music Festival** (p. 101).

Day 5: Bandelier National Monument

Head out from Santa Fe to **Bandelier National Monument** (p. 114) and hike among ancient ruins. Follow the Main Loop Trail as far up as you'd like, making sure you stop to climb the ladders to the kiva perched high on the canyon wall. Hikers should take the Falls Trail up Frijoles Canyon to a striking waterfall. From Bandelier, drive along the Rio Grande north to Taos. Spend the evening strolling around the **plaza** (p. 159) to get a feel for the town, perhaps stopping for a libation and to hear some local music at the Taos Inn's **Adobe Bar** (p. 135).

Day 6: Taos

Sports lovers have many options in this town. **Horseback rides** will take you out on the mesas or exploring the forests around the ski valley (p. 156). Alternatively, you may want to take a **llama trek** (p. 157) into the Rio Grande Gorge, or hike on one of the many trails in the **Carson National Forest** (p. 172). If it's ski season, you'll definitely want to spend the day at **Taos Ski Valley** (p. 152), or if you're visiting in the spring and the rivers are running, take the full-day heart-throbbing romp through the **Taos Box** (p. 157) or a half-day trip at Pilar.

Day 7: The High Road

On your last day, take a leisurely drive south toward Santa Fe along the **High Road** (p. 117), stopping at the churches along the way. In Chimayó don't miss **Ortega's Weaving Shop** (p. 117), or the **Santuario de Chimayo** (p. 117). And lunch on the patio at **Rancho de Chimayo** (p. 117) is a real treat. Depending on your plane reservations, spend the night in Santa Fe or Albuquerque.

An Active Tour of Northern New Mexico

SANTA FE ESSENTIALS

After visiting Santa Fe, humorist Will Rogers reportedly said, "Whoever designed this town did so while riding on a jackass backwards and drunk." Well, we can't argue with that. You, too, may find yourself perplexed when maneuvering through the meandering lanes and one-way streets, in this, the oldest capital city in the United States. But Santa Fe's crooked streets, combined with its stunning setting at the base of rugged mountains, provide a sense of exotic sophistication. On its historic central plaza, you'll see American Indians selling jewelry, locals cruising along in souped-up low-riders and vintage pickup trucks, and people young and old just hanging out. Such diversity, coupled with the variety of architecture—which ranges from Pueblo style to Romanesque to Gothic—prompted the tourism promotion people to label Santa Fe "The City Different."

Remember to pack your walking shoes, because exploring Santa Fe by foot is the best way to enjoy its idiosyncrasies. And if you do get lost, ask one of the roughly 70,000 people living here—7,000 feet above sea level—for directions.

ORIENTATION

Arriving

BY PLANE   Many people heading to Santa Fe choose to fly into the Albuquerque International Sunport, the state's largest airport. This is especially worthwhile if you are also visiting Albuquerque. The Sunport is about 66 miles from Santa Fe, a straight shoot via I-25. All major car rental companies operate out of Albuquerque Sunport; if you don't want to drive yourself, **Sandia Shuttle Express** (www.sandiashuttle.com; © **888/775-5696** or 505/474-5696) runs shuttles daily from the Sunport to Santa Fe. **New Mexico Rail Runner Express** (see below) also runs to Santa Fe, with a shuttle bus taking travelers from the airport to the train.

If you plan to skip Albuquerque, you can save time (but pay a bit more) by flying into the **Santa Fe Municipal Airport** (SAF; www.santafenm.gov/airport; ✆ **505/955-2903**), just outside the southwestern city limits off Airport Road. The airport has non-stop service from Dallas/Fort Worth and seasonally from Los Angeles with **American Airlines** (www.aa.com; ✆ **800/433-7300**), plus non-stop service from Denver with **United Airlines** (www.united.com; ✆ **800/864-8331**). From the Santa Fe Municipal Airport, **Roadrunner Shuttle** (www.roadrunnershuttleandcharter.com; ✆ **505/424-3367**) meets every commercial flight and takes visitors anywhere in Santa Fe. For car rentals, see p. 47.

BY TRAIN   Daily train service from Albuquerque to Santa Fe is provided by **New Mexico Rail Runner Express** (www.nmrailrunner.com; ✆ **866/795-7245**). **Amtrak** (www.amtrak.com; ✆ **800/872-7245**) has a daily east-west train, the *Southwest Chief,* running from Chicago to Los Angeles, which stops in Lamy, about 20 miles from Santa Fe. **Lamy Shuttle & Tours** (✆ **505/982-8829**) provides transportation between downtown Santa Fe and the train station. Cost is $20 per person one-way; reservations should be made at least 24 hours in advance.

BY CAR   I-25 skims past Santa Fe's southern city limits, connecting it along one continuous highway from Billings, Montana, to El Paso, Texas. I-40, the state's major east–west thoroughfare, which bisects Albuquerque, affords coast-to-coast access. (From the west, motorists leave I-40 in Albuquerque and take I-25 north; from the east, travelers exit I-40 at Clines Corners and continue 52 miles to Santa Fe on US 285.) For those coming from the northwest, the most direct route is via Durango, Colorado, on US 160, entering Santa Fe on US 84.

Visitor Information & Maps

Official **Santa Fe Visitor Information Centers** are located at the Convention Center, 201 W. Marcy St. (✆ **505/955-6200**); on the south side of the plaza in Plaza Galeria, 66 E. San Francisco St., Suite 3 (✆ **505/955-6215**); at the New Mexico Tourism Department, 491 Old Santa Fe Trail (www.newmexico.org; ✆ **505/827-7336**); and at the Santa Fe Depot, 410 S. Guadalupe St. (✆ **505/955-6230**). You can also log on to the visitor information website at www.santafe.org or call ✆ **800/777-2489.**

Free **city and official state maps** and other information can be obtained at tourist information offices, including the Santa Fe Visitor Information Centers (see above). Other good sources for maps and information are the **State Welcome Centers.** There's one you'll pass when driving from Albuquerque to Santa Fe on I-25, in a rest area about 17 miles south of Santa Fe at mile marker 269. This rest area is easily accessed heading north toward Santa Fe, but almost impossible to get to if you're driving south from Santa Fe to Albuquerque.

Members of the **American Automobile Association (AAA),** 2517 Zafarano Dr., Suite D (www.aaa.com; ✆ **877/222-1020** or 505/471-6620), can obtain free maps and other information from the AAA office. Other good regional and city maps can be purchased at area bookstores.

Santa Fe Orientation

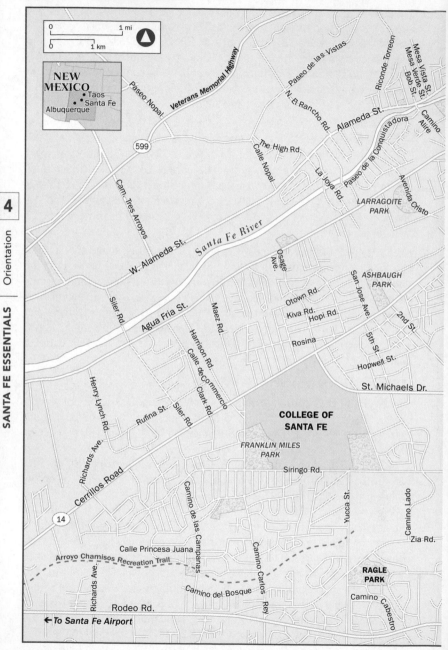

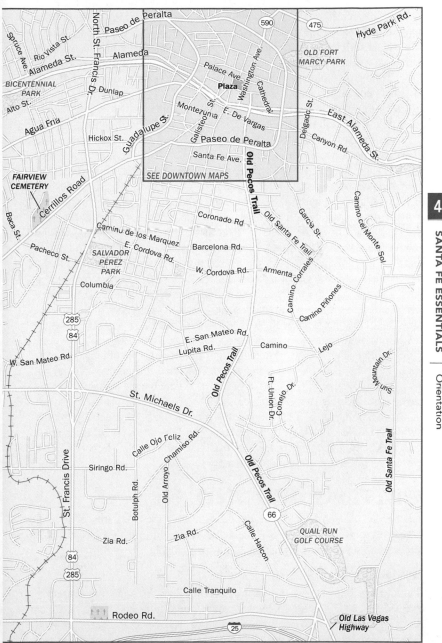

City Layout

MAIN ARTERIES & STREETS The limits of downtown Santa Fe are loosely demarcated on three sides by the horseshoe-shaped **Paseo de Peralta** and on the west by **St. Francis Drive,** otherwise known as US 84/285. **Alameda Street** follows the north side of the Santa Fe River through downtown. The State Capitol and other government buildings are on the south side of the river, while most buildings of historic and tourist interest are on the north, east of Guadalupe Street.

Santa Fe Plaza is Santa Fe's universally accepted point of orientation. Here, you'll find tall shade trees, lots of grass, and plenty of tourists. Its four diagonal walkways meet at a central fountain. If you stand in the center of the plaza looking north, you'll be facing the Palace of the Governors. In front of you is Palace Avenue; behind you, San Francisco Street. To your left is Lincoln Avenue, and to your right is Washington Avenue, which divides the downtown avenues into east and west. St. Francis Cathedral is the massive Romanesque structure a block east, down San Francisco Street. Alameda Street, which follows the Santa Fe River, is 2 full blocks behind you. To the south of the plaza is the **Santa Fe River,** a tiny tributary of the Rio Grande that runs most of the year. Near the intersection of Alameda Street and Paseo de Peralta, you'll find **Canyon Road,** a narrow, mostly one-way street packed with galleries and shops. Once it was the home of many artists, and today you'll still find some at work within gallery studios. A number of fine restaurants are in this district as well.

Leading southwest from the downtown area, beginning opposite the state office buildings on Galisteo Street, is **Cerrillos Road.** Once the main north-south highway, NM 14, connecting Santa Fe with Albuquerque, it is now a 6-mile-long motel and fast-food strip, most of which ends at the I-25 interchange. **St. Francis Drive,** which crosses Cerrillos Road 3 blocks southwest of Guadalupe Street, is a far more direct route to I-25, intersecting with the highway 4 miles southwest of downtown. The **Old Pecos Trail,** on the east side of the city, also connects downtown and the freeway. **St. Michael's Drive** crosses all three arteries south of downtown.

GETTING AROUND

The best way to see downtown Santa Fe, especially the plaza area, is on foot. Free **walking-tour maps** are available at Visitor Information Centers (see above), and several guided walking tours are available (see p. 87).

By Bus

Santa Fe's public bus system, **Santa Fe Trails** (www.santafenm.gov/transit; ℂ 505/955-2001), has ten routes; although primarily geared to the needs of Santa Fe residents, they are also an economical way for visitors to get around the city, with buses serving the plaza area, Museum Hill, and Cerrillos Road. One trip for adults costs $1; a one-day pass costs $2, and a 31-day pass costs

SANTA FE ESSENTIALS | Getting Around

$20. Rates are half that for seniors 60 and older and people with disabilities, and youths up to age 18 ride free. Fares must be paid in cash on the buses; checks and credit cards are accepted at the bus system office, 2131 Rufina Street. Visitors can pick up a map from any of the Visitor Information Centers. Most buses operate Monday to Friday 6am to 10pm and Saturday 8am to 8pm. There is limited service on Sunday and holidays.

By Car

Overall, you'll probably need a car in Santa Fe—there are quite a few places you'll want to go where driving yourself makes the most sense—but when exploring the plaza area, it's best to leave the car parked and do so on foot. (See our walking tour, p. 87.) **Street parking** is difficult to find during summer months, especially near the plaza. There are three metered parking lots within walking distance of the plaza: one at 100 E. Water Street a block south, which closes at night; and two 24-hour lots just south of St. Francis Cathedral, at 215 Cathedral Place and at 251 E. Alameda Street. In addition, there are two public parking garages near the plaza: at 216 W. San Francisco St. 2 blocks west, and at the convention center, 119 S. Federal Place 2 blocks north. At the Santa Fe Railyard, there's a parking garage at the north end, and a lot toward the south. Santa Fe Visitor Information Centers (see above) can give you a printed guide to Santa Fe parking areas.

> ### Driving Warning
>
> New Mexico has one of the highest per-capita rates of traffic deaths in the nation (mostly due to drunk driving), and also a high rate of uninsured motorists. It's a good idea to be especially cautious while driving, especially at intersections.

The State Highway and Transportation Department has a toll-free **Road Advisory Hotline** (⑦ **511** or 800/432-4269) and also a website—www. nmroads.com—that provides current information on road closures and driving conditions.

By Bicycle

Riding a bicycle is somewhat challenging in downtown Santa Fe due to its narrow streets and limited number of bike paths. However, it is a good way to get around for experienced city riders. You can rent bikes from **Mellow Velo,** 132 E. Marcy St. (www.mellowvelo.com; ⑦ **505/995-8356**) and **Bike-N-Sport,** 524 Cordova Rd. (www.nmbikensport.com; ⑦ **505/820-0809**).

[FastFACTS] SANTA FE

Airport See "Orientation," p. 42.

Car Rentals Avis has an outlet at the Santa Fe Airport (⑦ **505/471-5892**) and another at 1946 Cerrillos Rd. (⑦ **505/984-8109**) shared with **Budget** (⑦ **505/984-1596**). **Hertz** has an outlet at the airport (⑦ **505/471-7189**) and also at 2010 Cerrillos Rd., with the same phone number. **Enterprise** is located at 3961 Cerrillos Rd. (⑦ **505/424-1134**) and 1611 St. Michael's Dr. (⑦ **505/986-1414**).

Cellphones Cellphone coverage is good within the city limits but spotty in rural areas. Santa Fe prohibits the use of hand-held cellphones by drivers.

Currency Exchange You can exchange foreign currency at **Wells Fargo** at 241 Washington Ave. (© **505/984-0500**).

Doctors For a medical emergency, dial © **911.** For other medical issues a combination urgent and primary care facility is **Aspen Medical Center,** 3450 Zafarano Dr., Suite C, west of Cerrillos Rd. (www.aspenmedical center.com; © **505/466-5885**), open Monday to Friday 8am to 9pm and Saturday and Sunday 9am to 9pm.

Emergencies For police, fire, or medical emergencies, dial © **911.**

Hotlines Available hotlines include **Poison Control** (© **800/432-6866**) and **Sexual Assault** (© **505/986-9111**).

Internet Access Head to the **Santa Fe Public Library** and its two branch libraries for free Wi-Fi. See addresses below.

Libraries The **Santa Fe Public Library** is half a block from the plaza, at 145 Washington Ave. (www. santefelibrary.org; © **505/955-6781**). The Oliver La Farge Branch library is at 1730 Llano St., just off St. Michael's Drive, and the Southside Library is at 6599 Jaguar Dr., at the intersection of Country Club Road.

Newspapers The *New Mexican*—Santa Fe's daily paper—is the oldest newspaper in the West. Its main office is at 202 E. Marcy St. (www.santafenewmexican. com; © **505/983-3303**). The weekly *Santa Fe Reporter,* 132 E. Marcy St. (www.sfreporter.com; © **505/988-5541**), published on Wednesdays and available at stands all over town, is often more controversial, and its entertainment listings are excellent.

Police In case of emergency, dial © **911.** For all other inquiries, contact the **Santa Fe Police Department,** 2515 Camino Entrada (www.santafenm.gov/police; © **505/428-3710**). The **Santa Fe County Sheriff,** with jurisdiction outside the city limits, is at 35 Camino Justicia (© **505/986-2400**).

Post Offices The **main post office** is at 120 S. Federal Place, 2 blocks north and 1 block west of the plaza. It's open Monday to Friday 8am to 5:30pm and Saturday 9am to 4pm. The **Coronado Station branch** is at 2071 S. Pacheco St., and is open Monday to Friday 8am to 6pm and Saturday 9am to 4pm. For additional locations, see www.usps.com or call © **800/275-8777.**

Taxis Cabs are difficult to flag from the street, but you can call **Capital City Cab** (www.capitalcitycab.com; © **505/438-0000**). **Uber** (www.uber.com) also operates its ride-share business in Santa Fe.

WHERE TO STAY IN SANTA FE

The City Different offers a broad range of accommodations. From downtown hotels to Cerrillos Road motels, ranch-style resorts to quaint bed-and-breakfasts, the standard is almost universally high, and so are the prices.

Accommodations are often booked solid through the summer months, the Christmas holiday, and Easter, and most places raise their prices accordingly. Rates increase even more during Indian Market, the third weekend of August, and with some properties, even for the Albuquerque International Balloon Fiesta in early October. During these periods, it's essential to make reservations well in advance and to expect to pay premium. But this brings us to the other side of the coin: Those not particularly interested in Indian Market, the balloon fiesta, summer, or holiday events can save quite a bit by avoiding Santa Fe at these times. You'll also miss the crowds and long lines at

CHAIN MOTELS IN santa fe

In Santa Fe, you'll find a handy string of chain motels along Cerrillos Road, offering a decent alternative to the city's more expensive hotels if you want to save a few bucks. Although you won't be as close to Santa Fe Plaza as you might like, Santa Fe just isn't that big, so nothing's really all that far away. Note that the lower street numbers on Cerrillos Road—say, in the hundreds—are closer to the downtown attractions than the higher numbers, in the thousands, which are down at the south end of Cerrillos, near where it meets I-25.

We're fans of the La Quinta chain, in part because La Quintas generally accept pets with no extra charge—not to be confused with the $75 per night pet fee you'll pay at some downtown properties—but also because we have found these facilities to be clean, generally well-maintained, and a good value. Here the **La Quinta Inn ★★** is an especially attractive property. It's located at 4298 Cerrillos Rd. (www.lq.com; ℂ **800/753-3757**

or 505/471-1142), offers free Wi-Fi and all the usual amenities, with winter rates of $62 to $79 double and summer rates of about $100 double. Note that if you're eligible, La Quinta's AARP rates are often a bit lower than its AAA rates.

Other popular chains include the **Santa Fe Courtyard by Marriott ★★,** 3347 Cerrillos Rd. (www.santafe courtyard.com; ℂ **505/473-2800**), offering winter rates of $93 to $129 double and summer rates of $139 to $149 double; and **Super 8 Santa Fe ★,** 3358 Cerrillos Rd. (www.super8.com; ℂ **800/454-3213** or 505/471-8811), with year-round rates of $50 to $60 double.

There's also a **Motel 6 ★** at 646 Cerrillos Rd. (www.motel6.com; ℂ **800/ 899-9841** or 505/982-3551), with rates from $50 to $72 double; and another **Motel 6 ★** at 3695 Cerrillos Rd. (www. motel6.com; ℂ **800/899-9841** or 505/471-4140), with rates from $40 to $52 double.

restaurants. Lowest rates are usually from November through March, except for Christmas, of course. Be sure to check hotel websites for seasonal discounts and packages.

No matter the season, discounts are often available to seniors, affiliated groups, corporate employees, and others, especially at the chain motels (see above).

A little-known way to obtain relatively inexpensive lodging is to bed down in what are usually called **"camping cabins"** at commercial campgrounds. You'll need to bring your own linens and share the campground bathhouses, but these cabins can be very nice and are usually much more affordable than traditional motels and hotels. See "RV Parks & Campgrounds," p. 58.

A combined **city-state tax** of about 15% is added to every hotel bill in Santa Fe. And unless otherwise indicated, all recommended accommodations come with a private bathroom. Unless otherwise noted, parking is free.

RESERVATIONS SERVICES The best all-around reservation service in Santa Fe is the official Santa Fe website—**www.santafe.org**—where you can plunk in dates and other details, get a list of lodgings, locations, amenities, and rates, and if you so choose, book your room right there. It's operated by the Santa Fe Convention and Visitors Bureau. Click on "Accommodations" at the top of the page. If you are looking for a more personal Santa Fe experience, you might consider a privately owned casita, condo, or guesthouse, which you can find through **Santa Fe Stay** (www.santafestay.com; ℂ **800/995-2272** or 505/820-2468).

Downtown

With Santa Fe Plaza at the center, everything within the horseshoe-shaped Paseo de Peralta, along Canyon Road, and in and near the Railyard is considered downtown Santa Fe for the purposes of this book.

EXPENSIVE

Hotel St. Francis ★★   St. Francis of Assisi was a rich aristocrat who gave up a life of luxury to follow an ascetic path of devotion. The hotel named after him offers the best of these two extremes, combining a simple, historic aesthetic with modern luxury. Pillar candles flicker on the plaster walls and wide stone floors in the lobby, while the rooms are sparely but tastefully decorated, with high ceilings and casement windows. The three-story National Historic Register property offers a relaxed cosmopolitan vibe, with a multilingual concierge and high tea in the lobby every afternoon. (Don't miss the cherubs above the Victorian fireplace in the lobby, a motif that's repeated elsewhere.) Some of the rooms are small, as is the fitness center. The hotel has an acclaimed New Mexican restaurant, **Tabla de Los Santos,** and the **Secreto** wine and cocktail bar, with its sidewalk loggia, is a local favorite for a drink and street-side people-watching.

210 Don Gaspar Ave. www.hotelstfrancis.com. 80 units. ℂ **800/529-5700** or 505/983-5700. Doubles $99–$289. Parking $18 per day. Dogs accepted (2 maximum; $25 per day). **Amenities:** Restaurant; lounge; babysitting; concierge; exercise room; business center; room service; access to nearby spa; free Wi-Fi.

Inn and Spa at Loretto ★★★   Don't feel bad if you're 2 blocks from the plaza in downtown Santa Fe and suddenly think you've spotted an American Indian Pueblo. That's the Inn and Spa at Loretto, built in 1975 and styled after the multistory Taos Pueblo, all shadow-catching corners and flat roofs on the outside. Inside, it's an elegant hotel that enjoyed an extensive renovation in 2008. Unlike the real Taos Pueblo, the rooms are generously sized, with Native design touches like kiva fireplaces and modern amenities like iPod docks and slate-floored bathrooms. Some units have balconies—especially inviting are the ones on the northeast side with views of St. Francis Cathedral and the Loretto Chapel next door. Spring for a junior suite if you can, but be aware of parking and service fees. The **Living Room** lounge hosts live music in front of the fireplace Thursday, Friday, and Saturday nights, the **Luminaria** restaurant serves upscale Southwestern dishes, and the Spa Terre offers a long list of high-end treatments.

211 Old Santa Fe Trail. www.innatloretto.com. ℂ **800/727-5531** or 505/988-5531. Doubles $114–$299 plus $15 service fee. Valet parking $21 per day. Pets accepted (2 maximum, up to 65 pounds, $75 per stay). **Amenities:** Restaurant; lounge; concierge;

Downtown Santa Fe Accommodations

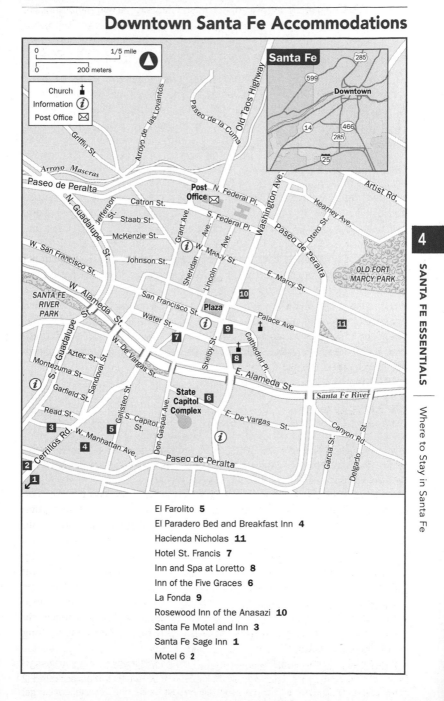

El Farolito **5**
El Paradero Bed and Breakfast Inn **4**
Hacienda Nicholas **11**
Hotel St. Francis **7**
Inn and Spa at Loretto **8**
Inn of the Five Graces **6**
La Fonda **9**
Rosewood Inn of the Anasazi **10**
Santa Fe Motel and Inn **3**
Santa Fe Sage Inn **1**
Motel 6 **2**

24-hour exercise room; 24-hour business center; outdoor pool (heated year-round); room service; spa, free Wi-Fi.

Inn of the Five Graces ★★★   Nestled in the historic Barrio de Analco, a few blocks from the plaza, this Relais & Chateaux hotel is one of the most plush properties in Santa Fe, which is saying a lot. It's named after the Eastern concept of the five senses—sight, sound, touch, smell, and taste—that must be honored to fully experience life. This setting stimulates them all—flower-filled courtyards, bubbling fountains, and artifacts the owners have brought back from Latin America and Central and South Asia, creating a unique "East meets West" atmosphere that wouldn't be too out of place in Bali or Kashmir. Owner Sylvia Seret's tile mosaics adorn the suites' kitchens and bathrooms, along with kilim rugs and carved teakwood beds. Most accommodations have fireplaces, and some have soaking tubs or steam showers. With all this flair, it's the little touches—personal handwritten notes and weather forecasts, fires laid in the fireplaces every evening—that elevate the service to "best-in-your-life" levels (just ask some of the many repeat guests). Suites on the north side of the street are larger, while less expensive rooms are (unsurprisingly) smaller. The inn boasts the **315 Restaurant and Wine Bar** next door, a Tibetan spa treatment room, and wine and cheese every other afternoon.

150 East De Vargas St. www.fivegraces.com. ✆ **866/992-0957** or 505/992-0957. 24 units. Doubles $550–$750, suites from $750. Includes full breakfast and afternoon treats. Pets accepted ($75 per day). Limited rooms for children under 5. **Amenities:** Restaurant; lounge; room service; exercise room; valet laundry; 24-hour concierge; free Wi-Fi.

La Fonda ★★★   According to the historical record, there has been a *fonda*, or inn, at this location—on the southeast corner of the plaza—almost since Santa Fe was founded in 1607. This incarnation was built in 1922 by famed Santa Fe architect John Gaw Meem, with help from Southwest designer Mary Elizabeth Jane Colter. It served as a railway hotel and a Harvey House over the years, lending more weight to its claim of being the oldest and best-known hotel in Santa Fe. This is definitely an iconic place, once the end of the Santa Fe Trail and now a high-end hotel that still oozes history, from the cafe in its time warp–tiled lobby to its Pueblo Revival tower. The property is filled with art and antiques—and often ogling visitors, at least in the lobby—and boasts an unusually high level of personal service. All the rooms were totally renovated in 2013, keeping warm design touches like painted headboards but adding modernizations such as better climate controls. The hotel's famous **Bell Tower Bar,** the best place in town to enjoy a sunset cocktail from spring through fall, was also expanded.

100 E. San Francisco St. www.lafondasantafe.com. ✆ **800/523-5002** or 505/982-5511. 180 units. Doubles $129–$374. Children 12 and under stay free in parent's room. Parking $16 per day. Pets accepted (under 40 pounds, $25 per pet per night). **Amenities:** Restaurant; 2 lounges; babysitting; on-site car rentals; concierge; exercise room; hot tub; outdoor heated pool (open year-round); room service; sauna; spa, 24-hour business center; free Wi-Fi.

Rosewood Inn of the Anasazi ★★   From the outside, this boutique hotel could pass for something out of the 19th century, all weathered wood beams and adobe-colored walls. Inside, it's a tasteful, posh hotel, with an excellent restaurant and bar, a cozy library with overstuffed chairs, and a lobby decorated with primitive art, flagstone floors, and spindly cacti. The rooms feature Navajo rugs, kiva-style gas fireplaces, and other warm touches like iron candleholders (and, thank you, humidifiers). A few have balconies. Remodels in 2006 and 2013 seem to have only elevated the furnishings, along with the level of service. This is the kind of place where the folks at the front desk greet you by name and there's a pair of oatmeal raisin cookies on your pillow every evening. This atmosphere of luxurious intimacy doesn't come cheap, and you'll also have to forgo features like hot tubs and pools, but for a high-end choice right off the plaza, the Rosewood Inn of the Anasazi is very hard to top.

113 Washington Ave. www.rosewoodhotels.com/en/inn-of-the-anasazi-santa-fe. © **505/988-3030** or 888/767-3966. 58 units. Doubles $196–$595, suites from $855. Valet parking $20 per day. Pets accepted ($50 per day). **Amenities:** Restaurant; lounge; concierge; library/boardroom; business center; room service; free Wi-Fi.

MODERATE

Santa Fe Motel & Inn ★★   The Santa Fe Motel & Inn boasts a central location and reasonable prices, always a good combination in this pricey city. Although technically a motel, it feels like a B&B, with friendly service, antique furnishings, and a full hot breakfast included in the rates. (Fresh cinnamon rolls definitely hit the spot first thing in the morning.) The rooms are tastefully decorated in Southwest style, with fresh flowers and radiant baseboard heat, and most have kitchenettes with fridges and stoves. For a little more, reserve one of three historic casitas with a bit more Santa Fe charm and private patios.

510 Cerrillos Rd. www.santafemotel.com. © **800/930-5002** or 505/982-1039. Rooms $109–$209, includes breakfast. Free parking. **Amenities:** Free Wi-Fi.

INEXPENSIVE

Santa Fe Sage Inn ★   This two-story motel right next to Whole Foods supermarket is a good deal with a central location, only 6 blocks from the plaza. The property fills three buildings just south of the Railyard district, and is more tastefully decorated and generally nicer than many of its budget-to-midrange competitors. Rooms are simply decorated, many with American Indian–style rugs and wooden furnishings. There's even a small swimming pool. Make sure to ask for a room on the second floor, in the back, for the quietest night.

725 Cerrillos Rd. www.santafesageinn.com. © **866/433-0335** or 505/982-5952. Rooms $94–$159, includes breakfast. Parking $5 per day. Pets accepted ($15 per pet per day). **Amenities:** 24-hour exercise room; 24-hour business center; coin-op laundry; seasonal heated outdoor pool; free Wi-Fi.

Outside Downtown

Santa Fe's main artery from downtown south to I-25 and Albuquerque is Cerrillos Road, NM 14. Once the main route to and from Albuquerque, NM 14 becomes very scenic south of I-25, as it skirts the mountains on the east. North of I-25, however, it's a commercial strip with lots of chain hotel and fast-food options. It's about 5¼ miles from the plaza to the Santa Fe mall at the corner of Cerrillos and Rodeo roads, which marks the southern boundary of the city. Most motels are on this strip, although several of them are to the east, closer to St. Francis Drive (US 84) or the Las Vegas Highway.

MODERATE

El Rey Inn ★   This enchanting, historic adobe motel is pure old Santa Fe. It opened in 1936 with 12 rooms on the original Route 66. It has the traditional northern New Mexico thick adobe walls, corner kiva fireplaces, massive log vigas, beautiful woodwork, and understated southwestern furnishings. Some suites have kitchenettes. The El Rey sits on 5 nicely landscaped acres, with delightful patio areas with umbrella tables, pots of flowers, and a fountain. In 2003, the National Wildlife Federation awarded the inn Backyard Wildlife Habitat status. No two rooms are alike—fun for repeat visitors—and you'll want to request a room back from busy Cerrillos Road. The best units here surround the Spanish colonial courtyard, with upscale amenities. The two-story inn does not have an elevator, so those with mobility issues should specify ground floor.

1862 Cerrillos Rd. www.elreyinnsantafe.com. © **800/521-1349** or 505/982-1931. 86 units. Doubles $93–$215; suites $155–$295. Rates include continental breakfast. **Amenities:** Exercise room; 2 hot tubs; outdoor pool (summer only); children's playground; sauna; free Wi-Fi.

Hyatt Place Santa Fe ★★   No "Santa Fe charm" here, but a very nice, modern hotel with spacious and well-appointed rooms sporting light colors, large windows, and separate living and sleeping areas. It's the sort of place you could move into long-term, and although its main purpose is to serve business and extended-stay guests, the Hyatt Place also works well for vacationers. Rooms have king beds and an oversize sofa-sleeper or sofa, and because it caters to business travelers, each unit has a separate work area and remote printing. Located near the south end of Cerrillos Road, it is not within

Accommodations & Dining on Cerrillos Road

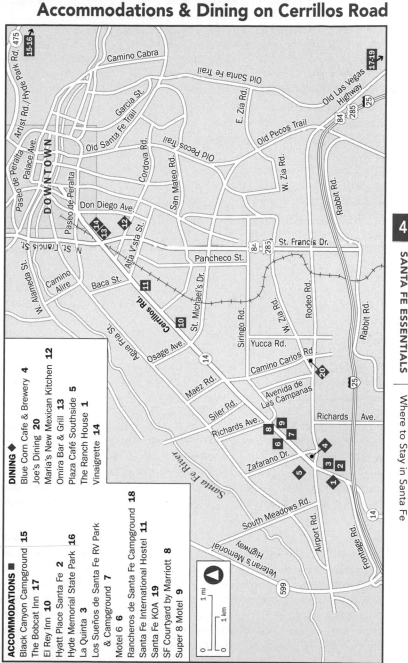

ACCOMMODATIONS ■

Black Canyon Campground **15**
The Bobcat Inn **17**
El Rey Inn **10**
Hyatt Place Santa Fe **2**
Hyde Memorial State Park **16**
La Quinta **3**
Los Sueños de Santa Fe RV Park & Campground **7**
Motel 6 **6**
Rancheros de Santa Fe Campground **18**
Santa Fe International Hostel **11**
Santa Fe KOA **19**
SF Courtyard by Marriott **8**
Super 8 Motel **9**

DINING ◆

Blue Corn Cafe & Brewery **4**
Joe's Dining **20**
Maria's New Mexican Kitchen **12**
Omira Bar & Grill **13**
Plaza Café Southside **5**
The Ranch House **1**
Vinaigrette **14**

walking distance of most of Santa Fe's attractions, but there is complimentary shuttle service to anywhere within 5 miles of the hotel.

4320 Cerrillos Rd. www.hyattplacesantafe.com. 92 units. © **800/993-4751** or 505/474-7777. Doubles $90–$154. Children 18 and younger free. Rates include breakfast. Pets accepted (2 maximum, up to 50 pounds, for up to 1 week; $75 per stay). $100 cleaning fee for stays more than 1 week. **Amenities:** Restaurant; concierge; 24-hour exercise room; heated indoor pool; 24-hour business center; 24-hour room service; free Wi-Fi.

INEXPENSIVE

Santa Fe International Hostel ★ This non-profit offers the most affordable lodging we can recommend in Santa Fe, and, although simple and basic in true hostel style, the accommodations here are quite pleasant. You can choose from a basic dormitory bed to a small private room with bath (shower only, no tub). There are also private rooms with shared bath and private rooms with half baths (sink and toilet only). The common bathhouses have private showers, and all the private rooms have functioning door locks. Each dormitory is single sex and sleeps four to seven people. The entire hostel, including grounds, is non-smoking and alcohol-free, and photo IDs are required of all guests. Food, beverages, and sleeping bags are not permitted in the rooms. There is no maid service; all guests are required to clean their rooms before they leave and help clean the common areas. Also available is a small efficiency apartment at $60 per night single or double. Because the mission of the hostel is to support educational travel, lodging is not available to New Mexico residents.

1412 Cerrillos Rd., across from the Santa Fe Indian School. www.hostelsantafe.org. © **505/988-1153.** Dorm bed $20, doubles with shared bath $35, with half bath $40, with private 3/4 bath $45. Children under 13, $5. **Amenities:** Communal kitchen stocked with food staples (free); coin-op laundry; Wi-Fi $2 per day.

Bed & Breakfasts

If you prefer a homey, intimate setting to the sometimes impersonal ambience of a large hotel, one of Santa Fe's bed-and-breakfast inns may be right for you. All those listed here are in or close to the downtown area and offer comfortable accommodations at expensive to moderate prices.

The Bobcat Inn ★★ This delightful little B&B is a bit out of the center of things, but if you're looking for a quiet place to hole up and enjoy warm hospitality and delicious breakfasts, this is where you want to be. And as a bonus, the Bobcat Inn is a great value. There are five rooms and two detached guesthouses on 10 acres with views of the Ortiz Mountains. There's even an actual bobcat trail behind the place, where the wild cats sometimes can be seen in the spring. The rooms and common area are decorated with colorful but low-key Southwest furniture, weaving, and art. Some units have kiva fireplaces, and one has a whirlpool tub. The guesthouses both have private patio decks. Breakfasts here are special, and varied. Especially popular are the spinach portabella frittata and the blueberry and macaroon bread pudding with warm apricot sauce. *Note:* The Bobcat Inn is located on a hill and guests will need 4X4 vehicles or chains during winter snowstorms.

442 Old Las Vegas Hwy. www.nm-inn.com. ℂ **505/988-9239.** 7 units. Doubles $120–$149, includes breakfast. Children over 6 welcome. **Amenities:** Access to nearby fitness center with swimming pools and tennis courts; guest computer; free Wi-Fi.

El Farolito ★★★   One of the best B&Bs in Santa Fe—an intimate compound of gardens and sunny walled patios—is only a few blocks from the plaza. Rooms are outfitted in different styles, including Western, folk art, Spanish colonial, American Indian, and Santa Fe. All share a tasteful artistic sensibility, as well as features like beeswax-rubbed walls and hand-carved furniture. Seven units have kiva fireplaces, with wood provided free October 15 to May 1, and the Santa Fe Suite has a gas fireplace usable year-round. All units have either shared or private garden patios. Service is top-notch and attentive. Homemade cookies, biscotti, and beverages are available all day, but save room for the buffet-style breakfast, which includes fresh fruit, gourmet coffee, and a hot main dish such as a frittata or eggs with corned beef hash.

514 Galisteo Dr. www.farolito.com. ℂ **888/634-8782** or 505/988-1631. 8 units. Doubles $160–$240, suite $275. Rates include breakfast. **Amenities:** Babysitting by appointment; free Wi-Fi.

El Paradero Bed and Breakfast Inn ★★   This early-19th-century adobe farmhouse may well be Santa Fe's most colorful B&B, on the inside at least. All units are decorated with rugs, weaving, art, and other bright touches in a rainbow southwestern palette—warm reds, muted yellows, inviting greens—that's tasteful, not overwhelming. Some of the rooms feature skylights, balconies, and real kiva fireplaces. The two suites are in a separate building, a turn-of-the-century brick coachman's house, and feature kitchenettes and porches. The owners are a great resource for advice on activities and dining; they can sometimes even secure hard-to-get reservations. The inn has a library and common room for guests, with a TV, fireplace, and full lineup of board games.

220 W. Manhattan Ave. www.elparadero.com. 15 units. ℂ **866/558-0918** or 505/988-1177. Doubles $110–$200, suites $170–$215, includes full breakfast and afternoon tea. Minimum stays Apr–Oct. Dogs accepted in some rooms ($20 per night). Children 3 and older welcome. **Amenities:** Concierge; free Wi-Fi.

Hacienda Nicholas ★★   What's better than a classic upscale Santa Fe hacienda just a short walk from the Plaza? One with reasonable rates, natural and organic breakfasts, and a spa across the street. The Hacienda Nicholas offers top-shelf service and a Southwest meets South of France design aesthetic, with lace curtains, four-poster beds of wrought iron or carved wood, New Mexico art and furnishings, and Mexican tiles in the bathrooms. The three suites each have fireplaces and doorways that open onto the interior courtyard. This shared area is mirrored by the Great Room inside, which also has a fireplace. Afternoon wine and cheese and access to a nearby health club—as well as the luxury spa across the street, operated by the same owners—make this B&B a great choice in this city with so many. (The owners also rent four cottages nearby, with rates of $150 to $225.)

320 E. Marcy St. www.haciendanicholas.com. 7 units. ☎ **888/284-3170** or 505/986-1431. Doubles $110–$165, suites $160–$240. Rates include full breakfast and early evening wine and cheese. Pets accepted ($20 per stay). Children 12 and older welcome. **Amenities:** Access to health club; free Wi-Fi.

RV Parks & Campgrounds

There are several commercial RV parks plus camping in a state park and the nearby national forest for RVers and tenters visiting Santa Fe. For the commercial campgrounds, rates vary by type of site and season, with the highest rates usually from Memorial Day weekend through Labor Day weekend and even higher during special events. Be sure to book ahead at busy times. All of the campgrounds and RV parks listed here accept pets in the campsites, and the commercial campgrounds have specific dog-walking areas.

Black Canyon Campground ★★ This Santa Fe National Forest campground, administered by the national forest's Española District, is next to Hyde Memorial State Park (see below). Due to its closeness to Santa Fe and beautiful forest setting, it is one of the region's most popular federal campgrounds and can fill up quickly. There are 36 drive-in RV and car sites and 6 walk-in tent sites; several of the drive-in sites are doubles that can accommodate small groups of up to 16 individuals. A very pleasant 1-mile-loop hiking trail leaves from the back of the campground. There is a campground host on-site but no dump station or electric hookups. Reservations are available (www.recreation.gov; ☎ **877/444-6777** or 518/885-3639).

Off Hyde Park Rd., Santa Fe. www.fs.fed.us/r3/sfe. ☎ **505/438-5300** or 505/753-7331 (Española District office). 42 units. $10 per night. Closed Nov–Apr. **Amenities:** Vault toilets; drinking water.

Hyde Memorial State Park ★★★ If you can do without the amenities of a commercial campground and just want the beauty and serenity of camping in a mountain forest, this is the spot for you. Located about 8 miles from downtown Santa Fe, it feels like it's 100 miles from the city lights and sounds. The campsites are what you would expect in a national park, and there are even seven with electric hookups. Hyde Memorial has 4.2 miles of hiking trails, a playground, and a visitor center. In winter you can cross-country ski and snowshoe. Elevations at the park range from 8,300 feet to 9,400 feet, so expect cool to cold nighttime temperatures, even in summer.

740 Hyde Park Rd. From Paseo de Peralta, head north on Bishops Lodge Rd. 2 blocks, turn right onto Artist Rd., which becomes Hyde Park Rd. www.nmparks.com. ☎ **505/983-7175.** 50 campsites. $10 basic campsite, $14 with electric hookup. **Amenities:** Picnic tables; group shelters; vault toilets; water.

Los Sueños de Santa Fe RV Park & Campground ★ This commercial RV park offers full RV hookups at all sites and has all the usual commercial campground amenities, including a very nice outdoor pool, open in summer. There are trees, a picnic table at each site, and a covered pavilion for campers' use. The park has a convenient location, just 5 miles south of the plaza, but it's on Cerrillos Road, one of Santa Fe's busiest thoroughfares.

3574 Cerrillos Rd. www.lossuenosrv.com. ℭ **505/473-1949.** 95 RV sites. $41.50–$51 daily. **Amenities:** Free cable TV; grills; outdoor heated pool (Memorial Day–Labor Day); restrooms; showers; vending machines; propane; free Wi-Fi.

Rancheros de Santa Fe Campground ★★ Among northern New Mexico's most scenic commercial campgrounds, Rancheros de Santa Fe sits on 22 acres of piñon and juniper, with open and wooded sites for motor homes and trailers of all sizes, plus secluded tent sites nestled among the trees. It offers close to a national forest or national park experience with all the amenities you'd expect in a commercial campground. A bit of trivia: Part of the 1978 Clint Eastwood film, *Every Which Way But Loose,* was filmed in the campground. Camping cabins, which share the campground's bathhouse, are also available ($45 to $52 double).

736 Old Las Vegas Hwy. (I-25 exit 290, east ½ mile). www.rancheros.com ℭ **505/466-3482.** 127 sites. Tent sites (no hookup) $22–$25; RV hookup sites $31–$44. Rates for 2 people; $3 for additional people over 3 years old. Bathhouse and store closed Nov–mid-Mar, some full hookup RV sites remain open Nov–mid-Mar for $25 per night. **Amenities:** Cable TV hookup (full RV hookup sites only); grills; grocery store; coin-op laundry; nature trails; nightly movies mid-May–Sept; picnic tables; playground; outdoor pool (summer only); propane; recreation room; gift shop; restrooms; showers; free Wi-Fi.

Santa Fe KOA ★ A member of the well-known and respected KOA chain, this commercial campground provides exactly what you would expect from a KOA except there's no pool. But it does have trees. About 11 miles northeast of Santa Fe, it sits among the foothills of the Sangre de Cristo Mountains in northern New Mexico's pine-filled high desert. It offers the usual amenities and some attractive camping cabins, where you'll use your own linens and share bathhouses with other campers. But the cabins are inexpensive and have porch swings, and you have a choice of air conditioning or not.

934 Old Las Vegas Hwy. (I-25 exit 294, west ¼ mile). www.koa.com. ℭ **800/562-1514** or 505/466-1419 for reservations. 62 campsites. RV hookup sites $42.50–$51.50, tent sites $28–$38; cabins $58–$63. Maximum RV or vehicle/trailer length 65 feet. Closed early Nov–Feb. Pets accepted in some cabins ($10 per night). **Amenities:** Cable TV hookup; dump station; gift shop; game room; coin-op laundry; picnic tables; playground; propane; restrooms; showers; free Wi-Fi.

WHERE TO EAT IN SANTA FE

Santa Fe abounds in dining options, with hundreds of restaurants in all categories. That's the good news. What's the bad news? There are hundreds of restaurants in all categories, and the fierce competition means that not all will survive. We suggest calling ahead to check not only on whether a particular restaurant is still there, but what the current hours are, since restaurants here frequently change their hours of operation.

Many of the long-time favorites serve traditional northern New Mexican cuisine, which emphasizes spicy chile sauces. If you're not used to spicy food, you may want to ask the servers how hot the chile is; many restaurants will either bring you a sample to taste before ordering, or put the chile on the side. There are also a variety of American restaurants here, as well as those specializing in European, Mexican, South American, and Japanese cuisine. Especially during peak tourist seasons, dinner reservations may be essential. Reservations are always recommended at better restaurants.

In New Mexico you'll find that many restaurants serve beer and wine but no spirits; that's because a beer and wine license is easier to obtain and cheaper than a full liquor license. In the listings below, we note which restaurants have full bar service.

Looking for a familiar chain? Many are on the south end of town, on or near Cerrillos Road. You'll find **Olive Garden** ★ at 3781 Cerrillos Rd. (www.olivegarden.com; ℂ **505/438-7109**); **Outback Steakhouse** ★ at 2574 Camino Entrada (www.outback.com; ℂ **505/424-6800**); **Applebee's Grill & Bar** ★★ at 4246 Cerrillos Rd. (www.applebees.com; ℂ **505/473-7551**); and **Red Lobster** ★ at 4450 Rodeo Rd. (www.redlobster.com; ℂ **505/473-1610**). If you're getting in late, leaving early, or just hungry at 3am, there's a 24-hour **Denny's** ★★ at 3004 Cerrillos Rd. (www.dennys.com; **505/471-2152**). An excellent choice for a healthy sandwich or soup to take back to your room or on a hike is the well-respected chain **Panera Bread** ★★★, with its Santa Fe branch at 3535 Zafarano Dr. (www.panerabread.com; **505/471-9396**).

Santa Fe Restaurants

For restaurants in the downtown and Canyon Road areas, see map, p. 61. For restaurants in the Cerrillos Road area, see map, p. 55.

EXPENSIVE

Bouche French Bistro ★★★ FRENCH   This is the closest you'll get to dining at a genuine Parisian neighborhood bistro without a trip across the Atlantic, and our top Santa Fe choice for a special occasion splurge. Award-winning chef and author Charles Dale—born in France to American parents—opened Bouche French Bistro in 2013. Today you'll often see him at work in the open kitchen. The restaurant is located in a nondescript 75-year-old building somewhat off the beaten path. Inside, the small, simply decorated dining room is cozy, with rustic furnishings, long banquettes, and a wood-burning fireplace. There's also a delightful outdoor patio for warm-weather dining. The menu is short but varied. There is a nightly fish selection, plus chicken, pork, and beef choices, all prepared French style. Choices include beef short ribs "Pot au Feu" with horseradish crème; coq au vin with mashed potatoes, carrots, and pearl onions; pumpkin ravioli with duck confit, cinnamon broth, and sage; and our favorite, steak au poivre with pommes frites. For dessert, you won't go wrong with the demerara crème brulee. Beer and wine are available.

451 W. Alameda St. (entrance on W. Water St.). www.bouchebistro.com. ℂ **505/982-6297.** Reservations recommended. Main courses $16–$34. Tues–Sat 5:30–9:30pm.

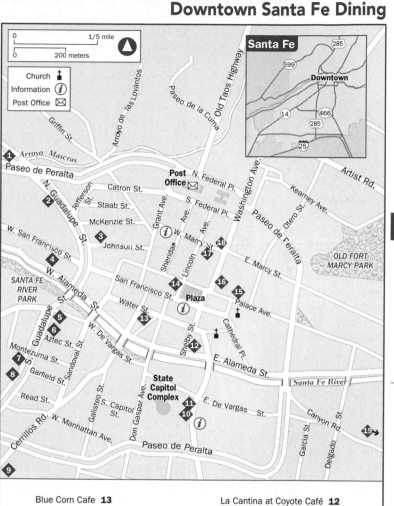

Blue Corn Cafe **13**
Bouche French Bistro **4**
The Bull Ring **17**
The Burrito Company **16**
Clafoutis **2**
The Compound **19**
Cowgirl BBQ **6**
Il Piatto Italiano
   Farmhouse Kitchen **18**
Kohnami **5**

La Cantina at Coyote Café **12**
The Pink Adobe **11**
Pizza Centro **7**
Plaza Cafe **14**
Rio Chama Steakhouse **10**
Santa Fe Bar & Grill **1**
Shake Foundation **9**
The Shed **15**
Shohko Cafe **3**
Tomasita's **8**

The Bull Ring ★★★ STEAKHOUSE   There are quite a few northern New Mexico restaurants that serve good steak, but for the very best you'll have to go to the Bull Ring. For years, the Bull Ring, then located next to the state Capitol, was famous as the hangout of the state legislature and other New Mexico movers and shakers. Then, in 1995, it moved downtown near the plaza, but more importantly, owner Harry Georgeades decided to change the menu, which had been good but not a standout, to feature the best beef available. Today, the Bull Ring serves USDA prime beef, corn-fed and hand-cut daily. The large dining room is simply decorated—you can't help but notice the large pieces of pottery—with nicely upholstered chairs and circular booths. You can also eat in the bar or, in warm weather, in the outside patio. Beef is the star here, of course, but you'll find a good selection of other entrees as well. For lunch, our choice is the locally famous half-pound Bull Burger, served with hand-cut fries. Or you might prefer the blackened salmon salad, with the fresh salmon just lightly blackened, or possibly a BLT or fried chicken. For dinner, you'll probably want beef, such as the 12-ounce filet, 14-ounce New York strip, or 16-ounce prime rib. Steaks are served sizzling in butter—you can specify extra butter or none. Other dinner options include a steak and lobster combo, grilled salmon filet, and lamb chops. Portions are generous, and service is excellent. Monday through Friday from 3 to 6pm there are appetizer and beer and wine specials during happy hour, and the Bull Ring offers full liquor service.

150 Washington Ave. in the courtyard of New Mexico Bank and Trust. www.santafebull ring.com. ℭ **505/983-3328.** Main courses lunch $11–$18, dinner $28–$50, bar menu items mostly under $20. Tues–Fri 11:30am–2:30pm and 5–10pm, Sat–Mon 5–10pm.

The Compound ★★★ CONTEMPORARY AMERICAN   Among Santa Fe's fine-dining classics, after a brief closure the Compound reopened in 2000 under executive chef/owner Mark Kiffin, who was named James Beard Best Chef of the Southwest in 2005. Kiffin kept the old white adobe walls, brightened with folk art chosen by designer Alexander Girard (of Folk Art Museum fame), but revamped the menu completely. Traditional regional ingredients brought to the area by the Spanish are joined by Mediterranean influences to create dishes like wild mushrooms and organic stone-ground polenta with black truffle relish. The menu also includes organic Scottish salmon, braised lamb shank, and grilled beef tenderloin. Even lunch entrees are a cut above, from the house-cured pastrami sandwich to the Wagyu beef burger. (If you order the latter, don't pass on the roasted poblanos and white cheddar.) Definitely try the bittersweet chocolate cake for dessert. The Compound's prices put it in splurge-only territory for many, but the elegant-yet-comfortable setting and friendly service make this an excellent choice in a city full of high-end possibilities.

653 Canyon Rd. www.compoundrestaurant.com. ℭ **505/982-4353.** Main courses lunch $13–$24, dinner $26–$46. Mon–Sat noon–2pm and 5–9pm, Sun 5–9pm.

Il Piatto Italiano Farmhouse Kitchen ★★★ ITALIAN   You'll think you've been transported to the Italian countryside when you step inside this upscale Italian restaurant, located 1 block north of the Plaza. Large front windows and a sidewalk patio make this eatery a sunny favorite for lunch. Chef Matt Yohalem sources as many ingredients as possible from local farms, ranches, and dairies, and although the portions aren't huge, they are tasty. For dinner, try the pumpkin ravioli with brown sage butter, pine nuts, and parmigiana; the spaghetti Bolognese with pork, prosciutto, and beef; or the prosciutto-wrapped Idaho trout. Pasta dishes are available in either appetizer or entree sizes. At lunch there are smaller versions of some of the dinner items plus sandwiches, burgers, and several pizzas, including the Pizzetta Siciliana, with anchovies, olives, capers, and sustainable Northwest shrimp. The atmosphere here is a suitably Santa Fean mix of formal and casual, with white tablecloths tipping it a bit toward the former. An extensive wine list draws from the seemingly bottomless recesses of the house's custom wine cave. There's happy hour daily from 4:30 to 6pm with half-price appetizers and wine specials, and a second happy hour with wine and food specials from 9 to 10:30pm.

95 W. Marcy St. www.ilpiattosantafe.com. © **505/984-1091.** Main courses lunch $10–$16, dinner $23–$35. Wed–Sat 11:30am–10:30pm, Sun–Tues 4:30 10:30pm.

Omira Bar & Grill ★★ BRAZILIAN   Even if you've never made it down to Rio, you can still experience an authentic Brazilian *churrascaria* (barbecue) at this family-friendly place near the Railyard. Although vegetarians are welcome—the set meal price includes unlimited trips to the organic soup and salad bar—Omira is really for carnivores. Waiters wander from table to table bearing spits of fresh-grilled chicken, pork, beef, lamb, and sausage, slicing pieces onto your plate until you beg them to stop. The restaurant uses only locally raised New Mexico beef, lamb, and pork, which it hand-cuts daily. The decor is plain but tasteful, and there's live guitar music on some evenings. Kids love the meal-comes-to-you aspect, and parents appreciate the extensive wine and Belgian craft beer selection.

1005 S. St. Francis Dr. www.omiragrill.com. © **505/780-5483.** Lunch $18 including salad bar, $12 salad bar only; dinner $28 including salad bar, $18 salad bar only. Tues–Sun 11am–2:30pm and 5–9pm.

The Pink Adobe ★★ NEW MEXICAN/AMERICAN   Named for the pink hue of its 350-year-old adobe walls, the Pink Adobe has been a local favorite since it was opened by New Orleans transplant Rosalea Murphy in 1944. Each of several small dining rooms has its own kiva fireplace, and the hand-carved wood furnishings and heavy log vigas add to the building's historic charm. In typical northern New Mexico fashion, even some traditional American dishes get spiced up a bit, such as the grilled salmon, which is prepared with chile. The restaurant's most popular (and most expensive) selection, steak Dunigan, is a charbroiled 13-ounce New York strip, topped with sautéed mushrooms and, of course, green chile. Looking for traditional northern New Mexico cuisine? Try the Plato Mexicano, a filling sampler that includes a cheese enchilada, chile relleno, and chicken taco, with red or green chile, rice, posole, and pinto beans. The chile served here is extra hot; if in doubt, ask for a sample before ordering. Weekend brunch offers a variety of egg dishes, French toast, and the like from 8am, and from 11am adds burgers, chicken salad, and several enchiladas. The restaurant's signature dessert is hot French apple pie topped with rum hard sauce. The Pink Adobe's Dragon Room Bar is a real local hangout.

406 Old Santa Fe Trail. www.thepinkadobe.com. © **505/983-7712.** Main courses dinner $18–$30, brunch $11–$15. Tues–Sun 5:30–9pm; brunch Sat–Sun 8am–2pm; bar Tues–Sun 4pm–midnight.

Rio Chama Steakhouse ★★ STEAK/SEAFOOD   Among the best places in Santa Fe for prime rib, this steakhouse is loaded with Santa Fe charm, with soft adobe walls, lots of wood, and a handmade tin chandelier; the bar has the atmosphere of a mountain lodge. There's a limited amount of prime rib nightly, so get there early. The prime rib is a ribeye beef roast brined with herbs and spices for 48 hours, grilled whole over an open flame, and slow-roasted. It's accompanied by the steakhouse's signature whipped horseradish cream and natural jus, and served with mashed potatoes and green beans. The dinner menu also includes several beefsteaks, an elk tenderloin with port-wine juniper-berry sauce, and wild salmon with maple butter sauce. At lunch there are sandwiches, salads, burgers, and entrees such as fish and chips and grilled salmon The weekend bunch features egg dishes, including country-fried prime rib and eggs and house-made corned beef hash with eggs, a six-cheese fondue with dipping vegetables, and burgers. Full liquor service is available.

414 Old Santa Fe Trail. www.riochamasteakhouse.com. © **505/955-0765.** Main courses lunch $11–$18, dinner $11–$39, weekend brunch $11–$18. Mon–Fri 11am–2pm and 5–10pm, Sat–Sun 11am–3pm and 5–10pm.

Shohko Cafe ★★★ SUSHI/JAPANESE   Ordering raw fish this far from the ocean is always a bit of a gamble, but Santa Fe's favorite sushi restaurant is a sure thing. The atmosphere here combines Asian minimalism with the Old West, juxtaposing rice-paper screens with viga ceilings. (The 150-year-old adobe building, with 3-foot-thick walls, used to be a brothel.) The menu is excellent across the board: noodles, tempura, sushi, sashimi, you name it. Even the beef teriyaki is great, with its delicately spiced sauce. The seafood tempura tower is big enough to share. Highly recommended is the shrimp-stuffed green chile tempura, combining the best of East and West in one crunchy bite. It's not cheap here, and the service can be relaxed, but the intimate setting and extensive list of sakes help make Shohko a worthy indulgence. Beer, wine, and sake are served. *Note:* The restaurant has a fragrance-free policy.

321 Johnson St., just off Guadalupe St. www.shohkocafe.com. © **505/982-9708.** Main courses lunch $10–$21, dinner $15–$37. Mon–Thurs 11:30am–2pm and 5:30–9pm, Fri 11:30am–2pm and 5:30–9:30pm, Sat 5–9:30pm.

MODERATE

Cowgirl BBQ ★ AMERICAN/BARBECUE   Good food in a fun and funky cafe atmosphere: low ceilings, lots of photographs of cowgirls and other western memorabilia covering the adobe walls, and something sparkly

FAMILY-FRIENDLY restaurants

Blue Corn Cafe (p. 68)   A relaxed atmosphere and their own menu pleases kids, while excellent brewpub beer pleases parents.

Cowgirl BBQ (see above)   A casual atmosphere, lots of old photos of cowgirls, and the ice cream baked potato makes for a fun time for kids and their parents.

Plaza Café (p. 70)   Burgers, sandwiches, a funky atmosphere, and an old-fashioned ice cream–style counter make this a kids' favorite.

in the wall paint. There's patio dining in warm weather. The service is good and the menu includes solid American fare plus some excellent—albeit hot—southwestern choices. We recommend the mesquite-smoked baby back ribs, grilled salmon filet with bourbon glaze, or one of the fajitas platters—choose from chicken breast, flatiron steak, or portobello mushroom. The adventurous might want to try the locally raised yak meatloaf. Save room for a fun dessert: ice cream baked potato—a chunk of good vanilla ice cream molded into the shape of a potato, rolled in cocoa, placed in a pool of chocolate sauce, and topped with whipped cream and shaved pistachios, and a square of golden frosting tucked into it like a pat of butter. There are lunch specials on weekdays, beer specials every day, and happy hour daily from 3 to 6pm. Beer and wine are served.

319 S. Guadalupe St. www.cowgirlsantafe.com. ℂ **505/982-2565.** Main courses lunch $8–$18, dinner $8–$23. Mon–Thurs 11:30am–10:30pm, Fri 11:30am–11pm, Sat 11am–11pm, Sun 11am–10:30pm. Bar Mon–Thurs until midnight, Fri–Sat until 1am, Sun until 11:30pm.

Joe's Dining ★★ AMERICAN   It used to be called Joe's Diner, a name we liked better, but whatever they call it, this casual and comfortable eatery is unpretentious and easy to like. Decor is '50s diner, complete with red vinyl upholstery and a checkerboard linoleum floor. The menu is old-time diner as well, although what's surprising is that the food quality is definitely a step or two above what you might expect. The owners are committed to using sustainable, local ingredients as much as possible, and claim to be the biggest restaurant buyer of farmers' market products in Santa Fe. We believe them. Try the herb-grilled organic chicken, grass-finished New Zealand lamb, or one of the nifty burgers such as the bourbon chutney burger. There are weekday lunch specials, including meatloaf on Wednesdays and fish and chips on Fridays, and Friday evenings feature prime rib. Joe's also serves pizzas and good basic breakfasts.

2801 Rodeo Rd. www.joesdining.com. ℂ **505/471-3800.** Main courses breakfast $5.50–$16, lunch and dinner $7–$29, Sunday brunch $8–$16, pizzas from $9. Daily 7:30am–9pm. Closed Thanksgiving, from 3pm Christmas Eve, all day Christmas, and Boxing Day (December 26).

Kohnami ★ JAPANESE   This reasonably priced sushi restaurant does a good job with the usual suspects: sushi, sashimi, miso soup, and tempura. The menu also includes sukiyaki, katsu (deep-fried cutlets of fish, pork, or chicken) and *dolsotbap* (rice cooked in a hot stone pot with a spicy sauce). The lunch bento boxes are a deal for this expensive city: $8.50 gets you a California roll, chicken teriyaki, tempura, rice, miso soup, and a small salad. Sit at one of the enclosed tatami tables for the full Japanese experience, or if it's nice out, ask for a seat out back where paper lanterns hang under a gazebo.

313 S. Guadalupe St. www.kohnamisantafe.com. © **505/984-2002.** Sushi rolls $6–$13, main courses $8.50–$18. Mon–Thurs 11:30am–9:15pm, Fri–Sat 11:30am–9:30pm, Sun noon–9pm.

La Cantina at Coyote Café ★★ SOUTHWESTERN   To try chef Eric DeStefano's contemporary southwestern fare without the high prices of his well-known Coyote Café, head to its adjacent rooftop cantina. Open in the summer only, the colorful painted terrace offers a fun social scene with cocktails and reasonably priced food choices. Try the Baja-style fish tacos; the beef burger with pickled Fresno chile, sharp cheddar, and crispy fried Vidalia onions; or the ginger chile pork ribs.

132 W. Water St. www.coyotecafe.com/cantina. © **505/983-1615.** Main courses $12–$21. Apr–Oct daily 11:30am–9:30pm.

Maria's New Mexican Kitchen ★ NEW MEXICAN   Maria's was opened back in 1952, which explains its somewhat odd location just off the busy intersection of Cordova Road and St. Francis Drive. No matter—Maria's is a Santa Fe tradition, with creaking wood floors and dependable New Mexican comfort food like blue corn enchiladas, tacos, grilled trout, and burgers. Specialties also include spare ribs, baked slowly in a mild red chile barbecue sauce; and fajitas—beef, chicken, shrimp, or vegetarian—cut into bite-size strips and sautéed, served with a cup of soupy beans, guacamole, pico de gallo, and house-made flour tortillas. Maria's is famous for its margaritas—a separate menu lists several hundred choices, all made with 100% agave tequila. For the full experience, sit in the cozy bar area, lit with wagon-wheel lights and neon beer signs, and tuck into chile rellenos and a Silver Coin margarita.

555 West Cordova Rd. www.marias-santafe.com. © **505/983-7929.** Main courses lunch $8.50–$15.95, dinner $11.50–$17.95. Daily 11am–10pm.

The Ranch House ★★★ BARBECUE   For our money, this is the best barbecue in Santa Fe, maybe in all of northern New Mexico. Chef Josh Baum was so successful at his smaller restaurant, Josh's BBQ, that he had to move and expand in 2011. The result is the classy-yet-casual Ranch House, housed in a handsome Santa Fe–style building with two spacious, well-lit dining rooms and two outdoor dining areas. The menu focuses on slow-smoked dishes made with hormone- and antibiotic-free meats, along with great green chile brisket burritos and pulled pork. The red chile honey sauce on the baby back ribs is the perfect blend of Texas and New Mexico flavors, and the smoking is done with Texas brown oak. For those in your group not fond of barbecue, there are also grilled salmon and steaks on the menu, plus salads and sandwiches galore. The portions are generous, and almost all the barbecued items come with a side of zingy green chile cornbread. There is a full bar, and barbecue is also sold by the pound to go.

2571 Cristo's Rd. (at Cerrillos Rd.). www.theranchhousesantafe.com. ✆ **505/424-8900.**
Main courses lunch $8–$12, dinner $10–$28. Sun–Thurs 11am–9pm, Fri–Sat 11am–10pm.

Santa Fe Bar & Grill ★★ SOUTHWESTERN/AMERICAN   Everything's colorful in this Mexican-themed restaurant, with a busy open kitchen, handcrafted Mexican furniture, and walls decorated with still-life paintings and copper and ceramic pots. The menu here is more Mexican than New Mexican, blending foods such as squash, beans, and chile with everything from beef brisket to Pacific oysters and salmon. Specialties include the Santa Fe rotisserie chicken with a chipotle chile aioli; blue corn vegetable enchiladas; and our favorite—the grilled Mexican steak tacos, marinated sirloin steak served on soft corn tortillas with fire-roasted salsa and guacamole. Half-pound burgers are available at both lunch and dinner, and the Sunday brunch features breakfast burritos, huevos rancheros, or for the non-adventurous in your group, plain old bacon and eggs or French toast. The restaurant has eight micro-brewed beers on tap, a good selection of wines by the glass, and an excellent selection of Mexican tequilas from which you can indulge in one of their specialty margaritas.

187 Paseo de Peralta, in Devargas Mall. www.santafebargrill.com. ✆ **505/982-3033.**
Main courses lunch $9–$13, dinner $9–$20. Daily 11am–10pm.

The Shed ★★★ NEW MEXICAN   The long lines, even at lunch, are proof enough that this local institution just east of the plaza is something special. The restaurant is set inside a rambling hacienda, built in 1692, and decorated with bright, folky paintings. The Shed is known for its shaded brick patio and its rich and spicy New Mexican cooking. The red chile is a regular local prizewinner, best displayed with the house's signature enchiladas. Another sure bet is the green chile stew, brimming with pork and potatoes. Sandwiches and burgers are also offered at lunch, but not dinner. Every traditional entree is served with blue corn tortillas and, oddly, garlic bread, which is a restaurant tradition. Save room for a piece of homemade mocha cake, one of Santa Fe's best desserts. Full liquor service is available. The margaritas are something special.

113½ E. Palace Ave. www.sfshed.com. ✆ **505/982-9030.** Main courses lunch $8–$12, dinner $10.75–$24. Mon–Sat 11am–2:30pm and 5:30–9pm.

Vinaigrette ★★ SALAD   Tucked away off Cerrillos Road, this casual salad bistro offers up-to-the-minute-fresh ingredients in concoctions like duck confit tossed with baby arugula, and "Eat Your Peas," with bacon and Asiago cheese mixed with sweet green peas. Much of the produce comes from the owner's 10-acre farm in Nambe. Proteins such as lemon-herb chicken breast, grilled flank steak, diver scallops, or grilled tofu are also available. Seasonal salad options are always changing—watch for the winter kale with ricotta and chicken when it's available. Several healthy sandwiches are also on the menu, including a hot turkey sandwich and a tuna melt. Vinaigrette's dining room has a modern, playful atmosphere, with red chairs and a green-tiled wine bar. On the back patio you can eat under an old apricot tree. Beer and wine are available.

709 Don Cubero Alley. www.vinaigretteonline.com. © **505/820-9205.** Main courses $10–$19. Mon–Sat 11am–9pm.

INEXPENSIVE

Blue Corn Cafe ★ NEW MEXICAN/BREWPUB   This is a good spot for lunch or dinner, especially on warm days when you can dine outside under an umbrella in the attractive but protected patio overlooking historic Water Street. Inside, the dining room looks like an upscale New Mexico cafe should look, with large windows, wood tables and chairs, tile floors, and light-colored walls decorated with New Mexico art. The restaurant is known for its fajitas—chicken, steak, portobello mushroom, shrimp, or a surf and turf—served with grilled onions and bell peppers, spicy salsa, sour cream, guacamole, cheese, and to wrap it all up in, a warm flour tortilla. The flatiron steak melt is also good, grilled to order, topped with roasted green chile and asadero cheese, and served with a cheese enchilada. Had enough spicy northern New Mexico food for a while? Then there's the fish and chips, dipped in the brewery's own amber ale batter and served with fries and jicama-lime slaw; or the basic brewery burger, hand-pattied Angus beef served on a brioche bun with a choice of sides. There's also a surprisingly good selection of salads. The cafe's sister restaurant, the **Blue Corn Cafe & Brewery,** with a somewhat different menu, is reviewed below.

133 W. Water St. www.bluecorncafe.com. © **505/984-1800.** Reservations accepted for parties of 6 or more. Main courses $10–$12. Daily 11am–10pm.

Blue Corn Cafe & Brewery ★★ NEW MEXICAN/BREWPUB   This sister restaurant to the Blue Corn Cafe downtown (see above) is where they actually brew the beer—about 1,200 barrels a year—so it's appropriate that the first thing you see as you walk in are the huge copper-clad tanks. The rest of the decor is also total brewpub, with beige adobe-style walls, heavy wood ceiling beams supporting herringbone boards, comfy booths (better than the wood chairs at the tables), and a large two-sided fireplace. There's also a busy bar where you can watch your favorite sports team, although the young crowd that congregates there can get a bit noisy, especially when their team scores or there's a bad umpire call. Although there are some similarities, the menu here is different than the downtown Blue Corn. The emphasis here is on locally grown and produced food made from scratch daily, and items with New Mexico ingredients are marked with a tiny New Mexico flag. The menu changes seasonally, but you'll always find burgers, beer-battered fish and chips, and northern New Mexico specialties such as lamb tacos, tamales, or the signature Blue Corn's Big Burrito—an extra-large tortilla rolled with refried pinto beans, cheddar and jack cheeses, lettuce and tomato, and smothered with chile and melted cheese. You can add chicken, beef, carnitas, tofu, or calabacitas tamales if you so choose. We also recommend the New Mexican shepherd's pie—topped with green chile, of course—and the pub steak, when available. Among the brewery's beers are its oatmeal stout, which won a gold medal in the 2007 Great American Beer Festival, and the very serious Road Runner IPA, with lots of hops and a 6.9% alcohol level. In summer there's outdoor dining.

4056 Cerrillos Rd. at Rodeo Rd. www.bluecorncafe.com. C **505/438-1800.** Main courses $9.95–$16.95. Daily 11am–10pm.

The Burrito Company ★ AMERICAN/NEW MEXICAN   Located just off of Santa Fe Plaza, this family-owned fast-food eatery has been a favorite of locals and tourists alike since it opened in 1978. It's noisy, busy, and fun, with red vinyl booths and colorful Mexican-style murals on the walls. You order at the counter, find a place to sit, and they bring you your food. Most breakfast items are served all day, including the popular breakfast burrito, either with or without meat; and the you'll-only-find-this-in-Santa-Fe Washington Street Burrito: scrambled egg whites, sautéed spinach, tomatoes, turkey bacon, and avocado, rolled in a whole-wheat tortilla and topped with New Mexico–style chile and Swiss cheese. Lunch items include burritos, tacos, burgers, several sandwiches, some tasty and even healthy salads, and to honor the chef-owner's Salvadoran roots, the El Salvador Combo—two house-made corn masa *pupusas* stuffed with squash, beans, and cheese, plus one chicken tamale wrapped in a banana leaf, and served with a side of mixed rice and beans. The dog-friendly patio is a great people-watching spot. Beer and wine are available.

111 Washington Ave. www.burritocompanysf.com. C **505/982-4453.** Main courses $6.50–$9.95. Summer, Mon–Fri 7:30am–4:30pm, Sat–Sun 8am–5pm; rest of year, Mon–Fri 7:30am–4pm, Sat–Sun 8am–4pm; extended hours during Spanish Market and Indian Market.

Clafoutis ★★ FRENCH BAKERY   Looking for a cheery bakery that serves light-as-air baguettes, rich French onion soup, flaky-crusted quiches, and breakfast crepes that melt in your mouth? Well, here it is. Everything about this bakery says "French country kitchen," except, perhaps, the welcoming attitude of the owners and servers. The dining room is small and a bit cramped, and seems even smaller when there's a long line for the takeout. Decor is rustic and homey, with herb jars and wooden utensils, and the cooking is simple but rich. Try the classic croque madame or croque monsieur sandwiches, with creamy béchamel sauce and homemade organic bread.

402 N. Guadalupe St. C **505/988-1809.** Most items $6–$11. Mon–Sat 7am–4pm.

Pizza Centro ★ PIZZA   Tucked away inside the Santa Fe Design Center, Pizza Centro turns out an excellent hand-tossed New York–style pizza in a suitably modern, no-frills setting. The restaurant makes its own dough and marinara sauces, with a menu full of specialty combos named after New York neighborhoods, like the Soho (roast chicken, mushroom, sun-dried tomato, onion, truffle oil, and fresh basil) and the Central Park (spinach, sun-dried tomato, basil, garlic, and ricotta). There's also the Hell's Kitchen: sausage, flash-fried eggplant, jalapeño, roasted red pepper, and feta. There are vegetarian selections and gluten- and dairy-free options as well. Sandwiches, calzones, and salads round things out. There's also outside dining at picnic tables. Beer and wine are served. Other branches of Pizza Centro can be found at 3470 Zafarano Dr., off Cerrillos Road (© **505/471-6200**) and in the Eldorado Agora Center, 7 Avenida Vista Grande (© **505/466-3161**).

Inside the Santa Fe Design Center, 418 Cerrillos Rd. www.pizzacentronys.com. © **505/988-8825**. Pizzas $12–$25. Daily 11:30am–8:30pm.

Plaza Cafe ★★★ AMERICAN/NEW MEXICAN/GREEK

Santa Fe's oldest continuously operating restaurant, opened in 1905 by Greek immigrants the Ipiotis brothers, offers the best diner food in Santa Fe. It's served in a suitably funky atmosphere, too, with colorful ceiling lights, linoleum-top tables, a neon wall clock, old black-and-white photos, and a soda-fountain-style counter with red vinyl-covered stainless steel stools. Plaza Cafe serves traditional American and New Mexican breakfasts—the blue corn piñon pancakes make a nice change—or go with the traditional ham and eggs or a "build your own omelet." Lunch and dinner items include the tortilla soup—avocado, tortilla strips, and Mexican cheeses—plus a good choice of salads and specialties such as chicken-fried steak, spicy fish and chips, grilled chicken, burgers, and sandwiches. The restaurant claims that the recipe for its spaghetti sauce is over 100 years old. There are also several Greek items available, including moussaka—a casserole of eggplant, spiced meat, and a creamy béchamel sauce. Beer and wine are available.

54 Lincoln Ave. www.thefamousplazacafe.com. © **505/982-1664**. Main courses $9.95–$22. Daily 7am–9pm.

Plaza Café Southside ★★★ AMERICAN/NEW MEXICAN

Next to a movie theater off Cerrillos Road at the south end of Santa Fe, this sister restaurant to the downtown Plaza Cafe may be out of the way, but it's worth the trip. The wide-open restaurant has a 1950s diner look, with strong colors, vintage black-and-white photos, and a mural with a sort of Day of the Dead motif. Oh, there's also a row of old automobile hubcaps on the wall. Breakfasts here are special, ranging from the traditional bacon and eggs to pancakes and French toast. The yogurt parfait features layers of fresh fruit, honey-flavored Greek yogurt, and house-made pumpkin-seed granola. There are also breakfast burritos, huevos rancheros, and other New Mexican dishes. For lunch and dinner there are burgers, a good choice of salads, sandwiches, and New Mexican dishes such as an enchilada platter. (Note that the Plaza Café Southside serves only cage-free eggs.) The menu warns diners that its red and green chile sauces come either medium hot or extra hot; you can ask for a sample or request that your sauce be served on the side. Most baked goods are prepared in-house, and they serve the very best restaurant sticky bun we have ever eaten. There is a full bar.

3466 Zafarano Dr., at the back of the San Isidro Plaza shopping center. www.plazacafe*southside.com. © **505/424-0755.** Main courses $8.95–$21. Sun–Thurs 8am–9pm, Fri–Sat 8am–10pm.

Shake Foundation ★ BURGERS & SHAKES   This is fast-food Santa Fe style, and one of the top spots to get a genuine New Mexico–style green chile cheeseburger. The burgers aren't huge, but they are tasty. All the patties are made with a mix of prime sirloin and brisket, the fresh-cut shoestring fries are perfectly crispy, and all food is prepared to order. You can also get a lamb or turkey burger, a deep-fried portobello mushroom burger stuffed with muenster cheese, or a fried oyster sandwich with red chile mayo. Yes, the Shake Foundation has just about everything … except a dining room. Step up to the window to order and sit at a picnic table outside under the awning, or in your car, or you can opt to take your food back to your room. Save room for an Adobe Mud Shake made with Taos Cow organic ice cream—topped with piñon nuts, of course. No alcohol is served.

631 Cerrillos Rd. www.shakefoundation.com. © **505/988-8992.** Burgers and sandwiches $3.95–$7.50. Mon–Thurs 11am–7pm, Fri–Sat 11am–8pm, Sun 11am–6pm.

Tomasita's ★★ NEW MEXICAN   Occupying a 19th-century former railroad depot on the "Chile Line," this local standby cooks up fresh red and green chile every day. No surprise, then, that both are often voted the best in Santa Fe, and the lines here often stretch out the door. Tomasita's has been run for over 40 years by the same family, so they know what they're doing, using recipes handed down from generation to generation. Tomasita's reflects its brick railroad station origins on the outside; inside, it's a homey place with hanging chile *ristras* (a string of dried chile peppers), brass light fixtures, brick walls, colorful art, high windows, and light wood accents. There's also a pleasant outdoor patio. The food is nothing fancy, just solid northern New Mexican cooking, as in the combination plate: a red chile cheese enchilada, taco, Spanish rice, posole, pinto beans, and green chile. Entrees come with one of the best sopapillas in the city, served with honey butter. Known for its margaritas, Tomasita's has full liquor service. New Mexico's only all-female mariachi band plays every Tuesday at 7:30pm.

500 S. Guadalupe St. www.tomasitas.com. © **505/983-5721.** Main courses $7–$16. Mon–Thurs 11am–9pm, Fri–Sat 11am–10pm.

EXPLORING SANTA FE

One of the oldest cities in the United States, Santa Fe has long been a center for the creative and performing arts, so it's not surprising that most of the city's major sights are related to local history and the arts. The city's Museum of New Mexico, art galleries and studios, historic churches, and cultural sights associated with local American Indian and Hispanic communities all merit a visit. It would be easy to spend a full week sightseeing in the city without ever heading out to any nearby attractions.

WHAT TO SEE & DO IN SANTA FE

The Top Attractions

Georgia O'Keeffe Museum ★★★ MUSEUM   Some artists will always be connected to specific places: Ansel Adams to Yosemite, Claude Monet to his gardens at Giverny, and Georgia O'Keeffe to New Mexico. O'Keeffe (1887–1986) fell in love with the Southwest deserts in the 1930s, and in 1949 she moved from the East Coast to Abiquiu, about 70 miles northwest of Santa Fe. Her paintings of flowers, skulls, and stark landscapes, simultaneously voluptuous and semi-abstract, made her an international art icon who is now considered the "Mother of American Modernism." This museum, set in a former Baptist church, holds the largest collection of her works in the world. In keeping with O'Keeffe's style, the museum's interior features stark white walls and paintings displayed in minimalist silver frames that the artist herself designed. While you're here, you can also book guided tours of her historic home and studio in Abiquiu, which is just south of I-84, slightly more than an hour's drive away.

217 Johnson St. www.okeeffemuseum.org. ✆ **505/946-1000.** Adults $12, students 18 and older $10, free for children 17 and under. Daily 10am–5pm (Fri until 7pm). Closed New Year's Day, Easter, Thanksgiving, and Christmas.

New Mexico History Museum ★★★ MUSEUM   There aren't many parts of the U.S. that have a deeper, richer cultural history than New Mexico, and this museum is one of the best places to explore it. From prehistoric tribes and more modern American

Downtown Santa Fe Attractions

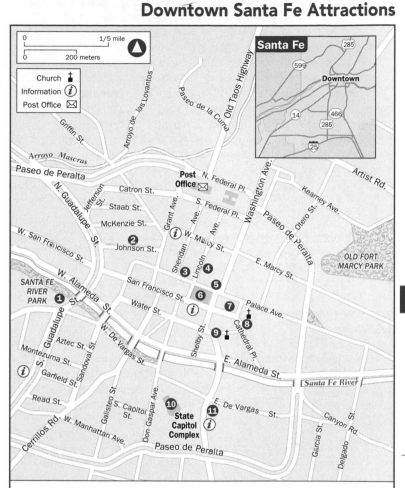

Georgia O'Keeffe Museum **2**
Loretto Chapel Museum **9**
Mission of San Miguel **11**
Museum of Contemporary Native Arts **7**
New Mexico History Museum **4**
New Mexico Museum of Art **3**
New Mexico State Capitol (Roundhouse) **10**
Palace of the Governors **5**
Santuario de Nuestra Señora de Guadalupe **1**
St. Francis Cathedral **8**
Santa Fe Plaza **6**

Indian tribes to the various waves of Spanish, Mexican, European, and American colonists and settlers that have swept through, New Mexico has seen it all. Fittingly, this 96,000-sq.-ft. history museum is a lot bigger than it looks from the outside. It was opened in 2009 as part of the state's 400th anniversary celebration, anchoring a complex that includes the Palace of the Governors, the Palace Print Shop & Bindery, the photo archives, and the Fray Angelico Chavez History Library. It's worth at least half a day's browsing, with immersive, interactive exhibits (permanent and changing) on cowboys, indigenous cultures, the Santa Fe Trail, Spanish colonial religious icons—you name it. All the displays are clearly laid out, with photos, historical artifacts, and videos to help explain the complex tapestry of New Mexican time.

113 Lincoln Ave. www.nmhistorymuseum.org. © **505/476-5200.** Adults $9, free for children 16 and under. Daily 10am–5pm (closed Mon Nov–Apr). Free admission 5–8pm every Fri May–Oct and on first Fri of the month Nov–Apr. Closed New Year's Day, Easter, Thanksgiving, and Christmas.

New Mexico Museum of Art ★★ MUSEUM "New Mexico" and "art" go together like, well, any two things that go very, very well together. This immensely photogenic state has inspired artists for centuries, so assembling a representative regional collection was no small task. This museum, formerly the Museum of Fine Arts, does an admirable job with its 20,000-piece permanent collection. Visitors here find drawings, paintings, photographs, furniture, prints, and sculptures by the usual suspects—Georgia O'Keeffe, Ansel Adams, Ernest Blumenschein—and many others, including Francisco de Goya, Gustave Baumann, and artists commissioned during the New Deal. Rotating exhibits change from month to month. The 1917 building itself is a work of art, one of the oldest Pueblo Revival structures in the city, featuring a wonderfully peaceful inner courtyard with flowers, WPA murals, sculptures, and flowing water. This is a nice place to easily pass an hour or two.

107 W. Palace (at Lincoln Ave.). www.nmartmuseum.org. © **505/476-5072.** Adults $9, free for children 16 and under. Daily 10am–5pm (closed Mon Nov–Apr). Free admission 5–8pm every Fri May–Oct and on first Fri of the month Nov–Apr. Closed New Year's Day, Easter, Thanksgiving, and Christmas.

Palace of the Governors ★★ HISTORIC SITE In an ancient city filled with lots of oldest this and oldest thats, the Palace of the Governors, on the north side of Santa Fe's plaza, is the granddaddy of them all. It was built in 1610 as the original capital of the Spanish colony of New Mexico, making it the oldest continually occupied public building in the United States. Today it's part of the New Mexico History Museum complex, which also includes the Museum of New Mexico Press, the Fray Angélico Chávez History Library, and extensive photo archives. As you can imagine, the palace's 15,000-object collection spans centuries, including everything from conquistador helmets and native hide paintings to a stagecoach and a clock hit by a bullet during Pancho Villa's raid on Columbus, New Mexico, in 1916. The building itself is perhaps the greatest historical artifact of them all, having been the seat of four distinct regional governments—Spain, Mexico, the

Confederacy, and the Territory of New Mexico—and under the rule of no fewer than 100 governors. (Glass panels in the floor reveal ongoing excavations.) Visitors who feel overwhelmed by all this history can have it elucidated by daily free docent-led tours. Outside, under the palace's distinctive portal, registered American Indian vendors sell jewelry, pottery, and more, all of which has met strict authenticity controls. You can see the highlights in about an hour, but if you're interested in history, this place could fill days.

105 W. Palace Ave. www.palaceofthegovernors.org. © **505/476-5100.** Adults $9, free for children 16 and younger. Daily 10am–5pm (closed Mon Nov–Apr). Free admission 5–8pm every Fri May–Oct and on first Fri of the month Nov–Apr. Closed New Year's Day, Easter, Thanksgiving, and Christmas.

Santa Fe Plaza ★★ HISTORIC LANDMARK This public space has been the heart and soul of Santa Fe since the city was established in 1610. Like most New Mexico plazas, it was originally designed as a meeting place, and it has been the site of innumerable festivals and other historical, cultural, and social events. Long ago the plaza was a dusty hive of activity as the staging ground and terminus of the Santa Fe Trail. Today, those who congregate here enjoy some of the best people-watching in New Mexico. Live music and dancing are often staged on the gazebo/bandstand in summer, and at Christmastime the plaza is decked out with lights.

At the corner of San Francisco St. and Lincoln Ave. Open daily 24 hrs.

Museum Hill

As the real estate people like to say, it's all about "location, location, location." Museum Hill is a group of museums with Spanish Colonial and American Indian themes—which, of course, could be said for a great many museums in northern New Mexico. What makes Museum Hill special, however, is that they're so close together, it's easy to see all four of the major museums here in a single morning or afternoon. For information on other things to see and do on Museum Hill, see **www.museumhill.net**.

Museum of Indian Arts and Culture ★★ MUSEUM The Southwest's unique legacy of American Indian culture is the focus of this state-run museum, which traces the culture's development from ancient times to the modern day through artifacts, music, video, and live demonstrations. A tunnel-like entrance, symbolizing the *sipapu* portal between spiritual worlds, leads into a collection of over 70,000 items—centuries-old pottery, silver jewelry, intricate weaving, even painted automobiles—created by native craftspeople. There's a recreation of a trading post and a traditional Pueblo kitchen, and the outstanding multimedia "Here, Now and Always" exhibition combines story, song, artifacts, and the voices of indigenous elders to tell the complex, ongoing story of these people and their place in the United States.

710 Camino Lejo. www.indianartsandculture.org. © **505/476-1269.** Adults $9, free for children 16 and under. Daily 10am–5pm (closed Mon Nov–Apr). Free admission 5–8pm every Fri May–Oct and on first Fri of the month Nov–Apr. Closed New Year's Day, Easter, Thanksgiving, and Christmas.

Museum of International Folk Art ★★★ MUSEUM Kids will love the collection of handmade objects—mostly toys—that fill the Girard Wing of this world-class museum. It's the nucleus of a collection of over 100,000 dolls, masks, dioramas, animals, and other objects gathered from over 100 countries and donated by architect and interior designer Alexander Girard and his wife Susan. Perusing the display cases feels like soaring over carefully crafted miniature worlds. There's a play area and hands-on craft section for itchy fingers, as well as a gift shop that's almost overwhelming in its colorful selection. Other museum sections include the Hispanic Heritage Wing, rotating exhibits in the Neutrogena Wing, and Lloyd's Treasure Chest in the basement, where you can get a peek into what museum conservators do behind the scenes. This branch of the Museum of New Mexico is the main destination on Museum Hill, and for good reason: There's nowhere else like it in the world. Expect to spend at least an hour here, although if you have kids, you might end up staying the whole afternoon.

706 Camino Lejo. www.moifa.org. © **505/476-1200.** Adults $9, free for children 16 and under. Daily 10am–5pm (closed Mon Nov–Apr). Free admission 5–8pm every Fri May–Oct and on first Fri of the month Nov–Apr. Closed New Year's Day, Easter, Thanksgiving, and Christmas.

Museum of Spanish Colonial Art ★ MUSEUM Thank the Spanish Colonial Art Society, founded in Santa Fe in 1925, for the unequaled collection on display here. This is the only museum in the U.S. dedicated to Spanish colonial art, with a prime spot on Museum Hill next to the Folk Art and Indian Arts and Culture museums. It's a (relatively) small building, meaning only a fraction of the 3,700-piece collection is visible at a time, but that includes holy images

If you get hungry while visiting the **Museum of Indian Arts & Culture, the Museum of International Folk Art,** the **Wheelwright Museum of the American Indian,** or the **Museum of Spanish Colonial Art** (all located together, on a hilltop southeast of the Plaza), you can subdue that growling stomach at the **Museum Hill Café ★,** 710 Camino Lejo (www.museumhillcafe.net; ⓒ **505/984-8900**). It's open daily for lunch from 11am to 3pm, with upscale Santa Fe selections including salmon tostadas, curried lentil stew, a grilled turkey sandwich, and of course, the almighty burger.

called *retablos* (painted) and *santos* (carved), furniture, weaving, ceramics, and tinwork that date to between the 16th and 20th centuries. A trip here feels like visiting the house of a very dedicated collector. There's even a "costume corner" where kids can dress up in replica historic clothing. The gift shop sells works by artists who gather for the Traditional Spanish Market every July.

750 Camino Lejo. www.spanishcolonialblog.org/museum. ⓒ **505/982-2226.** Adults $8, free for children 15 and under. Daily 10am–5pm (closed Mon early Sept–late May). Closed New Year's Day, Easter, Thanksgiving, and Christmas.

Wheelwright Museum of the American Indian ★★ MUSEUM   Up on Museum Hill, the Wheelwright is a compact but high-quality museum of contemporary and historic American Indian art. The building is shaped like a traditional octagonal Navajo hogan, complete with a doorway facing the rising sun. Founded in 1937 with the help of a Navajo medicine man, the collection's original aim was to preserve Navajo cultural artifacts. Since then it has expanded to include works by living artists of all Indian cultures, including stunning weaves, beadwork, jewelry, basketwork, paintings, and even film screenings and storytelling. Three or four exhibits rotate through every year. On the lower level, the Case Trading Post is a gift shop modeled on the classic posts that served as stores, banks, and meeting places across the Western frontier. Some of the items, like kachina dolls and silver jewelry, are quite expensive, but it also has some more affordable items.

704 Camino Lejo. www.wheelwright.org. ⓒ **505/982-4636.** Adults $5, free for children 11 and under or students with ID. Free admission for all the first Sun of every month. Mon–Sat 10am–5pm, Sun 1–5pm.

More Attractions
MUSEUM

Museum of Contemporary Native Arts ★★ MUSEUM   After a few days in New Mexico, it's good to be reminded that Indian art is more than just pottery, blankets, and kachina dolls. This museum is the place for it: the largest assemblage of contemporary native art in the country, located right in the heart of downtown Santa Fe, 1 block from the Plaza. Representing hundreds of tribes, the 7,500-item collection includes photographs, paintings, prints, and much more. Many of the works embody the struggle to bridge the old and

Greater Santa Fe Attractions

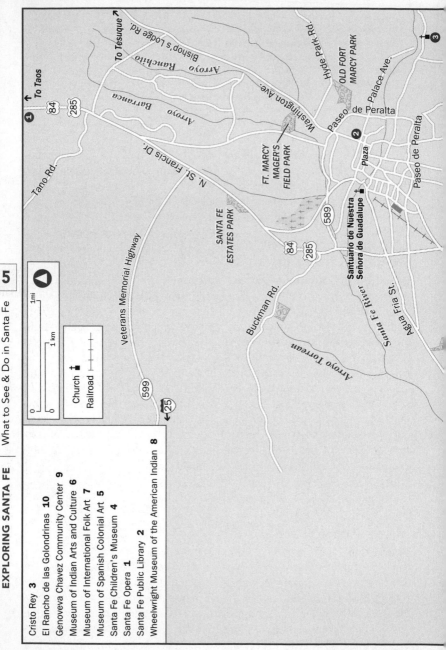

Cristo Rey **3**

El Rancho de las Golondrinas **10**

Genoveva Chavez Community Center **9**

Museum of Indian Arts and Culture **6**

Museum of International Folk Art **7**

Museum of Spanish Colonial Art **5**

Santa Fe Children's Museum **4**

Santa Fe Opera **1**

Santa Fe Public Library **2**

Wheelwright Museum of the American Indian **8**

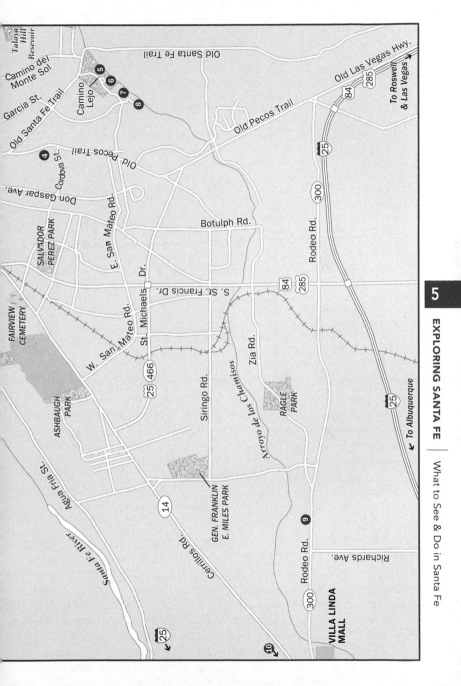

FETISHES: gifts OF POWER

According to Zuni lore, in the early years of human existence, the Sun sent down his two children to assist humans, who were under siege from earthly predators. The Sun's sons shot lightning bolts from their shields and destroyed the predators. For generations, Zunis, traveling across their lands in western New Mexico, have found stones shaped like particular animals, and Zuni legend maintains that these stones are the remains of those long-lost predators, still containing their souls or last breaths.

In many shops in Santa Fe, you too can pick up a carved animal figure called a *fetish*. According to belief, the owner of the fetish is able to absorb the power of that creature. Many fetishes were long ago used for protection and power while hunting. Today, a person might carry a bear for health and strength, or an eagle for keen perspective. A mole might be placed in a home's foundation for protection from elements underground, a frog buried with crops for fertility and rain, or a ram carried in the purse for prosperity. For love, some locals recommend pairs of fetishes—often foxes or coyotes carved from a single piece of stone.

Many fetishes, arranged with bundles on top and attached with sinew, serve as an offering to the animal spirit that resides within the stone. Fetishes are still carved by many of the pueblos. A good fetish is not necessarily one that is meticulously carved. Some fetishes are barely carved at all, as the original shape of the stone already contains the form of the animal. When you have a sense of the quality and elegance available, decide which animal (and power) suits you best. American Indians caution, however, that the fetish cannot be expected to impart an attribute you don't already possess. Instead, it will help elicit the power that already resides within you. An excellent source for fetishes is **Keshi ★,** 227 Don Gaspar Ave. (www.keshi.com; ℂ **505/989-8728**). Expect to pay $30 to $75 or more for a good one.

---

new, the traditional and the modern, such as David Sloan's silkscreened images of endangered species and their Navajo names over lithographed reproductions of old 1970s *Navajo Times* newspaper ads. Don't miss the outdoor sculpture garden, featuring works by Allan Houser.

108 Cathedral Place. www.iaia.edu. ℂ **505/983-1777.** Adults $10; seniors (62 and older), students, and children 16 and under $5. Mon and Wed–Sat 10am–5pm, Sun noon–5pm. Closed New Year's Day, Easter, Thanksgiving, and Christmas.

CHURCHES

Cristo Rey ★ CHURCH This Catholic church (Christ the King), a huge adobe structure, was built in 1940 to commemorate the 400th anniversary of Coronado's exploration of the Southwest. Parishioners did most of the construction work, even making adobe bricks from the earth where the church stands. The local architect John Gaw Meem designed the building, in mission style, as a site to preserve some magnificent stone *reredos* (altar screens) created by the Spanish during the colonial era, which were recovered and restored in the 20th century.

1120 Canyon Rd. www.cristoreysantefe.parishesonline.com. ℂ **505/983-8528.** Free admission. Mon–Fri 8am–5pm; Mass Sat 4:30pm and Sun 10am.

Loretto Chapel Museum ★★ CHURCH/MUSEUM   This Gothic church, modeled after Sainte-Chapelle in Paris, was built for the Sisters of Loretto between 1873 and 1878. It would have been just another beautiful old church in this religious city if not for what happened near the end of its construction. Workers realized there wasn't space to access the choir loft, 22 ft. high, by a normal staircase—a ladder was the only thing that would fit. The nuns prayed for nine days to St. Joseph, patron saint of carpenters, for a better solution. On the ninth day, as the story goes, a mysterious stranger arrived on a donkey with a toolbox, looking for work. Using only a saw, a square, and water to season the wood, he built an elegant spiral staircase over the next few months, then disappeared before they could pay him. Was it St. Joseph himself? Who knows, but the staircase is a marvel of engineering and aesthetics, with two full 360-degree turns and no visible means of support. Even more amazing, it was built using wooden pegs, not nails. Today, the deconsecrated chapel is run as a private museum with a small gift shop. It's a quick visit here, but worth the stop.

207 Old Santa Fe Trail (btw. Alameda and Water sts.). www.lorettochapel.com. © **505/982-0092.** Adults $3, free for children 6 and under. Mon–Sat 9am–4:30pm, Sun 10:30am–4:30pm. Chapel closes for special events; call for current schedule.

Mission of San Miguel ★ CHURCH   If you really want to get the feel of Spanish colonial Catholicism, visit this church. You won't be disappointed. Built around 1610, the church has massive adobe walls, high windows, an elegant altar screen (erected in 1798), and a 780-pound San José bell (now found inside), which was cast in Spain in 1356. It also houses buffalo-hide and deerskin Bible paintings used by Franciscan missionaries in the 1600s. It is believed to be the oldest active church in the United States. Anthropologists have excavated near the altar, down to the original floor that some claim to be part of a 12th-century pueblo.

401 Old Santa Fe Trail (at E. De Vargas St.). www.sanmiguelmission.org. © **505/983-3974.** Adults $1, free for children 6 and under. Mon–Fri 10am–2pm; Mass Sun 2pm in Latin, 5pm in English.

Santuario de Nuestra Señora de Guadalupe ★ CHURCH   This church, built between 1776 and 1796 at the end of El Camino Real by Franciscan missionaries, is believed to be the oldest shrine in the United States honoring the Virgin of Guadalupe, the patron saint of Mexico. Better known as Santuario de Guadalupe, the shrine has adobe walls that are almost 3 feet thick; the deep-red plaster wall behind the altar was dyed with oxblood in traditional fashion when the church was restored early in the 20th century. It is well worth a visit to see photographs of the transformation of the building over time; its styles have ranged from flat-topped pueblo to New England town meeting and today's northern New Mexico style. On one wall is a famous oil painting, *Our Lady of Guadalupe,* created in 1783 by the renowned Mexican artist José de Alzibar. Painted expressly for this church, it was brought from Mexico City by mule caravan. One of Santa Fe's newest landmarks, the graceful 12-foot, 4,000-pound statue of Our Lady of Guadalupe by Mexican sculptor Georgina "Gogy" Farias was erected in front of the church in 2008.

100 S. Guadalupe St. © **505/983-8868.** Donations appreciated. Mon–Fri 9am–4pm. Call for current Mass schedule.

St. Francis Cathedral ★★ CHURCH   Santa Fe's grandest religious structure is an architectural anomaly in Santa Fe because its design is French. Just a block east of the plaza, it was built between 1869 and 1886 by Archbishop Jean-Baptiste Lamy in the style of the great cathedrals of Europe. French architects designed the Romanesque building—named after Santa Fe's patron saint—and Italian masons assisted with its construction. The small adobe Our Lady of the Rosary chapel on the northeast side of the cathedral, however, has a Spanish look. Built in 1807, it's the only portion that remains from Our Lady of the Assumption Church, founded along with Santa Fe in 1610. The new cathedral was built over and around the old church. Don't miss the wooden icon set in a niche in the wall of the north chapel, **Our Lady of Peace,** which is believed to be the oldest representation of the Madonna in the United States. Rescued from the old church during the 1680 Pueblo Rebellion, it was brought back by Don Diego de Vargas when the Spanish colonists reconquered the capital 12 years later—thus, the name. Today, Our Lady of Peace plays an important part in the annual Feast of Corpus Christi in June and July. Take some time also to admire the cathedral's **front doors,** which feature 16 carved panels of historic note and a plaque memorializing the 38 Franciscan friars who were martyred during New Mexico's early years. There's also a large bronze statue of Archbishop Lamy himself; his grave is under the main altar of the cathedral.

13 Cathedral Place, at San Francisco St. www.cbsfa.org. © **505/982-5619.** Donations appreciated. Mon–Thurs 8:30am–4pm, Fri 8:30am–noon. Check website or call for Mass and confession schedule.

PARKS & REFUGES

Old Fort Marcy Park ★ PARK   Marking the 1846 site of the first U.S. military reservation in the Southwest, this park overlooks the northeast corner of downtown. Only a few mounds remain from the fort, but the Cross of the Martyrs, at the top of a winding brick walkway from Paseo de Peralta near Otero Street, is a popular spot for bird's-eye photographs. The cross was erected in 1920 by the Knights of Columbus and the Historical Society of New Mexico to commemorate the Franciscans killed during the Pueblo Rebellion of 1680. It has since played a role in numerous religious processions.

617 Paseo de Peralta (or travel 3 blocks up Artist Rd. and turn right).

Randall Davey Audubon Center ★★ NATURE CENTER   Named for the late Santa Fe artist who willed his home—originally an 1847 sawmill—to the Audubon Society, this wildlife refuge occupies 135 acres at the mouth of

SANTA FE'S french connection

In the 19th century, New Mexico, including Santa Fe, was first ruled by Spain, then Mexico, and finally the United States. So how is it that one of the most influential and important people of that time was a Frenchman?

Bishop Jean-Baptiste Lamy was the first bishop and archbishop of the Diocese of Santa Fe. Born in 1814 to a religious family in Lempdes in Auvergne, a region in southern France, Lamy entered a seminary that specialized in training priests for foreign missions, and in 1839 Lamy and a small group of priests and nuns made their way to America. Lamy's first assignment was to a parish in Danville, Ohio, where he oversaw the construction of several churches.

After the New Mexico Territory became part of the United States, the Catholic Church leadership petitioned the Vatican to establish a provisional diocese in New Mexico. The Vatican did so in 1850, and Lamy was rewarded for his work in Ohio by being appointed vicar. When the Diocese of Santa Fe was officially created in 1853, he was appointed its bishop.

While bishop of Santa Fe, Lamy was known for his many confrontations with the local Mexican clergy, many of whom he considered too worldly. He didn't like or trust them and they didn't like or trust him. These confrontations included a long-running dispute with Father Antonio José Martinez of Taos, whom Lamy excommunicated in 1858. Martinez, however, refused to recognize the excommunication and continued to celebrate Mass in private chapels.

Lamy disliked New Mexico's adobe architecture, so in the 1860s when it came time to build the St. Francis Cathedral, Lamy chose a stone Romanesque style instead. He also was responsible for the Gothic style of Loretto Chapel (p. 81).

Elevated to archbishop by the Vatican in 1875, Lamy retired in 1884 and died in Santa Fe in 1888. Perhaps his widest fame came after his death, as the model for Willa Cather's 1927 novel *Death Comes for the Archbishop.*

Santa Fe Canyon. Just a few minutes' drive from the plaza, it's an excellent escape. More than 125 species of birds and 120 types of plants live here, and varied mammals have been spotted—including black bears, mule deer, mountain lions, bobcats, raccoons, and coyotes. Trails winding through more than 100 acres of the nature sanctuary are open to day hikers, although no dogs are allowed. Tours of Davey's home are available, and guided birding walks are led several times a week; call for the schedule. There's also a natural history bookstore on-site.

1800 Upper Canyon Rd. http://nm.audubon.org/randall-davey. © **505/983-4609.** Adults $2, children 12 and younger $1. Mon–Sat 8am–4pm.

Santa Fe Canyon Preserve ★★★ NATURE PRESERVE   Covering some 525 acres just 2 miles from Santa Fe Plaza, this peaceful preserve managed by the Nature Conservancy has hiking and biking trails, the remnants of an historic Victorian-era dam, wildflowers, ponderosa pine, and a grove of cottonwoods and willows. Some 140 species of birds call it home, there are deer and an occasional bear, and beavers, plus their dams and lodges, are a common sight. There's a 1.3-mile Interpretive Loop Trail through the Santa

Fe River Riparian area, meandering along the remains of the Two Mile Dam to an overlook of a pond—all that's left of the reservoir that once served Santa Fe. The **Dale Ball Foothill Trail System,** which runs through the Santa Fe Canyon Preserve, includes some 22 miles of multi-use trails, and these trails connect to several other trails, including the 5.2-mile Atalaya Trail, the 1.5-mile Dorothy Stewart Trail, and the 1.3-mile Interpretive Loop Trail discussed above. Note that dogs and bicycles are not permitted in the preserve except on the Dale Ball Foothill Trail System.

Cerro Gordo Rd., at its intersection with Upper Canyon Rd. www.nature.org. © **505/988-3867.** Free admission. Daily sunrise–sunset.

Santa Fe River Park ★★ PARK   This is a lovely spot for an early morning jog, a midday walk beneath the trees, or perhaps a sack lunch at a picnic table. The green strip follows the midtown stream for about 10 miles as it meanders between Patrick Smith Park and Camino Real Park near NM 599. Contact the city of Santa Fe for more information and to get a city trail map.

www.santafenm.gov. © **505/955-6706.** Free admission. Open 24 hrs.

HISTORIC SITES
El Rancho de las Golondrinas ★★ HISTORIC HOME   A fascinating
place to visit anytime, and especially during its festivals and other special events, El Rancho de las Golondrinas takes us back to New Mexico's Spanish Colonial and Territorial days. The 200-acre ranch includes an 18th-century hacienda, with the rooms surrounding a central placita where most day-to-day living and working took place, plus a 19th-century home complete with outbuildings. Numerous other buildings—molasses mill, blacksmith shop, wheelwright shop, schoolhouse, and several water-powered grist mills—round out the story of life in Spanish Colonial and Territorial New Mexico. The ranch was an important overnight stop on the 1,000-mile Camino Real, or Royal Road, between Mexico City and Santa Fe. Craft demonstrations take place and there are live farm animals to see. A walk around the entire property is 1¼ miles, with amazing scenery. A free daily guided tour is offered at 10:30am, except during special events. Check the website for the festival schedule; they're worth fitting into your travel schedule.

334 Los Pinos Rd. Take exit 276 from I-25, go north on NM 599, turn left on W. Frontage Rd. then right on Los Pinos Rd. www.golondrinas.org. © **505/471-2261.** Adults $6, seniors (62 and older) and children 13–18 $4, free for children 12 and under. Higher fees during special events. June–Sept Wed–Sun 10am–4pm.

New Mexico State Capitol (Roundhouse) ★★ LANDMARK   This
is the only round capitol building in the U.S. Built in 1966, it's designed in the shape of a Zia Pueblo emblem, or sun sign, which is also the state symbol and is on the state flag. (See "The Sun Worshippers of New Mexico," p. 25). Surrounding the capitol is a lush 6½-acre garden boasting more than 100 varieties of plants, including roses, plums, almonds, nectarines, Russian olive trees, and sequoias. Inside you'll find standard functional offices and public areas

with art by New Mexico artists. Check out the Governor's Gallery and the Capitol Art Collection. Guided tours are available by appointment. All tours and self-guided brochures are free.

490 Old Santa Fe Trail, at Paseo del Peralta. www.nmlegis.gov. © **505/986-4589.** Free admission. Open for self-guided tours Mon–Fri 7am–6pm, and also holidays and Sat 9am–5pm Memorial Day–Aug. Free parking Mon–Fri at 420 Galisteo St.

Organized Tours

Walking is the best way to see downtown Santa Fe, and we highly recommend the self-guided walking tour below. But if you prefer a guide who can fill you in on the historic tidbits of this old city, the best is **Historic Walks of Santa Fe ★** (www.historic walks of Santa Fe.com; © **505/986-8388**), on the plaza at 66 E. San Francisco St. Many of the guides are local museum docents. The daily tours cost $14 per person (free for children under 16 with an adult) and last 1 hour and 45 minutes, starting several times daily at various downtown hotels. Well-behaved dogs are welcome. The company also offers various special tours, including a ghost tour, shopping tour, and a Canyon Road art tour. Details are on the company's website.

Feet getting sore but don't want to fight the Santa Fe traffic? An open-air tour of the city with **Loretto Line ★** (www.toursofsantafe.com; © **505/982-0092, ext. 1**) may solve the problem. The company has been running tours here since 1992. Tours last a little over an hour, covering the main historic sites and other places of interest, and are offered daily from mid-March through October. They depart at 10am, noon, and 2pm from the Loretto Chapel and a half-hour later from La Fonda Hotel. The cost is $15 for adults and $12 for children 12 and under with an adult.

Classes & Workshops

If you're looking for something to do that's a little off the beaten tourist path, you might consider taking a class.

You can master the flavors of Santa Fe with an entertaining 3-hour cooking class at the **Santa Fe School of Cooking ★**, 125 N. Guadalupe St. (www.santafeschoolofcooking.com; © **800/982-4688** or 505/983-4511). The class teaches about the flavors and history of traditional New Mexican and contemporary Southwestern cuisines. Prices are in the $78 to $98 range and are offered several times each week; call or check the website for the current schedule.

If southwestern art has you hooked, you can take a drawing and painting class led by a Santa Fe artist. Students sketch such outdoor subjects as the Santa Fe landscape and adobe architecture. In case of inclement weather, classes are held in the studio. Classes generally last for 3 hours, and art materials are included in the fee, which starts at $138. Private lessons can also be arranged, and all levels of experience are welcome. Contact **Jane Shoenfeld's Art Adventures in the Southwest ★** (www.skyfields.net; © **505/986-1108**).

Also see "Special-Interest & Escorted Trips," p. 234.

Especially for Kids

Don't miss taking the kids to the **Museum of International Folk Art** (p. 76), where they'll love the international dioramas and the toys. Kids are sure to enjoy **El Rancho de las Golondrinas** (p. 84), a living 18th- and 19th-century Spanish village comprising a hacienda, a village store, a schoolhouse, and several chapels and kitchens.

The Genoveva Chavez Community Center ★ RECREATION CENTER On the south side of Santa Fe, this city-run full-service family recreation center offers many options for kids. The complex includes a 50m pool, a leisure pool, a therapy pool, an ice-skating rink, three gyms, a workout room, racquetball courts, and an indoor running track, as well as a spa and sauna. It also has a variety of youth programs including Playzone, drop-in babysitting for children 2 to 6 years old. For hours, prices, and more information, check the center's website.

3221 Rodeo Rd. www.chavezcenter.com. ℰ **505/955-4000.**

Santa Fe Children's Museum ★ MUSEUM This museum offers interactive exhibits and hands-on activities in the arts, humanities, and science. The most notable features include a 16-foot climbing wall that kids—outfitted with helmets and harnesses—can scale, and a 1-acre southwestern horticulture garden, complete with animals, wetlands, and a greenhouse. This fascinating area serves as an outdoor classroom for ongoing environmental educational programs. Special programs and hands-on sessions with artists and scientists are regularly scheduled.

1050 Old Pecos Trail. www.santafechildrensmuseum.org. ℰ **505/989-8359.** Admission $7.50; free for infants under 1 year old. Tues–Sat 10am–6pm, Sun noon–5pm. Shorter hours in winter.

Santa Fe Public Library ★ LIBRARY/COMMUNITY CENTER Special programs, such as storytelling and magic shows, can be found here, especially in summer. Check the website or call for the current schedule. The main library is in the center of town, 1 block from the plaza.

145 Washington Ave. www.santafelibrary.org. ℰ **505/955-6781.** Mon–Thurs 10am–8pm, Fri–Sat 10am–6pm, Sun 1–5pm.

A SANTA FE STROLL

Santa Fe Plaza is the heart and soul of the city. For centuries it's where residents would come to shop, eat, and meet, and although in recent times the plaza has become a mecca for tourists as well as residents, it's still where you must go if you're going to say you saw Santa Fe. Because everything is so close (and because parking is sometimes a challenge) it's best to leave your car at your hotel or in a lot and explore the plaza area on foot.

START:	The plaza
FINISH:	Loretto Chapel
TIME:	1 to 5 hours, depending on the length of visits to the museums and churches
BEST TIMES:	Any morning before the afternoon heat, but after the American Indian traders have spread out their wares at the Palace of the Governors

1 The Plaza

This historic square (see "The Top Attractions," p. 72) offers a look at Santa Fe's everyday life as well as many types of architecture, ranging from the Pueblo-style Palace of the Governors to the Territorial-style row of shops and restaurants on its west side.

Facing the plaza on its north side is the:

2 Palace of the Governors

Today the flagship of the New Mexico state museum system, the Palace of the Governors (p. 74) has functioned continually as a public building since it was erected in 1610 as the capitol of Nuevo Mexico. Every day, American Indian artisans spread out their crafts for sale beneath its portal.

At the corner of Lincoln and Palace aves., you'll find the:

3 New Mexico Museum of Art

Located at 107 W. Palace Ave., this museum (p. 74) holds works by Georgia O'Keeffe and other famed 20th-century Taos and Santa Fe artists. The building is a fine example of Pueblo revival–style architecture.

Virtually across the street is the:

4 Delgado House

This Victorian mansion (at 124 W. Palace Ave.) is an excellent example of local adobe construction, modified by late 19th-century architectural detail. It was built in 1890 by Felipe B. Delgado, a merchant most known for his business of running mule and ox freight trains over the Santa Fe Trail to Independence and the Camino Real to Chihuahua. The home remained in the Delgado family until 1970. It now belongs to the Historic Santa Fe Foundation.

If you continue west on Palace Avenue, you'll come to a narrow lane— Burro Alley—jutting south toward San Francisco Street, with an interesting burro sculpture.

Head back to Palace Ave., make your way north on Grant Ave., and turn left on Johnson St. to the:

5 Georgia O'Keeffe Museum

Opened in 1997, this museum (see p. 72) houses the largest collection of O'Keeffe works in the world. The 13,000-square-foot space is the only

Walking Tour: The Plaza Area

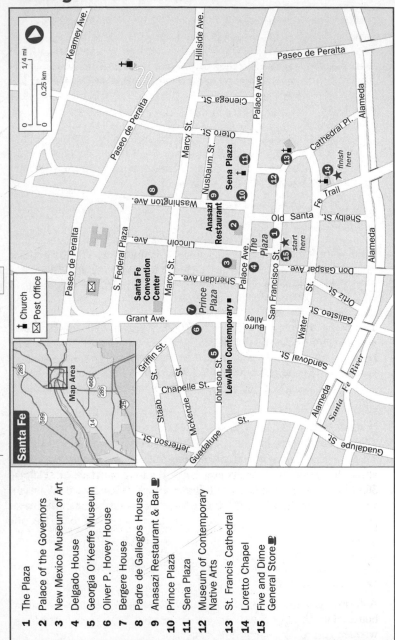

Church
⊠ **Post Office**

1 The Plaza
2 Palace of the Governors
3 New Mexico Museum of Art
4 Delgado House
5 Georgia O'Keeffe Museum
6 Oliver P. Hovey House
7 Bergere House
8 Padre de Gallegos House
9 Anasazi Restaurant & Bar 🍴
10 Prince Plaza
11 Sena Plaza
12 Museum of Contemporary Native Arts
13 St. Francis Cathedral
14 Loretto Chapel
15 Five and Dime General Store 🛍

museum in the United States dedicated solely to one internationally known woman's work.

Head back to Grant Ave. and continue north to Griffin St., where you'll find the:

6 Oliver P. Hovey House

Constructed between 1857 and 1859 in Territorial style, this adobe, located at 136 Griffin St., is unique because it is actually painted brick. It's not surprising that a man like Hovey, a local low-level politician known primarily for his pretentious and flamboyant ways, would go to the trouble to dress up a home in such a fancy style (red brick was a rare commodity in this outpost town back then), but such stunts might be what made people call him the Great Lord Hovey, when he was no lord at all.

Just to the east and across Grant Ave. is the:

7 Bergere House

Built around 1870, this house, at 135 Grant Ave., hosted U.S. President Ulysses S. Grant and his wife Julia during their 1880 visit to Santa Fe.

Proceed north on Grant and turn right on Marcy. On the north side of the street is the Santa Fe Community Convention Center. Three blocks farther east on Marcy, through an office and restaurant district, turn left on Washington Ave. Walk a short distance to 227–237 Washington Ave., where you'll see the:

8 Padre de Gallegos House

This house was built in 1857 in the Territorial style. Padre de Gallegos was a priest who, in the eyes of newly arrived Archbishop Jean-Baptiste Lamy (p. 83), kept too high a social profile and was therefore defrocked in 1852. Gallegos later represented the territory in Congress and eventually became the federal superintendent of American Indian affairs.

Reverse course and turn south again on Washington Ave., passing en route the public library.

9 Anasazi Restaurant & Bar ☕

This is a good time to stop for refreshments at Anasazi Restaurant & Bar at the Rosewood Inn of the Anasazi, 113 Washington Ave. (© **505/988-3030**). During the summer, you'll find a variety of drinks served on the veranda, and in the winter the atmospheric bar inside can be quite cozy.

Leaving the Rosewood Inn of the Anasazi, you'll notice the entrance to the Palace of the Governors Museum Shop, across the street, a good place to purchase quality regional memorabilia. As you approach the plaza, turn left (east) on Palace Ave. A short distance farther on your left, at 113 E. Palace Ave., is:

10 Prince Plaza

A former governor's home, this Territorial-style structure, which now houses **The Shed** (a great lunch or dinner spot; p. 67), once had huge wooden gates to keep out tribal attacks.

5

EXPLORING SANTA FE | Walking Tour: The Plaza Area

Next door is:

11 Sena Plaza

This city landmark offers a quiet respite from the busy streets, with its parklike patio. **La Casa Sena** restaurant (a good place to stop for lunch or dinner) is the primary occupant of what was once the 31-room Sena family adobe hacienda, built in 1831. The Territorial legislature met in the upper rooms of the hacienda in the 1890s.

Turn right (south) on Cathedral Place to no. 108, which is the:

12 Museum of Contemporary Native Arts

Here you'll find the most comprehensive collection of contemporary American Indian art in the world (p. 77).

Across the street, step through the doors of the:

13 St. Francis Cathedral

Built in Romanesque style between 1869 and 1886 by Archbishop Lamy, this is Santa Fe's grandest religious edifice. It has a famous 17th-century wooden Madonna known as Our Lady of Peace (p. 82).

After leaving the cathedral, walk around the backside of the illustrious La Fonda Hotel (p. 52)—south on Cathedral Place and west on Water St.—to the intersection of the Old Santa Fe Trail. Here, at the northwest corner of the Inn and Spa at Loretto (p. 50), you'll find the:

14 Loretto Chapel

This chapel (p. 81) is more formally known as the Chapel of Our Lady of Light. Archbishop Lamy (p. 83) was also behind the construction of this chapel, built for the Sisters of Loretto. It is remarkable for its spiral staircase, which has no central or other visible support, although any competent stair builder can explain how it was constructed.

This ends the walking tour. Follow Old Santa Fe Trail north, back to the Plaza.

15 Five and Dime General Store ☕

By now you may be tired and hungry, so head to a small store called Five and Dime General Store, 58 E. San Francisco St. (© **505/992-1800**), near where F. W. Woolworth's, the now-defunct legendary five-and-dime store, once stood. Like Woolworth's, the store serves a cherished local delicacy called Frito Pie: a bag of Fritos smothered in chile con carne, served in a plastic bag with a spoon and a napkin.

SPORTS & RECREATION

Set between the granite peaks of the Sangre de Cristo Mountains and the subtler volcanic Jemez Mountains, and with the Rio Grande flowing through, the Santa Fe area offers outdoor enthusiasts many opportunities to play. This is the land of high desert, where temperatures vary with the elevation, allowing for a full range of activities throughout the year.

If the weather turns against you but you still want to keep up with your exercise routine, stop by the **Genoveva Chavez Community Center,**

If you're one of those people who wants it all, and you don't mind spending money to have someone organize everything, consider hooking up with **Santa Fe Mountain Adventures ★★** (www.santafemountainadventures.com; ✆ **800/965-4010** or 505/988-4000). The company offers programs that combine outdoor adventures with arts and cultural experiences, and possibly a spa treatment. You might start the day with fly fishing or white-water rafting, and then in the afternoon take a cooking or pottery-making class. Families especially enjoy the guided "geocaching" adventure, a scavenger hunt using a global positioning device. Prices start at $79 per person for a half-day.

3221 Rodeo Rd. (www.chavezcenter.com; ✆ **505/955-4000**), a city-run full-service recreation center on the south side of Santa Fe (p. 86).

Biking

You can cycle along main roadways and paved country roads year-round in Santa Fe, but be aware that traffic is particularly heavy around the plaza. Mountain-biking interest has blossomed here and is especially popular in the spring, summer, and fall; the high-desert terrain is rugged and challenging, but mountain bikers of all levels can find exhilarating rides.

The Santa Fe Visitor Information Centers (p. 43) can supply you with bike maps. You can also download bike maps from the city of Santa Fe's website (www.santafenm.gov) as well as a map of the city's bicycle parking areas with racks. You can rent bikes from **Mellow Velo,** 132 E. Marcy St. (www.mellowvelo.com; ✆ **505/995-8356**) and **Bike-N-Sport,** 524 Cordova Rd. (www.nmbikensport.com; ✆ **505/820-0809**).

Some of the best mountain-biking here is in the **Dale Ball Foothill Trail System ★★** (see below). **Another good option for biking or hiking is the 3.7-mile paved Arroyo de los Chamisos Trail ★,** which meanders through the southwestern part of the city and is easily accessible to those staying in hotels along Cerrillos Road. It follows a chamisa-lined arroyo and has good mountain views. Begin at Santa Fe High School on Yucca St. or on Rodeo Rd. near Sam's Club.

Bird-Watching

The best bird-watching in Santa Fe is at the Nature Conservancy's **Santa Fe Canyon Preserve ★★★** and the nearby **Randall Davey Audubon Center ★★** (see "Parks & Refuges," p. 82).

Fishing

In the lakes and waterways around Santa Fe, anglers typically catch trout, bass, perch, and kokanee salmon. The most popular fishing holes are the Cochiti and Abiquiu lakes, as well as the Rio Chama, Pecos River, and the Rio Grande. For a weekly fishing report plus information on licenses and special

5

EXPLORING SANTA FE

Sports & Recreation

fishing proclamations, check with the **New Mexico Department of Game and Fish** (www.wildlife.state.nm.us; ☏ **505/476-8000**).

For gear, licenses, and experienced guides, contact **High Desert Angler,** 460 Cerrillos Rd. (www.highdesertangler.com; ☏ **505/988-7688**).

Golf

Among golf courses in the Santa Fe area are the 18-hole **Marty Sanchez Links de Santa Fe ★★,** 205 Caja del Rio (www.linksdesantafe.com; ☏ **505/955-4400**); the 18-hole **Santa Fe Country Club ★** on Airport Rd. (www.santafecountryclub.com; ☏ **505/471-2626**); and **Towa Golf Club ★,** Buffalo Thunder Resort, 12 miles north of Santa Fe on US 285/84 (www.buffalo thunderresort.com; ☏ **505/455-9000**), which has 27 holes and splendid views of the Jemez and Sangre de Cristo mountains. Avid golfers don't mind the drive to the highly rated 18-hole **Cochiti Golf Club ★,** 5200 Cochiti Hwy., Cochiti Pueblo, about 35 miles southwest of Santa Fe via I-25 and NM 16 and 22 (www.pueblodecochiti.org; ☏ **505/465-2239**).

Hiking

For in-town hiking and walking, the hands-down top spots are the Nature Conservancy's **Santa Fe Canyon Preserve ★★★,** which connects you with the **Dale Ball Foothill Trail System ★★,** and the nearby **Randall Davey Audubon Center ★★** (see "Parks & Refuges," p. 82). Trails in the Dale Ball Foothill Trail System are open to those with leashed dogs.

It's hard to decide which of the 1,000 or so miles of nearby national forest trails to tackle. Among the most popular areas are the **Pecos Wilderness,** with 223,000 acres, and the 58,000-acre **Jemez Mountain National Recreation Area.** Information on these and other U.S. Forest Service areas is available from the **Santa Fe National Forest,** 11 Forest Ln. (www.fs.usda.gov/santafe; ☏ **505/438-5300.**

A popular hike in the national forest is the **Borrego Trail ★,** which runs 22 miles through aspens and ponderosa pines up onto Borrego Mesa. For those not inclined to go the distance, there's a pretty creek about 4 miles up that makes a good turnaround point. It's easy to find the trail head: head up Hyde Park Rd. toward Ski Santa Fe, just over 8 miles from the city.

Also on Hyde Park Rd. near Ski Santa Fe is **Hyde Memorial State Park ★★,** New Mexico's first state park, with a nice campground, a playground, visitor center, toilets, and 4.2 miles of hiking trails. These include the half-mile **Waterfall Trail ★,** which follows a small creek to—you guessed it—a pretty waterfall, and the **West Circle Trail ★★,** a difficult 2.2-mile hike with a 1,000-foot elevation gain in 1 mile; the pay-off is splendid views of Santa Fe through the pines. The park day use fee is $5 per vehicle. For information, see www.nmparks.com or call ☏ **505/983-7175.**

Horseback Riding

Trips ranging from a few hours to overnight can be arranged by **Santa Fe Detours ★,** 54½ E. San Francisco St. (www.sfdetours.com; ☏ **800/338-6877** or 505/983-6565). You'll ride with experienced wranglers and see the West like cowboys did more than 100 years ago. Also providing horseback rides of varying lengths is **Broken Saddle Riding Company** ★ (www.brokensaddle.com; ℂ **505/424-7774**), based in the historic mining town of Cerrillos, with rides through the stunning Galisteo Basin south of Santa Fe.

Indoor Climbing

The two-story-high walls of the cavernous **Santa Fe Climbing Center** ★ (825 Early St.; www.climbsantafe.com; ℂ **505/986-8944**) are covered with foot- and handholds, making it a perfect place to practice your rock climbing out of the rain, snow, or blazing sun. There's a bouldering room and a top rope/lead climbing room with routes for all levels of climber. You can rent climbing shoes and harnesses for $3.50 each; a daily pass costs $14 for adults, $12 for students age 12 to 24, and $10 for children 11 and under. Call for hours.

Skiing

There's something available for every ability level at **Ski Santa Fe** ★ (www.skisantafe.com; ℂ **505/982-4429**), about 16 miles northeast of Santa Fe at the end of Hyde Park Rd. While not on par with Taos or the resorts in Colorado, it's still a fun place to ski. Lots of locals ski here, particularly on weekends, so if you can, go on a weekday. It's a good family area and fairly small—you can easily split off from and later reconnect with your group. Built on the upper reaches of 12,000-foot Tesuque Peak, the area has an average annual snowfall of 225 inches and a vertical drop of 1,725 feet. Seven lifts, including a 5,000-foot triple chair and a quad chair, serve 79 trails. Base facilities, at 10,350 feet, center on **La Casa Lodge,** with a cafeteria, lounge, ski shop, and boutique. A restaurant, **Totemoff's,** has a mid-mountain patio. The ski area is open daily from 9am to 4pm, usually from Thanksgiving to early April, depending on snow conditions. Full-day lift tickets are $72 for adults, $58 for ages 13 to 20, $52 for children 12 and under, and $55 for seniors 62 to 71. Tickets are free for kids fewer than 46 inches tall (in their ski boots), and for seniors 72 and older. For 24-hour reports on snow conditions, call ℂ **505/983-9155.**

5

EXPLORING SANTA FE

Sports & Recreation

If traveling, skiing, or other activities have left you weary, Santa Fe has a number of relaxation options. **Absolute Nirvana Spa & Gardens** ★★, 106 Faithway St. (www.absolutenirvana.com; © **505/983-7942**) offers imaginative Indo-Asian spa "experiences" as well as massages and facials. Their signature treatment, the Javanese Lulur, includes a full-body massage with jasmine oil, a sandlewood/rice powder exfoliation and yogurt/honey wrap, followed by a steam shower and decadent rose petal bath, all accompanied by tea, fruit, and a house-made truffle. The spa is open Sunday to Thursday 10am to 6pm and Friday and Saturday 10am to 8pm. Prices start at $95, with most around $250 for a 2-hour session. Another option with a more Japanese bent is **Ten Thousand Waves** ★★, a spa about 3 miles northeast of Santa Fe on Hyde Park Rd. (www.tenthousandwaves.com; © **505/982-9304**). This

serene retreat, nestled in a grove of piñon trees, offers hot tubs, saunas, and cold plunges, plus a variety of massage and other bodywork techniques. Bathing suit bottoms are required in the communal hot tub, suits are optional in the women's communal tub, and you can stay in either for as long as you like for $24. Private hot tubs cost $35 to $45 an hour per person, and a private spa suite is available for $57 per person for 90 minutes. You can also arrange therapeutic massage, hot-oil massage, in-water *watsu* massage, herbal wraps, salt glows, facials, dry brush aromatherapy treatments, Ayurvedic treatments, and the much-praised Japanese Hot Stone Massage. From July through October the spa is open daily 10:30am to 10:30pm (however, it opens at noon on Tuesdays). Winter hours are shorter, so call ahead. Reservations are recommended, especially on weekends.

Cross-country skiers find seemingly endless miles of snow to track in the **Santa Fe National Forest,** especially along Hyde Park Rd., and there are also suitable trails in **Hyde Memorial State Park** (see "Hiking," p. 92).

Swimming

There are several public city-run pools in Santa Fe, in addition to the many at local hotels and motels. The **Bicentennial Outdoor Swimming Pool,** 1121 Alto St. (© **505/955-4778**), is the only public outdoor pool, but it's closed in the winter. Public indoor pools open year-round include the pool in the **Fort Marcy Recreation Complex,** 490 Bishop's Lodge Rd. (© **505/955-2500**) and at the **Genoveva Chavez Community Center** (p. 86). For additional information, see the City of Santa Fe website, www.santafenm.gov.

SANTA FE SHOPPING

Shopping in Santa Fe can be both exciting and intimidating, with myriad shops and galleries greeting you at seemingly every turn. You could easily spend several days wandering among the shops and not see them all, but with perseverance, a good eye, and a bit of luck, you should be able to find that special item or items that will make a perfect gift or be the perfect remembrance of your time in the Land of Enchantment.

Your first port of call should be Santa Fe Plaza, the heart of Santa Fe for more than four centuries. Traders battled the heat and dangers of the Santa Fe Trail every year to bring their goods here, as had earlier traders bringing goods from Mexico along the Camino Real. In and around the Plaza you'll find everything from fine art to folk art to kitschy souvenirs. On the north side of the plaza, under the portal of the Palace of the Governors, American Indians display their jewelry, pottery, hand-tooled leather, and other transportable goods for sale. They'll be happy to talk with you about their wares.

Don't forget the museum shops, often excellent places to find top-quality crafts. Galleries selling a superb range of fine art cluster along Canyon Rd. If you're still not shopped out, head to some of the small shopping malls scattered about the city, such as DeVargas Center (see p. 97).

And don't worry about having to lug your purchases home. Practically every shop and gallery will be happy to ship them for you.

The Top Art Galleries

Allan Houser Gallery ★★ Considered one of the most important American artists of the 20th century, the late Allan Houser, a Chiricahua Apache, was a fine painter and teacher, but is probably best known for his bronze sculptures. You can see and purchase them here. 125 Lincoln Ave., Ste. 112. www.allanhouser.com. ✆ **505/982-4705.**

Bellas Artes ★ Contemporary and imaginative, the paintings, wall hangings, and sculptures in this gallery are fascinating and thought-provoking. 653 Canyon Rd. www.bellasartesgallery.com. ✆ **505/983-2745.**

Charlotte Jackson Fine Art ★★ With the works of more than two dozen artists, this contemporary gallery shows a wide variety of styles, and presents clever themed exhibits such as "Black Magic," "Field of Dreams," and "All that Glitters." 544 S. Guadalupe St. www.charlottejackson.com. ✆ **505/989-8668.**

Chiaroscuro Gallery ★ Contemporary fine art and photography are the specialties here, such as colorful images by Gayle Crites and fascinating (and even more colorful) glass sculptures by Flo Perkins. 702 and 708 Canyon rds. www.chiaroscurogallery.com. ✆ **505/992-0711.**

Gerald Peters Gallery ★★★ What many consider to be Santa Fe's top gallery displays a wide range of fine art. Works here include classic Western, 20th-century American modernism, contemporary, naturalism, sculpture, photography, and works on paper, with the founders of the Taos Society of Artists and Santa Fe Art Colony well represented. 1005 Paseo de Peralta. www.gpgallery.com. ✆ **505/954-5700.**

La Mesa of Santa Fe ★ More than 50 contemporary artists and crafts workers create splendid ceramic plates, bowls, glassware, and accessories, such as Sally Bachman's colorful pillows, wood figures and masks by Hopi artist Gregory Lomayesva, and glass wall sculptures by Melissa Haid. 225 Canyon Rd. www.lamesaofsantafe.com. ✆ **505/984-1688.**

Heavy-duty shopping can be tiring, so if you need a recharge, stop at **Ecco ★★**, 105 E. Marcy St. (www.eccogelato.com; *© **505/986-9778***), for Santa Fe's best espresso (hot or cold) and some authentic Italian gelato. Open 7am to 9pm Monday, Thursday, and Friday; 8am to 10pm Saturday; and 8am to 7pm Sunday.

LewAllen Galleries ★★   Among Santa Fe's top galleries, this spot displays works by modernists from the late 1800s to the mid–20th century, plus contemporary artists, in a magnificent 14,000 square-foot space. You'll see a variety of paintings, sculptures, and works on paper and glass. 1613 Paseo del Peralta. www.lewallencontemporary.com. *© **505/988-3250.***

Manitou Galleries ★   Contemporary representational paintings, many depicting the Southwest, are the theme at this large gallery, which also has prints, sculpture, glass, and extremely fine jewelry. Manitou Galleries also has an outlet at 225 Canyon Rd. (*© **877/986-9833** or 505/986-9833). 123 W. Palace Ave. www.manitougalleries.com. *© **800/283-0440** or 505/986-0440.

Morning Star Gallery ★★   Looking for genuine American Indian artworks? This is the place to come. From Navajo blankets over a hundred years old to works by today's young Pueblo potters and silversmiths, everything that's American Indian is represented here. 513 Canyon Rd. www.morningstargallery.com. *© **505/982-8187.***

Peyton Wright Gallery ★   To see a wide variety of art in one place, stop at this fine gallery, housed in an historic building near the plaza. Although it specializes in 20th-century postwar and modern American art, it also has a fine collection of Spanish Colonial devotional art, Spanish Colonial silver, and works from around the world. 237 E. Palace Ave. www.peytonwright.com. *© **800/879-8898** or 505/989-9888.

Photo-Eye Gallery ★   Contemporary photography is the main thrust of this excellent gallery, but there are also some earlier works. Photography styles vary considerably, with both established and beginning photographers represented; it's practically guaranteed that you'll see photos you love as well as some works that you think belong in the trash can. Photo-Eye also has a bookstore at 376 Garcia St. (*© **505/988-5152**). 541 S. Guadalupe St. www.photoeye.com. *© **505/988-5159**, ext. 202.

Shidoni Foundry and Galleries ★★   It's well worth the drive 5 miles north of Santa Fe to Shidoni Foundry, where the indoor galleries display the works of close to 150 contemporary American artists; outside are 8 acres of sculpture gardens. The foundry produces works of art in bronze; you can take self-guided foundry tours on weekdays (noon to 1pm, $5 per person), or on Saturdays you can watch 2,000-degree molten bronze being poured into ceramic molds ($10 per person). Times for the Saturday Bronze Pour and self-guided tours vary, so call Friday. 1508 Bishop's Lodge Rd., Tesuque. www.shidoni.com. ✆ **505/988-8001.**

Malls & Shopping Centers

DeVargas Center ★★ In 2015, when Sanbusco Market was bought by a charter school, many of its merchants came here, beefing up the appeal of this large adobe-style shopping center. In addition, Blessings Cooperative, with some 40 separate vendors, opened here. All of this adds up to a glorious shopping arena. N. Guadalupe St. and Paseo de Peralta. www.devargascenter.com. ✆ **505/982-2655.**

Santa Fe Arcade ★★ The Arcade has been drawing visitors and locals alike since 2004 to browse its three stories of shops. The atmosphere is sleek, a far cry from the Woolworth's that once lived here. Some 60 spaces offer everything from showy Western wear to hip clothing, Peruvian knick-knacks to fine Indian jewelry. Fun for everyone. 60 E. San Francisco St. on the Plaza. ✆ **505/988-5792.**

Markets

Santa Fe Farmers' Market ★★ A large space with a list of vendors as long as your arm, this farmers' market has everything from fruits, vegetables, and flowers to cheeses, cider, and salsas. If you're an early riser, wander through and enjoy good coffee and excellent breakfast burritos. Open from 8am to 1pm on Saturdays year-round, also on Tuesdays from May through November, plus occasional special market days. In the Santa Fe Railyard, off Paseo de Peralta. www.santafefarmersmarket.com. ✆ **505/983-4098.**

Tesuque Flea Market ★ If you're a flea-market enthusiast, you'll love this place. Over 500 vendors offer just about everything—used cowboy boots, clothing, jewelry, books, rugs, and furniture, to name a few. It lies below and on the north side of the Santa Fe Opera about 8 miles north of the city, and is open from 9am to 4pm Friday to Sunday, March to late December. 15 Flea Market Rd., exit 171 off US 84/285. www.pueblooftesuquefleamarket.com. ✆ **505/670-2599.**

More Shopping A to Z
BOOKS

Collected Works Bookstore & Coffeehouse ★ Stop in for an espresso, or if caffeine isn't your friend, an organic apple cider or chai. While you're sipping, peruse the many shelves containing books on the Southwest, travel, nature, cooking, and even novels. The shop offers readings, book signings, and occasional lectures. 202 Galiseo St. www.cwbookstore.com. ✆ **505/988-4226.**

Garcia Street Books ★ Here you can browse a fine selection of titles on the Southwest and collectibles, plus biographies, cooking, and more, although there isn't much in the way of novels. The staff is very knowledgeable and happy to help. 376 Garcia St. www.garciastreetbooks.com. ✆ **505/986-0151.**

CRAFTS

Davis Mather Folk Art Gallery ★   The brightly colored animals are real eye-catchers—this small shop is filled with them, not to mention the crazy snakes all over the wall. There is Mexican, New Mexican, and Navajo folk art, and a few other things thrown in just for variety. 141 Lincoln Ave. at Marcy St. www.davismatherfolkartgallery.com. ✆ **505/983-1660.**

Nambé Outlet ★   First sand-cast and handcrafted at the Nambé Pueblo, this alloy has since been fashioned into almost every cooking, serving, and decorating piece imaginable. It's quite lovely, but also quite soft, so be sure to ask about the care required to keep it shining. 104 W. San Francisco St. www.nambe.com. ✆ **505/988-3574.** Also at 924 Paseo de Peralta. ✆ **505/988-5528.**

FOOD

Cheesemongers of Santa Fe ★   Well over a hundred domestic and international cheeses can be found here, plus cured meats and antipasti—and then there's the breads. The shop is small but the offerings are huge. 130 E. Marcy St. www.cheesemongersofsantafe.com. ✆ **505/795-7878.**

The Chile Shop ★★   Chile ristras, dried chile powder and pods, chile jelly (it's great with cream cheese and crackers), green chile stew mix—everything chile can be found in this fun little shop. It also stocks cookbooks, pottery, dinnerware, table linens, and other housewares. 109 E. Water St. www.thechileshop.com. ✆ **505/983-6080.**

Oleaceae ★★   The many flavors of olive oil and balsamic vinegar in this shop are astounding. You can taste before purchasing—the combination of honey ginger vinegar and Japanese roasted sesame olive oil is astonishing. Also available are mustards, jams, and sauces, plus skin and beauty products. Old Santa Fe Trail at the La Fonda Hotel. www.oleaceaeoliveoil.com. ✆ **505/795-7780.**

Señor Murphy Candy Maker ★   Everybody knows that chocolate is the most important food group. And Señor Murphy's law is to always use the best and freshest ingredients in small, handmade batches. Add to that the southwestern flavors of chile and piñon nuts, and you have an unbeatable combination. Señor Murphy has another shop at 100 E. San Francisco St. (La Fonda Hotel). www.senormurphy.com. ✆ **505/982-0461.** Also in the DeVargas Center (✆ **505/780-5179**).

More Than Dinosaurs

A timeless adventure tucked into a small space, **Dinosaurs & More,** 137 W. San Francisco St., upstairs in Ste. 5 (www.meteoritefossilgallery.com; ✆ **505/988-3299**), caters to children of all ages, even those simply young at heart. Rockhound Charlie Snell has been hunting and collecting fossils, minerals, and meteorites for 25 years. He displays and sells them here, paying special attention to children's curiosity. At the back of the shop, kids can participate in the archaeology by brushing and scraping away rock and dust from real dinosaur bones.

FOR THE HOME

Artesanos Imports Company ★ Colorful tiles from Mexico, for every imaginable use from house numbers to countertops, are found here. There's a huge selection of Talavera tile and pottery, as well as light fixtures and many other accessories for the home. 1414 Maclovia St., west of Cerrillos Rd. and a bit south of the St. Michael's Dr. intersection. www.artesanos.com. ℰ **505/471-8020.**

Casa Nova ★ Amidst this wild gathering of unusual yet attractive furnishings and accessories, you'll find everything from tableware to jewelry, furniture to weavings—all in geometric patterns or bright colors. 530 S. Guadalupe St. (in the Gross Kelly Warehouse). www.casanovagallery.com. ℰ **505/983-8558.**

Green River Pottery ★★ This studio and gallery features stoneware ceramics by Theo Helmstadter, whose works are wheel-thrown from New Mexico clay, highly fired, and designed for daily use. His designs are simple, usable, and elegant, from teaware to platters and bowls, large-scale vessels and jars. The studio also offers workshops, classes, and individual sessions. 1710 Lena St. www.greenriverpottery.com. ℰ **505/614-6952.**

Jackalope ★★ You have to see this to believe it. Innumerable items from India, Mexico, Thailand, Bali, Africa, China, and Egypt are carried at this international bazaar, with clothing and jewelry, pottery and textiles, garden decor and folk art, furniture and fountains spread all over. It's fascinating and fun. The owner has been traveling and buying stuff to sell here since 1976. 2820 Cerrillos Rd. www.jackalope.com. ℰ **505/471-8539.**

Stone Forest ★★ You'll find marvelously crafted designs for the bath, kitchen, and garden sculpted from stone, bronze, copper, iron, and wood in this out-of-the-way shop behind the railway station. 213 South St. Francis Dr. www.stoneforest.com. ℰ **505/986-8883.**

GIFTS & SOUVENIRS

Cutlery of Santa Fe ★★ These knives are almost too beautiful to use—but use them you should. The variety runs the gamut from practical to decorative, functional to fun in this tiny shop wedged into a corner of La Fonda Hotel. 107 Old Santa Fe Trail. ℰ **505/982-3262.**

Double Take ★★ Since its opening in 1987, the Double Take has become the choice for many travelers, locals, collectors, and bargain hunters. There's a bit of everything, from the ordinary to the extraordinary—Western stuff, fetishes, home furnishings, affordable vintage and designer women's clothing, accessories, books, and more. Come in and browse. 321 S. Guadalupe St. www.santafedoubletake.com. ℰ **505/989-8886.**

El Nicho ★★ This delightful shop boasts an abundance of lovely wood carvings, most at quite reasonable prices. Other handcrafted items are here as well, and the owner/shopkeeper is very personable. A perfect place to find a souvenir of your trip. 227 Don Gaspar Ave. ℰ **505/984-2830.**

JEWELRY

Tresa Vorenberg Goldsmiths ★★   Over 30 artists are represented in this fine jewelry store. The pieces are stunning, with some delightfully imaginative designs. All are handcrafted, and custom commissions are welcome. 656 Canyon Rd. www.tvgoldsmiths.com. ✆ **505/988-7215.**

WEARABLES

Back at the Ranch ★   You want cowboy boots? This is the place for you, with an incredible array of handmade boots, plus chic Western wear. 209 E. Marcy St. www.backattheranch.com. ✆ **505/989-8110.**

O'Farrell Hat Company ★★   O'Farrell's has been making custom felt hats for 30 years. The fit, style and shape, materials, and skill and craftsmanship that go into each hat makes an O'Farrell hat just about the best you can find. 111 E. San Francisco St. www.ofarrellhatco.com. ✆ **505/989-9666.**

Overland Sheepskin Company ★   For leather coats, blazers, hats, purses, or other finely made leather items, plus sheepskin slippers, coats, and more, this is the place to visit. Overland has been making these goods since 1973. 74 E. San Francisco St. www.overland.com. ✆ **505/983-4727.**

5 | THE PERFORMING ARTS IN SANTA FE

The performing arts have recently become so strong, they almost eclipse the visual art scene in Santa Fe. Numerous companies call the City Different home, including the world-renowned Santa Fe Opera, and there are also festivals galore. Many companies perform in a variety of venues, and ticket prices vary tremendously. Specifics are available on websites, or by calling the phone number listed.

Dance Companies

Aspen Santa Fe Ballet ★   This company brings classically trained dancers and choreographers from around the world to produce new and adventuresome pieces in both Santa Fe and Aspen, Colorado. Performances take place at the **Lensic Performing Arts Center** (p. 101). www.aspensantafe ballet.com. ✆ **505/983-5591.**

Major Performing Arts Companies

Desert Chorale ★★   This marvelous vocal group performs a wide range of music from medieval polyphony to contemporary works. Singers from all over the United States audition for a place in the 24-member ensemble. There are summer and winter festivals, with performances at various locations in Santa Fe and throughout the Southwest. www.desertchorale.org. ✆ **800/244-4011** or 505/988-2282.

Sangre de Cristo Chorale ★   This fine ensemble includes in its repertoire music from 11th-century chant to classical, ethnic, and folk, right up to

A HOME FOR THE arts

Since a multimillion-dollar renovation completed in 2001, this Moorish-style 1931 movie palace has come alive again as the **Lensic Performing Arts Center** (211 W. San Francisco St.; www.lensic. org; ✆ **505/988-7050**). Its year-round events calendar offers everything from theater, music, and dance performances to literary happenings, films, and lectures. There's a complete schedule at their website.

contemporary. Concerts are performed both in Santa Fe and Los Alamos. www.sdcchorale.org. ✆ **505/455-3707**.

Santa Fe Opera ★★★ For over 40 years, opera lovers have been leaving the big cities to come to the City Different to enjoy superb opera in a spectacular setting. Although it has a roof these days, the open-air feel remains, with the amphitheater's sides still open, as well as the back of the stage (depending on the opera being performed). When there's a lightning storm—as there often is in this desert setting—it can certainly add to the drama taking place on stage. Many patrons come early to enjoy a "tailgate picnic" in the parking lot before heading in to the performance. Views are breathtaking in all directions, with lights winking on all around as the sun sets. The staging and costumes are always stupendous, and the singers sublime. Five operas are presented each year, in repertory, July and August. Near the end of the season, the apprentice artists take the stage in two performances consisting of a scene from each of the operas. For anyone not already an opera buff, this can be a terrific introduction to this magical music. 7 miles north of Santa Fe off U.S. 84/285 exit 168; follow the signs to the parking lot. www.santafeopera.org. ✆ **800/280-4654** or 505/986-5900.

Santa Fe Pro Musica Chamber Orchestra & Ensemble ★★ Pro Musica brings together outstanding musicians to delight and educate audiences of all ages. With a season running from September to May, it offers a variety of classical music programs in historic Santa Fe venues, including performances by orchestra, string quartet, chamber ensemble, and some on baroque instruments. www.santafepromusica.com. ✆ **505/988-4640**.

Santa Fe Symphony Orchestra and Chorus ★ Founded in 1984, this professional group continues to offer great performances of classical and popular works. The season runs from September to May. www.santafesymphony. org. ✆ **800/480-1319** or 505/983-1414.

Music Festivals & Concert Series

Santa Fe Chamber Music Festival ★★ This festival brings together exceptional artists from around the world. Concerts are offered from mid-July to mid-August in the St. Francis Auditorium and the Lensic Performing Arts Center, with programs featuring new music by a composer in residence, plus free youth concerts, preconcert lectures, and open rehearsals. www.sfcmf.org. ℂ 505/982-1890.

Theater Companies

Santa Fe Playhouse ★ Established in 1922, this is the "oldest continually running theater west of the Mississippi." The annual Fiesta Melodrama lampoons local news and politics, and has been entertaining crowds while embarrassing politicians since the state was just 7 years young. 142 E. De Vargas St. www.santafeplayhouse.org. ℂ **505/988-4262.**

Theater Grottesco ★★ This troupe creates a new kind of performance that is visual, explosive, and full of surprise. Expect to be shocked, confused, confounded, and, above all, struck silly with laughter. Performances take place at whatever venue seems most appropriate. www.theatergrottesco.org. ℂ **505/474-8400.**

SANTA FE NIGHTLIFE

In addition to the clubs and bars listed below, a number of hotels and restaurants have bars and lounges that get lively after the sun goes down (see "Where to Stay in Santa Fe," p. 48). Entertainment schedules vary, and cover charges for entertainment usually range from nothing to $5, with an occasional special performance charging more.

Cava Santa Fe Lounge ★★ Billing itself as the Santa Fe community living room, this bar in the Eldorado Hotel & Spa has an excellent wine list, good food, and live entertainment most Wednesday through Saturday evenings. The type of music varies, but it won't be heavy metal. At the Eldorado Hotel & Spa, 309 W. San Francisco St. www.eldoradohotel.com. ℂ **505/988-4455.**

Cowgirl BBQ ★★ If you're going to bump into someone you know in Santa Fe, chances are it'll be at the Cowgirl. It's that kind of place: raucous, sprawling, and popular with visitors, locals, and even the occasional local-ish celebrity. There's a great front patio (heated and enclosed in winter, open in the summer) and a kid-friendly eating area in the back with a playground. Inside are pool tables and a rambling bar/dining room with daily live music and a menu of barbecue favorites. For drinks, try a green chile margarita with a red chile salt rim, or a "lava lamp," which mixes a beer float with a margarita. See you at the Cowgirl! 319 S. Guadalupe St. www.cowgirlsantafe.com. ℂ **505/982-2565.**

Del Charro Saloon ★ What's better than cozying up with a margarita next to a fireplace on a chilly Santa Fe evening? A margarita made with 100% agave tequila and real juice, that only sets you back $6.50—a rarity in this pricey town—which you can enjoy at this laid-back saloon attached to the Inn of the Governors. The burgers and the green chile chicken chowder are both tasty and satisfying, whether you're by the fire or at one of the copper-topped tables in the semi-enclosed patio dining room. At the Inn of the Governors, 101 W. Alameda St. www.delcharro.com. ℂ **505/954-0320.**

El Farol ★★   This old adobe cantina seems like the kind of place where a cowboy might just ride his horse up to the bar. According to local legend, that sort of thing actually used to happen back when this was the original Canyon Road watering hole. There has been a bar in this location since 1835, making it the oldest in this very old city, and the bar has retained its historic atmosphere, from its low-beamed ceiling to the colorful, rustic wall paintings and well-worn bar stools. The food menu includes high-end tapas and other Spanish and Mexican fare, and there are cocktail specialties every night. Come for the drinks, stay for the live music seven nights a week, including blues, jazz, and who knows what? Every Saturday brings a flamenco dinner show ($25). 808 Canyon Rd. www.elfarolsf.com. ℂ **505/983-9912.**

Santa Fe Brewing Company ★   You may have already seen Santa Fe Brewing's beers at a supermarket or liquor store, but it's always better when you go straight to the source. The brewery's tasting room is off Highway 14 at the south end of Santa Fe, away from the hubbub of downtown. It's an unpretentious spot with outdoor tables and the occasional food truck parked outside. The focus is on beer, of course, with over a dozen varieties available. There are seasonal brews and other unusual varieties like the Kickin' Chicken bourbon barrel-aged barley wine and a really good Black IPA. Saturday afternoon is the best time to come—that's when they offer free tours and tastings of small-batch brews. 35 Fire Pl. www.santafebrewing.com. ℂ **505/424-3333.**

Second Street Brewery ★★   After a hot summer hike or a day on the ski slopes, nothing hits the spot like a pint of ale and a plate of loaded potato skins. Second Street Brewery offers both in a convivial setting, often with live music on weekends. There are eight drafts on tap—the cream stout is a standout—plus a menu of serviceable bar fare like turkey wraps and fish and chips. If you can't choose among the brews, order a sampler. This is the original Second Street location and it's a big, lively space, especially when the music is happening in the evenings; the second location, at 1607 Paseo del Peralta, #10 (ℂ **505/989-3278**), offers similar fare. 1814 Second St. www.secondstreet brewery.com. ℂ **505/982-3030.**

Secreto Lounge ★★★   The bar in the historic Hotel St. Francis (p. 50) is a not-so-secret destination for an expertly made craft cocktail. The staff uses local herbs, fruits, and spirits in many of the concoctions, like the signature Spicy Secreto, a combination of cachaça liquor, elderflower liqueur, cucumber, lime juice, and jalapeño. Of all the drinks, the best may be the Smoked Sage Margarita, especially enjoyable while people-watching on the outdoor patio. Inside, wooden-cross light fixtures provide a faux-rustic vibe. Guests can order food from the hotel restaurant—try the baked goat cheese or the roasted-corn green-chile chicken chowder. The service can be somewhat casual, so don't plan to be anywhere else in a hurry. Inside the Hotel St. Francis, 210 Don Gaspar Ave. www.secretolounge.com. ℂ **505/983-5700.**

Vino del Corazon Wine Room ★   At this tasting room just off the plaza, owners Erica and Richard Hart offer eight of their own New Mexico–made vintages to sample. It's a short but diverse list, ranging from a Chardonnay and Riesling to Red Chili Cabernet Sauvignon and the sweet-spicy Santa Fe Siesta Red. New Mexico isn't Napa, but the overall quality is quite respectable. Each tasting (four for $10) comes with either a chocolate truffle or a tray of cheese and crackers. Sit outside on the patio or inside on crimson couches—either way, this is a comfy spot to enjoy a sip. 235 Don Gaspar Ave., Suite 6. www.vinodelcorazon.com. © **505/216-9469.**

EXCURSIONS FROM SANTA FE

One of the things that makes Santa Fe such a popular destination is the variety of things to see and do, not just in the city but in the surrounding area. So after you've seen what seems like every American Indian pot, piece of Hispanic folk art, and work of fine art in the world, take a break and hit the road. Head to a pueblo or two to see where those pots are actually made and the people who make them, check out the birthplace of the atomic bomb, or poke around historic ruins that show the clashes of cultures in New Mexico's past, as well as some old Spanish villages that have barely changed in a hundred years along the High Road to Taos.

Exploring the Northern Pueblos

Of the eight pueblos in northern New Mexico, six of them—Tesuque, Pojoaque, Nambe, San Ildefonso, San Juan, and Santa Clara—are within about 30 miles of Santa Fe. Picuris (San Lorenzo) is on the High Road to Taos (p. 117), and Taos Pueblo is just outside the town of Taos (see Chapter 7, p. 146).

You can easily get to each of the six pueblos described in this section in day trips from Santa Fe. While you may not have time to visit them all, if you only have one day free, you can get a good feel for the ancient Indian lifestyle by combining visits to San Ildefonso, with its broad plaza, and Ohkay Owingeh (San Juan), the birthplace of Pope (Poh-*pay*), who led the Pueblo Revolt of 1680.

For additional information on each of these pueblos, plus others in the state, go to **www.indianpueblo.org/19pueblos.** At the bottom of the page, click on the name of the pueblo that interests you. All the pueblos are closed to the public periodically; call to check their schedules and current hours.

Pueblo Etiquette

Personal dwellings and/or important historic sites at pueblos must be respected as such. Don't climb on the buildings or peek into doors or windows. Don't enter sacred grounds, such as cemeteries and kivas. If you attend a dance or ceremony, remain silent while it is taking place and refrain from applause when it's over. Many pueblos prohibit photography or sketches; others require you to pay a fee for a permit. If you don't respect the privacy of the people who live there, you'll be asked to leave.

Bandelier National Monument **2**
Los Alamos **3**
Nambe Pueblo **9**
Ohkay Owingeh Pueblo **5**
Pecos National Historic Park **12**
Picuris Pueblo **6**
Pojoaque Pueblo **8**
Puye Cliff Dwellings **4**
San Ildefonso Pueblo **10**
Santa Clara Pueblo **7**
Tesuque Pueblo **11**
Valles Caldera National Preserve **1**

TESUQUE PUEBLO ★

Excavations confirm that a pueblo has existed here since at least the year A.D. 1200; accordingly, this pueblo is now on the National Register of Historic Places. The 800 residents at Tesuque (Te-*soo*-keh) Pueblo (✆ **505/983-2667**), about 9 miles north of Santa Fe on US 84/285, remain faithful to their traditional religion, rituals, and ceremonies.

When you come to the welcome sign at the pueblo, turn right, go a block, and park on the right. You'll see the plaza off to the left. There's not a lot to see; in recent years renovation has brought a new look to some of the homes around it. There's a big open area where dances are held, and the **San Diego Church,** completed in 2004 on the site of an 1888 structure that burned down. It's the fifth church on the pueblo's plaza since 1641. Visitors are asked to remain in this area. You'll find many crafts at a gallery on the plaza's southeast corner; some Tesuque women are especially known for their skilled pottery. Ignacia Duran's black-and-white and red micaceous pottery and Teresa Tapia's miniatures and pots with animal figures are especially noteworthy.

You'll know that you're approaching the pueblo when you see a large store near the highway. If you're driving north and you get to the unusual Camel Rock formation and a large roadside casino (**Camel Rock Casino,** www.camelrockcasino.com; © **505/984-8414**), you've missed the pueblo entrance. Admission to the pueblo is free; photography, sketching, and painting are not permitted.

POJOAQUE PUEBLO ★

Though small and without a definable village, Pojoaque (Po-*hwa*-keh) Pueblo (www.pojoaque.org; © **505/455-2278**) is important as a center for traveler services; in fact, Pojoaque, in its Tewa form, means "water-drinking place." It's about 6 miles farther north of Tesuque Pueblo on US 84/285, at the junction of NM 502. The historical accounts of the Pojoaque people are sketchy, but we do know that in 1890 smallpox took its toll on the Pojoaque population, forcing most of the pueblo residents to abandon their village. Since the 1930s, the population has gradually increased, and in 1990, a war chief and two war captains were appointed. Today, the **Poeh Cultural Center and Museum** (www.poehcenter.org; © **505/455-3334**), on US 84/285, operated by the pueblo, provides a good roadside peek into pueblo arts, offering a museum, cultural center, and artists' studios. It's situated within a complex of adobe buildings, including the three-story Sun Tower. There are frequent artist demonstrations, exhibitions, and, in the warmer months, traditional ceremonial dances. Indigenous pottery, embroidery, silverwork, and beadwork are available for sale at the Pojoaque Pueblo Visitor Center nearby.

Feast Days Through the Year

Each pueblo has its own special feast days throughout the year; visiting a pueblo on its feast day can be a very special experience indeed, because you'll see the pueblo people celebrating in a very genuine way—these dances are the real thing, not some show for tourists. However, be aware that there are often special restrictions, such as no photography, and some areas of the pueblos will be off-limits to outsiders. Here's a calendar of the northern pueblos' feast days: **January 23: San Ildefonso Pueblo**'s San Ildefonso Feast Day features buffalo and deer dances. **June 24: Ohkay Owingeh Pueblo**'s San Juan Feast Day features buffalo and Comanche dances. **August 9 and 10: Picuris Pueblo** celebrates San Lorenzo Feast Days. **August 12: Santa Clara Pueblo** has corn and harvest dances on Santa Clara Feast Day. **Late August or early September: San Ildefonso Pueblo** performs corn dances, which commemorate fertility in all creatures—humans, animals, and plants. **October 4: Nambe Pueblo** celebrates Saint Francis of Assisi Feast Day with buffalo and deer dances. **November 12: Tesuque Pueblo** observes San Diego Feast Day with harvest, buffalo, deer, flag, or Comanche dances. **December 12: Pojoaque Pueblo** celebrates the annual feast day of Our Lady of Guadalupe with a buffalo dance. **December 25: Ohkay Owingeh Pueblo** performs the Matachine dance (p. 27), depicting the subjugation of the Pueblo people by the Spaniards, followed on **December 26** by a turtle dance ceremony. For feast days at **Taos Pueblo,** see p. 148.

Admission to the pueblo is free; photography, sketching, and painting are not permitted. The pueblo also operates a casino, **Cities of Gold Casino** (www.citiesofgoldcasino.com; 𝒞 **800/455-3313**).

NAMBE PUEBLO ★

The name means "mound of earth in the corner," and this 700-year-old Tewa-speaking pueblo, with a solar-powered tribal headquarters, sits at the foot of the Sangre de Cristo range. Drive north on US 84/285 about 3 miles from Pojoaque to NM 503, turn right, and travel until you see a sign for Nambe Falls. Turn right on NP 101 for another 2 miles to reach Nambe Pueblo (www.nambepueblo.org; 𝒞 **505/455-2036,** or 505/455-2304 for the Ranger Station). Only a few original pueblo buildings remain, including a large round kiva, used today in ceremonies. Pueblo artisans make woven belts, beadwork, and brown micaceous pottery. A favorite reason for visiting the pueblo is to see the small herd of bison; a 2-mile trail loops around the bison pasture. The **Nambe Falls Recreation Area,** usually open April through October, includes **Nambe Falls,** a stunning three-tier drop through a cleft in a rock face about 4 miles beyond the pueblo. You can reach the falls via a 15-minute hike on a rocky, clearly marked path that leaves from the picnic area. A recreational site at the reservoir offers fishing, boating (non-motor boats only), hiking, camping, and picnicking.

Admission to the pueblo is free, admission to the recreation area is $10 per vehicle. Photography, filming, and, sketching are prohibited in the pueblo but not the recreation area.

SAN ILDEFONSO PUEBLO ★★

Rebellious San Ildefonso was one of the last pueblos to succumb to the reconquest spearheaded by Don Diego de Vargas in 1692; from the pueblo, you can see the volcanic Black Mesa, which came to be considered a symbol of the San Ildefonso people's strength. Through the years, each time San Ildefonso felt itself threatened by enemy forces, the residents, along with members of other pueblos, would hide out up on the butte, returning to the valley only when starvation set in. From Pojoaque, head west on NM 502 and drive about 6 miles to the turnoff for San Ildefonso Pueblo (www.sanipueblo.org; 𝒞 **505/455-3549**), or *Pox Oge,* as it is called in its own Tewa language, meaning "place where the water cuts down through"—possibly named such because of the way the Rio Grande cuts through the mountains nearby. This pueblo has a broad, dusty plaza, with a kiva on one side, ancient dwellings on the other, and a church at the far end. It's nationally famous for its matte-finish, black-on-black pottery, developed by tribeswoman María Martinez in the 1920s. A few shops surround the plaza, and the **San Ildefonso Pueblo Museum** is tucked away in the governor's office beyond the plaza. The pueblo also has a 4½-acre fishing lake surrounded by *bosque* (Spanish for "forest"), usually open for day use April to October.

Admission costs $10 per car, and there are additional fees for photography, sketching or painting, and fishing.

THE GREAT PUEBLO revolt

By the 17th century, the Spanish subjugation of the Native Americans in the region had left them virtual slaves, forced to provide corn, venison, cloth, and labor. They were also forced to participate in Spanish religious ceremonies and to abandon their own religious practices. Under no circumstances were their ceremonies allowed; those caught participating in them were severely punished. In 1676, several Puebloans were accused of sorcery and jailed in Santa Fe. Later they were led to the plaza, where they were flogged or hanged. This incident became a turning point in Indian-Spanish relations, generating an overwhelming feeling of rage in the community. One of the accused, a San Juan Pueblo Indian named Pope, became a leader in the Great Pueblo Revolt of 1680, which led to freedom from Spanish rule for 12 years.

OHKAY OWINGEH PUEBLO (SAN JUAN) ★

The largest of the Tewa-speaking pueblos and headquarters of the Eight Northern Indian Pueblos Council (www.enipc.org; ℭ **505/747-1593**), Ohkay Owingeh (formerly called San Juan Pueblo) is north on US 84/285; turn off on NM 68 just before Española, then drive north to NM 74. Ohkay Owingeh (ℭ **505/852-4400**) is situated on the east side of the Rio Grande, opposite the 1598 site of San Gabriel, the first Spanish settlement west of the Mississippi River and the first capital of New Spain. In 1598, the Spanish, impressed with the openness and helpfulness of the people of the pueblo, decided to establish a capital there (it was moved to Santa Fe 10 years later), making Ohkay Owingeh the first pueblo to be subjected to Spanish colonization. The Indians were generous, providing food, clothing, shelter, and fuel—they even helped sustain the settlement when its leader Conquistador Juan de Oñate became preoccupied with his search for gold and neglected the needs of his people. The leader of the eventual 1680 pueblo revolt against the Spanish (see box above) was from Ohkay Owingeh, although the revolt was organized in Taos and Ohkay Owingeh played no special role. Today the pueblo is known for its redware pottery, weaving, and painting, and you can also see its bison herd. Though many of the tribal members are Roman Catholics, most of the tribe still practice traditional religious rituals. Thus, two rectangular kivas flank the church in the main plaza, and *caciques* (pueblo priests) share power with civil authorities.

Admission is free; ask about fees for photography, sketching, or painting. The pueblo runs the **Ohkay Casino Resort Hotel** (www.ohkay.com; ℭ **877/829-2865** or 505/747-1668).

SANTA CLARA PUEBLO ★

There's an intriguing mix of the old and the new at the big Santa Clara Pueblo (ℭ **505/753-7326**), south of Española on NM 30. Its village sprawls across the river basin near the beautiful Black Mesa, rows of tract homes surrounding an adobe central area. Although it's in an incredible setting, the pueblo itself is not much to see; however, a trip through it will give a real feel for the contemporary lives of these people, where artisan elders work with children to teach them their native Tewa language, which is on the brink of extinction because so many now speak English. On the main route to the old village, stop by the visitor center, also known as the neighborhood center, to get directions to small shops that sell distinctive black incised Santa Clara pottery, red burnished pottery, baskets, and other crafts. One stunning sight here is the cemetery, on the west side of the church: Look over the 4-foot wall to admire this primitive site, with plain wooden crosses and some graves adorned with plastic flowers.

The past comes more to life at the well-preserved **Puye Cliff Dwellings** ★★ (www.puyecliffs.com; *©* **888/320-5008** or 505/917-6650), located on the Santa Clara Pueblo land (from the Puye Cliffs Welcome Center on NM 30, head about 7 miles west on Indian Route 601). You'll first visit the Harvey House and exhibit hall, which tells some of the history of the site. Separate tours take you to centuries-old cliff dwellings (this includes a fairly steep hike up to a 200-foot cliff face), and up to the top of the mesa. It's believed that these dwellings were occupied from the 900s to about A.D. 1580, and at its height Puye had about 1,500 residents and was the center for a number of villages on the Pajarito Plateau. The guides, descendants of those people, help interpret the site. Tour times vary, so check the website or call before going. The site is closed the week before Easter, June 13, August 12, and for Christmas Day. The full tour costs $35 for adults, $33 for children under 15 and seniors over 54. Lower fees are charged to just do parts of the tour.

Admission to the larger pueblo is free; inquire about permits for photography, sketching, and painting.

Pecos National Historic Park ★★

Preserving well over 1,000 years of human history, Pecos National Historical Park takes us from prehistoric times through Spanish colonization up to the early 20th century. Here, the National Park Service protects and interprets prehistoric American Indian ruins, a mission church built by Spanish conquistadors, a Santa Fe Trail trading post, the site of New Mexico's most decisive Civil War battle, and an early-20th-century cattle ranch.

Here's the history in a nutshell. Nomadic hunter-gatherers had been attracted to this area for thousands of years before pit houses began to appear in the 9th century. Then, in the 12th century, the pueblo of Pecos began taking shape. Although it started as one small village among about two dozen small villages in the Pecos Valley, protection and other issues initiated a move to consolidate the villages. By 1450, Pecos Pueblo had become one of the largest and most important southwestern pueblos, a walled compound standing five stories high that housed some 2,000 people. The people of Pecos grew corn, beans, squash, and cotton, and traded with Apaches and other Plains tribes, as well as other pueblos. By the late 1500s they were also trading with the Spanish, who visited Pecos in 1540 on their first foray into New Mexico in search of the fabled cities of gold.

GEORGIA O'KEEFFE & NEW MEXICO:
a desert romance

In June 1917, during a short visit to the Southwest, the painter Georgia O'Keeffe (born 1887) visited New Mexico for the first time. She was immediately enchanted by the stark scenery; even after her return to the energy of New York City, her mind wandered frequently to New Mexico's arid land and undulating mesas. However, it wasn't until coaxed by the arts patron and "collector of people" Mabel Dodge Luhan 12 years later that O'Keeffe returned to the multihued desert of her daydreams.

O'Keeffe was reportedly ill, both physically and emotionally, when she arrived in Santa Fe in April 1929. New Mexico seemed to soothe her spirit and heal her physical ailments almost magically. Two days after her arrival, Luhan persuaded O'Keeffe to move into her home in Taos. There, she would be free to paint and socialize as she liked.

In Taos, O'Keeffe began painting what would become some of her best-known canvases—close-ups of desert flowers and objects such as cow and horse skulls. "The color up there is different . . . the blue-green of the sage and the mountains, the wildflowers in bloom," O'Keeffe once said of Taos. "It's a different kind of color from any I've ever seen—there's nothing like that in north Texas or even in Colorado." Taos transformed not only her art, but her personality as well. She bought a car and

learned to drive. Sometimes, on warm days, she ran naked through the sage fields. That August, a new, rejuvenated O'Keeffe rejoined her husband, photographer Alfred Stieglitz, in New York.

The artist returned to New Mexico year after year, spending time with Luhan as well as staying at the isolated Ghost Ranch in Abiquiu, some 70 miles northwest of Santa Fe. She drove through the countryside in her snappy Ford, stopping to paint in her favorite spots along the way. Until 1949, O'Keeffe always returned to New York in the fall. Three years after Stieglitz's death O'Keeffe relocated permanently to New Mexico, spending each winter and spring in her house in Abiquiu and each summer and fall at nearby Ghost Ranch. Georgia O'Keeffe died in Santa Fe in 1986.

Much of her painting was inspired by the landscape in the Abiquiu area, and today, **Ghost Ranch Education & Retreat Center** (www.ghostranch.org; ✆ **877/804-4678** or 505/685-1000) offers guided tours to some of O'Keeffe's favorite spots. Tours are by bus, foot, or horse, and prices range from $34 to $85. To get to Abiquiu from Santa Fe, drive north on US 285/84 to Española. When the routes split, stay on US 84 north about 25 miles to Abiquiu. It's another 10 miles to the turn-off for Ghost Ranch; follow the signs to the Ranch office.

Although the Spanish conquistadors did not find gold, they did discover what they believed were souls that needed saving, and by the late 1500s began setting up missions to convert the Pueblo people to Christianity. In all, four mission churches were built at Pecos, including the last one, built in 1717, whose ruins remain today.

The people of Pecos and other New Mexico pueblos, however, did not appreciate being told by the Franciscan missionaries that their religious views and ceremonies, which they had practiced for centuries, were wrong. The demand that they pay tribute to this new religion was bad enough, but that was soon compounded by the introduction of European diseases and a drought and resultant famine. Eventually, the native peoples had had enough. In the Pueblo Revolt of 1680, the scattered pueblos joined forces to drive the Spanish back to Mexico. At Pecos, the priest was killed and the mission church, which had been the most impressive in the region, was destroyed. On the site of the mission's living quarters, the Pecos people defiantly built a kiva, their own traditional ceremonial chamber, which had been forbidden under Spanish rule.

The Spaniards returned 12 years later to retake New Mexico. Although their reconquest required bloodshed at some pueblos, the takeover of Pecos Pueblo was peaceful, and a new Pecos mission, built on the ruins of the old one, was the first mission reestablished after the revolt. The Franciscans now treated the Indians better, but disease, raids by other Indian tribes, and other problems led to the decline of Pecos. In 1838, its few final tribal members abandoned Pecos to join Jemez Pueblo, about 80 miles to the west. Pecos Pueblo and its mission then fell into ruin.

Today, the visitor center's **museum** contains exhibits on the pueblo, missions, and other aspects of the park, including a number of prehistoric Indian and Spanish Colonial artifacts that were discovered during excavations. A 12-minute introductory film is shown, and there is also a bookstore. A **1.25-mile round-trip self-guiding trail** leads from the visitor center through the ruins of Pecos Pueblo and the Spanish mission church. The two reconstructed kivas in the pueblo may also be entered. A trail guide is available at the visitor center.

There's also a **self-guided 2.3-mile Civil War Battlefield Trail,** which takes in two sites from the Battle of Glorieta Pass, which took place in March 1862; it is considered the decisive battle of the Civil War for New Mexico in that it prevented the Confederates from overrunning the Southwest. Sign up at the visitor center, where you will receive the gate code for access to the trail. A trail map costs $2. In late March there is a **Civil War Weekend,** with a living history encampment, black powder demonstrations, and talks by historians.

The park also includes several early ancestral Puebloan ruins, the remains of a 19th-century Spanish settlement, a section of the Santa Fe Trail (complete with wagon wheel ruts), and a stage station along the trail. Some of these sites can be seen only on **guided van tours** ($2 per person). These tours also visit the **Forked Lightning Ranch,** a working cattle ranch in the early 1900s. The van tours are offered year-round but fill quickly in summer, so call ahead for reservations.

Pecos National Historical Park is open daily 8am to 6pm (until 5pm Labor Day to Memorial Day). It's closed New Year's Day, Thanksgiving, and Christmas. Admission costs $7 for people 16 and over and is free for children under 16. For information, see www.nps.gov/peco or call the park visitor center (© **505/757-7241**). The park is about 25 miles east of Santa Fe. Take I-25 south to exit 307, then go 4 miles north on NM 63 to the park entrance.

Los Alamos

Pueblo tribes lived in the rugged Los Alamos area for well over 1,000 years, and an exclusive boys' school operated atop the 7,300-foot plateau from 1918 to 1943. But the fascination most Americans have with this town stems from the **Los Alamos National Laboratory,** established here in secrecy during World War II to develop the world's first atomic bombs.

Code-named Site Y of the Manhattan Project, the hush-hush Los Alamos project was led by director J. Robert Oppenheimer, later succeeded by Norris E. Bradbury. Thousands of scientists, engineers, and technicians worked here to produce the pioneering—and controversial—atomic bombs, which were instrumental in bringing World War II to an end in two mighty explosions at Hiroshima and Nagasaki, Japan. The community remained completely under federal government ownership until the 1960s, when the residents were finally allowed to buy land and buildings. But this town of 12,000 people remains a "government town" today, with its main purpose still being scientific research into nuclear energy for weaponry, energy production, and medicine, as well as space, atmospheric studies, supercomputing, and theoretical physics.

Sitting on the Pajarito Plateau, between the Jemez Mountains and the Rio Grande Valley, Los Alamos is about 35 miles west of Santa Fe and about 65 miles southwest of Taos. From Santa Fe, take US 84/285 north approximately 16 miles to the Pojoaque junction, then turn west on NM 502. As NM 502 enters Los Alamos from Santa Fe, it follows Trinity Drive, where accommodations, restaurants, and other services are located. Central Avenue parallels Trinity Drive and has restaurants, galleries, shops, and museums.

The Los Alamos Chamber of Commerce operates the **Los Alamos Meeting & Visitor Bureau,** 109 Central Park Sq. (www.visitlosalamos.org; ℂ **800/444-0707** or 505/662-8105), across from the Bradbury Science Museum (see below). It's open Monday through Friday 9am to 5pm, Saturday from 9am to 4pm, and Sunday 10am to 3pm. The visitor bureau produces one of the best visitor guides in the state, with real information and very little "aren't we wonderful!" gushing. You can view it online, ask for a hard copy to be mailed to you, or pick one up at most northern New Mexico visitor centers.

Bradbury Science Museum ★★ Both educational and fun, this fine museum, operated by Los Alamos National Laboratory, has exhibits not only on the development of the atomic bomb, but also some fascinating displays about work done at the lab since World War II, including exhibits on some of the lab's research on the human genome, medical uses of nuclear energy, and biomagnetism. Overall, there are more than 40 interactive exhibits, plus two films. Among exhibits not to miss are "Algae to Biofuels: Squeezing Power from Pond Scum" and "Nanotechnology: The Science of the Small." There's also a good exhibit on lasers and displays on supercomputers, including the vintage Cray 1A supercomputer, which was state of the art back in 1977. You can see a 1939 letter from Albert Einstein to President Franklin Roosevelt, suggesting research into uranium as an energy source, and exhibits on Fat Man and Little Boy, the two bombs that were dropped on Japan.

1350 Central Ave., at 15th St. www.lanl.gov/museum. ℂ **505/667-4444.** Free admission. Tues–Sat 10am–5pm, Sun–Mon 1–5pm. Closed New Year's Day, Thanksgiving, and Christmas.

A work in progress, the **Manhattan Project National Historical Park** is being developed to focus on the World War II development of the atomic bomb, and includes U.S. Department of Energy facilities in Los Alamos, where the bombs were designed; Hanford, Washington, site of plutonium production; and Oak Ridge, Tennessee, site of uranium enrichment. As of this writing there are no areas of the park open to the public in Los Alamos, but planning is in the works. For information, see the National Park Service website, **www.nps.gov/mapr**.

Fuller Lodge & Art Center ★ Built in 1928 as the dining hall for the Los Alamos Ranch School, Fuller Lodge was designed by prominent architect John Gaw Meem, who personally chose the 771 massive pine trees used in its construction. Step inside to see the vertical-log and stone building with a 19-foot ceiling, stone fireplace, New Mexico weavings, and period decor. There are exhibit rooms upstairs, and in an adjacent wing the art center displays the works of northern New Mexico artists in changing exhibits. The art center also has a good gallery shop and offers art classes. Arts and crafts fairs are presented here in August and October; there's also a very popular Affordable Art Show each December.

2132 Central Ave. www.fullerlodgeartcenter.com. © **505/662-1635.** Free admission. Mon–Sat 10am–4pm.

Los Alamos Historical Museum ★★ As presented here, the human history of Los Alamos and the Manhattan Project is just as fascinating, or maybe more so, than the scientific milestones that occurred here. There are exhibits on area geology, the prehistoric peoples who lived in the area, the Los Alamos Ranch School, and an excellent exhibit called "The Manhattan Project—Life in the Secret City," presenting the perspective of the people who were part of the project. The museum is housed in a restored log and stone building, constructed in 1918, that was first an infirmary and then a guest cottage for the Los Alamos Ranch School and the Manhattan Project. A free self-guided walking tour of the Los Alamos Historic District is available here (or download it at www.visitlosalamos.org), or you can buy tickets for a

LOS ALAMOS, hollywood style

Los Alamos and the creation of the world's first atomic bombs have gotten a lot of publicity recently with the TV show *Manhattan*, set in Los Alamos and filmed in New Mexico. It's okay, although a bit too much of a soap opera. A much better drama, and a more accurate account of the Manhattan Project, is the 1989 film *Fat Man and Little Boy*, starring Paul Newman. The title comes from the code names given to the two bombs made in Los Alamos, which were eventually dropped on Hiroshima and Nagasaki, Japan.

5

EXPLORING SANTA FE

Excursions from Santa Fe

docent-guided tour, offered Mondays, Fridays, and Saturdays at 11am (adults $10, ages 13–17 $5, free for children 12 and under with a ticketed adult). *Note:* A renovation project to the museum building is underway at press time, with expected completion by fall 2016. In the meantime, the museum is in a temporary location at 475 20th Street. Check the website or call to find out where it is during your visit.

1050 Bathtub Row (next to Fuller Lodge). www.losalamoshistory.org. © **505/662-6272** (Los Alamos Historical Society); © **505/662-4493** (museum's temporary home). Free admission. May–mid-Oct Mon–Fri 9:30am–4:30pm, Sat–Sun 11am–4pm; mid-Oct–Apr Mon–Fri 10am–4pm, Sat–Sun 11am–4pm. Closed New Year's Day, Easter, Thanksgiving, and Christmas.

Pajarito Mountain Ski Area ★   Started in the late 1950s as a ski club for employees of Los Alamos National Laboratory and other locals, this fun little resort is rarely crowded and offers good tree skiing and great bump skiing. There are 300 acres of cleared skiable terrain with 40 named trails, a terrain park, five lifts, and a rope tow. Trails are rated 20% easy, 50% intermediate, and 30% difficult. It has a vertical drop of 1,440 feet from the peak elevation of 10,440 feet.

397 Camp May Rd., 7 miles west of Los Alamos via NM 502. www.skipajarito.com. © **505/662-5725.** Full-day lift tickets adults $29–$49, ages 13–20 and seniors 60–69 $13–$30, children 7–12 $29–$34, free for children 6 and under and seniors 70 and older. Check website for seasonal hours.

Bandelier National Monument ★★★

Less than 15 miles south of Los Alamos via NM 4, Bandelier National Monument is in many ways the antithesis of that controversial 20th-century site: It offers an up-close look at prehistoric American Indian ruins, several hikes—including one to a picturesque waterfall—and opportunities to see New Mexican wildlife.

The main reason to come here is to see the fascinating 13th-century ancestral Puebloan ruins, including a large pueblo, cliff dwellings, and a variety of rock art. The 1.2-mile **Main Loop Trail** begins just outside the visitor center/museum and leads through the ruins of **Tyuonyi Pueblo**—an almost perfectly round pueblo, built in the 1300s and occupied into the early 1500s, which once had about 400 rooms. By the time Spanish explorers arrived later in the 16th century, it had already been abandoned. Anthropologists believe that the pueblo was a mix of one, two, and three stories, built around a large central plaza in which there were three small kivas, underground ceremonial chambers. There were probably no windows on the compound's exterior walls, and only one ground-level exterior entrance.

From Tyuonyi Pueblo, the trail continues to a series of **cliff dwellings,** built into a south-facing canyon wall that caught the warming winter sun. From here you have a choice of a level, easy walk with views up at the cliff dwellings, or a paved but somewhat steep and narrow trail along the cliff side, with ladders providing access to some of the dwellings. Canyon walls here are composed of tuff, a soft, pinkish volcanic rock that weathers easily, producing holes that the prehistoric residents enlarged for storage and living quarters. These caves were often used as back rooms of more formal houses, constructed on the cliff face from talus, the broken chunks of rock deposited at the cliff base. One talus home has been reconstructed.

Continuing along the trail, you'll come to **Long House,** believed to have been a condominium-style community. Extending about 800 feet along the side of the cliff are rows of holes dug into the rock to support roof beams, called vigas, which show clearly the outline of the multistoried cliff dwelling. Also along the cliff side are a number of petroglyphs and a large pictograph, likely created by people standing on roofs. (Petroglyphs are designs chipped or pecked into a rock surface, while pictographs are images painted onto a rock surface.) Above the pictograph is a tall, narrow cave which is the summer home to a colony of bats.

From the Long House cliff dwellings, the path turns to return to the visitor center via a shady **nature trail,** with signs describing the area's plant and animal life. A side trail leads to another cliff dwelling called **Ceremonial Cave,** a natural cave that was enlarged by the prehistoric residents, who constructed clusters of rooms and a small kiva. Located about 150 feet above the canyon floor, it is accessed by a level dirt trail plus a steep 140-foot climb up a series of ladders and steps. This side trip adds about 1 mile round-trip to the Main Loop Trail.

Several other sections of the monument are well worth visiting. Beginning near the visitor center, the easy-to-moderate **Falls Trail hike** offers wonderful scenery and the possibility of seeing wildlife as it follows the Frijole Canyon—named for the beans ancestral Puebloans grew here—to two picturesque waterfalls, passing through a lush forest of juniper, ponderosa pine, and cottonwoods; in the falls area, yucca, cactus, and sagebrush predominate. The trail crosses Frijoles Creek on wooden bridges several times. It's an easy 1.5 miles to the dramatic Upper Falls, which plunges 70 feet; at the falls viewing area, you'll turn around and head back. About 12 miles north of the main entrance, the **Tsankawi Trail** is a 1.5-mile loop that is generally easy and fairly level, but it does include some narrow passages between rocks and involves climbing a 12-foot ladder. Passing among juniper, piñon, brush, and yucca, the trail offers views of petroglyphs including images of birds, humans, and four-pointed stars, as well as the mounds of dirt and rock that mark the unexcavated ruins of a pueblo, probably built in the 1400s, which contained about 350 rooms.

In addition to the park's main trails there are about 70 miles of backcountry trails, most of which are in the **Bandelier Wilderness,** a designated wilderness area that comprises over 70% of the monument's 32,737 acres. The terrain is rugged, with steep canyons, but trails take hikers to relatively secluded sections of the monument where there are additional archeological sites and excellent chances of seeing wildlife. Seen year-round are Steller's jays, western scrub jays, northern flickers, common ravens, canyon wrens, pygmy nuthatches, and both spotted and canyon towhees. In the warmer months, look for western bluebirds, violet-green swallows, white-throated swifts, broad-tailed hummingbirds, and turkey vultures. In wooded areas you're likely to see various squirrels, including Abert's, rock, golden-mantled ground, and red; plus their cousins, the least and Colorado chipmunks. Also watch for coyotes, raccoons, porcupines, mule deer, and elk. Numerous lizards inhabit the drier areas, plus a few snakes, including the poisonous western diamondback rattler. Detailed maps, additional information, and the required permits for overnight trips can be obtained at the visitor center.

For delightful forest **camping,** head to Juniper Campground, in a forest of junipers, with more than 90 nicely spaced campsites, each with a picnic table and fireplace. There are no RV hookups or showers, but there are restrooms with flush toilets and an RV dump station. Reservations are not accepted, but the campground seldom fills. Cost is $20 per night.

From late May through late October, daily between 9am and 3pm, park visitors are required to park at the **White Rock Visitor Center** (www.nps.gov/band, ✆ **505/672-3861, ext 517**), along NM 4 on the way into the park, and ride the **free shuttle,** which delivers you to the Main Loop Trail, main visitor center, and the trail head for Falls Trail. The shuttle runs about every 30 minutes on weekdays and every 20 minutes on weekends. Before 9am and after 3pm, you can drive into the park if you have a disability tag on your vehicle, if you're going to Juniper Campground, if you're on a bicycle, if you have a pet in your vehicle, or if you are an overnight backpacker. Park admission is $20 per car or truck, $15 motorcycles, $10 individuals and bicycles. No pets are allowed on trails, and the park is closed New Year's Day and Christmas.

Valles Caldera National Preserve ★★

Talk about a big boom: This delightful, peaceful area of forests, meadows, peaks, and valleys, with elk by the thousands and historic ranch buildings, was created some 1.25 million years ago by a tremendous volcanic eruption from what scientists tell us is one of only three super volcanoes in the United States. The eruption created a huge crater, which is the heart of this nearly 89,000-acre preserve, purchased by the federal government in 2000 and transferred to the National Park Service in late 2015. It's about 14 miles west of Los Alamos, on NM 4.

The name, Valles Caldera, refers to the numerous valleys (*valles* in Spanish) that occupy the caldera—a large crater formed by the volcanic eruption. The caldera is over a half-mile deep and from 12 to 15 miles wide. Scientists say that eruptions from this volcano released some 50 cubic miles of ash and rock, more than 16 times the material that spewed from Mount St. Helens when it erupted in 1980.

After becoming a private ranch in 1860, the area had remained off-limits to the public except for some guided elk hunts. Ranch owners also did timber harvesting; there are still miles of old logging roads providing relatively easy access to much of the ranch's backcountry now that it is open to the public. Today, the Valles Caldera is known primarily for its magnificent herds of elk—estimated at more than 5,000 animals—but it is actually home to a wide range of wildlife, including mule deer, mountain lions, black bear, golden-mantled squirrels, chipmunks, and coyotes. Birds here include mourning doves, black-chinned hummingbirds, violet-green swallows, mountain blue-birds, and peregrine falcons. There are 54 miles of hiking and biking trails (also open to cross-country skiers in winter), plus some 30 miles of trout streams. The visitor center (www.nps.gov/vall; © **505/670-1612;** closed Christmas and Thanksgiving) is along the main road, about 2 miles in from the main entrance. Admission to the park is $20 per vehicle.

The High Road to Taos ★★

The quick way to Taos from Santa Fe is about 70 miles on a route that partly follows the Rio Grande. It's a pretty enough drive, especially scenic in summer when the river is dotted with colorful rafts. But an alternate route, only about a dozen miles longer, offers a much deeper sense of the region's history, as it winds through historic Spanish colonial villages known for beautiful weaving, where you'll also see some of the most picturesque churches in the Southwest.

Both routes go to Española via US 285, but where the shorter route continues north on NM 68, the High Road (www.highroadnewmexico.com), takes off east from Española on NM 76, wandering through the mountains. Your first stop will be in the tiny village of **Chimayó,** settled in 1598. Be sure to stop at **Ortega's Weaving Shop ★★** (www.ortegasdechimayo.com; © **877/351-4215** or 505/351-4215), where the ninth generation of weavers still work the looms. They produce a wide range of woven items, from large rugs and blankets to vests and coats, plus small items including placemats, coasters, and purses. Considering the work and skill involved, prices here are quite reasonable. There are several other interesting shops here, including **Chimayó Trading and Mercantile ★,** along NM 76 (www.chimayoarts.com; © **800/248-7859** or 505/351-4566), a delightfully cluttered store with local arts and crafts, Pueblo pottery, and Navajo and Hopi crafts. Chimayó is also your best bet for food between Santa Fe and Taos. **Rancho de Chimayó Restaurante ★★★** (300 Juan Medina Rd./County Rd. 98, www.ranchodechimayo.com; © **505/351-4444**) serves authentic northern New Mexico food for lunch and dinner daily and breakfast Saturday and Sunday. Some items can be hot (that's spicy hot), so ask your server for suggestions if you have a tender tummy. The restaurant is open daily May to October, closed Mondays the rest of the year. It also has two shops, one with beautiful but very pricey high-end jewelry and pottery, the other with more affordable items, including a wonderful Rancho de Chimayó cookbook.

Nearby, off NM 76 on County Rd. 98, the inspiring **El Santuario de Chimayó ★★** (15 Santuario Dr., www.elsantuariodechimayo.us; © **505/351-9961**), built in the early 1800s, is visited annually by thousands of people seeking relief from medical problems by means of what many consider the "miraculous dirt" found in a corner of the chapel. An active Roman Catholic church, it is open to the public, with free admission, from 9am to 6pm May through September and 9am to 5pm the rest of the year. Check the website for the Mass and confession schedule. If you click on the website's "Holy Pilgrimage" section, you will see a map and descriptions of the other historic churches in the area.

Continuing east and north on NM 76, you soon come to the village of **Truchas,** one of the most isolated of the Spanish colonial towns, which was the scene for much of Robert Redford's 1988 movie *The Milagro Beanfield War*, based on the novel by Taos author John Nichols, who also wrote the screenplay. There are spectacular mountain views from here, and some good art galleries. A short detour, just south of Truchas, leads to **Cordova,** a tiny village known for its woodcarvers.

Back on NM 76, the next village to stop in is **Las Trampas,** home to the **Church of San Jose de Gracia,** one of the most beautiful churches built during the Spanish Colonial period. For background information, see the website of El Santuario de Chimayó, above.

The road continues through the mountains, passing through the village of **Chamisal** before arriving in **Peñasco.** On NM 76 near its intersection with NM 75, you can stop to visit **Picuris Pueblo** (www.picurispueblo.org; ✆ **575/587-2519**), set in what is called "The Hidden Valley." A few of the original mud-and-stone houses still stand, as does a lovely church, the Mission of San Lorenzo, which has been in use for over 200 years. There is a striking above-ground ceremonial kiva called "the Roundhouse," believed to have been built at least 700 years ago, and some excavated kivas and storerooms are on a hill above the pueblo. Visitors often see the small herd of bison that roam freely on tribal lands. The Picuris people make pottery from micaceous clay that is similar to the pottery at Taos Pueblo. Self-guided tours through the old village ruins cost $5, with an added $15 fee if you want to use a camera. The pueblo is open to visitors Monday through Friday from 8am to 5pm.

Continue on toward Taos via NM 518. This particularly scenic route takes you into the Carson National Forest to the **U.S. Hill Scenic Overlook** and then to **Ranchos de Taos,** where you can turn right and follow the main drag into Taos, or turn left and head back to Santa Fe following the Rio Grande via NM 68.

HIGH ON art

If you really like art and want to meet artists, check out one of the **Art Studio Tours** held in the fall in the region. Artists spend months preparing their best work, and then open their doors to visitors. Wares range from pottery and paintings to furniture and woodcarvings to *ristras* and dried-flower arrangements. The most notable tour is the **High Road Studio Art Tour** (www.highroadnewmexico.com) in mid- to late September. If you're not in the region during that time, watch newspapers (such as the *Santa Fe New Mexican*'s Friday edition, "Pasatiempo") for notices of other art-studio tours.

TAOS ESSENTIALS

Ringed on the north and east by the Sangre de Cristo range of the Rocky Mountains, Taos spreads west toward the Rio Grande Gorge, a canyon so narrow it's like a knife-cut in the sagebrush-covered mesa. If you're driving up from Santa Fe, you'll find the most dramatic view of the gorge in late afternoon. As you top that final hill, pull into the parking area on your right: If the lighting's just right, the panorama is unforgettable.

Located about 70 miles north of Santa Fe, this town of almost 6,000 residents combines 1960s hippiedom (thanks to communes set up in the hills back then) with the ancient culture of Taos Pueblo, where some people still live without electricity and running water, as their ancestors did at least 700 years ago. There are even some people here who completely eschew materialism, living "off the grid" in half-underground houses called earthships. But there are plenty of more mainstream attractions as well—Taos boasts some excellent restaurants, a lively arts scene, world-class music, and incredible opportunities for outdoor action, including world-class skiing.

For a town of its size, Taos has an incredibly colorful history. Throughout the Taos Valley, ruins and artifacts attest to an American Indian presence dating back 5,000 years. The Spanish first visited this area in 1540 and colonized it in 1598, although as late as the 1680s and 1690s, three rebellions at Taos Pueblo challenged Spanish rule. During the 18th and 19th centuries, Taos was such an important trade center that New Mexico's annual caravan to Chihuahua, Mexico, couldn't leave until after the annual midsummer **Taos Fair,** which French trappers had been attending since 1739. Even though the Plains tribes often attacked the pueblos at other times, they would call a temporary truce each year so they could attend the market festival. By the early 1800s, Taos had become a meeting place for American mountain men, the most famous of whom, Kit Carson, made his home in Taos from 1826 to 1868.

Taos remained loyal to Mexico during the U.S.–Mexican War of 1846 and rebelled against its new U.S. landlord in 1847, even killing newly appointed governor Charles Bent in his Taos home. The town was eventually incorporated into the Territory of New Mexico in 1850, but only a few years later, during the Civil War, Taos fell into Confederate hands for 6 weeks; afterward, Carson and two other men raised the Union flag over Taos Plaza and guarded it day and night. Since that time, Taos has had the honor of flying the flag 24 hours a day.

In 1898, two East Coast artists—Ernest Blumenschein and Bert Phillips—discovered the community by accident while looking for a place to get a broken wagon wheel repaired. They were enthralled with the dramatic, varied effects of sunlight on the land, the picturesque adobe homes, the dramatic church in Ranchos de Taos, and the prominent shape of Taos Pueblo, all of which they captured on canvas. By the early 1900s more artists made their way to Taos, and the **Taos Society of Artists** was founded. Since then the town has gained a worldwide reputation as an artistic and cultural center. It is estimated that more than 15% of the population in Taos today are painters, sculptors, writers, or musicians, or in some other way earn their income from artistic pursuits.

The town of Taos is merely the focal point of rugged 2,200-square-mile Taos County. Two features dominate this sparsely populated region: the high desert mesa, split in two by the 650-foot-deep chasm of the **Rio Grande,** and the **Sangre de Cristo** range, which tops out at 13,161-foot Wheeler Peak, New Mexico's highest mountain. From the forested uplands to the sage-carpeted mesa, the county is home to a large variety of wildlife. The human element includes American Indians who still live in ancient pueblos, and Hispanic farmers who continue to irrigate their farmlands using centuries-old methods.

There's a laid-back attitude here, even more pronounced than the general *mañana* attitude for which New Mexico is known. Many Taoseños live to play—and that means outdoors. Some work at the ski area all winter (skiing whenever they can) and work for rafting outfitters in the summer (to get on the river as much as they can). Others are into rock climbing, mountain biking, and backpacking. Yet Taos doesn't feel like an outdoor sports resort—its strains of Hispanic and American Indian heritage give it a richness and depth that most resort towns lack.

Taos' biggest task these days is trying to balance the things that make it so attractive—clear air, laid-back attitudes, outdoor recreation—with a constant stream of newcomers and the development that always accompanies growth.

ORIENTATION

Arriving

BY PLANE Most people opt to fly into **Albuquerque International Sunport** (see p. 232), rent a car, and drive up to Taos from there. The drive takes approximately 2½ hours. If you'd rather be picked up at Albuquerque International Sunport, call **Faust's Transportation, Inc.** (© **575/758-3410**), which offers trips between the Sunport and Taos Mondays through Saturdays (the Taos-Albuquerque run leaves at 7:30am, the Albuquerque-Taos run at 1:30pm). The **Taos Regional Airport** (www.taosairport.org; © **575/758-4995**) is about 8 miles northwest of town on US 64, but as of this writing, there were no regular flights connecting to Albuquerque or anywhere else.

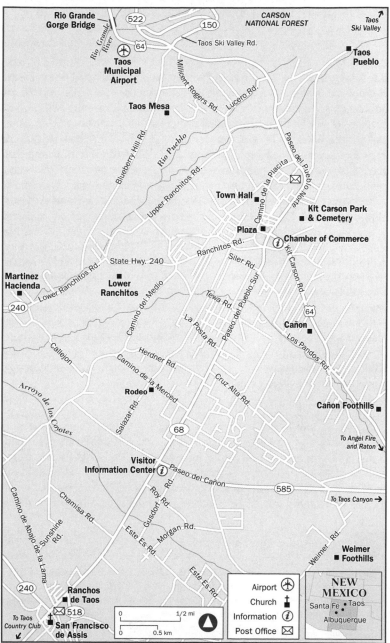

Rio Grande
Gorge Bridge

522

150

CARSON
NATIONAL FOREST

Taos
Ski Valley

Rio Grande River

64

Taos Ski Valley Rd.

Taos
Pueblo

Taos
Municipal
Airport

Millicent Rogers Rd.

Lucero Rd.

Taos Mesa

Blueberry Hill Rd.

Rio Pueblo

Upper Ranchitos Rd.

Paseo del Pueblo Norte

Camino de la Placita

Town Hall

Kit Carson Park
& Cemetery

Plaza

Chamber of Commerce

Ranchitos Rd.

Siler Rd.

Kit Carson Rd.

Martinez
Hacienda

240

State Hwy. 240

Lower Ranchitos Rd.

Lower
Ranchitos

Camino del Medio

Tewa Rd.

Paseo del Pueblo Sur

La Posta Rd.

Cañon

64

Los Pandos Rd.

Callejon

Herdner Rd.

Camino de la Merced

Cruz Alta Rd.

Arroyo de los Cootes

Rodeo

Salazar Rd.

Cañon Foothills

68

To Angel Fire
and Raton

Visitor
Information Center

Paseo del Cañon

585

To Taos Canyon →

Camino de Abajo de la Lama

Chamisa Rd.

Sunshine Rd.

Roy Rd.

Gusdorf Rd.

Este Es Rd.

Morgan Rd.

Weimer Rd.

Weimer
Foothills

Este Es Rd.

Airport

Church

Information

Post Office

NEW
MEXICO

Santa Fe
Taos

Albuquerque

240

Ranchos
de Taos

518

To Taos
Country Club

San Francisco
de Assis

0   1/2 mi

0   0.5 km

BY BUS/TRAIN   Another option is to take the **New Mexico Rail Runner** train from Albuquerque to Santa Fe and connect at the Santa Fe Depot with the North Central Regional Transit District (NCRTD) shuttle bus service to Taos, where you connect with the Taos Chile Line (see p. 123). Shuttle service is free Monday through Friday and $5 one-way on weekends. Call ℂ **866/206-0754** or check www.ridethebluebus.com for schedules and routes.

BY CAR   Most visitors arrive in Taos by car, via either NM 68 or US 64. Northbound travelers on I-25 should exit at Santa Fe, follow US 285 to Española, and then continue on the divided highway when it becomes NM 68. Taos is about 79 miles from the I-25 junction. Southbound travelers on I-25 should exit about 6 miles south of Raton and follow US 64 West about 95 miles to Taos. Coming from the Four Corners area, take US 64 East from Farmington, about 214 miles. Snow often closes this route in winter between Tres Piedras and Chama, but you can get around the closure by detouring up to Colorado. (Check road and driving conditions by calling the state's **Road Advisory Hotline** at ℂ **800/432-4269**, or check out www.nmroads.com.)

Visitor Information

The official **Taos Visitor Center** is located at 1139 Paseo del Pueblo Sur (www.taos.org; ℂ **800/348-0696** or 575/758-3873) at its intersection with Paseo del Canon (NM 585), an easy stop on your drive in from Santa Fe. You can get a free Taos map here, as well as information and maps about the Carson National Forest. The center is open daily 9am to 5pm; closed New Year's Day, Easter Sunday, Thanksgiving, and Christmas. The **Taos County Chamber of Commerce,** at 108 Kit Carson Rd. (www.taoschamber.com; ℂ 575/751-8800), is open Monday to Friday 9am to 5pm in summer and 1 to 5pm in winter. It's closed on major holidays.

City Layout

The center of town—and Taos' first traffic light—is **Taos Plaza,** just west of the intersection of US 64 (Kit Carson Road) and NM 68, **Paseo del Pueblo Sur.** US 64 proceeds north from the intersection as **Paseo del Pueblo Norte**, and continues out to the Rio Grande Gorge Bridge and beyond. **Camino de la Placita (Placitas Road)** circles the west side of downtown, passing within a block of the other side of the plaza. Many of the streets that connect these

---

Warning for Drivers

En route to many recreation sites, reliable paved roads often give way to rough forest roads, where gas stations and cafes are virtually non-existent. Four-wheel-drive vehicles are recommended on much of the unpaved terrain of the region, and are imperative in snow. If you're doing any off-road adventuring, it's wise to go with a full gas tank, extra food and water, and warm clothing—just in case. At the higher-than-10,000-foot elevations of northern New Mexico, sudden summer thunderstorms are frequent, and even freak summer snowstorms can occur.

thoroughfares are narrow and winding lanes lined with traditional adobe buildings, many of them over 100 years old.

Around the plaza are shops and galleries, plus the historic La Fonda Hotel (p. 126), facing the central green that occasionally offers live entertainment on summer evenings. There are more shops, galleries, and museums within a few blocks of the plaza. The area is best traversed on foot.

Two other areas of interest are the **Ranchos de Taos** area, a few miles south of the plaza, and **Arroyo Seco**, about 6 miles north.

GETTING AROUND

By Car

Taos is best explored by private vehicle. Although there are a lot of attractions and restaurants within walking distance of Taos Plaza, there are some really good spots away from the plaza that we hope you won't miss. Aside from a few too many potholes, roads are fairly decent, and most are paved to the areas you'll want to visit. Finding a place to park in downtown Taos is usually not too difficult, although it can be a problem during the summer rush, when an unceasing stream of tourists' cars rolls north and south through town. Street parking is metered, as are several of the lots closest to the plaza; there's a free lot a few blocks east on Kit Carson Road (US 64), and another off Placitas Road just west of Taos Plaza, where there's also room for RVs.

By Bus & Shuttle

If you're in Taos without a car, you're in luck because there's free local bus service, provided by **Taos Chile Line** (www.ridethebluebus.com; ℭ **575/751-4459**). Buses run from 7:30am to 5:30pm daily, every 35 to 45 minutes. Two simultaneous routes run southbound from Taos Pueblo and northbound from the Ranchos de Taos Post Office. Each route makes stops at the casino and various hotels in town, as well as at Taos RV Park.

By Bicycle

Bicycle rentals are available from **Gearing Up Bicycle Shop,** 129 Paseo del Pueblo Sur (www.gearingupbikes.com; ℭ **575/751-0365**); rentals run $35 for a full day and $25 for a half-day for a mountain bike with front suspension. The store's open Monday through Saturday from 10am to 6pm in summer; call for winter hours.

[FastFACTS] TAOS

Airport See "Orientation," above.

Car Rentals Car rental agencies in Taos are **Hertz,** 5 Airport Way (ℭ **575/751-3119**), and **Enterprise,** 1354 Paseo del Pueblo Sur (ℭ **575/751-7490**).

Cellphones Cellphone coverage is good within the town of Taos but spotty in rural areas. A seldom-enforced law prohibits the use of hand-held cellphones by drivers.

Doctors For a medical emergency, dial ℭ **911.** Walk-in medical services are available at **Taos Urgent Care,** 330 Paseo del Pueblo Sur, Unit C (© **575/758-1414**). Full-service adult medicine is available at **Taos Medical Group,** 1399 Weimer Road, Ste. 200 (© **575/758-2224**). For complete family care, call **Family Practice Associates of Taos,** 630 Paseo del Pueblo Sur, Ste. 150 (© **575/758-3005**).

Emergencies Dial **911** in case of emergency.

Hotlines The **Crisis Hotline** (© **575/758-9888**) is available for emergency counseling.

Internet Access You can surf the web and check your e-mail using the Wi-Fi at **Purple Sage Cafe,** 1381 Paseo del Pueblo Sur (www. thepurplesagecafe.com; © **575/751-0562**); and **Wired? Cafe,** behind Albertsons at 705 Felicidad Lane (www.wiredcoffeeshop. com; © **575/751-9473**). The **Taos Public Library,** 402 Camino de la Placita (www.taoslibrary.org; © **575/758-3063** or 575/737-2590) and most lodgings in and around town offer free Internet access.

Newspapers *The Taos News* (www.taosnews.com; © **575/758-2241**) is published every Thursday.

Police In case of emergency, dial © **911.** All other inquiries should be directed to the **Town of Taos Police Department,** 400 Placitas Road (© **575/758-2216**), or for inquiries outside town limits, to the **Taos County Sheriff** (© **575/737-6480**).

Post Offices The main **Taos post office** is at 318 Paseo del Pueblo Norte (© **575/758-2081**), a few blocks north of the plaza traffic light; it's open Monday to Friday 8:30am to 5pm. An annex to the Taos post office is located inside Albertsons on Paseo del Pueblo Sur, which is also open Saturday mornings. There are smaller offices in **Ranchos de Taos** (© **575/758-3944;** Mon–Fri 8:30am–5pm, Sat 9am–noon) and **El Prado** (© **575/758-4810;** Mon–Fri 8am–4:30pm, Sat 8:30–11:30am).

WHERE TO STAY IN TAOS

A small town with a big tourist market, Taos has thousands of rooms in hotels, motels, condominiums, and bed-and-breakfasts. There are two high seasons in Taos: winter (the Thanksgiving-to-Easter ski season, except for January, which is notoriously slow except for Martin Luther King weekend) and June through October. In the slower seasons—January through early February and April through early May—when competition for travelers is steep, rates may be lower, and you may even be able to bargain your room rate down. Book well ahead for ski holiday periods, especially Christmas and spring break.

Hotels/Motels

One of the advantages of a relatively small town is that it has fewer streets, and that makes everything easier to find. In the town of Taos, most lodging is along the main drag—Paseo del Pueblo Sur and Paseo del Pueblo Norte, with a few on Kit Carson Road.

EXPENSIVE

El Monte Sagrado ★★★ One of the premier properties in the state, the "Sacred Mountain" resort has an eco-friendly focus, with a lush landscape full of flowing water (recycled, of course) that's centered on a tranquil "Sacred Circle" of grass and trees. Accommodations range from standard Taos Mountain rooms to small, self-contained casitas to suites, including eight bi-level two-bedroom suites. The varied interior design draws inspiration from everywhere from the Southwest and South America to Morocco and Tibet. Suites

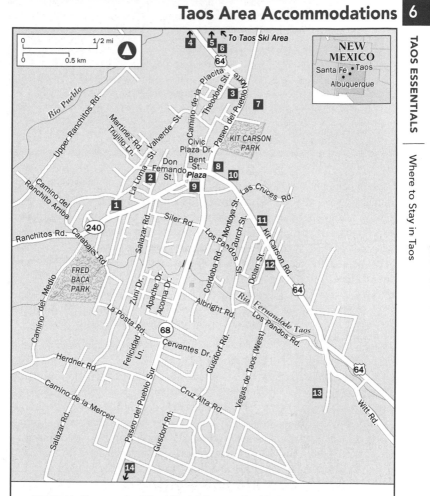

Abominable Snowmansion Skiers' Hostel **5**
Adobe & Pines Inn **14**
Adobe and Stars Bed and Breakfast Inn **5**
Adobe Sun God Lodge **14**
Carson National Forest **4**
Casa Benavides Bed & Breakfast Inn **10**
El Monte Sagrado **11**
El Pueblo Lodge **3**
Hacienda del Sol **6**
Hampton Inn Taos **14**
The Historic Taos Inn **8**

Hotel La Fonda de Taos **9**
Inn on La Loma Plaza **1**
Inn on the Rio **12**
Kachina Lodge **7**
La Posada de Taos **2**
Old Taos Guesthouse **13**
Quality Inn **14**
Sagebrush Inn & Suites **14**
Taos Monte Bello RV Park **5**
Taos Valley RV Park
    and Campground **14**

CHAIN MOTELS in taos

boast either a patio or balcony, private of course, and virtually every room has stunning views of Taos Mountain and the surrounding landscape. The over-the-top luxury suites are the real draws here, all with wet bar, kiva fireplace, huge bathrooms, and decor that would make Indiana Jones jealous. A plus is that El Monte Sagrado is within fairly easy walking distance of Taos Plaza. For food and drink, stop in the **De la Tierra** restaurant (p. 135) and the **Anaconda Bar** (p. 164).

317 Kit Carson Rd. www.elmontesagrado.com. ℂ **888/213-4419** or 575/758-3502. 84 units. Rooms and casitas $116–$458, suites from $200. Valet parking $12. **Amenities:** Restaurant; bar; concierge; health club; whirlpool tub; indoor pool; free Wi-Fi.

The Historic Taos Inn ★★ The name is no hyperbole: Some of the buildings that make up the Historic Taos Inn were bought by the town's first physician in the 1890s, and the guest list has included Greta Garbo and British author D. H. Lawrence. The buildings surround a small plaza, which was enclosed in the mid-1930s to become the inn's delightful lobby. In the middle of the lobby is a fountain encircled by vertical vigas rising two-and-a-half-stories to a stained glass cupola. Across the lobby from the carved reception desk is the **Adobe Bar** (p. 135), still a local gathering place with live music nightly, and to the left of the front door is the entry to **Doc Martin's** (p. 135) restaurant, popular for business lunches, special celebrations, and just a good meal. The hotel encompasses both the older buildings, where the rooms can be pretty small and even low-ceilinged, and the newer Helen's House, with fancier digs done up in contemporary southwestern decor like Saltillo tile floors and kiva fireplaces. The whole package radiates warm Old Taos character, overlaid with a modern comfort level.

125 Paseo del Pueblo Norte. www.taosinn.com. ℂ **888/518-8267** or 575/758-2233. 44 units. $75–$275. **Amenities:** Restaurant; lounge; access to nearby health club; whirlpool tub; room service; free Wi-Fi.

Hotel La Fonda de Taos ★ The only hotel right on Taos Plaza has roots that date back to 1820, when a hotel first appeared on this spot. Famous guests over the years have included Judy Garland, Tennessee Williams, and D. H. Lawrence (his presence lingers on in the "D. H. Lawrence Forbidden Art Museum," where you can see nine of his oil paintings risqué enough to be confiscated by police in 1929, if pretty tame by modern standards). The rooms, while not huge, have undeniable historic elegance, with hand-tiled bathrooms and fireplaces in some. (Rooms 201 and 301 overlook the plaza itself.) If you want more space, opt for a larger suite, or spring for the luxury penthouse on the top floor (1 to 4 bedrooms that go for $500 to $1,400). The property is right in the middle of the action, Taos-wise at least, so expect some noise from the plaza, although a policy of no kids under 8 helps keep the interior ruckus to a minimum. Although there is an elevator, many rooms are only stair-accessible, so contact the hotel directly if accessibility is an issue.

108 South Plaza. www.lafondataos.com. (C) **800/833-2211** or 575/758-2211. Rooms $119–$259, suites $179–$229, penthouse $500–$1,420. Children under 8 not permitted. **Amenities:** Restaurant; coffee shop; lounge; free Wi-Fi.

MODERATE

El Pueblo Lodge ★ The sign and vibe may say "old school," but this budget lodge about a half-mile north of the plaza doesn't scrimp on comfort. Rooms in the 1940s South Building and in the "Casita," the original 1920s motor lodge, ooze with Route 66 atmosphere—the three in the Casita don't even have A/C. Units in the newer West Building are larger, with kiva-style fireplaces. There's also a three-bedroom condo with full kitchen facilities. Rates include continental breakfast and cookies in the afternoon. All in all, this is a good value, especially considering that it's within walking distance of the plaza.

412 Paseo del Pueblo Norte. www.elpueblolodge.com. (C) **800/433-9612** or 575/758-8700. 50 units. Double $100–$135, includes continental breakfast. Pets welcome. **Amenities:** Seasonal pool; hot tub; fitness room; coin-op guest laundry; BBQ grills; horseshoe pits; free Wi-Fi.

Inn on the Rio ★★ There is no shortage of lodgings in Taos that qualify as quaint, charming, occasionally even adorable. It takes a little something special to rise above the crowd, as the Inn on the Rio does. Away from the hustle and bustle of downtown Taos in the foothills of the Sangre de Cristo Mountains, the inn provides a relaxing setting by old rustling cottonwoods along the bank of the Rio Fernando or by an outdoor pool. Each room is unique, with colorful decor and touches such as hand-carved log beds, western memorabilia, and American Indian–style wall hangings. Each of the private bathrooms has been whimsically hand-painted by area artists. The gracious hosts, Robert and Julie, cook up gourmet breakfasts, keep the hot tub bubbling, and make every guest feel like an actual guest instead of a paying client.

910 E. Kit Carson Rd. 1.5 mi. east of Taos Plaza. www.innontherio.com. (C) **800/737-7199** or 575/758-7199. 12 units. $115–$225, includes full breakfast. Ski and summer packages. **Amenities:** Outdoor pool; whirlpool tub; free Wi-Fi.

Sagebrush Inn & Suites ★★★ This sprawling property about three miles south of town has two main draws: its quiet location amid the sagebrush away from downtown, and a wide range of accommodations from cozy historic rooms with kiva fireplaces (in the original 3-story adobe building) to executive suites with all modern conveniences for the business traveler. The seasonal pool is located in the large original tree-shaded courtyard, and there's a second, more intimate courtyard with rooms and suites behind the conference center. Many units have their own patios or balconies, and the view of Taos Mountain to the north is stupendous. The spacious lobby bar livens up at night with country music and dancing.

1508 Paseo del Pueblo Sur. www.sagebrushinn.com. 🕐 **800/428-3626** or 575/758-2254. 97 units. Rooms and suites $79–$219, includes full breakfast. Pets accepted ($10 per pet per night). **Amenities:** Restaurant; bar; outdoor pool; 3 hot tubs; fitness center; free Wi-Fi.

INEXPENSIVE

Abominable Snowmansion Skiers' Hostel ★

Set in the picturesque village of Arroyo Seco just 8 miles north of Taos and 10 miles from Taos Ski Valley, the Snowmansion offers several low-cost lodging choices, from individual rooms with private or shared bathrooms to communal dorm rooms. There's a common space with a pool table, fireplace, and a full kitchen for guests to use. (You're welcome to pick produce from the garden in the summer; just leave something in the donation jar in exchange.) There are also four snug year-round cabins, and roomy but unheated tipis set up in the summer, complete with an outdoor kitchen. (There is camping, too.) The property is very clean as hostels go, with friendly owners, plenty of outdoor space, and a wider age range of guests than you might expect.

476 State Rd. 150. www.snowmansion.com. 🕐 **575/776-8298.** 80 beds. Dorm bunks from $26, cabins from $55, private rooms from $60 with shared bathroom, $65 with private bathroom. Dogs $15 per night per dog, no cats. **Amenities:** Pool table; library; free Wi-Fi.

Adobe Sun God Lodge ★★

Opened in the 1950s, the economical Sun God Lodge was "boutique" before boutique was a thing. It sits about five minutes' drive from Taos Plaza, with a beautiful grass courtyard surrounded by old trees and three separate sets of buildings: the original part, which has been updated but still keeps some of its southwest-motel ambience, and two newer sections. The most recent buildings have two stories, with porches and balconies, and some have kitchenettes and kiva fireplaces. The whole spread covers 1½ acres and is pretty much the opposite of a chain hotel: sprawling, landscaped, and full of character, down to the free tea and donuts in the lobby.

919 Paseo del Pueblo Sur. www.sungodlodge.com. 🕐 **800/821-2437** or 575/758-3162. 56 units. Doubles $65–$95, suites $115–$150. Pets accepted ($20 per pet per night). **Amenities:** Hot tub; picnic area; free Wi-Fi.

Kachina Lodge ★

Set on the north edge of town, this lodge, built in the early 1960s as a motor hotel, has considerable charm. Accommodations are spacious and comfortable, with southwestern decor such as carved wood chairs, tables, mirrors, and colorful walls. Rooms encircle a large grassy courtyard with several large blue spruce trees—a space just begging for kids to run free. On summer evenings, a Taos Pueblo family performs dances around a central fire, explaining the significance of the dance—a special treat for those interested in Pueblo rituals.

413 Paseo del Pueblo Norte. www.kachinalodge.com. ⓒ **800/522-4462** or 575/758-2275. 118 units. $69–$149 double. Rates includes full breakfast. Children 11 and under stay free in parent's room. **Amenities:** 2 restaurants; lounge; outdoor pool (summer only); indoor hot tub; free Wi-Fi.

Bed & Breakfasts

EXPENSIVE

Adobe & Pines Inn ★★★ You may feel you're taking a step back in time as you drive through the colorfully painted tall *latillas* (poles) that loom over each side of the entrance to this 3-acre property, built around an 1832 adobe hacienda half a mile south of San Francisco de Asis church in Ranchos de Taos. You enter its lobby through a short door after ducking under the low overhang of an 80-foot-long grand portal that stretches across the front. This is a perfect spot to rest in the evening and enjoy the changing light of the sunset reflected on the Sangre de Cristo Mountains. The grounds are lush in summer, with a stream—part of the original *acequia*, or irrigation ditch, system of Taos—flowing through and traversed by a charming old stone bridge. Five rooms are in the original hacienda building; all rooms are richly colored with sumptuous furnishings, and have at least one fireplace, plus private entrances. The most requested room is Puerta Rosa, with its large sunken bathroom where you can pamper yourself in a deep two-person soaking tub or a dry cedar sauna. Puerta Violeta on the second floor has its own oversize jetted tub and a private balcony where you'll feel as though you can pluck the stars right out of the velvet sky. Although it's close to the highway, once you're inside the thick-walled adobe building, the traffic sounds disappear.

4107 State Road 68, about 4 mi. south of Taos Plaza. www.adobepines.com. ⓒ **855/828-7872** or 575/751-0947. 8 units. $109–$219 double; $219–$249 suite. Rates include full breakfast. Pets accepted with prior arrangement, one-time $25 fee. **Amenities:** Concierge service; kitchenette (in some rooms); free Wi-Fi.

Adobe and Stars Bed and Breakfast Inn ★★ Perched on the mesa north of Taos on the road to Taos Ski Valley, this inn offers trendy southwestern-style hospitality in a serene setting. The common living and dining rooms have wide windows to bring in the expanse of sky and wide open landscape. Rooms have kiva fireplaces, private decks or patios, and hand-crafted southwestern-style furniture. Many have jetted tubs, and most of the downstairs rooms open onto the portal. The upstairs Polaris room has custom wrought-iron furniture and a wide window seat for star-gazing. Two other upstairs rooms, La Luna and La Puesta del Sol (sunset), can be combined with a mini-kitchen into a three-room suite, perfect for a family. La Luna boasts a two-person, heart-shaped jetted tub, and La Puesta del Sol has a private deck from which guests can take in the stupendous Taos sunsets. Breakfast ranges from New Mexican dishes such as green chile strata to gingerbread waffles with homemade strawberry syrup to quiche Lorraine. Throughout the day guests can enjoy coffee, tea, soda, and often homemade cookies, all found in the dining room.

8 mi. north of Taos on State Road 150 where it meets the Valdez Rim Rd. www.taos adobe.com. © **800/211-7076** or 575/776-2776. 8 units. $125–$189 double. Rates include full breakfast and refreshments. Pets under 50 lb. accepted ($10–$20 per pet). **Amenities:** Whirlpool tub; free Wi-Fi.

Casa Benavides Bed & Breakfast Inn ★★★ This eclectic place stretches the boundaries of what a B&B can be: 39 rooms spread across a multitude of properties, each done in a different style (and for different prices), but all sharing a traditional New Mexico aesthetic of wood-burning fireplaces and Mexican-tile bathrooms. (Guests can pick specific rooms from the website ahead of time.) The owners' families have lived in Taos for generations. They opened Casa Benavides in 1989 in what was an art gallery and artists' residence just a few blocks from Taos Plaza. The lounge and dining room are in the main building, with a patio and two outdoor hot tubs. Don't miss the homemade granola at breakfast.

137 Kit Carson Rd. www.taos-casabenavides.com. © **800/552-1772** or 575/758-1772. 39 units. $90–$175 double, includes breakfast and afternoon tea. **Amenities:** 2 hot tubs; courtyard; free Wi-Fi.

Hacienda del Sol ★★ The first thing you notice about the Hacienda del Sol is the magnificent mountain backdrop. Even though it's just off the main drag, the property edges up against Taos Pueblo land, which means the scenery is virtually unspoiled. It's easy to see why art patron Mabel Dodge Luhan bought the place in the 1920s as a private retreat and guesthouse. Eventually you'll notice the rest of it: the 200-year-old main house with two courtyards, arched doorways, curved adobe walls, and viga ceilings. All eleven rooms here are filled with antique furniture, original art, and quilts made by a local artist. (The newer rooms have nicer bathrooms and a bit more privacy.) Most rooms have kiva fireplaces, and some have private hot tubs and steam showers. All guests are welcome at the main outdoor hot tub. Gourmet breakfasts are cooked up by owner Gerd Hertel, who also hosts group cooking lessons. In 2014, the private "Southwest Villa" was added, with a full kitchen, heated floors, and French doors leading to a private garden bursting with flowers in the summer.

109 Mabel Dodge Ln. www.taoshaciendadelsol.com. © **866/333-4459** or 575/758-0287. 12 units. $160–$325 double; $200–$315 suite; $350 villa; includes breakfast. **Amenities:** Free Wi-Fi.

Inn on La Loma Plaza ★★ Hidden away on historic La Loma (the small hill) Plaza, this beautifully restored 200-year-old-plus hacienda is just minutes from Taos Plaza. Spacious common areas welcome guests with Old World charm melded to southwestern ambience, with high ceilings, antiques, local art, plants, and fountains. Each room has its own layout and personality, further refined by hand-crafted furniture, Mexican tiles, and fabrics. The two-room, second-floor Penthouse Suite, which has its own private curved stair entry, boasts two fireplaces, a two-person jetted tub, and a large walk-in shower with body sprays. The downstairs Junior Suite also has a two-person jetted tub and separate shower. Two studio rooms with kitchenettes can be combined with king rooms to create two-bedroom suites. Most rooms have balconies or terraces with wonderful views. Almost all rooms have traditional plaster walls, with the exception of the Happy Trails Room, the epitome of old cowboy with its knotty-pine paneling, brass bed, old chaps, and decorative hanging spurs. Breakfast offerings may include breakfast burritos, green chile strata, granola pancakes, or French toast made from croissants soaked in triple sec–laced cream.

315 Ranchitos Rd. www.vacationtaos.com. ℂ **800/530-3040** or 575/758-1717. 10 units. $165–$260 double; $285–$325 studio; $425–$600 suite. Children 12 and under stay free in parent's room. Rates includes full breakfast, afternoon snacks, beverages. **Amenities:** Concierge; workout room; free Wi-Fi.

MODERATE

La Posada de Taos ★★   Taos' first B&B, just 2 blocks west of the plaza, rests within a walled courtyard graced with shade trees and flowers. It's a charming restored 1905 hacienda-style adobe, with original art throughout and lots of northern New Mexico accents. The rooms in the oldest part of the building are the coziest, and all but one room has a kiva fireplace. Most have warm wood floors and decorative tile accenting architectural motifs. The Honeymoon House, or La Casa de la Luna Miel, is a two-room casita with its own entrance, a king bed with skylight overhead, and a two-person, tiled whirlpool tub. The Beutler boasts local handcrafted rugs and quilts, and El Solecito is a two-level suite with willow chairs and headboard. Sumptuous breakfasts include fresh fruit and juice, house-made granola, and a fresh-baked goodie such as chile-piñon scones, followed by a hot entree such as hash-brown–crusted quiche or breakfast tostada with black beans topped with an egg over easy.

309 Juanita Lane. www.laposadadetaos.com. ℂ **800/645-4803** or 575/758-8164. 6 units. $119–$199 double; $189–$229 casita. Rates include breakfast and afternoon snack. **Amenities:** Free Wi-Fi.

Old Taos Guesthouse ★   This hacienda-style B&B fills a two-centuries-old adobe home set high on the quiet outskirts of town. Each cozy room has a private entrance; some have fireplaces, mountain views, and kitchens, though the bathrooms tend toward the smaller side. There's a veranda over the well-tended courtyard for shade in the summer, and the views from the outdoor hot tub seem to go on forever. The friendly owners are diehard skiers, with dogs who are just as welcoming to kids and adults alike.

1028 Witt Rd. www.oldtaos.com. ℂ **800/758-5448** or 575/758-5448. 10 units. $139–$189 double. Rates include breakfast. **Amenities:** Massage room; spa; Jacuzzi; free Wi-Fi.

Ski Area Lodges & Condominiums

Taos Ski Valley began a major, multiyear construction project in the summer of 2014, and many of its lodgings are currently undergoing renovation, too. But everything remains open and available for your enjoyment. For more information on what's going on in Taos Ski Valley, see p. 152.

EXPENSIVE

The Bavarian Lodge ★   Sitting at the base of Kachina Peak at an elevation of 10,200 feet, the Bavarian strives for authentic European ambience rather than southwestern. The reception area and restaurant have an alpine feel, with carved and painted detailing, and Bavarian objets d'art. The upstairs rooms are comfortable and fairly spacious, with lofts for the kids, although the King Ludwig suite is furnished a bit over-the-top for our taste. The use of trompe-l'oeil in the Chalet is meant to invoke the atmosphere of Cinderella's castle a la Walt Disney. Relaxing on the sun deck is grand, especially on a sunny winter day, where you can recoup while watching the skiers before rejoining them.

100 Kachina Rd. www.thebavarian.com. ✆ **888/205-8020** or 575/776-8020. 4 units. Christmas holiday–New Year and spring break $400–$455; Nov–Christmas holiday and mid-Jan to Feb $305–$355; June–Sept $185–$205. Rates include breakfast. Closed Oct, Apr–May. **Amenities:** Restaurant; bar; free Wi-Fi.

Edelweiss Lodge & Spa ★★   This classy condominium property offers one-, two-, and three-bedroom condos, each individually furnished by their owners. All have fully equipped kitchens, living rooms, dining areas, washers and dryers, and gas fireplaces, with ski-in/ski-out convenience. Many have grand views of the ski slopes. Small hotel rooms are available as lock-outs from a larger condominium. Rooms are medium size with comfortable beds and medium-size baths. The on-site underground parking, full spa, excellent restaurant, and ski valet service all contribute to the appeal.

106 Sutton Place. www.edelweisslodgeandspa.com. ✆ **800/458-8754** or 575/737-6900. 31 units. Winter $220–$440 double, $275–$1,156 condo; summer $100 double, $160–$335 condo. **Amenities:** Restaurant; bar; concierge; health club and full spa; hot tub; sauna; boot lockers; free Wi-Fi.

Powderhorn Suites and Condominiums ★   This simply yet comfortably furnished multistory property is located just 500 feet from the base of Lift One. A range of rooms accommodate from 2 to 6 people. The condos and larger suites have full kitchens, smaller suites have kitchenettes, and many units have balconies and fireplaces. Weekly rates are available; there's no elevator.

5 Ernie Blake Rd. www.taospowderhorn.com. ✆ **800/776-2346** or 575/776-2341. 16 units. Ski season $105–$265 double, $115–$495 suite, $150–$545 condo; summer $85–$165 all room options. Weekly rates available. Valet parking. **Amenities:** Ski storage lockers; 2 hot tubs; coin-op laundry; free Wi-Fi.

Sierra del Sol Condominiums ★   Located slope-side and stream-side, these condos offer convenience year-round. From your private deck or balcony you'll have magnificent views of the surrounding mountains and Al's Run, the Lake Fork Stream, and the star-studded night sky. Condos range in size from an economical studio to luxurious three-bedroom/two-bath, and several have lofts with twin beds, making them perfect for families. Each is individually furnished by the owner and all have fully equipped kitchens.

13 Thunderbird Rd. www.sierrataos.com. ✆ **800/523-3954** or 575/776-2981. 31 units. Studio and 1-bedroom $144–$245; 2- or 3-bedroom $293–$440. **Amenities:** Babysitting; hot tub; sauna; riverside picnic tables & BBQ grills for summer use; free Wi-Fi.

Snakedance Condominiums and Spa ★★ Located less than 20 yards from Lift One, these elegant condos are individually decorated but consistent in quality. All have full kitchens with granite countertops, and all units have gas fireplaces. Sizes range from small studios to three-bedroom/three-bath units that sleep six to eight people. On-site massage services run the gamut from a gentle relaxing Swedish massage to deep tissue therapeutic massage. The Hondo Restaurant and Bar offers dining and entertainment most nights during the ski season, and is home to the annual Winter Wine Festival in late January.

110 Sutton Place. www.snakedancecondos.com. ℭ **800/322-9815** or 575/776-2217. 27 units. Winter $165–$410 studio or 1-bedroom, $350–$750 2- or 3-bedroom; Christmas holiday $375–$500 studio or 1-bedroom, $800–$1,100 2- or 3-bedroom; summer $100–$185, slightly lower for multi-night stays. **Amenities:** Restaurant and bar winter only; free airport transfers; ski valet with ski storage and boot dryers; exercise room; hot tub; sauna; spa; free Wi-Fi.

MODERATE

Alpine Village Suites ★★ This pet-friendly, family-owned hotel is just a few steps from the ski lifts, and includes within its "village" two ski shops (show your key at Cottam's and receive a 10% discount) and the Stray Dog Cantina, a popular family-friendly bar and restaurant. A variety of suites filled with rustic mountain charm can accommodate two to six people; private home rentals are also available, accommodating up to ten. All suites have kitchenettes; some rooms have fireplaces and balconies, and some suites have sleeping lofts for the young and nimble. All are attractively and comfortably furnished with southwestern touches. In addition, there's a wonderful massage and spa service.

100 Thunderbird Rd. www.alpine-suites.com. ℭ **800/576-2666** or 575/776-8540. 33 units. Ski season $150–$215 suite for 2, $216–$347 suite for 4, $216–$391 suite for up to 6; summer $90 suite for 2, $102–$132 suite for 4, $120–$270 suite for up to 6. Pets accepted ($20 per pet per day). Continental breakfast, summer only. Covered valet parking $15 per night (optional). **Amenities:** Hot tub; massage and spa services; sauna; ski lockers; free Wi-Fi.

Taos Mountain Lodge ★ Comfy and cozy describes this lodge, with a kiva fireplace in the reception area and two-storied post-and-beam condos. Located about a mile west of the village of Taos Ski Valley, the property backs up to the Carson National Forest, where you can snowshoe, snowmobile, and backcountry ski in winter. In summer there's hiking, mountain biking, and great trout fishing in the Rio Hondo just across the road. The loft suites can each accommodate up to six people, with large windows that practically bring the outdoors inside. Regular rooms have kitchenettes, with mini-fridges and stoves, and deluxe rooms have full kitchens.

1346 Taos Ski Valley Rd. (NM 150). www.taosmountainlodge.net. ℭ **866/320-8267** or 575/776-2229. 10 units. Mid-Nov–Mar $120–$275; Apr–Mid-Nov $85–$100. **Amenities:** Sauna; patio with BBQ grills; free Wi-Fi in reception area (not in rooms).

RV Parks & Campgrounds

Carson National Forest ★★ There are three national forest camping areas 4 to 7 miles east of Taos along US 64, and another six within 20 miles southeast via NM 518; these developed areas are open from Memorial Day to Labor Day. They range from woodsy, stream-side sites on the road to Taos Ski Valley to open lowlands with lots of sagebrush. Call or stop at the forest service office to discuss the best location for your needs and desires.

Carson National Forest Supervisor's Office, 208 Cruz Alta Rd. www.fs.fed.us/r3/carson. © **575/758-6200.** $6–$16 per night. No credit cards. Pets welcome. **Amenities:** Vault toilets; no Wi-Fi.

Taos Monte Bello RV Park ★★ Taos' newest RV park is located on 5 acres on the sagebrush-covered mesa 7 miles north of town. Every site offers 360° views of the Sangre de Cristo Mountains to the north and east, and unbeatable New Mexico sunset vistas to the west. The Rio Grande Gorge Bridge is just 5 miles west, and the centuries-old Taos Pueblo is 4 miles southeast. Our only complaint with the location is that its mesa-top setting can be windy. Sites are spacious, with plenty of room for slide-outs; the restrooms and showers are clean, and the convenience store, in addition to foodstuffs and curios, carries those pesky items that make life in an RV challenging, like awning tie-downs and hoses to replace one that's just sprung a leak. And if they don't have what you need, they can probably tell you where in town to find it. There's a 24-hour host on-site and security gates.

24819 US Hwy 64 W. www.taosmontebellorvpark.com. © **575/751-0774.** 19 sites, 16 with full hookups. Tents $20; water and electric only $32; full hookups $36–$38. Weekly and monthly rates available. Pets welcome. **Amenities:** Playground; horseshoe pit; hiking path; convenience store; coin-op laundry; dump station; free Wi-Fi.

Taos Valley RV Park and Campground ★ For almost-in-town camping, this is the place to be, just 2½ miles south of Taos Plaza but set back far enough on a side road that you won't be hearing traffic noises all night. It's well-maintained (very clean bathhouses), mostly open with some well-established trees, offers all the usual commercial campground amenities, and has grand views of the surrounding mountains. Each site has a picnic table and grill.

120 Este Es Rd., off NM 68 (a half-block east of Paseo del Pueblo Sur). www.taosrv.com. © **800/999-7571** or 575/758-4469. 91 sites. $27 tent; $32–$34 water and electric; $37–$42 full hookup. Pets welcome. **Amenities:** Playground; convenience store; coin-op laundry; dump station ($10 fee for those not camping here); propane; free Wi-Fi.

WHERE TO EAT IN TAOS

Taos offers great food in great comfort; nowhere is a jacket and tie mandatory. Alongside fine dining spots, you'll also find basic comfort food—northern New Mexico–style, of course. As in Santa Fe and Albuquerque, the chile can be hot (spicy hot), so if you're not sure your taste buds and stomach can handle it, ask for a sample before ordering. For many dishes you can also ask for your chile on the side and add a little bit at a time to your meal.

Reservations are recommended when the town's jammed in summer or during the height of ski season, especially for dinner.

Taos Area Dining
EXPENSIVE

De La Tierra ★★★ NEW AMERICAN   Located in El Monte Sagrado (p. 124), this high-end restaurant surrounds you in elegance, with plush leather seating, attractive Southwest artwork, and a light and airy feel. Breakfast offers such items as El Monte Benedict—topped with chipotle (chile) Hollandaise—plus the Taos Breakfast Burrito. At lunch you might try our favorite: the jalapeño burger (made with beef, chicken, or mushrooms), with avocado, bacon, pepper jack cheese, and roasted jalapeño, served on a ciabatta roll. They also offer a specialty pizza, interesting salads, and a nice white gazpacho. Dinner entrees include a tender filet mignon, chipotle barbecued pork ribs, and a number of fish items including grilled trout tacos. We didn't find the desserts quite as good as the rest of the meal, but they certainly aren't bad. The chef utilizes seasonal and local ingredients, including organic ones when he can. A lovely outdoor space for al fresco dining, The Gardens, is tucked inside the walls of the resort, and you can also eat in the Anaconda Bar (p. 164).

In the El Monte Sagrado Hotel, 317 Kit Carson Rd. www.elmontesagrado.com. © **800/828-8267** or 575/758-3502. Breakfast $8–$14; lunch $6–$20; dinner $18–$40. Breakfast Mon–Sat 7–11am; Sunday brunch and lunch Mon–Sat 11am–2pm; dinner 5–9pm Sun–Thurs, until 10pm Fri–Sat.

Doc Martin's ★★★ AMERICAN/NEW MEXICAN   Doc Martin's serves delicious and innovative meals in the former home and office of the first doctor in Taos, Dr. Thomas Paul Martin—also the place where painters Ernest Blumenschein and Bert Phillips plotted the beginnings of the Taos Society of Artists in 1912. The old adobe building oozes with Taos history, while keeping up-to-date in comfort and style. Changing local art graces the walls, tables are comfortably spaced, and there's a nice courtyard in back for warm-weather dining. There's also patio dining in front, along the street, if you don't mind a little traffic noise. This is where we come for our green chile cheeseburger and fries at lunch, although we also like Da' Classic—pastrami and Swiss on rye—or the blue corn chicken enchiladas and the local pulled pork tostada. The dinner menu offers local lamb shank braised in red wine, Doc's chile relleno (cheese-stuffed green chiles) platter, and the ever-popular pan-seared trout. The chef uses local and organic ingredients and wild game when available. The Adobe Bar, across the lobby from the restaurant, is often referred to as the "living room of Taos" and offers live music (a changing menu of bluegrass, jazz, gospel, Celtic, and folk) with no cover charge.

In the Historic Taos Inn, 125 Paseo del Pueblo Norte. www.taosinn.com. © **575/758-1977.** Breakfast $5–$10; lunch $7–$15; dinner $18–$30. Daily 5–9:30pm; Mon–Fri 7:30–11am and 11am–3pm; brunch Sat–Sun 7:30am–2:30pm.

El Meze ★★ SPANISH   New Mexico's culture owes much to Europe, of course, but it was also influenced by the greater Mediterranean. El Meze

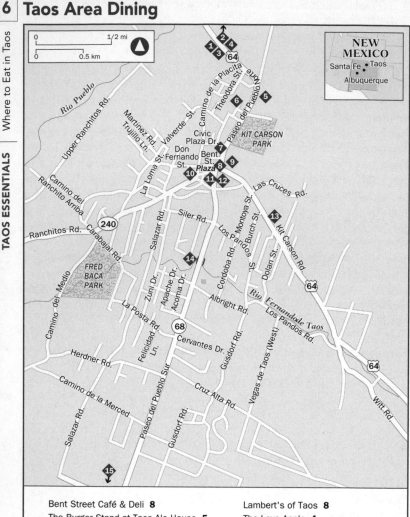

Bent Street Café & Deli **8**
The Burger Stand at Taos Ale House **5**
De La Tierra **13**
Doc Martin's **9**
El Gamal **10**
El Meze **2**
Eske's Brewpub **12**
The Gorge Bar & Grill **11**
Guadalajara Grill **15**
Gutiz **3**
La Cocina de Taos **15**

Lambert's of Taos **8**
The Love Apple **4**
Mantes Chow Cart **14**
Martyrs Steakhouse **7**
Michael's Kitchen **6**
Old Martina's Hall **15**
Orlando's New Mexican Café **1**
Pizaños **2**
Sabroso **2**
Taos Cow **2**
Taos Pizza Out Back **3**

("The Table" in Arabic) harks back to the rustic Spanish and Arabic roots of northern New Mexican cuisine. Owner and chef Fred Muller calls his hybrid menu "La Comida de las Sierras," or the food of the mountains, serving dishes like buffalo short ribs adovada, butternut squash and chickpea soup, and gazpacho with prickly pear granita. The results are simple and subtle but never boring. The wine list brims with Spanish tintos and riojas. The building itself, a gorgeously restored 1847 hacienda, offers sweeping sierra views from the patio and a typical classy-casual Taoseño atmosphere inside.

1017 Paseo del Pueblo Norte. www.elmeze.com. © **575/751-3337.** Main courses $16–$21. Tues–Sat 5:30–9:30pm.

Lambert's of Taos ★★ AMERICAN First opened back in 1989, this Taos favorite moved to this space on Bent Street (formerly the Apple Tree Restaurant) in 2013. From the Harris Ranch meats (the filet mignon practically melts in your mouth), to the excellent Apple Tree salad and mango chicken enchiladas, to rich desserts by pastry chef Michelle Myers (cinnamon bun bread pudding with rum sauce, yum), Lambert's offers fine dining in a spare, elegant setting. Too bad the service isn't always impeccable to match. For a more casual atmosphere, head upstairs to the Treehouse Bar & Lounge, with a view of the apple tree–shaded patio. Keep an eye out for the occasional surprises that turn up on the menu, such as red chile–dusted roasted rock shrimp.

123 Bent St. www.lambertsoftaos.com. © **575/758-1009.** Lunch $6–$13; dinner $23–$38. Daily 11:30am–2:30pm, 5:30pm–close.

Martyrs Steakhouse ★★★ STEAK/SEAFOOD Housed in a beautifully renovated adobe home 2 blocks north of Taos Plaza, Martyrs offers fine dining in an elegant atmosphere, but without pretension. You won't go wrong at lunch with the ABLT, an excellent BLT with the tasty addition of sliced avocado. The open-face prime rib sandwich is equally good, and Martyrs' signature Black Angus burger is served all day. The restaurant also usually offers a weekday $9 lunch special, one of the best deals in Taos. Dinners include lamb chops, tender steaks (the 12-ounce New York and 8-ounce filet mignon can't be beat), Scottish salmon, and seasonal fresh fish. There's a full bar, and an outdoor patio adds people-watching to your dining enjoyment. Note the dining room's exquisite etchings by famed Taos artist Gene Kloss, depicting Taos scenes from the 1940s through the 1970s.

146 Paseo del Pueblo Norte. www.martyrs-steakhouse.com. © **575/751-3020.** Lunch $12–$18; dinner $15–$33. Daily 11:30am–9pm.

Sabroso ★★ AMERICAN The 150-year-old adobe that once housed the well-loved Casa Cordova restaurant is now home to this classic après-ski destination, a favorite for special occasions. Start with a half-dozen Chesapeake Bay oysters, flown in twice a week, but know that steaks are the stars here. Chef Tim Wooldridge tracks down the best New Mexico beef he can find and cooks it over a wood-fired grill (even the wood is local). The braised buffalo short ribs with Asian cherry sauce are excellent, but you'll very likely be happy with just about anything grilled, from the salmon to the burgers. The wine list is extensive. The interior is classic northern New Mexican, fireplace and all. Head to the bar for comfortable couches, a more relaxed menu, and live music some nights.

470 NM 150 (Taos Ski Valley Rd.). www.sabrosotaos.com. ✆ **575/776-3333.** Main courses $19–$35. Daily 4:30pm–close. From town, head north on US 64, turn right onto NM 150 toward the ski valley.

MODERATE

El Gamal ★ VEGETARIAN/MIDDLE EASTERN One block behind Taos Plaza, this is the kind of place vegetarians love to stumble across: an unassuming Middle Eastern cafe that makes everything in-house. You know you're in for a treat from the first aromatic whiff of spices and baking bread when you step through the door. The ambience is part New Mexican, part Middle Eastern cafe. Check the chalkboard menu for the latest specials, or cover all of your bases with a sample platter of hummus, baba ganoush, tabouli, and Israeli couscous salad. The lentil quinoa burger may be the best vegetarian burger you've ever tasted. Little ones love the mint lemonade, and the kids' pizza-on-a-pita packs a spicy kick.

112 Dona Luz St. ✆ **575/613-0311.** Main courses $10–$29. Mon–Sat 9am–5pm, Sun 11am–3pm.

The Gorge Bar & Grill ★ NORTHERN NEW MEXICAN/AMERICAN Located on the upper floor of a shopping complex on the northeast corner of Taos Plaza, the outside balcony dining area overlooks the plaza and is a great place to watch what's going on (and to hear periodic live concerts in summer). The spacious main dining room has both tables and booths, and is a bit on the dark side. But the food is tasty, and everything is made from scratch using home-grown ingredients from around the state. We love their green chile stew, but it's quite spicy, so beware—you might want to ask for sour cream on the side to cool it down. The many sandwiches—burgers to chicken to fish—come with your choice of beer-battered fries, sweet potato fries, apple cider stew, or cottage cheese. If you're partial to fish and chips, the beer-battered cod is quite good. There's also a children's menu, and several interesting tacos—"the only food shaped like a smile!"

103 E. Plaza. www.thegorgebarandgrill.com. ✆ **575/758-8866.** Main courses $14–$25. Tues–Sun 5pm–close.

La Cocina de Taos ★★ NEW MEXICAN/AMERICAN Housed in an octagonal-shaped building, with long low windows, a central four-sided fireplace, and a floor slightly below ground level, La Cocina ("The Kitchen") serves good traditional northern New Mexico food. There's banco seating at tables along the walls, and southwestern decor complete with nichos for pottery and kachina dolls. In addition to the usual American foods like scrambled eggs, sandwiches and burgers, roast beef or turkey, there's fresh homemade soup daily, plus true northern New Mexican fare. Try the fajita plate (marinated beef or chicken grilled with onions and peppers), or our favorite, chile rellenos—roasted Hatch green chile stuffed with cheese and cooked in a secret batter. Almost all of the New Mexico dishes can be smothered with your choice of red or green chile, or "Christmas"—a combination of both.

1541 Paseo del Pueblo Sur, about 3 miles south of Taos Plaza. www.laconcinadetaos. com. ⓒ 575/758-4855. Breakfast $6–$12; lunch $7–$13; dinner $10–$25. Mon–Sat 7am–2pm, 5–9pm.

The Love Apple ★★ AMERICAN/FRENCH Named after the original French phrase for the tomato ("la pomme d'amour"), this small restaurant occupies a former chapel a short drive north of the plaza. It's a romantic setting, with twinkling lights and huge roof beams overhead. The emphasis is on regional, organic ingredients, with standout specialties like rainbow trout with lime and coriander and house-made sweet corn tamales. There are plenty of vegetarian options, an extensive wine list, and tempting desserts that change with the seasons.

803 Paseo del Pueblo Norte. www.theloveapple.net. ⓒ 575/751-0050. Main courses $14–$25. No credit cards. Tues–Sun 5pm–close.

Old Martina's Hall ★★ NEW MEXICAN/AMERICAN This historic adobe landmark, across the street from the famous San Francisco de Asis Mission Church in Ranchos de Taos, has hosted countless weddings and dances over the decades—including parties with guests like Dennis Hopper and Ricky Nelson—but fell into disrepair. German cosmetics manufacturer Martina Gebhardt brought it back to life and reopened it in 2012, and now the hall is once again a center of community life. In a classic Taos setting of warm adobe walls, bare beams, and wood floors, Chef Erica Miller blends international dishes and New Mexican flavors in offerings that include enchiladas, seafood pasta, and outstanding burgers. There's a full-to-bursting pastry case and, if you want to make a night of it (which we definitely recommend), a new oak dance floor for live music and two-step and tango nights.

4140 State Rd. 68. www.oldmartinashall.com. ⓒ 575/758-3003. Lunch $10–$16; dinner $15–$32. Mon and Wed–Sat 9am–9pm, Sun 9am–5pm. About 4 miles south of Taos Plaza.

family-friendly RESTAURANTS

Michael's Kitchen (p. 142) With a broad menu, comfy booths, and a very casual, diner-type atmosphere, Michael's Kitchen makes both kids and their parents feel at home.

Orlando's New Mexican Café (p. 142) The relaxed atmosphere and playfully colorful walls will please the kids almost as much as the tacos and quesadillas made especially for them.

Taos Cow (p. 142) Potpies and sandwiches will fill kids up before they dive into the all-natural ice cream at this cafe north of town.

Taos Pizza Out Back (p. 140) Pizza is a natural hit for both parents and kids; even better are all the odd decorations here, such as the chain with foot-long links hanging over the front counter.

Pizaños ★ PIZZA   Two friends from Utica, New York, brought their East Coast pizza know-how to Taos and the result is the best of both worlds: great pies and intriguing local flavors. Case in point? The Fire Twirler, with jalapeños, green chile, pepperoni, bacon, and pineapple. Other dishes also get high praise, including the spinach salad with house-made chipotle-lime vinaigrette, and the Adirondack sandwich with smoked gouda, Monterey pepper jack, and—of course—green chile. Sit on the back deck for great landscape views (sorry, no dogs).

23 NM 150. Head north from town on US 64, turn right onto NM 150 toward the ski valley, Pizaños is just ahead on the right. www.taospizza.com.✆ **575/776-1050.** Sandwiches $9–$11; pizzas $15–$32. Daily 11am–9pm.

Taos Pizza Out Back ★ PIZZA   It's hard to decide what's better at this popular and unpretentious pizza joint: the crispy thin crusts topped with sesame seeds, the homemade sauces, or the choice of creative assemblages like the Killer, with green chile, Gorgonzola, black olives, and sun-dried tomatoes. Either way, the slices are monstrous and the shop has a good selection of microbrews to wash them down. Sit outside on the patio on nice days, and don't be afraid to try the salads—the pesto dressing is excellent. They also do a brisk to-go business.

712 Paseo del Pueblo Norte. www.taospizzaoutback.com. ✆ **575/758-3112.** Pizzas $13–$28; pastas and calzones $9–$15. Sun–Thurs 11am–9pm, Fri–Sat 11am–10pm.

INEXPENSIVE

Bent Street Café & Deli ★ DELI/CAFE/INTERNATIONAL   This popular cafe, a short block north of the plaza, serves simple food in a country-home atmosphere. Outside, a flower box surrounds sidewalk seating that is heated in winter. Inside, wood floors and lots of windows provide a country-diner feel. The breakfast menu (served until 11am) features breakfast burritos, egg dishes, and fresh-baked breads; for lunch you can choose from 20 deli sandwiches, plus a "create-your-own" column, as well as a variety of salads. Their dark-brown bread matched with a changing selection of soups is one of their best offerings. If you'd like a picnic to go, the deli here offers carryout service, plus free delivery in the downtown area.

120 Bent St. in the John Dunn Shops. www.bentstreetdeli.com. ✆ **575/758-5787.** Breakfast $4–$10; lunch $4–$12. Mon–Sat 8am–4pm, Sun 10am–3pm.

The Burger Stand at Taos Ale House ★ BURGERS & BEER   The Burger Stand started out in Lawrence, Kansas, and in 2014 opened its third Stand here, right across from the Taos Post Office. Although you can get vegetarian, vegan, and gluten-free items, the burger reigns supreme, with eight choices, plus six varieties of fries and tasty beer-battered onion rings. A burger favorite is Fire, with fresh avocado and habañero-cactus jam. They also offer some "Hawt Doggz," and shakes and floats in addition to beer and wine.

401 Paseo del Pueblo Norte. www.taosburgersandbeer.com. ✆ **575/776-5522.** Main courses $4.50–$14. Daily 11am–11pm.

Eske's Brewpub ★ PUB FARE & BEER A place packed with locals is always a good sign, and this snug spot near the plaza is a prime example. Set in a 100-year-old adobe home, Eske's has a dozen beers on tap, a pleasant outdoor patio, and a short but respectable menu (try the lamb stew washed down with a green chile beer). Live entertainment is hosted on the outdoor patio. Every Thursday is international night, with fare from some far-flung part of the world, and Sundays bring "Blue Plate Special" dinners. There's even a kid's menu.

106 Des Georges Ln. Off Paseo del Pueblo Sur just south of Taos Plaza. www.eskes brewpub.com. ℂ **505/758-1517.** Main courses $7–$18. Mon–Thurs 4–10pm, Fri–Sun noon–10pm.

Guadalajara Grill ★ MEXICAN All too often, Mexican food—even in New Mexico—is a bland heaping of rice, beans, and sauces, generously portioned but often tasteless. Not here, where dishes such as the vegetarian Aztec quesadilla (with peppers, onion, scallions, and mushrooms) are crisp and spicy enough to make your lips sing. The fish tacos are often called the best in town, and you can order half-size plates for the kids. The fried ice cream is big enough for a table to share. There are two Guadalajara Grills in town; the other is at 822 Paseo del Pueblo Norte, but it doesn't have patio dining like this one. *Note:* This is Mexican food, the type you'll find in Mexico, and not the New Mexican food you'll find in most northern New Mexico restaurants.

1384 Paseo del Pueblo Sur. www.guadalajaragrilltaos.com. ℂ **575/751-0063.** Main courses $9–$14. Mon–Sat 10:30am–9pm, Sun 11am–9pm.

Gutiz ★★ LATIN/FRENCH They may be small and only serve breakfast (albeit all day) and lunch, but Gutiz still manages to turn out some of the best Parisian crepes, brie omelets, and cinnamon French toast imaginable. The open kitchen mixes French and Latin American cooking into something as colorful as the setting, with its lavender walls and contemporary art. Green chile sausage bowls, tapas (mostly seafood), and sandwiches on homemade bread are available for lunch, maybe with a spicy Mexican hot chocolate to finish up.

812B Paseo del Pueblo Norte. www.gutiztaos.com. ℂ **575/758-1226.** Main courses $7.50–$16. Tues–Sun 8am–3pm.

Mantes Chow Cart ★ NORTHERN NEW MEXICAN For years, Taoseños crowded around the actual Chow Cart parked in a grocery store lot to get their breakfast or lunch burrito of choice. Then Mante moved his operations into a building, so we now have less parking but the same food (and there's a picture of the original Chow Cart truck so you know you're at the right place). It's straight northern New Mexican basics: enchiladas, burritos, fajitas, rellenos, tacos—all with numerous options. This is an honest-to-goodness fast-food joint a la Taos, offering both drive-through and dine-in.

402 Paseo del Pueblo Sur. ℂ **575/758-3632.** Breakfast $4.35–$7.70; lunch and dinner $4–$11. Mon–Sat 7am–9pm, Fri open until 10pm.

Michael's Kitchen ★ NEW MEXICAN/BAKERY A local landmark for four decades or so, Michael's serves what some call the best green chile in town, but that's just the start. Breakfast, served all day, is actually the star attraction here, with choices like strawberry-banana-pecan pancakes and the "Moofy" (egg, ham, and cheese on a croissant), drawing folks from far out of town. The extensive and varied menu runs from Philly cheesesteaks and tuna melts to steaks and pork chops. It also features what Michael's calls "Health Food," a double order of fries with your choice of chile and cheese. There's also a full bakery turning out cakes, pies, breads, donuts, and cookies. Don't miss the pumpkin empanadas.

304 Paseo del Pueblo Norte. www.michaelskitchen.com. ℂ **575/758-4178.** Baked goods $3–$6; main courses $7–$14. Mon–Thurs 7am–2:30pm, Fri–Sun 7am–8pm.

Orlando's New Mexican Café ★★ NEW MEXICAN A family-run cafe in El Prado, about 2 miles north of the plaza, Orlando's doesn't cook anything too flashy, but what they do, they do well—witness the dozens of awards on the walls. Red and green chile are the standouts, but the *carne adovada* and taco salad are also popular with the crowds that pack the place at lunchtime. One way you can tell it's authentic New Mexican cooking is that they serve posole (hominy stew) instead of rice on the side. Definitely save time and space for a slice of frozen avocado pie, creamy and seasoned with lime, inside a graham cracker crust. *¡Delicioso!* Their sister cafe, **3one6 Station Café,** at 316 Paseo del Pueblo Sur (ℂ **575/737-0316**), a few blocks south of Taos Plaza, is on the site of a former gas station—hence the name—and although it has a totally different atmosphere, the menu is similar and equally tasty.

1114 Don Juan Valdez Ln. (on US 64). ℂ **575/751-1450.** Main courses $8–$13. Daily 10:30am–3pm and 5–9pm.

Taos Cow ★★ ICE CREAM/CAFE What could inspire skiers fresh off the mountain to stop for ice cream in Arroyo Seco? Taos Cow, that's what—a cafe that's been churning out all-natural, hormone-free ice cream since 1993, in flavors like maple walnut, piñon caramel, cafe ole (coffee with cinnamon and dark chocolate), and buffalo chip (vanilla with dark chocolate–covered coffee beans). But this spot offers more than just cones; you can also fuel up with an espresso or hot chocolate, grab a breakfast burrito for the road, or sit down for a fresh brie and turkey sandwich or quiche of the day. This is a must-stop on the way to the slopes or hiking trails—or on the way back.

485 NM 150, in the town of Arroyo Seco, about 8 miles north of Taos. www.taoscow.com. ℂ **575/776-5640.** Cones $3–$5; main courses $6–$10. Daily 7am–6pm.

EXPLORING TAOS

With a history shaped by pre-Columbian civilization, Spanish Colonialism, and the Wild West, boasting outdoor activities that range from hot-air ballooning to hiking to some of the West's best skiing, and graced by an abundance of artists, writers, and musicians, Taos has something to offer almost everybody. Its museums represent a world-class display of regional history and culture, and Taos Pueblo should be on everyone's must-do list.

WHAT TO SEE & DO IN TAOS

Top Attractions

Ernest L. Blumenschein Home & Museum ★★ MUSEUM/ HISTORIC HOME Talk about eclectic—this mishmash of pretty old and very old shows how the artists of the early–20th century lived and worked. Parts of this historic adobe building date from the 1790s; in 1919 it became the home and studio of Blumenschein, one of the founders of the Taos Society of Artists. The building, with its garden walls and courtyard, has been maintained much as it was when the artist and his family lived here, with period furnishings including European antiques and handmade Taos furniture in Spanish Colonial style. An extensive collection of works by early-20th-century Taos artists, including some by Blumenschein's wife, Mary, and daughter, Helen, are on display.

Note: **Taos Historic Museums** offers a $15 combination ticket (need not be used on the same day) to this and La Hacienda de los Martinez (see p. 145).

222 Ledoux St. www.taosmuseums.org. ℂ **575/758-0505.** Adults $8, children 6–16 $4, free for children 5 and under. Summer daily 9am–5pm; call for winter hours.

Harwood Museum of Art ★★★ MUSEUM Good things sometimes come in small packages, like this museum in the former home of Taos painter Burt Harwood. The high-ceilinged building is chock-full of works by artists from northern New Mexico and Latin America (Larry Bell, Ernest Blumenschein), but not so much that it's overwhelming. Many of the pieces were collected by Mabel Dodge Luhan, an important local art patron. Paintings from the early–20th century fill the ground floor; upstairs in the Hispanic

Taos Attractions

D. H. Lawrence Ranch **1**
Ernest L. Blumenschein
  Home & Museum **11**
Governor Bent House
  Museum **9**
Harwood Museum of Art **11**
Kit Carson Home
  and Museum **8**
Kit Carson Park
  and Cemetery **7**
La Hacienda
  de Los Martinez **12**
Millicent Rogers Museum **3**
Rio Grande Gorge Bridge **2**
San Francisco
  de Asis Church **13**
Taos Art Museum
  at Fechin House **6**
Taos Firehouse Collection **9**
Taos Plaza **10**
Taos Pueblo **5**
Taos Ski Valley **4**

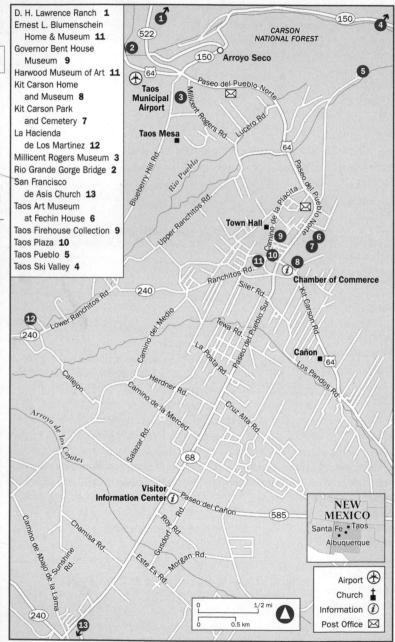

144

Traditions Gallery you'll find the largest public collection of sculptures by 20th-century artist Patrocino Barela, as well as Mabel Dodge Luhan's collection of *retablos* (paintings on wood of saints), 19th-century tinwork, and 19th- and 20th-century New Mexican furniture. The museum schedules changing exhibitions throughout the year, and the docents are very enthusiastic and helpful. You can see the highlights in 45 minutes to an hour.

238 Ledoux St. www.harwoodmuseum.org. (C) **575/758-9826.** Adults $10, seniors and students $8, 18 and under free. Mon–Sat 10am–5pm, Sun noon–5pm; closed Mondays Nov–Mar.

La Hacienda de Los Martinez ★★ HISTORIC SITE

To step back into New Mexico in the early–19th century, start at this imposing adobe complex. Built along the Rio Pueblo between 1804 and 1827 by a farmer and trader, this was the northern terminus of El Camino Real (the Royal Road), a major trade route that ran all the way to Mexico City. Thanks to occasional raids by Indian tribes, it's part residence, part fortress—notice the lack of windows in the outer walls—but still remarkably homey, with 21 rooms arranged around two courtyards, or *placitas*. Kids love exploring the colonial clothes, foods, and other items that fill the restored rooms (you can take a self-guided tour around the place). There's also a working blacksmith's shop and other living history–type crafts on display, especially on weekends. Old-time Taoseños tell stories of the ghosts that are supposed to haunt the hacienda; ask the docents and maybe some will share their stories.

Note: **Taos Historic Museums** offers a $15 combination ticket (need not be used on the same day) to this and the Ernest L. Blumenschein Home & Museum (see p. 143).

708 Hacienda Rd. (off NM 240/Lower Ranchitos Rd.). www.taoshistoricmuseums.org. (C) **575/758-1000.** Adults $8, under 16 $4, under 5 free. Mon–Sat 10am–5pm, Sun noon–5pm.

Millicent Rogers Museum of Northern New Mexico ★★★

MUSEUM   Thank Millicent Rogers, the late Standard Oil heiress, for popularizing the turquoise and silver American Indian jewelry that has become such a southwestern fashion standard. Her collection of jewelry and Navajo weavings forms the core of this museum. The wide-ranging exhibits include Hispanic, American Indian, and Anglo pieces from Pueblo jewelry to Apache baskets; Hopi *kachina* dolls; and more recent decorative tinwork. The museum boasts the largest public collection of works by San Ildefonso Pueblo potter Maria Martinez, arguably the Southwest's most famous American Indian potter. Another focus is carved Catholic images called *santos*, with many examples from master carvers of the 18th and 19th centuries. Rogers' own jewelry collection includes the famous "Tab Necklace," made of three pounds of Zuni-worked turquoise, for which she paid a mere $5,000 in the 1940s.

1504 Millicent Rogers Rd., off of US 64 about 3 miles north of Taos Plaza. www.millicent rogers.org. (C) **575/758-2462.** Adults $10, seniors $8, veterans and students 16–21 with ID $6, children 6–16 $2. Daily 10am–5pm (closed Mon Nov–Mar).

San Francisco de Asis Church ★★ CHURCH If this massive adobe edifice about 4 miles south of Taos looks familiar, it's because this Spanish Colonial church has inspired artists since it was built in 1816. Almost elemental in its strength and simplicity, the building's design is a classic mix of Spanish and native styles, with huge buttresses supporting the walls and twin bell towers adorned with white crosses. Ansel Adams and Georgia O'Keeffe are just two of the long list of artists who have immortalized the back of the church on film or canvas, and today it's practically a law that every Taos artist is required to try his or hand at finding a fresh way to portray it. Visitors are welcome when services aren't being held, but please remember this is a house of worship and not a museum. Photography is not permitted inside the church or the nearby parish hall, where you can watch a video about the church and view the "mystery painting"—an 1896 image of Christ that shows a mysterious glowing cross when the lights are dimmed.

60 St. Francis Plaza, Ranchos de Taos. ℂ **575/758-2754.** Free. Mon–Sat 9am–4pm.

Taos Art Museum at Fechin House ★ MUSEUM A rotating collection of 600 or so paintings, drawings, and prints by the Taos Society of Artists and the Moderns who followed them fills the former home of Russian émigré artist Nicolai Fechin (*Feh*-shin). Between 1927 and 1933, Fechin built this home for his family, carving and shaping it into a wonderful merging of Russian, American Indian, and Spanish motifs. The elaborate carved wooden doors, windows, and gates are his work. Visit Fechin's studio, take a break in the garden, and don't miss the museum store, which offers books on most of the artists, handcrafted pieces from Russia, plus many items crafted by New Mexico artists.

227 Paseo del Pueblo Norte. www.taosartmuseum.org. ℂ **575/758-2690.** Adults $8, seniors $7, children 6–12 $4, under 5 free. Tues–Sun 10am–5pm (closed at 4pm Nov–Apr).

Taos Pueblo ★★★ HISTORIC LANDMARK If you see nothing else in Taos, you must see this. The northernmost of New Mexico's 19 pueblos, Taos is the only living American Indian community designated both a World Heritage Site by UNESCO and a National Historic Landmark. This awe-inspiring five-story adobe structure has been home to Taos Indians since before

The Thing About Adobe...

Each June (usually the first two weeks), parishioners from **San Francisco de Asis Church** (see above) undertake the annual task of re-plastering its soft mud exterior walls. Built in Spanish Colonial times before foundations were common, the church was refurbished with an exterior coat of hard plaster several years ago—but it turned out that sealing the outer walls, with no foundation to protect them from ground moisture, allowed moisture to seep up inside the walls, melting the adobe from within. Off came the hard plaster, and back came the annual ritual. The church is closed during this work, but the workers are very friendly and happy to take a break and chat a bit, and watching them is a one-of-a-kind experience.

Columbus found and claimed his "New World" for Queen Isabella. Though the Tiwa were essentially a peaceful agrarian people, they also spearheaded the most successful revolt by American Indians. Launched by Pope (Poh-*pay*) in 1680, the uprising drove the Spanish from Santa Fe until 1692 and from Taos until 1698.

The largest multistory pueblo in existence, Taos remains home to about 150 people, who live without electricity or running water. Some 1900, more Taos Indians live nearby on other pueblo lands. Taos Pueblo is comprised of two main multistory buildings, one on each side of the Rio Pueblo de Taos, which is traversed by footbridges. The plaza runs along the river banks, and Taos Mountain stands sentinel to the northeast. Both structures are coated with a soft straw-and-mud plaster, requiring constant upkeep (if you're there on a winter morning after a snowfall, you'll see the inhabitants shoveling the snow off their flat roofs). This is a life that goes back centuries.

As you explore the pueblo, stop in shops and studios, buy some homemade fry-bread from a traditional *horno* oven, look into the **San Geronimo Chapel,** a handsome Roman Catholic church still in use today, and wander past the ruins of the nearby mission church and cemetery. The place is incredibly photogenic, but always ask permission before taking a photo of someone (some may request a small payment), and do not attempt entrance to kivas (underground sacred chambers) or any area marked as restricted. If you would like to try traditional feast-day meals, the **Tiwa Kitchen,** near the entrance to the pueblo, is a good place to stop.

Like many New Mexico pueblos, Taos has opened a casino. **Taos Mountain Casino** (www.taosmountaincasino.com; ✆ **888/946-8267**) is on the main road to Taos Pueblo and features slot machines, blackjack, and poker.

Note: Taos Pueblo is sometimes closed for a period of time in the spring for tribal rituals and at other unexpected times for private activities, so call ahead.

From Paseo del Pueblo Norte, travel north 2 miles on Veterans Hwy. www.taospueblo. com. ✆ **575/758-1028.** $10 adults, $5 students, children 10 and under free. Camera, video, and sketching fees subject to change on a yearly basis; be sure to ask about telephoto lenses and tripods, as the pueblo may not allow them; photography not permitted on feast days. Mon–Sat 8am–4:30pm, Sun 8:30am–4:30pm, with a few exceptions; closes at 4pm in winter. Guided tours available every 20 minutes beginning at 9am.

More Attractions

D. H. Lawrence Ranch ★ HISTORIC HOME   Although the controversial early-20th-century author D. H. Lawrence spent a total of just 11 months in New Mexico, the state made such an impression on him that he wrote "I think New Mexico was the greatest experience from the outside world that I have ever had. It certainly changed me forever. ... The moment I saw the brilliant, proud morning shine high up over the deserts of Santa Fe, something stood still in my soul." Today you can visit his retreat, the remote Kiowa Ranch on Lobo Mountain above San Cristobal, where he lived on and off between 1922 and 1925. His mornings were frequently spent writing at a small table under a mammoth pine tree—the Lawrence Tree. When he died in

feast days AT TAOS PUEBLO

Timed to celebrate the patron saints of the Catholic religion, feast days at Taos Pueblo also correspond to the traditional Pueblo religion's holy days. These fascinating religious ceremonies are open to the public, although no photography is allowed.

The most important is the **Feast of San Geronimo** (the patron saint of Taos Pueblo), September 29 and 30, which marks the end of the harvest season. This feast day is reminiscent of an ancient trade fair for the Taos Indians, when tribes from as far south as South America and as far north as the Arctic traveled here to trade for wares, hides, clothing, and harvested crops. Today the celebration is marked by foot races, pole climbs performed by traditional Indian clowns, and artists and craftspeople dressed like early traders.

The pueblo's Christmas celebration begins on **Christmas Eve,** with bonfires and a procession of the Blessed Mother. On **Christmas Day,** a variety of dances take place. These may include the **deer dance,** in which dancers act out a hunt, or the haunting **Matachine dances** (p. 27), an intriguing blend of native and Spanish traditions.

Other annual events include a turtle dance on **New Year's Day;** buffalo or deer dances on **Three Kings Day** (January 6); and corn dances on **Santa Cruz Day** (May 3), **San Antonio Day** (June 13), **San Juan Day** (June 24), **Santiago Day** (July 25), and **Santa Ana Day** (July 26).

A more recent tradition that's been going strong since 1985, the **Taos Pueblo Powwow** (www.taospueblopowwow.com) brings together tribes from throughout North America in early July. The celebration includes dances and a parade on tribal lands off NM 522. See p. 231 for details.

southern France in 1930 of tuberculosis, his wife Frieda returned to the ranch, where she eventually constructed the shrine to her husband. When she died in 1956, Frieda willed Kiowa Ranch to the University of New Mexico for educational, cultural, and recreational purposes, providing they made "a perpetual D. H. Lawrence Memorial and Foundation." The ranch has been sporadically open to the public since then; it was re-opened in July 2014 under the auspices of the University of New Mexico, the D. H. Lawrence Ranch Alliance, and the Taos Community Foundation. Besides the Lawrence Memorial and the Lawrence Tree, you can see Frieda's gravesite and two cabins. There is a small visitor center, and a docent tour can be arranged.

About 15 miles north of Taos on NM 522, in San Cristobal. www.dhlawrencetaos.org. For information, call Taos Community Foundation (✆ **575/737-9300**). Free admission. Open Apr–Oct, Thu–Sat 10am–2pm, Sun–Wed by appointment.

Governor Bent House Museum ★ HISTORIC HOME This small museum's claim to fame is that this is the exact spot where the New Mexico Territory's first American governor was murdered. The museum is housed in the residence of Charles Bent, a former trader who helped establish Bent's Fort in Colorado. He was killed during the 1847 Taos Pueblo and Hispanic revolt, while his wife and children escaped by digging through an adobe wall into the house next door. The original furnishings and personal effects were either looted or destroyed; items on display represent the era but not Governor Bent specifically.

117 Bent St. ✆ 575/758-2376. Adults $3, children 8–15 $1, free for 7 and under. Daily 9:30am–5pm (opens 10am in winter). Closed New Year's Day, Easter, Thanksgiving, and Christmas.

Kit Carson Home and Museum ★ HISTORIC HOME

Taos' most famous frontiersman bought this adobe home near the plaza as a wedding gift for his blushing bride Josefa Jaramillo in 1843. They lived here until 1868, when they both died a month apart. Today, three rooms have been restored and furnished as they were when the couple was in residence, including buffalo hides, leather clothes, and the famous scout's Spencer carbine rifle in a beaded leather case. Some people find the collection a little underwhelming, considering Carson's larger-than-life legacy, but a visit here does offer a quick glimpse of life during Taos' frontier heyday.

113 Kit Carson Rd. www.kitcarsonmuseum.org. ✆ 505/758-4945. Adults $7, seniors $6, teens and students $5, free for 12 and under. Daily 10am–5pm (closes at 4pm Nov-Feb). Closed Thanksgiving, Christmas, and New Year's days.

Kit Carson Park and Cemetery ★ PARK

Major community events are held in this pleasant park north of town, a relaxing grassy place to take a break while exploring Taos. At the southeast corner of the park you can wander around a cemetery, established in 1847, which contains the graves of many historical figures connected to the sites you'll be visiting: Kit Carson, his wife Josefa, the murdered Governor Charles Bent, the Don Antonio Martinez family, Mabel Dodge Luhan, and many others. Their lives are described briefly on plaques.

211 Paseo del Pueblo Norte. ✆ 575/758-8234. Free admission. Daily 24 hrs.

Rio Grande Gorge Bridge ★★ LANDMARK

This magnificent 1,272-foot-long bridge, west of the Taos airport, spans the mighty Rio Grande. At 650 feet above the canyon floor, it's one of America's highest bridges. If you can withstand the vertigo—and the vibration when a truck drives over—it's a grand view to the river below. Sometimes you can see rafters or kayakers skimming along the water, and occasionally you'll see a hot-air balloon dipping into the gorge. If you park in the rest area on the west side of the bridge and follow the West Rim Trail south, you'll get a grand view

Art Classes

If you're in Taos, why not be a famous Taos artist? To pursue an artistic adventure of your own, check out the variety of classes in such media as painting, American Indian pottery making, photography, and weaving offered by **Taos Art School ★** (www.taosartschool.org; ✆ 575/758-0350). Open since 1989, the school is a virtual campus in which classes are held wherever they need to be. For instance, a painting class on Georgia O'Keeffe may be held in Abiquiu, a pottery class outdoors at a local artist's home, or a painting class at an interesting church. Fees vary from class to class and usually don't include the cost of materials.

lowriders: CAR ART

While cruising northern New Mexico, and especially the Taos and Española areas, don't be surprised if you see the front of a car rise up off the ground and then sink down again, or if you witness another that appears to be scraping its underbelly on the pavement. These novelties are part of a car culture that thrives in northern New Mexico. Traditionally, the owners use American cars from the 1960s and '70s, which they soup up with hydraulic suspension systems, elaborate chrome, metal chain steering wheels, fancy paint, and sometimes even portraits of Our Lady of Guadalupe on the hood.

of the expanse of the bridge. You might even glimpse a few of the bighorn sheep that make the gorge their home. Movie trivia: The wedding scene in the 1994 movie *Natural Born Killers* was filmed here.

US 64, 10 miles west of Taos. Free admission. Daily 24 hrs.

Taos Firehouse Collection ★★ MUSEUM   Tucked away at the back of the Taos Fire Station, behind the fire trucks, hoses, and pool tables, is an unexpected trove of more than 100 paintings that's among the most eclectic collections in Taos. The works have only two things in common: all the artists lived and worked in the Taos area, and each piece was donated to the fire department. Just about every square inch of space in the fire department's recreation hall is covered with this somewhat haphazardly hung exhibit. It's a fascinating collection spanning more than a century of Taos art. Look for the delightfully whimsical painting by Eugene Dobos of a man dressed in a tux wearing a firefighter's helmet.

323 Camino de la Placita. © **575/758-3386.** Free admission. Mon–Fri 9am–4:30pm (unless everyone's out fighting a fire).

Organized Tours

Take a walk into Taos' past on a fun and informative walking tour of the historic downtown area with **Taos Historic Tours ★** (© **575/613-5508**). The 2-hour tours begin at the Gazebo on Taos Plaza and cost $15 per person, with a two-person minimum. Call to schedule your tour.

For a different kind of tour, especially if you like drama and imagination with your history, opt for a **Ghosts of Taos ★** walking tour (© **575/613-5330**), which gives an unusual slant on the historic areas of downtown. The charge is $20 per person, with discounts for families with children and groups. Call for availability.

SPORTS & RECREATION

Thanks to the federal government, the area around Taos is one big public playground, with forests, mountains, lakes and streams, and the sometimes mighty Rio Grande. There is hiking, camping, fishing, downhill and cross-country skiing, snowshoeing … the list goes on and on. Most of this public land is managed by two federal agencies with their headquarters in Taos. For information on many of the activities and locations discussed below, contact **Carson National Forest,** 208 Cruz Alta Rd. (www.fs.fed.us/r3/carson; ✆ 575/758-6200), or the **Bureau of Land Management,** 226 Cruz Alta Rd. (www.blm.gov/nm; ✆ 575/758-8851).

Downhill Skiing

Four alpine ski resorts are within an hour's drive of Taos; all offer complete facilities, including lodging, restaurants, equipment rentals, and just about every type of ski gear and clothing you might want to buy. Although exact opening and closing dates vary according to snow conditions, the season usually begins from mid-to-late November to early-to-mid December and continues into late March or early April. The basic ski pass prices are included below, but be sure to check each resort's website for special deals and packages.

Angel Fire Resort ★★   About 20 miles east of Taos, and over a mountain, Angel Fire is a good family-friendly ski area. The 80 runs are heavily oriented to beginner and intermediate skiers and snowboarders, although there is plenty for more advanced skiers and boarders. This is not an old village like you'll find at Taos and Red River (see below). Instead, it's a Vail-style resort, with a variety of activities other than skiing (see "The Enchanted Circle," p. 165). Snowmaking capabilities here are excellent, and there's a popular ski school. There's a 2,077-foot vertical drop from the summit (10,677 ft.) to the base (8,600 ft.). Two high-speed quad lifts whisk skiers to the top; there are also three double lifts and two surface lifts. Trails are rated 21% beginner, 56% intermediate, and 23% advanced, with four glade (tree trail) areas covering 30 acres designated as advanced. There are also three terrain parks, including Liberation Park at the summit, with multiple jumps, rails, fun-boxes, and other features for advanced riders. Cross-country skiing, snowshoeing, and snow-biking are also available.

www.angelfireresort.com. ✆ **800/633-7463** or 575/377-6401. Full-day lift ticket adults $62–$71, ages 13–17 $52–$61, ages 7–12 $42–$51; free for seniors over 69 and children under 7. Daily 9am–4pm from mid-Dec to late March.

Red River Ski & Snowboard Area ★★   This family-oriented ski and snowboard area, with most of its trails geared to intermediate and beginner skiers, is also nicely compact so that lodgers in the village of Red River can often walk out their doors and be on the slopes. Opened in 1959, the area doesn't have to depend on Mother Nature as much as most other ski areas— good snow is guaranteed early and late in the year by snowmaking equipment that can work on 85% of the runs. However, be aware that this human-made snow tends to be icy, and the mountain is full of inexperienced skiers, so you really have to watch your back.

There's a 1,600-foot vertical drop here to a base elevation of 8,750 feet. Lifts include two double chairs, three triple chairs, and a surface tow, with a capacity of close to 8,000 skiers per hour. There are 57 trails and one glade, rated 32% beginner, 38% intermediate, and 30% expert.

Locals in the area refer to this as "Little Texas" because it's so popular with Texans, Oklahomans, and other Southerners. A very friendly atmosphere, with a touch of redneck attitude, prevails.

www.redriverskiarea.com. ☏ **575/754-2223.** For lodging: www.redriver.org; ☏ **877/ 885-3885** or 575/754-1708. Full-day lift ticket adults $68, ages 13–17 $62, ages 4–12 $52, seniors 65–69 $52; free for seniors over 69 and children under 4. Daily 9am–4pm from Thanksgiving through March.

Sipapu Ski and Summer Resort ★   The oldest ski area in the Taos region, founded in 1952, Sipapu is located on NM 518 in the tiny village of Vadito, tucked into the mountains about 25 miles southeast of Taos. It prides itself on being a small, family-friendly ski area—small enough so your kids won't get lost—and claims to have the longest ski season in the state. It also has the lowest lift prices in the Taos area, with deep discounts for early- and late-season skiers; first-timers are welcomed with free ski lessons. A brand-new quad chairlift opened for the 2015–16 season, complementing two triple chairs, a platter lift, and two surface lifts. There's a vertical drop of 1,055 feet to the 8,200-foot base. Of Sipapu's 42 trails, 20% are for beginners, 40% are intermediate, and 40% are advanced; there are also three terrain parks.

www.sipapunm.com. ☏ **505/587-2240.** Full-day lift ticket adults $44, ages 13–20 $37, ages 7–12 $29, seniors 60–69 $29; free for seniors over 69 and children under 7. Daily 9am–4pm from late Nov through March.

Taos Ski Valley ★★★   This is the big one: New Mexico's best and most famous ski area; some would call it the preeminent ski resort in the southern Rocky Mountains. It was founded in 1955 by Swiss-German immigrant Ernie Blake, who had been managing Santa Fe Ski Basin and its sister ski area in Glenwood Springs, Colorado. Commuting between the two by small plane, Blake spotted the perfect place for a ski resort of his own as he flew over the abandoned mining site of Twining, north of Wheeler Peak and high above Taos. Owned and managed by several generations of Blakes for years, the resort was sold at the start of the 2013–14 ski season to Louis Bacon of Long Island, New York, founder and CEO of hedge fund company Moore Capital Management. Bacon pledged a $350-million, multi-year construction and improvement project, which began in the summer of 2014. This includes upgrades to practically every aspect of Taos Ski Valley, from new energy-efficient snowmaking equipment to construction of an 80-room hotel in the heart of the base area. Many privately owned lodgings are also undergoing renovation, but management assures us that while visitors will see construction during this time, everything will remain open and available.

So, why do you want to ski or snowboard Taos? For starters, there's its light, dry powder (usually more than 300 inches annually), one of the best ski schools in the country, and its personal, friendly service. And then there are the superb trails. Taos Ski Valley offers steep, high-alpine, high-adventure skiing, perfect for the expert skier, but beginners and intermediates aren't left out, either. Of the resort's 110 trails, 24% are for beginners, 25% are for intermediates, and 51% are for experts. Between the 12,481-foot Kachina Peak and the 9,207-foot base, the area has an uphill capacity of more than 15,000 skiers per hour on its five double chairlifts, three triples, four quads, and three surface tows.

There are numerous lodges and condominiums at Taos School Valley, with nearly 1,500 beds, and most offer ski-week and other packages. There are several restaurants on the mountain as well, in addition to the many facilities of Village Center at the base.

www.skitaos.org. © **575/776-2291** for general information; © **800/776-1111** for lodging reservations. Full-day lift ticket adults $63 $06, ages 13–17 $53–$75, ages 7–12 $48–$55, seniors 65–79 $53–$75; free for seniors over 80 and children 6 and under (with adult ticket purchase). Daily 9am–4pm from Thanksgiving to mid-April.

Cross-Country Skiing

There are dozens of popular Nordic trails in the **Carson National Forest,** which covers much of the area around Taos. One of the more popular trails is **Amole Canyon Trail # 10 ★★,** off NM 518 near the Sipapu Ski Resort. This is actually a stacked loop system of trails of various difficulty levels, with trail signs at intersections. Part of the system is groomed and tracked periodically. It's open to cross-country skiers and snowshoers, but closed to snowmobiles—a comfort to lovers of serenity. Details on this and numerous other trails are available from the Carson National Forest office (p. 151). Recreation officers there emphasize that these trails are not patrolled; for your personal safety, they recommend that you not go alone.

Just east of Red River, with 20.5 miles of groomed trails (in addition to 9.3 miles of trails strictly for snowshoers), the **Enchanted Forest Cross Country Ski Area ★★** (www.enchantedforestxc.com; © **575/754-6112**) sits on 400 acres of forestlands atop Bobcat Pass. There's even a 3.1-mile section where you can ski with your dog. In addition to cross-country ski and snowshoe rentals, the ski area rents pulk sleds—high-tech devices in which children are pulled by their skiing parents. The ski area offers a full ski shop and snack bar. Instruction in cross-country classic as well as freestyle skating is available. A yurt (Mongolian-style hut) is also available for a ski-in accommodation. Full-day trail passes, good from 9am to 4:30pm, are $18 for adults, $15 for teens 13–17, $15 for seniors 62–69, $9 for children 7–12, and free for seniors over 69 and children under 7.

For access to high-mountain terrain, the **Southwest Nordic Center ★** (www.southwestnordiccenter.com; © **575/758-4761**) offers rentals in a yurt that can accommodate 10 people, in what is called Bull of the Woods near

Taos Ski Valley. Skiers trek to the hut, carrying their clothing and food in backpacks, either accompanied by a guide or on their own (following directions on a provided map). The yurts are rented by the night and range from $100 to $145 per group. Guide service is extra. Call for reservations as far in advance as possible.

Adventure Ski Rentals & Snowboard Shop ★, 1337 Paseo del Pueblo Sur (www.adventureskishops.com; ✆ **800/433-1321** or 758/758-9292), should be able to set you up with whatever snow gear you need, from snowshoes to cross-country skis, with various packages available.

Other Sports & Recreation

BALLOONING

As in many other towns throughout New Mexico, hot-air ballooning is a top attraction. Recreational trips over the Taos Valley and Rio Grande Gorge are offered year-round by **Eske's Paradise Balloons ★** (www.taosballooning. com; ✆ **575/751-6098**) and **Pueblo Balloons ★** (www.puebloballoon.com; ✆ **575/751-9877**), and from June through September by **Taos Balloon Rides** (www.taosballoonrides.com; ✆ **575/224-6022**).

BIKING

The **West Rim Trail ★** is a scenic and easy 9-mile ride along the Rio Grande. To reach it, head west on US 64 and cross the Rio Grande Gorge Bridge, pulling into the rest area. The trail head is marked, but watch for people walking their dogs off-leash (despite a county-wide leash ordinance). Or start at the trail's southern end: Head south on NM 68 for 17 miles to Pilar; turn west onto NM 570 and travel along the river for 6¼ miles. Cross the bridge and drive to the top of the ridge. Watch for the trail marker on your right.

If you're looking for a technical and challenging ride, try the steep **Devisadero Loop Trail 108 ★** in the Carson National Forest. This 5.1-mile trail, also used by hikers and horseback riders, is 3 miles east of Taos via Kit Carson Rd. (US 64), and provides splendid panoramic views of the Taos Valley. You can follow it to Devisadero Peak and stand guard to watch for invading Apaches, as the people of Taos Pueblo once did.

Bicycle rentals are available from the **Gearing Up Bicycle Shop ★,** 129 Paseo del Pueblo Sur (www.gearingupbikes.com; ✆ **575/751-0365**); daily mountain bike rentals start at $65. It's open Monday to Friday from 10am to 6pm, with trail maps available.

Annual touring events include Red River's **Enchanted Circle Century Bike Tour** (✆ **575/754-2366**) on the weekend following Labor Day.

FISHING

The rivers and streams of Taos County are great for fishing, and although you can go out on your own, we recommend going with a guide, who will know where the fish are biting. The family-owned **Taos Fly Shop ★★** (www.taos flyshop.com; ✆ **575/751-1312**), 338 Paseo del Pueblo Sur, has gear, maps, and knowledgeable people to help you; "Super Fly" Taylor Streit, who's been guiding in the area since 1980, runs the guiding side of things. Gear and guides are also available from **Dos Amigos Anglers** ★ (www.dosamigosanglers.net; © **575/758-4545**), 536 Paseo del Pueblo Norte, and **The Solitary Angler** ★ (www.thesolitaryangler.com; © **866/502-1700** or 575/758-5653). Licenses are required and can be purchased at local sporting goods and fly shops.

FITNESS FACILITIES

The **Taos Spa and Tennis Club** ★★, 111 Dona Ana Dr. (across from Sagebrush Inn; www.taosspa.com; © 575/758-1980), is a fully equipped fitness center that rivals any you'd find in a big city. It has a variety of cardiovascular machines, bikes, and weight-training machines, as well as saunas, indoor and outdoor Jacuzzis, a steam room, and indoor and outdoor pools. The club offers a wide range of exercise classes from yoga to Pilates to water fitness. In addition, it has tennis and racquetball courts. Therapeutic massage, facials, and physical therapy are available daily by appointment. Children's programs include a tennis camp and swimming lessons, and child care services are available some evenings. The spa is open Monday to Thursday 5am to 9pm, Friday 5am to 8pm, and Saturday and Sunday 7am to 8pm. The daily rate is $12, but short term memberships and multiple-day passes are available.

The **Northside Health and Fitness Center** ★, on the north side of town at 1307 Paseo del Pueblo Norte (© **575/751-1242**), is also a full-service facility, with free weights, and Cybex and cardiovascular equipment. It offers aerobics and yoga classes, indoor and outdoor pools, and four tennis courts, as well as children's and seniors' programs. The center is open weekdays 5am to 9pm and weekends 8am to 8pm. The daily rate is $12.

Also of note, with classes daily, is **Taos Pilates Studio** ★, 1103 Paseo del Pueblo Norte (www.taospilates.net; © **575/758-7604**).

GOLF

Golfers love the 18-hole course at the **Taos Country Club** ★, 54 Golf Course Dr., Ranchos de Taos (www.taoscountryclub.com; © **575/758-7300**), with its Jep Wille–designed course and four sets of tees. The rolling greens are edged and surrounded by a sea of sagebrush against a stunning backdrop of the Sangre de Cristo Mountains. Located off NM 68 and CR 110, just 6 miles south of Taos Plaza, it's a first-rate championship golf course designed for all levels of play. It has open fairways and no hidden greens, a driving range, practice putting and chipping greens, and instruction by PGA professionals. The country club also has a clubhouse with a restaurant and full bar. It's always advisable to call ahead, or book online, for tee times. Greens fees start at $65 in summer, and $43 spring and fall; cart and club rentals are available. Closed December to early May.

The par-72, 18-hole course at the **Angel Fire Resort Golf Course** ★ (www.angelfireresort.com; © **800/633-7463** or 575/377-3055) is surrounded by stands of ponderosa pine, spruce, and aspen. At 8,500 feet, it's one of the highest regulation golf courses in the world. It has a driving range, putting green, carts and clubs for rent, and a club pro who can give lessons. Greens fees start at $89 in summer, $65 spring and fall; tee times should be scheduled 7 days ahead.

HIKING

There are hundreds of miles of hiking trails in Taos County's mountain and high-mesa country. The trails are especially well traveled in the summer and fall, although nights turn chilly by September, and mountain weather is always changeable. Remember to take plenty of water and sunscreen, and wear stout hiking shoes and a hat. A snack is always advisable. For maps and advice on all **Carson National Forest** trails and recreation areas, look online (www.fs.fed.us/r3/carson) or visit the **U.S. Forest Service** office in Taos. Gear and advice are available from **Taos Mountain Outfitters,** 113 N. Plaza (www.taosmountainoutfitters.com; ✆ **575/758-9292**).

One of the easiest hikes to access is the **West Rim Trail ★,** which follows the rim of the Rio Grande Gorge. Drive west from Taos on US 64, crossing the Rio Grande Gorge Bridge, and turn left into the picnic area. Walking a short distance south along this trail affords a spectacular view of the full span of the bridge. The full trail is 9 miles long, but you can go however far as you like, remembering you have to hike the same distance back to your car!

The 19,663-acre **Wheeler Peak Wilderness ★★★** is a wonderland of alpine tundra, encompassing New Mexico's highest peak (13,161 ft.). A favorite (though rigorous) hike to Wheeler Peak's summit (15 miles round-trip with a 3,700-ft. elevation gain) makes for a long but exciting day. The trail head is at Taos Ski Valley (p. 152).

In Hondo Canyon, the popular **Italianos Canyon ★★** trail can get quite crowded on summer weekends. You'll walk among mixed conifers along its 3.5 miles; it gains 2,800 feet in elevation and affords access to Lobo Peak, Flag Mountain, and Gold Hill. The trail head is on the north side of NM 150, about 3 miles southwest of Taos Ski Valley and 8 miles from Arroyo Seco. Nearby **Yerba Canyon Trail ★,** just 2 miles west of Italianos along NM 150, boasts an abundance of aspen and willows along its southern stretch, gradually giving way to spruce and fir as you approach the ridge. It's 4 miles long, with an elevation gain of 3,700 feet. Both of these trails follow a drainage path, which means avalanches are a possibility in winter and early spring. Both trails are open to horseback riding and back-country camping also.

HORSEBACK RIDING

The expansive sage mesas and tree-covered mountains around Taos make it a fun and exciting place to ride. **A.A. Taos Ski Valley Wilderness Adventures ★** (www.aataosskivalleyadventures.com; ✆ **575/751-6051**) offers a variety of guided rides along the mountain trails of the ski valley. There's something for everyone regardless of ability or experience. A 3-hour adventure (2 hours of actual riding) starts at $65 per person; overnight rides start at $145.

Horseback riding is also offered in summer by **Rio Grande Stables** (www. lajitasstables.com; ✆ **575/776-5913**). Rides last from 1 hour to all day, exploring forested trails and open mesas. The 2-hour sunset ride is breathtaking. Prices start around $90 per person, and longer rides include food.

HUNTING

Hunters in **Carson National Forest** bag deer, turkey, grouse, band-tailed pigeons, and elk by special permit. Hunting seasons vary year to year, so it's important to inquire ahead with the New Mexico **Game and Fish Department** in Santa Fe (www.wildlife.state.nm.us; ℰ **505/476-8000**).

ICE SKATING

In winter there's ice skating at the **Taos Youth and Family Center ★★**, 407 Paseo del Cañon, 2 miles south of the plaza and about ¾ mile off Paseo del Pueblo Sur (www.taosyouth.com; ℰ **505/758-4160**). Cost is $3 for adults and $2 for children, which includes skate rentals. Hours are Monday through Friday from 10am to 5pm, Saturdays from 2 to 5pm, and Sundays from 1 to 4pm, although weekend hours may be shortened during hockey season.

JOGGING

The paved paths and grass of **Kit Carson Park** (p. 149) provide a quiet place to stretch your legs.

LLAMA TREKKING

For a taste of the unusual, you might want to try letting a llama carry your gear and food while you walk and explore, free of any heavy burdens. They're friendly, gentle animals that have keen senses of sight and smell. Often, other animals such as elk, deer, and mountain sheep are attracted to the scent of the llamas and will venture closer to hikers if the llamas are present. **Wild Earth Llama Adventures ★★** (www.llamaadventures.com; ℰ **800/758-5262** or 575/586-0174) offers a "Take a Llama to Lunch" day hike—a full day of hiking into the Sangre de Cristo Mountains, complete with a gourmet lunch, for $115. Wild Earth also offers a variety of custom multiday wilderness adventures tailored to trekkers' needs and fitness levels, starting at $425 per person for 2 days. Children 11 and under receive discounts. Camping gear and food are provided. On the trips, experienced guides provide information about native plants and local wildlife, as well as natural and regional history of the area.

RIVER RAFTING

Half- or full-day white-water rafting trips down the Rio Grande and Rio Chama originate in Taos and can be booked through a variety of outfitters in the area. The wild and wonderful **Taos Box ★★★**, a steep-sided canyon south of the Wild Rivers Recreation Area, offers a series of class IV rapids that rarely let up for some 17 miles. The water drops up to 90 feet per mile, providing one of the most exciting 1-day white-water tours in the West. May and June, when the water is rising, is a good time to go. Experience is not required, but you will be required to wear a life jacket (provided), and you should expect to get wet.

Several experienced rafting companies in Taos are **Cottam's Rio Grande Rafting** (www.cottamsriograndrafting.com; ℰ **800/322-8267** or 575/758-2822), **Los Rios River Runners** (www.losriosriverrunners.com; ℰ **800/544-1181** or 575/776-8854), and **Far Flung Adventures** (www.farflung.com; ℰ **800/359-2627** or 575/758-2628). Note that only experienced river runners should attempt these waters without a guide. Check with the **Bureau of Land**

GETTING PAMPERED: the spa scene

For a luxurious pampering, head to **Ojo Caliente Mineral Springs Resort and Spa ★★★** (ojospa.com; ✆ **800/222-9162** or 505/583-2045), about 45 minutes southwest of Taos in the village of Ojo Caliente. You'll find 11 sulfur-free mineral pools, a seasonal mud pool, and a full-service day spa. There's also a restaurant and wine bar, plus lodging and camping on premises.

In Taos, **El Monte Sagrado ★★** (www.elmontesagrado.com; ✆ **800/828-8267** or 505/758-3502) offers a variety of treatments to its guests (see p. 124). And you can get a massage at **Spirits of Beauty ★★** (www.spiritsofbeauty.com; ✆ **575/758-1158**) and **Taos Spa and Tennis Club ★** (see "Fitness Facilities," p. 155).

Management (www.blm.gov/nm; ✆ **575/758-8851**) to make sure that you're fully equipped to go white-water rafting. Have them check your gear to make sure that it's sturdy enough—this is serious rafting and kayaking!

ROCK CLIMBING

Mountain Skills (www.climbingschoolusa.com; ✆ **575/776-2222**) offers rock-climbing instruction for all skill levels, from beginners to more advanced climbers, who would like to find the best area climbs.

SKATEBOARDING

Try your board at **Taos Youth and Family Center** (see "Ice Skating," p. 157), which includes an in-line-skate and skateboarding park, open when there's no snow or ice. Admission is free.

SNOWMOBILING

Traversing the hiking and horseback trails of the ski valley on a snowmobile makes for some of the best rides anywhere. Big Al of **A.A. Taos Ski Valley Wilderness Adventures** (www.aataosskivalleyadventures.com; ✆ **575/751-6051**) knows these trails inside and out, and he'll take you on the ride of your life. It doesn't matter if you've never been on one of these machines before. Big Al prides himself on providing personal service to ensure that you'll enjoy every minute. Rides start at $74 for 2 hours. Call to reserve.

SWIMMING

The Town of Taos **Youth and Family Center** (see "Ice Skating," p. 157) includes the **Taos Aquatic Center** (✆ **575/737-2583**), which has an excellent pool and slide. Swim sessions cost $3 adults and $2 children, and times are set aside for recreational swimming, lap swimming, water aerobics, and toddler swim times. Check the website for the current schedule.

TENNIS

The **Taos Spa and Tennis Club** has four courts, and the **Northside Health and Fitness Center** has three tennis courts (see both under "Fitness Facilities," p. 155). In addition, there are four free public courts in Taos—two at **Kit**

Carson Park, on Paseo del Pueblo Norte, and two at **Fred Baca Memorial Park,** on Camino del Medio, south of Ranchitos Rd.

TAOS SHOPPING

For those who love to shop, Taos offers countless choices. The place to start is **Taos Plaza,** with shops all around, plus a restaurant or two and even the La Fonda Hotel (p. 126). After perusing what the plaza has to offer, head east on **Kit Carson Road,** then north on Paseo del Pueblo several blocks, taking a side trip down **Bent Street**—so named not because of the sharp bend about two-thirds of the way down, but rather because the first governor of the territory lived here (see p. 148).

Once you've finished with downtown Taos, head south to **Ranchos de Taos** and the shops and galleries on the plaza behind San Francisco de Asis Church. Finish up with a visit to the charming village of **Arroyo Seco,** about 5 miles north of Taos along NM 150. While you're there, stop by the lovely 1834 church, La Santísima Trinidad, tucked away a short walk off the highway.

Galleries and shops are generally open daily in summer and closed Sundays or one day mid-week in winter. Hours vary but generally run from 10am to 5 or 6pm. Some artists show their work by appointment only.

Art

Act I Gallery ★   This gallery has a diverse selection of works in a variety of media and subject matter. You'll find watercolors, *retablos,* furniture, paintings, Hispanic folk art, pottery, glass art, jewelry, and sculpture. 218 Paseo del Pueblo Norte. www.actonegallery.com. ✆ **877/228-1278** or 575/758-7831.

Envision Gallery ★   Offering contemporary art with an elaborate sculpture garden, this is a fun place to browse for works on paper or of clay. Lyman Whitaker's wind sculptures catch the eye of everyone driving by on US 64. 1405 Paseo del Pueblo Norte (in the Overland Sheepskin Complex), El Prado. www.envisiongallery.net. ✆ **505/751-1344.**

Michael McCormick Gallery ★★   Nationally renowned artists dynamically play with southwestern themes in the works at this gallery, steps from the plaza. Especially notable are the bright portraits by Miguel Martinez. 106C Paseo del Pueblo Norte. www.mccormickgallery.com. ✆ **800/279-0879** or 575/758-1372.

Mission Gallery ★★★   Since its opening in 1962, Rena Rosequist has built the gallery's reputation by identifying and displaying quality works of art by painters and sculptors who lived and worked in Taos. Much of the works she has shown were by Taos Modernists such as Emil Bisttram, Andrew Dasburg, and Earl Stroh. The gallery is located in the former home of Taos Society of Artists co-founder Joseph Henry Sharp. 138 Kit Carson Rd. ✆ **575/758-2861.**

Navajo Gallery ★★★   This historic centuries-old adobe was once R. C. Gorman's home/studio/gallery. Today it showcases the artist's widely varied

sipping WHILE SHOPPING

While wandering the shops in the plaza area, be sure to stop in at **La Chiripada Winery & Vineyards** ★, 103 Bent St. (www.lachiripada.com; ✆ 575/751-1311). The tasting room offers a variety of samples that may include a rich pinot noir or chardonnay. The wine is made in Dixon, south of Taos, and offers a taste of the 400-year-old wine-making tradition in the region. While tasting, check out the ceramics and paintings made by the vintners themselves. La Chiripada also has a tasting room at the vineyard in Dixon (NM 75, 2.5 miles from NM 68) itself well worth a visit.

work: acrylics, lithographs, silk screens, giclees, bronzes, tapestries, hand-cast ceramic vases, etched glass, and more. 210 Ledoux St. and 104 S. Plaza. www.rcgormangallery.com. ✆ **575/758-3250.**

Nichols Taos Fine Art Gallery ★ Here you will find traditional works in all media, including Western and cowboy art. 403 Paseo del Pueblo Norte. ✆ **575/758-2475.**

R. B. Ravens ★★ Looking for old Navajo rugs and pottery? You'll find those and a variety of other fine crafts and works of art at this longtime gallery, located in an old home with raw pine floors and hand-sculpted adobe walls in Ranchos de Taos Plaza. 4146 NM 68 (across from St. Francis Church Plaza), Ranchos de Taos. www.rbravens.com. ✆ **575/758-7322.**

Robert L. Parsons Fine Art ★★★ Located in the 1859 Ferdinand Maxwell home, this gallery displays works of the early Taos and Santa Fe artists, including Nicolai Fechin, Joseph Sharp, and O. E. Berninghaus. Fine Pueblo pottery and antique Navajo blankets dress the space as well. 131 Bent St. www.parsonsart.com. ✆ **575/751-0159.**

Books

Brodsky Bookshop ★ Come here for the exceptional inventory of fiction, nonfiction, southwestern and American Indian studies, children's books, used books, cards, tapes, and CDs. 226A Paseo del Pueblo Norte. www.facebook.com/brodsky-bookshop. ✆ **575/758-9468.**

Children

Twirl ★★ This is an adventure as well as a terrific place to shop. A play structure, hobbit home, and fountain entertain kids while those of all ages hunt for musical instruments, toys, and clothing. 225 Camino de la Placita. www.twirlhouse.com. ✆ **575/751-1402.**

Crafts

Taos Blue ★ You can't miss this gallery at the corner of Bent Street, with its colorful metal flower sculptures in the front yard and string of huge canister bells hanging from the portal. Inside you'll find fine American Indian and contemporary handcrafts, plus cards and wearables, jewelry, and fetishes. 101A Bent St. www.taosblue.com. ℭ **575/758-3561.**

Weaving Southwest ★★ In addition to contemporary tapestries by New Mexico artists, one-of-a-kind rugs, blankets, and pillows, you can purchase lovely hand-dyed yarns for your own projects here. 487 NM 150, Arroyo Seco. www.weavingsouthwest.com. ℭ **575/758-0433.**

Fashion

Artemisia ★ Advertising "Happy clothers for artful souls," this shop delivers, with wearable art in bold colors, all hand-woven or hand-sewn, all for women. 115 Bent St. www.artemisiataos.com. ℭ **575/737-9800.**

Mariposa Boutique ★★ Color and quality are the bywords here, with a bit of southwestern charm thrown in for style. Clothing and accessories for both girls and women. 120F Bent St. in the John Dunn Shops. www.johndunnshops. com. ℭ **575/758-9028.**

Overland Sheepskin Company ★ You can't miss the romantically weathered barn just off the highway in a meadow a few miles north of town. Inside, you'll find anything you can imagine in leather: coats, gloves, hats, and slippers. The coats here are exquisite, from oversize ranch styles to tailored blazers in a variety of leathers from sheepskin to buffalo hide, plus elegant Italian calfskin. NM 522. www.overland.com. ℭ **575/758-8820.**

Furniture & Home

At Home in Taos ★ If you're looking to brighten your abode, head to this brilliant shop in McCarthy Plaza just off a corner of the main plaza. You'll find colorful, handmade placemats and bowls as well as bags made from recycled materials. Plus cards and pottery, and even some lovely little earrings made by the daughter of the owner. 117 S. Plaza. www.facebook.com/athomeintaos. ℭ **575/751-1486.**

Country Furnishings of Taos ★★ Here, you'll find unique hand-painted folk-art furniture. The pieces are as individual as the styles of the local folk artists who make them. There are also home accessories, unusual gifts, clothing, and jewelry. 534 Paseo del Pueblo Norte. www.cftaos.com. ℭ **575/758-4633.**

Nambé ★ This company made a name for itself producing serving platters, picture frames, and candlesticks from a metal alloy. Over the years, Nambé has expanded into production of crystal and wood designs, all lovely for the home. 109 N. Plaza. www.nambe.com. ℭ **575/758-8221.**

Gifts & Souvenirs

Arroyo Seco Mercantile ★ This funky building is chock-full of cowboy hats, antiques, and country home items. 488 NM 150, Arroyo Seco. www. secomerc.com. ℭ **575/776-8806.**

Chimayo Trading del Norte ★ Specializing in Navajo weavings, pueblo pottery, and early Taos artists, this is a fun spot to peruse on the

Ranchos Plaza. There's also jewelry, sculptures, and baskets. 1 St. Francis Church Plaza, Ranchos de Taos. www.chimayotrading.com. ℂ **575/758-0504.**

El Rincón Trading Post ★   This century-old shop has a real trading-post feel. It's a wonderful place to find turquoise jewelry, whether you're looking for contemporary or antique. In the back of the store is a museum full of American Indian and Western artifacts. 114 Kit Carson Rd. ℂ **575/758-9188.**

Taos Gems and Minerals ★★   Locally owned and operated for several decades, this intriguing shop offers a huge assortment of stones, polished and not, in all shapes and sizes. There's jewelry, carvings, and lovely polished bowls with fossils, plus unique wooden vessels. Don't rush your visit here. The well-informed staff is pleased to answer your questions and help you find the perfect piece to take home. 637 Paseo del Pueblo Sur. www.facebook.com/taosgemsminerals. ℂ **575/758-3910.**

Taos Rockers ★   Wander among the myriad minerals and fossils, gems and jewelry in this fascinating shop. Additionally, there are healing stones and crystals, rough and polished geodes, mineral lamps and candleholders. Something for everyone. 229 Camino de la Placita. www.taosrockers.com. ℂ **575/758-2326.**

Touchstone Mineral & Fossil Gallery ★   This fine showroom, one of four in the Touchstone chain, offers an adventure into an ancient world of stunning geodes and fossils, both decorative and functional. Look for jewelry and fetishes here as well. 110 S. Plaza. www.touchstonegalleries.com. ℂ **575/737-5001.**

Two Graces Gallery ★★   For a wide range of old and new, don't miss this place on the Ranchos Plaza. In this 250-year-old building, you'll find art, southwestern pottery, Indian kachinas, curios, jewelry, and books—mostly used but a few new—on Taos or the Southwest. 68 St. Francis Church Plaza, Ranchos de Taos. www.twograces.com. ℂ **575/758-4101.**

Jewelry

Artwares Contemporary Jewelry ★★   The gallery owners here call their contemporary jewelry "a departure from the traditional." True to this slogan, each piece here offers classic and unusual settings of sterling silver or gold, often combined with precious or semiprecious stones. Many present a new twist on traditional southwestern and American Indian designs. 129 N. Plaza. www.artwaresjewelry.com. ℂ **800/527-8850** or 575/758-8850.

Claireworks ★★★   Claire Haye has been designing her unique jewelry for several decades. She began her career as a ceramic sculptor, and her jewelry reflects this background in that each piece is a tiny sculpture or made up of a series of same. She offers her pieces in silver, bronze, or gold, accented with gemstones. Claire also creates marvelous bronze or painted steel sculptures for the home, plus ceramic murals. You can see a sampling outside the front of the shop. 482A NM 150, Arroyo Seco. www.claireworks.com. ℂ **888/219-6060** or 575/776-5175.

Musical Instruments

Taos Drum Company ★ Taos Drums has one of the largest selections of American Indian log and hand drums in the world. In addition to drums, the showroom displays log tables, lamps, and more than 60 styles of rawhide lampshades. As you drive south from town, watch for the tepees and drums on your right. 3956 NM 68, about 5 miles south of Taos Plaza. www.taosdrums.com. *©* **800/424-3786** or 575/758-3796.

Pottery & Tiles

Rottenstone Pottery ★ This small shop displays lovely ceramic mugs, plates, bowls, and other vessels, plus unique ceramic art. 486 NM 150, Arroyo Seco. www.rottenstonepottery.com. *©* **575/776-1042.**

Stephen Kilborn Pottery ★★ Visiting this shop in town is a treat, with the kitschy and unusual execution of the more often perceived as mundane designs on the plates, bowls, mugs, and tiles you'll find here. 136A Paseo del Pueblo Norte. www.stephenkilborn.com. *©* **575/750-5760.**

TAOS AFTER DARK

For a small town, Taos has its share of top entertainment. The resort atmosphere and the arts community attract performers, and the city enjoys annual programs in music and literary arts.

Many events are scheduled by the **Taos Center for the Arts (TCA),** 133 Paseo del Pueblo Norte (www.tcataos.org; *©* **575/758-2052**), at the Taos Community Auditorium. The TCA imports local, regional, and national performers in theater, dance, and concerts, and also hosts local performances in theater and music.

You can obtain information on current events in the *Taos News* (www.taosnews.com; *©* **575/758-2241**), published every Thursday. The **Taos County Chamber of Commerce** (www.taoschamber.com; *©* **575/751-8800**) is also a good resource, as is the **Taos Visitors Center** (www.taos.org; *©* **800/732-8267** or 575/758-3873).

The Performing Arts

Music from Angel Fire ★★ If you enjoy chamber music, be sure to attend one of the recitals presented by the Music from Angel Fire program. World-renowned performers appear in a short season that runs from mid-August to Labor Day. Based in the small resort town of Angel Fire (about 21 miles east of Taos, off US 64), the concert series also stages events in surrounding communities, including Taos. Angel Fire. www.musicfromangelfire.org. *©* **888/377-3300** or 575/377-3233.

Taos School of Music ★★★ If you're in Taos during the summer, you owe it to yourself to catch a performance by Taos School of Music. The school, located at Hotel St. Bernard in Taos Ski Valley, attracts the best and brightest young musicians every year, and takes them to the next level. The school runs from mid-June to mid-August, with students of violin, viola, cello, and piano working on chamber music pieces by both the known masters, such as Mozart and Bach, and contemporary chamber music composers. The 8-week **Chamber Music Festival,** an important adjunct of the school, offers 16 concerts and seminars for the public; performances are given by pianist Robert McDonald and ensembles including the Borromeo, St. Lawrence, and Brentano string quartets, plus the students themselves, all of whom are already playing at a professional level when they arrive at the school. Performances are held at the Taos Community Auditorium and the Hotel St. Bernard. www.taosschoolofmusic.com. ✆ **575/776-2388.**

The Club & Music Scene

Adobe Bar ★★   Nightly live music, with no cover charge, and some of the best margaritas in Taos draw folks to the small bar at the Taos Inn, across the lobby from the restaurant, Doc Martin's (p. 135). Music ranges from folk to jazz to bluegrass and beyond. The place is often packed, so get there early to grab some food and a drink and claim a place to sit. The Taos Inn, 125 Paseo del Pueblo Norte. www.taosinn.com/adobe_bar.html. ✆ **575/758-2233.**

Alley Cantina ★   One of Taos' old standby nightspots, the Alley Cantina has gone through various owners and names through the years, but it hasn't changed much. Parts of the building date back some 400 years, and of course there's the resident ghost—Teresina Bent, the daughter of the 19th-century territorial governor who was murdered less than a block away. There's an old saloon feel to the place, live music of some sort most nights, and good drinks and burgers. What more can you ask for? 121 Teresina Ln. www.alleycantina.com. ✆ **575/758-2121.**

Anaconda Bar ★★   The fanciest bar in Taos, the lounge at El Monte Sagrado is definitely **not** the spot for foot-stompin' beer drinkers to hang out, but it is a good place for a quiet drink and to pretend you're rich. There's a giant metallic snake sculpture high above and a huge saltwater aquarium. There is even live local music occasionally, very dignified, of course. The El Monte Sagrado Hotel, 317 Kit Carson Rd. www.elmontesagrado.com/dining/lounge/. ✆ **575/758-3502.**

KTAOS Solar Restaurant & Bar ★★   Look for the solar panels at the start of the road to Taos Ski Valley to find this family-friendly bar, which is flanked by two operating radio stations. Watch the DJs at work and, if it's nice out, send the kids to play on the grassy knoll outside, pre-stocked with toys. The tacos are great, especially the Baja fish and pork habanero, and there's usually live music happening indoors or out. If the staff isn't too busy, they just might give you a tour of the solar-powered stations. 9 State Rd. 150. www.ktaos.com/StationBar. ✆ **575/758-5826** ext. 206. Sun–Thurs 4–9pm, Fri–Sat 4–11pm.

Sagebrush Grill & Cantina ★★   For years one of the most popular bars in Taos, this is where locals go Friday and Saturday nights to practice their two-steppin' in a genuine Old West setting, complete with a rustic wooden dance floor. 1508 Paseo del Pueblo Sur. www.sagebrushinn.com. ✆ **575/758-2254.**

Taos Mesa Brewing ★★   That hangar-like building near the tiny airport north of Taos isn't for planes—it's actually a microbrewery, restaurant, and live-music venue with both indoor and outdoor stages. The building itself was inspired by the eco-friendly construction techniques used in the off-the-grid "earthships," half-buried and built from dirt-filled tires, just across the Rio Grande Gorge Bridge to the west. The dozen or so handcrafted beers on tap are good enough to distract you from the mountain-view sunsets and, even better, they're super-cheap at happy hour. There's live music most nights, often free, but sometimes there's a cover charge of $5 to $7 (higher for the occasional big-name group). 20 ABC Mesa Rd. www.taosmesabrewing.com. ℂ **575/758-1900.**

EXCURSIONS FROM TAOS

The Enchanted Circle ★★

This just might be the perfect driving tour. The 84-mile Enchanted Circle loop winds through some of northern New Mexico's most spectacular mountain scenery—including views of 13,161-foot Wheeler Peak, the state's highest point—with stops at towns rich in history and culture, such as the old Hispanic villages of Arroyo Hondo and Questa and the Wild West mining town of Red River. You'll roll through a pass that the Apaches, Kiowas, and Comanches once used to cross the mountains to trade with the Taos Pueblo people; travel along the base of some of New Mexico's tallest peaks; then skim the shores of a high mountain lake at Eagle Nest before heading back to Taos along the meandering Rio Fernando de Taos. Although you can drive the entire loop in 2 hours, most folks prefer to take 5 or 6 hours, stopping in Red River or Eagle Nest for lunch.

Traveling north from Taos via NM 522, it's a 9-mile drive to **Arroyo Hondo,** the remains of an 1815 land grant along the Rio Hondo. Along the dirt roads that lead off NM 522, you may find a windowless *morada* or two, marked by plain crosses in front—places of worship for the still-active Penitentes, a somewhat secretive religious order known for self-flagellation. In the 1960s, Arroyo Hondo was also the site of the New Buffalo hippie commune. Over the years, the commune's members have dispersed throughout northern New Mexico, bringing an interesting creative element to the food, architecture, and philosophy of the state. This is also the turnoff point for trips to the Rio Grande Box, an awesome 1-day, 17-mile white-water run for which you can book raft and kayak trips.

En route north, the highway passes near **San Cristobal,** where a side road turns off to the **D. H. Lawrence Ranch** (p. 147) and **Lama,** former home of another 1960s commune.

Next, NM 522 passes through **Questa,** most of whose residents are former employees of a nearby molybdenum mine that ceased operations in 2014. Mining molybdenum (an ingredient in light bulbs, television tubes, and missile systems) was controversial; several groups complained about the water

Excursions from Taos

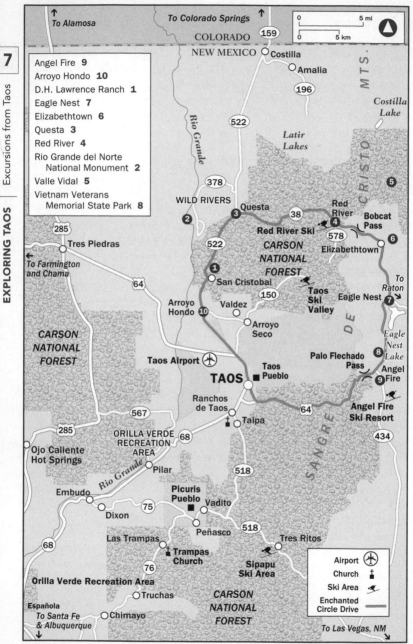

Angel Fire **9**
Arroyo Hondo **10**
D.H. Lawrence Ranch **1**
Eagle Nest **7**
Elizabethtown **6**
Questa **3**
Red River **4**
Rio Grande del Norte
    National Monument **2**
Valle Vidal **5**
Vietnam Veterans
    Memorial State Park **8**

To Alamosa

To Colorado Springs

COLORADO
NEW MEXICO

159

0   5 mi
0   5 km

Costilla

Amalia

196

522

Rio Grande

Latir
Lakes

*Costilla
Lake*

378

WILD RIVERS

Questa

38

Red
River

Bobcat
Pass

522

Red River Ski

578

CARSON
NATIONAL
FOREST

Elizabethtown

285

Tres Piedras

←
*To Farmington
and Chama*

64

San Cristobal

Arroyo
Hondo

Valdez

150

Arroyo
Seco

Taos
Ski
Valley

Eagle Nest

To
Raton

*Eagle
Nest
Lake*

Palo Flechado
Pass

Angel
Fire

**CARSON
NATIONAL
FOREST**

Taos Airport ✈

TAOS

Taos
Pueblo

**Angel Fire
Ski Resort**

Ranchos
de Taos

567

† Talpa

64

434

285

ORILLA VERDE
RECREATION
AREA

68

Ojo Caliente
Hot Springs

Rio Grande

Pilar

518

Embudo

75

**Picuris
Pueblo**

Vadito

Dixon

Peñasco

518

Tres Ritos

68

Las Trampas

† Trampas
Church

Sipapu
Ski Area

76

Orilla Verde Recreation Area

CARSON
NATIONAL
FOREST

Española
*To Santa Fe
& Albuquerque*
↓

Truchas

Chimayo

To Las Vegas, NM

Airport ✈
Church †
Ski Area 🎿
Enchanted
Circle Drive

S A N G R E   D E   C R I S T O   M T S .

pollution it produced. The process raked across hillsides along the Red River, using ground water, and although the mine's owners treated the water it used before returning it to the river, studies showed that it adversely affected the fish life. Now that the mine is closed, a major clean-up is underway, but the scars along the hillsides will be visible for years. About 3 miles north of Questa along NM 522, you can turn west onto NM 378 to reach the **Rio Grande del Norte National Monument** (p. 169). Another 20 miles north of Questa on NM522, the village of **Costilla** is the turnoff point for four-wheel-drive jaunts and hiking trips into **Valle Vidal** (p. 170).

However, to continue the Enchanted Circle loop, turn east at Questa onto NM 38 for a 12-mile climb to **Red River.** This rough-and-ready 1890s gold-mining town has parlayed its Wild West image into a pleasant resort village that's especially popular with families from Texas and Oklahoma. At 8,750 feet, Red River is a center for skiing, snowmobiling, fishing, hiking, off-road driving, horseback riding, mountain biking, river rafting, and other outdoor pursuits. Frontier-style celebrations, honky-tonk entertainment, and even staged shootouts on Main Street are held throughout the year. Though it can be a charming and fun town, Red River's restaurant scene does not compare to what you'll find in Taos, but it's still a good spot for lunch if the clock and your stomach say it's time.

From Red River, it's a beautiful 16-mile drive over the 9,850-foot Bobcat Pass to the village of **Eagle Nest,** especially pretty in fall when the aspen trees turn bright yellow. Nestled in the Moreno Valley on the shore of Eagle Nest Lake, Eagle Nest is another Old West town that tries to capitalize on its heritage. Gold was mined in the area as early as 1866, starting in what is now the ghost town of **Elizabethtown,** about 5 miles north; Eagle Nest itself (pop. just under 300 on a good day) wasn't incorporated until 1976. If you turn onto US 64, you'll pass by Eagle Nest Lake, where the 4-square-mile **Eagle Nest Lake State Park** (www.nmparks.com; ✆ **575/377-1594**) stretches out below the village. Facilities include restrooms, camping (19 sites), a boat ramp and a dock, and a visitor center. The lake is considered one of the top trout producers in the United States and attracts ice fishermen in winter as well as summer

ghosts **OF ELIZABETHTOWN**

Although only a few trodden clues remain, the gold-mining Elizabethtown once boasted 7,000 residents and was the first seat of Colfax County. It was called Virginia City when founded in 1865, but the name was changed to honor Elizabeth Moore, daughter of a leading citizen. What has become known as E-town had plenty of gold-town perks: five stores, two hotels, seven saloons, and three dance halls. By the early 1900s, much of the gold had run out, and in 1903 fire blazed through the town, leveling much of it. Today, visitors can still see the stone walls of a hotel, some foundations, and remnants of a cemetery. It's on the west side of NM 38, about 10 miles east of Red River, just before you get to the Eagle Nest turnoff.

anglers. It's too cold for swimming, but sailboaters and windsurfers ply the waters when it isn't covered in ice. The park is also a good spot for seeing various birds, and there's a 1.2-mile hiking trail.

If you're heading to Cimarron or Denver, proceed east on US 64 from Eagle Nest. But if you're circling back to Taos, continue southwest on NM 38 and US 64. Shortly before the Agua Fría junction, you'll see the **Vietnam Veterans Memorial State Park,** C.R. B-4, Angel Fire (www.nmparks.com; © 575/377-2293). It's a stunning structure with curved white walls soaring high against the backdrop of the Sangre de Cristo Range. Consisting of a chapel and an underground visitor center, it was built by Dr. Victor Westphall in memory of his son, David, a marine lieutenant killed in Vietnam in 1968. The 6,000-square-foot memorial houses exhibits, videos, and memorabilia. It also has a changing gallery of photographs of Vietnam veterans who lost their lives in the Southeast Asian war, but no photo is as poignant as this inscription written by young David Westphall, a promising poet:

> Greed plowed cities desolate.
> Lusts ran snorting through the streets.
> Pride reared up to desecrate
> Shrines, and there were no retreats.
> So man learned to shed the tears
> With which he measures out his years.

If you like the clean efficiency of a resort complex, you may want to plan a night or two at **Angel Fire,** farther south on US 64, some 21 miles east of Taos. Opened in the late 1960s, this resort offers a hotel, condominiums, and cabins. Winter is the biggest season, especially with skiing families. In spring, summer, and fall, **Angel Fire Resort** (p. 151) offers golf, tennis, hiking, mountain biking (you can take your bike up on the quad lift), fly-fishing, river rafting, and horseback riding. There are other fun family activities, such as a video arcade, a miniature golf course, theater performances, and, throughout the year, a variety of festivals, including a hot-air balloon festival, Winterfest, and concerts of both classical and popular music. For more information on the Moreno Valley, including accommodations and restaurant listings, contact the **Angel Fire Chamber of Commerce** (www.angelfirechamber.org; © 800/446-8117 or 575/377-6353).

Returning to US 64, turn left (south) to return to Taos. Soon the road reenters the **Carson National Forest,** and you begin a slow, winding, mountain drive through a forest of firs and pines. The road seems to point straight up to Palo Flechado Pass, at 9,101 feet elevation. Its name is Spanish for "tree pierced with arrows," and in the 18th and 19th centuries, the pass was used by American Indians, Spaniards, and Anglo-Americans traveling from the eastern plains to the trading center of Taos. From here it's all, or at least mostly, downhill, past a number of U.S. Forest Service recreation sites, including some good spots for picnicking, camping, hiking, cross-country skiing, and snowshoeing. Finally, you arrive back in Taos via Kit Carson Road, which delivers you to the historic Taos Plaza.

Rio Grande del Norte National Monument ★★★

Created by Presidential Proclamation in March 2013, this vast Bureau of Land Management property encompasses about 17% of Taos County, or a quarter-million acres, stretching from the New Mexico/Colorado border south to Pilar along the Rio Grande. Here can be found rugged, wide-open plains dotted with sagebrush, a deep chasm carved by the Rio Grande over millennia, and ancient volcanic mounds with piñon and juniper covering the slopes. Ute Mountain climbs to 10,093 feet and the Rio Grande flows 600 to 800 feet below the rim. Rocky Mountain elk, mule deer, pronghorn, and Rocky Mountain bighorn sheep often winter in the monument, and can frequently be seen traversing it. Evidence of ancient man crop up everywhere—petroglyphs, prehistoric dwelling sites, and other archeological finds—and more recent human activity is evidenced by abandoned homesteading from the 1930s. For 21st-century visitors, recreation opportunities abound: hiking, mountain biking, camping, picnicking, hunting, fishing, canoeing, kayaking, river rafting, or soaring aloft in a hot-air balloon.

A good starting place is **Orilla Verde Recreation Area,** near the community of Pilar, 14 miles south of Taos via NM 68 and NM 570, along the banks of the Rio Grande. Views here range from rugged mesas to deep canyons carved by the river. Anglers catch native brown trout, German brown trout, rainbow trout, and northern pike, and there is an easy-to-moderate 1.25-mile (one-way) hiking trail that leads past prehistoric petroglyphs, and also offers wonderful scenic views. You'll find picnic tables, a visitor center with a variety of exhibits, and easy access to a relatively calm section of the Rio Grande, especially inviting to those with small inflatable boats. There are both primitive campsites ($5 per night) and developed campsites ($7 per night for one vehicle, $10 for two), as well as a limited number with RV electric hookups ($15 per night). Drinking water and restrooms are available.

The scenery's more rugged at **Wild Rivers Recreation Area,** which sits on a plateau above the Rio Grande, with trails leading into the gorge. It's north

rock art **IN THE RIVER GORGE**

Modern-day outdoor types weren't the first to explore the dramatic gorges of the **Wild Rivers Recreation Area,** so don't be surprised if you find petroglyphs on its boulders and rock faces. One especially good site is accessed by hiking into the gorge from the Big Arsenic Springs Campground. **Warning:** The hike, which is only a little over a mile each way, is rated moderate to difficult because of the 1,000-foot elevation change—not bad going down, but a little rough coming back up. Look for a big round rock near the river, which stands about 7 feet high: It's covered with a wealth of petroglyphs, including numerous animal images, which are believed to have been created between A.D. 1000 and 1600. It can be difficult to find, so ask for directions at the visitor center before you start the hike.

of Taos, past the community of Questa along NM 522 and then NM 378, which takes you west to the recreation area. The level mesa top provides a point from which you can look down into the awesome canyons where the Rio Grande and Red rivers converge. About two dozen miles of hiking trails traverse the area, including several leading down from the mesa campgrounds to the Rio Grande (the only way to get down to the river). The recreation area also has several mountain-biking trails, and fishing for northern pike and brown and rainbow trout. There are river-view campsites along the canyon rim ($7 per night for one vehicle, $10 for two), with water and toilets but no showers or RV hookups.

A **Rio Grande del Norte National Monument** map is available for download and there is more detailed information on the monument's website, **www.blm.gov/nm/riograndedelnorte.** The monument is open year-round, with day-use hours of 6am to 10pm, and a daily fee of $3 per vehicle for those staying 30 minutes or more.

The Valle Vidal ★

If you want to get away from it all and spend a few days fishing, hiking, and camping, or just take a long but scenic day trip from Taos, this unit of the Carson National Forest may be the place for you. It offers plenty of wide open spaces, sparkling lakes, tall pines, snow-capped peaks, historic sites, and some of the best wildlife viewing in the area.

Valle Vidal covers about 100,000 acres to the north of Red River. Access is via US 64 and the communities of Eagle Nest and Cimarron to the east, and from NM 522 and the towns of Costilla and Amalia to the west. The main route through the unit is Forest Road 1950. For maps and information, contact the **Carson National Forest** (p. 151).

Back in the late 19th century this was a busy place, dotted with pioneer logging and ranching communities, and although it is far from pristine today after years of ranching and logging, the Valle Vidal offers a rugged beauty, with opportunities for all sorts of outdoor adventures, or just a wonderful place to relax. The remains of pioneer ranch houses and railroad beds convey a feeling that this is the genuine Old West.

The scenery is spectacular, but what sets the Valle Vidal apart is the richness and diversity of its wildlife. At last count there were well over a thousand elk and several hundred mule deer, wild turkeys, hawks, bobcats, cougar, beaver, coyotes, and black bear. Abert's squirrels are often seen on the east side, and bald eagles occasionally pass through.

The Valle Vidal also contains one of the largest pure stands of bristlecone pines in the Southwest, a species considered the world's oldest living tree. Located northwest of **Clayton Corral,** about a half-mile off Forest Road 1950, the stand includes what is believed to be the world's largest bristlecone, a healthy 76-footer with a trunk almost 4 feet across.

There are few marked hiking trails in Valle Vidal, but numerous old logging roads lead to pioneer homesteads, railroad buildings, and cemeteries. In fact, of about 350 miles of dirt roads open when Valle Vidal was donated to the Forest Service in 1982, all but 42 miles are now closed to motor vehicles, and available for hiking, mountain biking, and horseback riding. The area's pioneer heritage is especially evident at the imposing **Ring Ranch House,** along Forest Road 1950 in the eastern section of the park. In the 1890s, this two-story log building was headquarters for a 320-acre ranch, and home to Irish immigrant Timothy Ring, his wife Catherine, and seven daughters. An interpretive trail leads about a half-mile from **McCrystal Campground** to the ranch house, with photo exhibits that describe the history of the ranch.

Anglers catch Rio Grande cutthroat trout in the unit's 67 miles of streams, with the best luck usually in Costilla Creek and Middle Ponil Creek, plus the Shuree Ponds, which also contain rainbow trout. All streams are catch and release and other special regulations apply. One of the two Shuree Ponds is open for fishing only by children under 12. Valle Vidal is also a popular hunting destination during the fall elk season.

There are 96 campsites in two shady campgrounds—**Cimarron Campground,** off FR 1910 at 9,400 feet elevation, and **McCrystal Campground,** off FR 1950 at 8,100 feet. Both have grills, picnic tables, vault toilets, and horse corrals, but no showers or RV hookups. Cimarron also has drinking water (McCrystal does not). Camping costs $16 at Cimarron; $12 at McCrystal.

Chama ★★

Sitting at the base of 11,403-foot Brazos Mountain and surrounded by some of the most beautiful mountain scenery in the West, Chama has a wonderful location. At 7,850 feet above sea level, this former mining town of about 1,000 people is one of New Mexico's highest communities, which helps explain why it gets so much snow every winter and the chilly nights that are the rule even in July. The town's main claim to fame today is as a base for year-round outdoor recreation—fishing, hunting, hiking, cross-country skiing, snowshoeing, snowmobiling; you name it—plus, and it's a big plus, the absolutely wonderful narrow-gauge Cumbres & Toltec Scenic Railroad (see below).

Chama is on US 64/84 at its junction with NM 17, about 89 miles from Taos. Much of the 2-to-3-hour drive there is a beautifully scenic route through the mountains of the Carson National Forest. Note that in winter, snow often causes road closures, so check road conditions (see p. 151) before heading out.

In 1880, the Denver and Rio Grande Western Railroad began construction on a rail extension from Alamosa, Colorado, to Durango, Colorado, by way of Chama. The first rail travel began in February 1881, and for the next 30 years, Chama was a wild little place, complete with honest-to-goodness holdups of the payroll train, lots of saloons, and a great influx of both good guys and bad guys. You can get a walking-tour brochure, describing about two dozen points of interest in the Chama railroad yards, from the 1899 depot in Chama.

A registered National Historic Site owned by the states of Colorado and New Mexico, the **Cumbres & Toltec Scenic Railroad** (500 S. Terrace Ave., www.cumbrestoltec.com, ✆ **888/286-2737** or 575/756-2151) steam train runs through some incredible mountain scenery 64 miles between Chama and Antonito, Colorado, passing through forests of pine and aspen, past striking rock formations, and over the magnificent Toltec Gorge of the Rio de los Pinos. At 10,015 feet elevation, it tops Cumbres Pass. Halfway through the trip, at Osier, Colorado, the New Mexico Express from Chama meets the Colorado Limited from Antonito, and they stop to exchange greetings, engines, and passengers. A buffet lunch is served (included with all fares), and from there, passengers either board the Colorado train and continue on to Antonito (later returning to Chama by van) or re-board the New Mexico train to return to Chama. Both trips are nearly full-day events (there are also half-day trips, dinner trips, and other special itineraries). Seating is assigned, in three levels of train cars: basic coach cars with comfortable bench seating, deluxe tourist cars with extra room and individual seating, and parlor cars (open only to those 21 and older), which are top-of-the line, restored historic cars with lounge-style comfort. All three are enclosed, and passengers can walk through the train to the snack car, restrooms, and the gondola car—an open-air car that provides the best cinders-in-your-face views. Special cars with wheelchair lifts are available with a 7-day advance reservation. Tickets costs $99 to $185 for adults and $49 to $79 for children under 12; reservations are highly recommended. The train runs late May to mid-October; trains leave Chama daily at 10am; vans depart for Antonito at 8:30am.

Meanwhile, the woods, streams, and lakes of the **Carson National Forest** offer practically unlimited opportunities for hiking, mountain biking, cross-country skiing, snowshoeing, snowmobiling, camping, fishing, and hunting. Information, including contact information for local outfitters and guides, is available at the **state visitor center in Chama** (northwest corner of the junction of US 64/84 and NM 17, ✆ **575/756-2235**), and at the **Chama Valley Chamber of Commerce** website (www.chamavalley.com). For details on activities in the national forest, contact the Carson's **Canjilon Ranger Station,** located in the community of Canjilon, about 33 miles south of Chama via US 84 and NM 115 (www.fs.usda.gov/carson; ✆ **575/684-2489**).

South of Chama are two lovely state parks with big lakes that offer lots of recreation opportunities. **El Vado Lake State Park** (27 miles south of Chama via US 64/84 and NM12; www.nmparks.com, ✆ **575/588-7247;** day use fee $5 per vehicle) centers on a 3,200-acre lake where you'll see all varieties of boats, from high-powered speedboats to sailboats and even some canoes and small inflatables. Swimming is permitted, although there are no designated swimming areas and water temperatures are somewhat chilly. Anglers catch rainbow and German brown trout, kokanee salmon, and channel catfish. There are also hiking trails and plenty of wildlife viewing. The park's campgrounds

THE lake-to-lake CONNECTION

El Vado Lake and Heron Lake are connected by the 5.5-mile **Rio Chama Trail,** a lovely hiking trail open to foot travel only. It's a great opportunity to view wildlife such as wild turkeys, peregrine falcons, red-tail hawks, Clark's nutcrackers, white-throated swifts, scrub jays, and mountain bluebirds, as well as the occasional elk and mule deer. From its El Vado Lake trail head, the trail follows the Rio Chama to a mesa on the south side of the river, which offers tree-framed views of both El Vado and Heron lakes. The trail then winds down the side of the canyon, through a piñon-juniper forest, and crosses the Rio Chama on a cable footbridge before leading up a steep set of redwood stairs to the Heron Lake trail head. Note that while the trail is relatively flat and easy for the first 5 miles from El Vado Lake, it's moderately strenuous for the last half-mile.

have 80 campsites (19 with electric hookups), restrooms with showers, and an RV dump station; camping fees are $8 to $14 per campsite. *Note:* The park is closed December through March.

Heron Lake State Park (640 NM 95, 20 miles south of Chama via US 64/84 and NM 95; www.nmparks.com; © **575/588-7470;** day use fee $5 per vehicle) has an even bigger lake, tucked away in a mountain forest of ponderosa pines, piñons, and junipers. The lake, which covers 5,900 acres, is roughly 4 miles long and 3 miles wide, a broad expanse that gives sailboats plenty of tacking room. A marina has a dock and slips for rent on a nightly basis, but no boat rentals or supplies, although there are businesses within a few miles of the park that offer canoe, fishing, and pontoon boat rentals, plus groceries and camping and fishing supplies. Swimming is permitted anywhere in the lake. Although there are no established trails, cross-country skiers can ski along some of the lesser-used roads that are not plowed; snowshoers can traipse along the hiking trails, or just head out across the fields and through the woods. There are 250 developed campsites, including 54 with electric hookups; camping fees are $8 to $14 per site. The park has restrooms with showers and an RV dump station.

ALBUQUERQUE ESSENTIALS

As the gateway to northern New Mexico, Albuquerque is often regarded simply as the portal through which most domestic and international visitors pass before traveling on to Santa Fe and Taos. But don't sell this city short. Albuquerque is a comfortable city, easy to explore, with a small-town attitude and relaxed environment. It's also an economical place to visit, with some of the lowest lodging and meal prices in the state. It's a smart idea to spend a day or a week here—or even make Albuquerque your base camp for exploring the region.

From the rocky crest of Sandia Peak at sunset, one can see the lights of this city of more than a half-million people spread out across 16 miles of high desert. As the sun drops beyond the western horizon, it reflects off the Rio Grande, flowing through Albuquerque more than a mile below. This waterway is the bloodline for the area, the feature that made it possible for a city to spring up in this vast desert. Nowadays, however, as the population swells, the farming communities that lined its banks are giving way to subdivisions and shopping centers. With continuing sprawl on the west side of the city, more means for transporting traffic have been built across the river.

The railroad, which set up a major stop here in 1880, prompted much of Albuquerque's initial growth, but that economic explosion was nothing compared with what happened after World War II. When Albuquerque was designated a major national center for military research and production, people from across the nation and around the world came for jobs. And as the city grew, it became a trading center for New Mexico and beyond. Look closely, and you'll see Anglo ranchers, American Indians, and Hispanic villagers stocking up on goods to take back to the New Mexico boot heel or the Texas panhandle.

ORIENTATION

Arriving

BY PLANE　The **Albuquerque International Sunport** (ABQ; www.cabq.gov/airport; © **505/244-7700**) is in the southcentral part of the city, between I-25 on the west and Kirtland Air Force Base

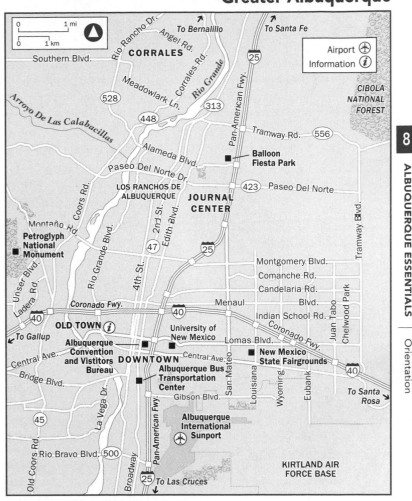

on the east, just south of Gibson Boulevard. Sleek and efficient, the airport is served by most national airlines.

There's an **Albuquerque Visitor Center** desk on the lower level at the bottom of the escalator across from Carousel #4. Information is available 24 hours, and it's staffed daily 9:30am to 8pm, except Saturdays when it closes at 4:30pm.

Once you land at the airport, you'll need to either rent a car or use a shuttle service to get anywhere. Many Albuquerque hotels have courtesy vans to meet their guests. In addition, **Sunport Shuttle** (www.sunportshuttle.com; ✆ **505/883-4966**) runs vans to and from city hotels. Limousine service is available from **American Limousine** (© 505/877-7576) and **Carey Southwest Limousine** (© 505/766-5466).

BY TRAIN   Amtrak's *Southwest Chief* arrives and departs daily to and from Los Angeles and Chicago, stopping once westbound and once eastbound. The station is at the Alvarado Transportation Center, 300 2nd St. SW (at the corner of Lead and Second; www.amtrak.com; © **800/872-7245**). The **New Mexico Rail Runner Express** (www.nmrailrunner.com; © **866/795-7245**) runs trains daily from various points in Albuquerque to various ones in Santa Fe, with connecting buses to the Albuquerque International Sunport and to Taos.

BY BUS   Greyhound (www.greyhound.com; © **800/231-2222** or 505/243-4435) arrives and departs from the Alvarado Transportation Center, 100 1st St. SW.

BY CAR   Albuquerque is intersected by two major interstates, the east-west I-40 and the north-south I-25. I-40 heads 164 miles west to Flagstaff, Arizona, and 284 miles east to Amarillo, Texas; I-25 passes through Santa Fe and goes on north to Denver, Colorado (440 miles), or goes south from Albuquerque to El Paso, Texas (270 miles).

Visitor Information

The main office of the **Albuquerque Convention and Visitors Bureau** is at 20 First Plaza Center NW #601 (www.itsatrip.org; © **800/284-2282** or 505/842-9918). It's open Monday to Friday 8am to 5pm. There are information centers at the airport (see above), and in Old Town at 303 Romero St. NW, Suite 107, open daily, hours vary by season. Tape-recorded information about current local events is available from the bureau after 5pm weekdays and all day Saturday and Sunday (© **800/284-2282**).

City Layout

Albuquerque's sprawl takes a while to get used to. A visitor's first impression is of a grid of arteries lined with shopping malls and fast-food eateries, with residences tucked behind on side streets.

The center point of all this is the crossroads—referred to locally as the "Big I"—of I-25 north-south and I-40 east-west. In the southwest quadrant formed by that intersection, you'll find both **downtown Albuquerque** and **Old Town,** site of many tourist attractions. Lomas Boulevard and Central Avenue, a.k.a. Historic Route 66 (US 66), flank downtown on the north and south. They come together 2 miles west of downtown near **Old Town Plaza,** the historical and spiritual heart of the city. Lomas and Central continue east across I-25, staying about half a mile apart as they pass by the **University of New Mexico** and the **Expo New Mexico** fairgrounds. The airport is directly south of the UNM campus, about 3 miles via Yale Boulevard. Kirtland Air Force Base—site of Sandia National Laboratories—is an equal distance south of the fairgrounds, on Louisiana Boulevard.

A bit north of the Big I, **Menaul Boulevard** runs east-west and is the focus of midtown and uptown shopping, as well as the hotel districts. The other major east-west thoroughfare in the northeast quadrant is **Montgomery Boulevard,** about 1.5 miles north of Menaul. As Albuquerque expands northward, the **Journal Center** business park area, about 3 miles north of Montgomery along the west side of I-25, is expanding. East of Eubank Boulevard lie the **Sandia Foothills,** where the alluvial plain slants a bit more steeply toward the mountains.

When looking for an address, it is helpful to know that Central Avenue divides the city into north and south, and the railroad tracks—which run just east of First Street downtown—comprise the dividing line between east and west. Street names are usually followed by a directional: NE, NW, SE, or SW.

MAPS Comprehensive Albuquerque street maps are available from the Convention and Visitors Bureau (© **800/284-2282** or 505/842-9918), and also from **AAA,** 10501 Montgomery Blvd., NE (www.aaa.com; © **888/716-2492**), if you're a member.

GETTING AROUND

Albuquerque is easy to get around, thanks to its wide thoroughfares and grid layout, combined with its efficient transportation systems.

By Bus

ABQ Ride (www.cabq.gov/transit; © **505/725-3100**) cloaks the arterials with its city bus network. Call for information on routes. Standard bus fares are $1 for adults, 35 cents for students aged 10 through high school and seniors 62 and over, but you can also buy a variety of unlimited-ride bus passes, including a 1-day pass ($2), a 2-day pass ($4), and a 3-day pass ($6), which can be bought directly on any bus.

By Car

Albuquerque is a good place to have a car, in large part because attractions, restaurants, and even lodgings are spread out through the city. Also, it's a fairly easy city to drive in once you get the hang of its peculiarities, as mentioned in "City Layout," above. Traffic can be pretty stiff during rush hour, generally from 7:30 to 9:30am and 4 to 6pm, but isn't bad the rest of the time.

Parking is generally not difficult in Albuquerque. Meters operate weekdays 8am to 6pm and are not monitored at other times. Only the large downtown hotels charge for parking.

[FastFACTS] ALBUQUERQUE

Airport See "Orientation," above.

Car Rentals The following national car rental firms have pickups at the Albuquerque airport: **Alamo** (www.alamo.com; © **505/842-4057**); **Avis** (www.avis.com; © **505/842-4080**); **Budget** (www.budget.com; © **505/247-3443**); and **Hertz** (www.hertz.com; © **505/842-4235**). Close to the airport is **Thrifty,** 2039 Yale Blvd. SE (www.thrifty.com; © **505/842-8733**), with easy shuttle service.

Cellphones Cellphone coverage is good within the city limits but spotty in rural areas. Albuquerque prohibits the use of hand-held cellphones by drivers.

Currency Exchange Foreign currency can be exchanged at **Wells Fargo Bank,** 200 Lomas Blvd. NW; ✆ **505/766-6415.**

Doctors For a medical emergency, dial ✆ **911.** There are a number of walk-in urgent care centers in Albuquerque, including **NextCare Urgent Care,** 5504 Menaul Blvd. NE (www.nextcare.com; ✆ **505/ 348-2868**), open Monday through Friday 8am to 8pm and Saturdays and Sundays from 9am to 4pm. To find a doctor, check with the **Greater Albuquerque Medical Association** (www. gamamed.org; ✆ **505/821-4583**), which has an online "Find a Doc" feature.

Emergencies For police, fire, or ambulance, dial ✆ **911.**

Hotlines The following hotlines are available in Albuquerque: rape crisis (✆ **505/266-7711**), poison control (✆ **800/222-1222**), and suicide (✆ **505/247-1121**).

Internet Access Free high-speed Internet access is available at all branches of the **Albuquerque/Bernalillo County Public Library** (see below).

Library There are 18 branches of the **Albuquerque/Bernalillo County Public Library,** including the main branch at 501 Copper Ave. NW, between Fifth and Sixth streets (✆ **505/768-5140**). You can find the locations of other library branches at **www. abclibrary.org**.

Liquor Laws The legal drinking age is 21 throughout New Mexico. Bars may remain open until 2am Monday to Saturday and until midnight on Sunday. Wine, beer, and spirits are sold at licensed supermarkets and liquor stores.

Lost Property Contact the city police at ✆ **505/ 768-2229.**

Newspapers The daily newspaper is the **Albuquerque Journal** (www.abqjournal.com; ✆ **505/823-4400**). You can pick up the **Alibi** (www.alibi. com; ✆ **505/346-0660**), Albuquerque's alternative weekly, for free at newsstands all over town. It offers entertainment listings and alternative views on a variety of subjects.

Police For emergencies, call ✆ **911.** For other business, contact the **Albuquerque City Police** (✆ **505/ 242-2677** or the **New Mexico State Police** (✆ **505/ 841-9256**).

Post Offices The main Albuquerque U.S. Post Office is at 1135 Broadway Blvd. NE (✆ **505/346-8051**). To find additional post office locations, see www.usps.com or dial ✆ **800/275-8777.**

Taxis You won't find cabs to be hailed on the street here, but **Yellow Cab** (✆ **505/247-8888**) serves the city and surrounding area 24 hours a day. **Uber** (www.uber.com) also operates its ride-share business here.

WHERE TO STAY IN ALBUQUERQUE

Finding a place to sleep in Albuquerque usually isn't difficult. There are plenty of hotels and motels, and you'll find that most are far less pricey than those in Santa Fe or even Taos. The only downside to the Albuquerque lodging scene is that, with a few exceptions, it's really boring. There are numerous chain motels, all pretty much the same as you would find in any other area. Sure, they'll put a few local prints on the walls and use deep red and brown colors for bedspreads and drapes so they can say the rooms have southwestern decor, but that's about it. We suggest that unless you want to stay in one of the high-end properties or a neat bed and breakfast, you stick with a reputable chain.

Albuquerque Accommodations

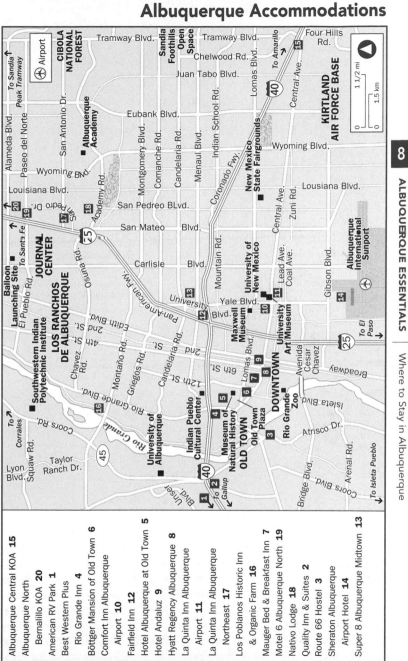

Albuquerque Central KOA **15**
Albuquerque North
   Bernalillo KOA **20**
American RV Park **1**
Best Western Plus
   Rio Grande Inn **4**
Böttger Mansion of Old Town **6**
Comfort Inn Albuquerque
   Airport **10**
Fairfield Inn **12**
Hotel Albuquerque at Old Town **5**
Hotel Andaluz **9**
Hyatt Regency Albuquerque **8**
La Quinta Inn Albuquerque
   Airport **11**
La Quinta Inn Albuquerque
   Northeast **17**
Los Poblanos Historic Inn
   & Organic Farm **16**
Mauger Bed & Breakfast Inn **7**
Motel 6 Albuquerque North **19**
Nativo Lodge **18**
Quality Inn & Suites **2**
Route 66 Hostel **3**
Sheraton Albuquerque
   Airport Hotel **14**
Super 8 Albuquerque Midtown **13**

chain hotels in ALBUQUERQUE

You don't need us to describe the dozens of chain motels—you've probably seen them before—but we can give you some of the locations, contact information, and current rates. All of these properties offer free Wi-Fi. The rate ranges quoted here do not include the special event times mentioned above.

We're fans of the **La Quinta** chain (www.lq.com; © **800/753-3757**), in part because La Quintas generally accept pets with no extra charge, and also because we've found these facilities to be clean, generally well-maintained, and a good value. Albuquerque has five La Quintas, with rates usually from $62 to $79 double. We suggest the **La Quinta Inn Albuquerque Airport ★★**, 2116 Yale Blvd. SE (© **505/243-5500**), and the **La Quinta Inn Albuquerque Northeast ★**, 5241 San Antonio Dr. NE (© **505/821-9000**).

Choice Hotels (www.choicehotels.com; © **877/424-6423**) includes quite an array of motel brands, including EconoLodge, Comfort Inn, Quality Inn, Sleep Inn, and Rodeway Inn. Choice has 18 properties in Albuquerque, with rates mostly between $40 and $70 per night. We recommend the **Comfort Inn Albuquerque Airport ★★,** 1801 Yale Blvd. SE (© **505/242-0036**), and the **Quality Inn & Suites ★**, 6100 West Iliff Rd. (© **505/836-8600**).

Other popular chains include **Super 8** (www.super8.com; © **800/454-3213**), with four motels in Albuquerque, including the **Super 8 Albuquerque Midtown ★**, 2500 University Blvd. NE (© **505/888-4884**), with rates from $43 to $58 double. **Motel 6** (www.motel6.com; © **800/899-9841**) has eight motels in Albuquerque. One of its nicest is the **Motel 6 Albuquerque North ★**, 8510 Pan American Freeway NE (© **505/821-1472**), with rates from $46 to $55 double.

While Albuquerque lodging is usually a very good value, beware of special events—specifically, the New Mexico Arts and Crafts Fair (late June), the New Mexico State Fair (September), and especially the Albuquerque International Balloon Fiesta (early October). At these times lodging will not only be hard to find, but rates will be higher, sometimes double. The solution? If you want to participate in those events, grin and bear it. But if you don't really care about the arts and crafts fair, state fair, or the balloon fiesta, plan your New Mexico trip at some other time.

A **tax** of approximately 15.4% is added to every hotel bill.

Hotels/Motels
EXPENSIVE

Hotel Albuquerque at Old Town ★★   Elegant southwestern furnishings, authentic art, and excellent service make this hotel, just steps from Old Town, a good choice. Although not large, the rooms are quite comfortable, and south-facing ones overlook Old Town. Many of the rooms have private balconies, offering great views of mountains or mesa; and junior suites have a separate sitting area. If you come during the Balloon Fiesta (p. 209), request a room on the north side so you can watch the display in total comfort. The spacious high-ceilinged lobby is a grand place to meet friends. Patrons receive a "Local Treasures" discount card (one per room), good at some 80 local attractions, restaurants, bars, shops and galleries; and complimentary walking tours of Old Town are offered seasonally on Saturdays. The Hotel Albuquerque also offers wedding planning services, either in its own 19th-century-style non-denominational chapel or another Albuquerque venue.

800 Rio Grande Blvd. NW. www.hotelabq.com. © **800/237-2133** (reservations only) or 505/843-6300. 188 units. $99–$174 double, junior suites from $199. Children stay free in parent's room. Free parking. **Amenities:** 2 restaurants; lounge; concierge; exercise room; whirlpool tub; outdoor pool (summer only); room service; in-room massage; free Wi-Fi.

Hotel Andaluz ★★★   This luxury boutique hotel, built by New Mexico native Conrad Hilton, opened in 1939 as the first Hilton Hotel in the state and is on the National Register of Historic Places. In 2008 it was completely renovated to the tune of $30 million. The lobby is lusciously modern, with its soaring ceiling, intimate alcoves, and a central fountain. The elegant guest rooms are decorated in a contemporary fusion of cool colors balanced by warm earth tones, with polished wood and rich stone, and boast environmentally sustainable custom furniture and allergen-free carpets. The rooftop bar and patio provides sweeping views of the city and mountains to the east plus lively entertainment many evenings.

125 2nd St. NW, at Copper Ave. www.hotelandaluz.com. © **877/987-9090** or 505/842-9090. 107 units. $159–$179 double, suites from $199. Self-parking $10/day, valet parking $16/day. Pets accepted with fee, call for pricing. **Amenities:** Restaurant; lounge; nightclub; concierge; exercise room; room service; free Wi-Fi.

Hyatt Regency Albuquerque ★★   Conveniently located for the business or leisure traveler in the heart of downtown, this Hyatt offers luxury at affordable prices. In the lobby, a delightful fountain sparkles in the light from a pyramidal skylight; wander the hotel's public areas to view its extensive art collection. The spacious guest rooms have a welcoming warm New Mexico style with cushy bedding and either a mountain or city view, plus an ergonomic work area. You'll find the epitome of luxury in the Presidential Suite with its own wet bar; great views from the separate living room, dining room, and bedrooms; and an indulgent marble bath complete with marble jetted tub and walk-in shower.

330 Tijeras Ave. NW. www.hyatt.com. © **800/233-1234** or 505/842-1234. 395 units. $114–$159 double; suites from $179. Self-parking $12, valet parking $20. **Amenities:** Restaurant; bar; concierge; fitness center; outdoor rooftop pool and hot tub; room service; sauna; free Wi-Fi.

Nativo Lodge ★   In general, the accommodations at this full-service hotel on the north side of town are modest, though comfortable: Attractively decorated in an American Indian theme, each room has a small balcony and a desk, with bathrooms that are small but functional. What lifts the Nativo Lodge into a higher category, however, is its eight "Artist" rooms, which are something unique indeed: "large-scale, livable installation works of art" commissioned from contemporary Indian artists. Each room is one of a kind, and staying in one will immerse the visitor in the designing artist's vision. The lounge can get noisy in the evenings on weekends, so try to get a room that's not too close if you don't plan to be part of the festivities. Guests receive a "Local Treasures" discount card (one per room), good at some 80 local attractions, restaurants and bars, shops, and galleries.

6000 Pan American Fwy. NE, just east of I-25 exit 230. www.nativolodge.com. © **888/628-4861** or 505/798-4300. $79–$200 double. Free parking. **Amenities:** Restaurant; lounge; exercise room; whirlpool tub; indoor/outdoor pool; room service; free Wi-Fi.

MODERATE

Best Western Plus Rio Grande Inn ★★   A short walk from Old Town, this attractive, Pueblo-style building has a lobby decorated in distinctly southwestern fashion. As it's close to the interstate, try for a quieter, south-facing room. The medium-size rooms are accessed from interior corridors and have warm earth-tone colors on the walls and handcrafted southwestern furniture. One room option is outfitted with a king-size Murphy bed, giving you more room when it's tucked away during the day. With a restaurant on-site and a lovely fenced pool, this is a good family choice.

1015 Rio Grande Blvd. NW, on the south side of I-40 exit 157. www.riograndeinn.com. © **800/959-4726** or 505/843-9500. $110–$150 double. Free parking. Pets accepted ($20 per night). **Amenities:** Restaurant; free airport transfer; exercise room; hot tub; outdoor pool (heated year-round); free Wi-Fi.

Sheraton Albuquerque Airport Hotel ★   This 15-story building is easy to spot, just 200 yards from the airport. It offers simply decorated but comfortable rooms, with grand views from the upper floors, and some noise from all the planes. Business travelers particularly like this hotel as it has a 24-hour business center with free Wi-Fi. The restaurant serves a variety of American and southwestern dishes.

2910 Yale Blvd. SE. www.sheratonalbuquerqueairport.com. © **505/843-7000.** 276 units. $90–$189 double. Free parking. Pets accepted (free up to 40 lb., over 40 lb. $75). **Amenities:** Restaurant; lounge; concierge; fitness center; business center; outdoor pool (summer only); Wi-Fi $13 per day in room, free in business center.

INEXPENSIVE

Fairfield Inn ★   A contemporary southwestern lobby complete with fireplace welcomes guests to this Marriott-owned hotel. Rooms are light and bright, and kept exceptionally clean. Each has a balcony or terrace. As it's nestled into the NE quadrant of the intersection of I-40 and I-25, you might want to request an east-facing room to avoid the noise and view of the highway.

1760 Menaul Blvd. NE. www.fairfieldinn.com. © **800/228-2800** or 505/889-4000. 188 units. $89–$99 double. Children 18 and under stay free in parent's room. Free continental breakfast. Free parking. **Amenities:** Fitness center; indoor pool; free Wi-Fi.

Route 66 Hostel ★★   Simple and basic in true hostel style, this facility is housed in a building that partly dates to 1905. The single-sex dorm rooms are standard hostel style, with bunk beds, and sleep five to eight people. Each has its own bathroom. There are also private rooms with shared bathrooms and private rooms with private bathrooms (shower only). The communal kitchen is stocked with various breakfast foods including dry cereals, pancake mix, and fresh eggs; those using the kitchen are expected to clean up when they're finished. There are no laundry facilities on-site but there is a coin-op laundry about a block away. For those without cars, it's good to know that the hostel is reasonably close to the bus and train stations.

51012 Central Ave. SW. www.route66hostel.com. ℂ **505/247-1813.** 19 dorm beds, 9 private rooms. $20 dorm bed, $30 private room with shared bathroom, $40 private room with private bathroom. Plus $10 refundable towel and key deposit. **Amenities:** Communal kitchen stocked with breakfast food staples (free); free Wi-Fi.

Bed & Breakfasts

Böttger Mansion of Old Town ★★★ This stunning Victorian mansion houses an historic inn in historic Old Town, decorated with historic memorabilia from the coming of the railroad to Route 66. Is that enough history for you? Most of the rooms are named for an interesting and lesser-known historical figure, and include a thumbnail bio for your edification. In summer, the flower-filled courtyard attracts hummingbirds, finches, and other birds, and is shaded by 100-year-old trees. Among its choice rooms, there's the first-floor Route 66 Suite, with its own sunroom; the Edward Burton Cristy room (named for the architect who redesigned this elegant B&B), decorated in blue and white with yellow accents to celebrate New Mexico's azure blue sky, puffy white clouds, and golden aspen; and the Bernard Rodey room (named for the territorial legislator who founded the University of New Mexico), which is full of historic photos, a map of UNM, and statehood cartoons. Breakfasts are as elegant as the decor, starting with fresh-roasted coffee (or tea if that's your preference), juice, and fresh fruit. The entree might be a savory green chile quiche, blue corn pancakes with toasted pine nuts, or the scrumptious blueberry French toast casserole. And there's generally breakfast sausage, ham, or bacon, plus scones or biscuits.

110 San Felipe NW. www.bottger.com. ℂ **800/758-3639** or 505/243-3639. 7 units. $104–$179 double. Rates include full breakfast and snacks. Free reserved parking space. **Amenities:** Free Wi-Fi.

Los Poblanos Historic Inn & Organic Farm ★★ Renovated in the 1930s to a design by architect John Gaw Meem, this bed and breakfast is listed on the National Registry of Historic Places. Located in northwestern Albuquerque in the village of Los Ranchos de Albuquerque, with the Rio Grande flowing southward just over a block west, it's set on 25 acres of formal flower gardens, ancient cottonwoods, fields of lavender, and organic vegetable gardens. Rooms in the original ranch house offer king, queen, or twin beds and have kiva fireplaces, hardwood floors, and antique New Mexican furnishings. The newer Meem guest rooms and suites were designed to remain true to the original architectural designs, with high ceilings, Mexican tiled baths, and views of the gardens. The slightly upscale Greely Suites were created from original 1930s buildings and have private patios, separate living rooms, and spacious bathrooms. The Farm rooms and suites are a bit different, with pitched tin roofs and simpler decor, yet the same 1930s feel, with wood-burning fireplaces, hardwood floors, and a central courtyard with a delightful fountain. Several Farm units have private patios. At breakfast, guests can enjoy fresh eggs, honey, and fruits and vegetables from the fields just outside. The Carne Adovada is definitively New Mexican: red chile–braised pork, roasted potatoes, caramelized onions, plus two eggs any style.

4803 Rio Grande Blvd. NW, Los Ranchos de Albuquerque. www.lospoblanos.com. © **866/344-9297** or 505/344-9297. 20 units. $180–$345 double, suites from $270. $25 additional person. Rates include full breakfast. Free parking. **Amenities:** Restaurant; bike rentals; fitness center; concierge; outdoor pool (summer only); free Wi-Fi.

Mauger Bed & Breakfast Inn ★★   This restored Queen Anne home, built in 1897, offers a delightful place to relax within easy walking distance of Old Town. Listed on the National Register of Historic Places, this former residence of wool baron William Mauger is noted for its rich woodwork, etched glass, and high ceilings. All rooms are decorated with period furnishings. Bathrooms have showers only—the mini-suite has a double-headed shower for two—and one ground-floor room is especially designed for those with small or medium-size dogs, with a dog door that opens onto a fenced side yard. It's located on a quiet street between Lomas Boulevard and Central Avenue, close to both downtown attractions and Old Town. Treats of cheese, wine, and other beverages are offered in the evenings, and a full gourmet breakfast is served each morning in indoor and outdoor dining rooms.

701 Roma Ave. NW. www.maugerbb.com. © **800/719-9189** or 505/242-8755. 10 units. $89–$159 double, suites from $129. Rates include full breakfast and evening refreshments. Free parking. Dogs accepted by prior arrangement ($20 fee). **Amenities:** Free Wi-Fi.

RV Parks & Campgrounds

Albuquerque Central KOA ★   A good location—not in the middle of the noisy city but close enough so you don't spend all your time driving—this RV park and campground has all the amenities you'd expect in a commercial campground and even a few extras, such as a miniature golf course and horse-shoe pits. It's set in the foothills east of Albuquerque, with easy access off I-40, has good mountain views and some shade trees, and has large sites to accommodate big rigs. The camping cabins are especially nice, although the best ones, with private bathrooms, are a bit pricey. Linens are provided for the cabins with bathrooms but not for the ones that share the campground bathhouses.

12400 Skyline Rd. Off I-40 exit 166. NE. www.koa.com. © **800/562-7781** or 505/296-2729. $30–$35 tent site, $43–$70 RV site, $59–$135 cabin. Rates for up to 2 people. Pets accepted ($10–$20 per night in cabins). **Amenities:** Bathhouse; convenience store; horseshoe pits; outdoor pool (open mid-May through mid-October); indoor hot tub; coin-op laundry; miniature golf (extra fee); playground; propane; free Wi-Fi.

Albuquerque North Bernalillo KOA ★★   This is one of our favorite KOAs, with more than 1,000 cottonwood and pine trees for shade, lots of flowers in summer, and very friendly and helpful hosts. At the foot of the mountains, 14 miles north of Albuquerque, it has plenty of amenities. Guests

CRUISING corrales

If you're heading north, enjoy a leisurely drive along tree-lined streets through meadows and apple orchards by taking the road through Corrales. Home to farmers, artists, and affluent landowners, this is an enchanting place to roam through shops and galleries and, in the fall, sample fruits and vegetables from roadside stands. Two excellent restaurants, both serving imaginative new American cuisine, sit on the main street. **Indigo Crow ★**, 4515 Corrales Rd. (© **505/898-7000**), serves lunch and dinner Tuesday to Saturday 11:30am to 9pm, and brunch and dinner on Sunday 10am to 9pm. **Hannah & Nate's ★★**, 4512 Corrales Rd. (www.hannahandnates.com; © **505/898-2370**), serves delectable

breakfasts, salads, and sandwiches. It is open daily 7am to 2pm. If you'd like to stay in the village, contact the **Sandhill Crane Bed-and-Breakfast ★**, 389 Camino Hermosa (www.sandhillcrane bandb.com; © **800/375-2445** or 505/898-2445).

The town also has a nature preserve and a historic church. In September, the Harvest Festival is well worth the trip. For more information about Corrales, contact Corrales Village (www.corrales-nm.org; © **505/897-0502**).

To get to the village, head north on either I-25 or Rio Grande Boulevard, turn west on Alameda Boulevard, cross the Rio Grande, and turn north on Corrales Road (NM 448). The village is just a few minutes up the road.

---

enjoy an outdoor cafe and free outdoor movies in summer. Six camping cabins are also available.

555 Hill Rd., Bernalillo off I-25 exit 240. www.koa.com. © **800/562-3616** or 505/867-5227. $26–$28 tent site; $34–$43 RV site, depending on hookup; $43–$54 cabin. Rates include pancake breakfast and are valid for up to 2 people. Additional person $3. Children 6 and under free with parent. Pets accepted. **Amenities:** Restaurant; coin-op laundry; playground; outdoor pool (summer only); store; free Wi-Fi.

American RV Park ★ About 10 miles west of downtown on the higher west mesa, this RV park has nice views of the Sandia Mountains and the city lights at night. There are some shade trees and grass, but it's still pretty hot in high summer. There's a nice pool, two bathhouses, and a hot tub.

13500 Central Ave. SW. Off I-40 exit 149. www.americanrvpark.com. © **800/282-8885** or 505/831-3545. 236 sites. $35–$41 per day including continental breakfast; monthly rates available; lodges $109–$119. Pets accepted. **Amenities:** 2 bathhouses; outdoor pool; covered hot tub; horseshoe pits; playground; coin-op laundry; propane; store; free Wi-Fi.

WHERE TO EAT IN ALBUQUERQUE

Albuquerque may not be the first American city that comes to mind when you think of fine dining destinations, but that's not to say you can't have a memorable meal or two while visiting. There are excellent high-end restaurants such as the Rancher's Club of New Mexico (p. 188), quite a few really good moderately priced eateries, and some bargain joints that serve tasty, inexpensive, and sometimes even relatively healthy grub.

Many of the most interesting restaurants here serve traditional northern New Mexican cuisine, which emphasizes spicy chile sauces. We certainly hope you'll try some, because to truly experience northern New Mexico, you will want to experience the foods as well as the sights and sounds. However, those not used to spicy food may want to ask the servers how hot the chile is—you'll note that in New Mexico we use the word "hot" to mean spicy, which doesn't have anything to do with actual temperature. Many restaurants will either bring you a sample to taste before ordering, or put the chile on the side, so you can add a bit at a time.

Looking for a familiar restaurant chain? Albuquerque has them all. **Applebee's Grill & Bar ★★ has nine outlets in Albuquerque, including one at 2600 Menaul Blvd. NE** (www.applebees.com; ✆ **505/883-2846**). **Olive Garden ★** has three restaurants in town, including one at 6301 San Mateo Blvd. NE (www.olivegarden.com; ✆ **505/881-8425**). There's a good **Outback Steakhouse ★** at 4921 Jefferson St. NE (www.outback.com; ✆ **505/884-8760**), and a **Red Lobster ★** restaurant at 5555 Montgomery Blvd. NE (www.redlobster.com; ✆ **505/884-4445**). If you're getting in late, leaving early, or just hungry at 3am, there are four 24-hour **Denny's ★★** in Albuquerque, including one at 2400 San Mateo Blvd. NE (www.dennys.com; ✆ **505/884-6574**). An excellent choice for a healthy sandwich or soup to take back to your room or on a hike is the well-respected chain **Panera Bread ★★★,** with four outlets in Albuquerque, including one at 6600 Menaul Blvd. NE (www.panerabread.com; ✆ **505/884-3040**).

Greater Albuquerque Dining
EXPENSIVE

High Finance ★★ AMERICAN   The views are the star attraction, plus the fact that you have to ride a tram to get here (see p. 198). The food and service have been up and down lately—although mostly up—but the views never change: the best in Albuquerque, from the top of Sandia Peak, at an elevation of 10,378 feet. You can see some 11,000 square miles of western New Mexico, with panoramic sunsets and nighttime city-light vistas that are simply phenomenal. The dining room is a bit dated, but attractive enough with tile floors, polished wood, and comfortable chairs. The main attraction: a wall of windows so every table has a good view. We recommend the steaks—in particular the 12-ounce New York strip and the 8-ounce filet, but the more adventurous may want to opt for the chicken parmesan (8-ounce chicken breast topped with house-made marinara sauce served over fettucine), the grilled salmon, or the pan-seared oven-finished breast of duck. There is full liquor service, with the bar open Monday and Tuesday from 2pm, the rest of the week from 10am for drinks and appetizers.

Atop Sandia Peak, accessible via Sandia Peak Aerial Tram. www.sandiapeakrestaurants. com. ✆ **505/243-9742.** Main courses lunch $10–$15, dinner $20–$38. Mon–Tues 4:30–close, Wed–Sun 11am–3pm and 4:30pm–close, last reservation at 8pm.

Albuquerque Dining

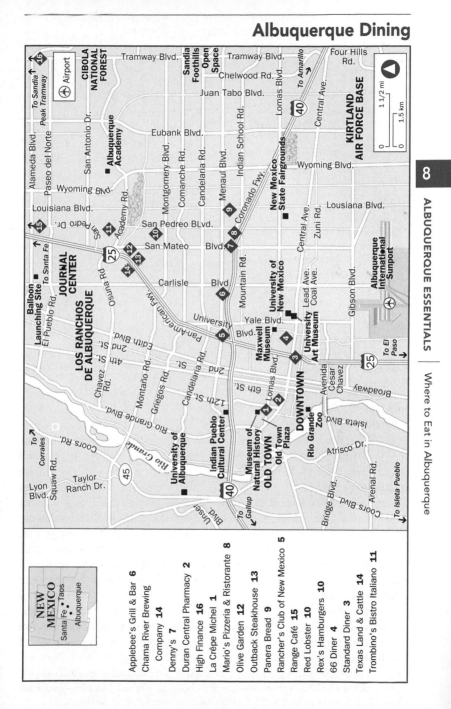

Applebee's Grill & Bar **6**
Chama River Brewing
  Company **14**
Denny's **7**
Duran Central Pharmacy **2**
High Finance **16**
La Crêpe Michel **1**
Mario's Pizzeria & Ristorante **8**
Olive Garden **12**
Outback Steakhouse **13**
Panera Bread **9**
Rancher's Club of New Mexico **5**
Range Café **15**
Red Lobster **10**
Rex's Hamburgers **10**
66 Diner **4**
Standard Diner **3**
Texas Land & Cattle **14**
Trombino's Bistro Italiano **11**

Rancher's Club of New Mexico ★★★ STEAK/SEAFOOD/GAME

Have a special occasion to celebrate? This is the spot. Albuquerque's best and most luxurious restaurant, the Rancher's Club boasts superb service in an elegant dining room with a refined ranch decor—lots of polished wood and a handsome stone fireplace. There are saddles and ranch memorabilia, and ranching photos by renowned New Mexico photographer Harvey Caplin. Cuisine is primarily steak, seafood, and game, prepared on a wood grill using mesquite, hickory, and other aromatic woods. Meats and other ingredients are from local farms and ranches as much as possible.

> ### Gastroblog
>
> For an in-depth look at Albuquerque's restaurants, check out **Gil's Thrilling (and Filling) Blog ★★** at www.nm gastronome.com/blog. Food critic and New Mexico native Gil Garduño has dined at more than 1,000 restaurants in northern New Mexico. In his blog he provides his personal in-depth accounts and ratings, of both the food and the experience of dining at most of them. You can spend hours reading up on his favorites, or just take a quick peek to get a recommendation.

You won't go wrong with anything on the menu, but the 18-ounce cowboy-cut bone-in ribeye and the wood-fired "hunters" mixed grill are especially tasty. You couldn't ask for better service—attentive without being invasive, and the staff are very knowledgeable about the food and the extensive wine list. There is live piano music in the lounge Wednesday through Saturday evenings. The Rancher's Club has full liquor service, and it's one of the few northern New Mexico restaurants with a dress code: business casual, men must wear collared shirts, and no shorts or beach sandals are permitted. This is also one of the few northern New Mexico restaurants where you really do need to make a reservation.

Inside the Crowne Plaza, 1901 University Blvd. NE. www.theranchersclubofnm.com. ⓒ **505/889-8071.** Main courses $30–$80. Mon–Thurs 5:30–9:30pm, Fri–Sat 5:30pm–10pm.

MODERATE

Chama River Brewing Company ★★ AMERICAN

Walking into this somewhat noisy and bustling brewpub, the first thing that grabs your attention is the large rough-rock fountain with a graceful bird sculpture. From here you're escorted either to the left into the bar, with a good view of the beer vats; or to right, into the slightly quieter dining room. Decor is typical brewpub—lots of wood, from the heavy beams on the ceiling to the wood-topped tables and accents. There are tables and comfortable booths, and the dinner menu is a step or two above the average brewpub. You'll find burgers, fish and chips, and fried chicken, of course, but also red chile–braised duck legs, house-smoked pork chops, and goat cheese–stuffed zucchini. Our favorites are the prime rib, and when available as a special, the blackened salmon. For an appetizer, you can't beat the green chile and ale fondue. The lunch menu features a variety of burgers plus sandwiches and salads. Happy hour (4 to

6pm) offers especially good appetizer and drink specials. There's a full bar, a good selection of wine, and the brewery's own beers.

4939 Pan American West Fwy. NE (I-25 exit 229, take frontage road south). www. chamariverbrewery.com. (© **505/342-1800.** Main courses lunch $6.50–$15, dinner $9.25–$28. Sun–Thurs 11am–10pm, Fri–Sat 11am–11pm.

La Crêpe Michel ★★ FRENCH   Among New Mexico's best French restaurants, this almost-hidden little gem of a cafe in Albuquerque's Old Town offers an imaginative, and for some, refreshing, change from the usual northern New Mexico cooking. In good cafe style, decor is simple, with dark red tablecloths and walls dotted with posters showing scenes from France. The menu, written in French, can be a bit confusing for those of us who don't understand the language, but for lunch there are some very nice salads, a quiche of the day, omelets, several sandwiches, and a variety of crepes. Dinner concentrates on the crepes. Steak frites are served at both lunch and dinner, and daily specials, such as salmon in wine sauce, are written on a chalkboard. There's also an outdoor patio.

400 San Felipe St., Old Town. www.lacrepemichel.com. (© **505/242-1251.** Main courses lunch $8–$14.50, dinner $11–$35. Tues–Sun 11:30am–2pm, Tues–Sat 6–9pm.

Range Café ★★ NEW MEXICAN/AMERICAN   Northern New Mexico comfort food done right is what you'll find at all three Range Cafés, this one in downtown Bernalillo, about 20 minutes north of Albuquerque. Here in the original Range there's more funky New Mexico ambience than the other two. It's in an old building, has tables and booths, hand-carved chairs, attractive artwork—some with a whimsical feel—and a pressed-tin ceiling. Food is mostly basic American, such as roast turkey and stuffing, grilled chicken breast, burgers, and the local favorite, Tom's meatloaf, but there are also New Mexican dishes and a few surprises. Try the Asian quinoa salad—quinoa tossed with fresh spinach, cabbage, carrots, jicama, cucumber, and sliced almonds, in a sesame ginger dressing. Breakfast, served until 3pm, is tops, and the Range also offers "Brinner," breakfast for dinner. We recommend the breakfast burrito with green chile and what the Range calls "the basic": eggs, potatoes, toast, and a choice of breakfast meat. There's a gift shop and full liquor service. The Albuquerque outlets, with the same menu but more modern buildings, are at 4401 Wyoming Blvd. NE (© **505/293-2633**) and 2200 Menaul Blvd. NE (© **505/888-1660**).

925 Camino del Pueblo (btw. I-25 exits 240 and 242), Bernalillo. www.rangecafe.com. (© **505/867-1700.** Main courses $7.50–$16. Sun–Thurs 7am–9pm, Fri–Sat 7am–9:30pm. Closed Thanksgiving and Christmas.

Standard Diner ★★ NEW AMERICAN   With every other moderately priced restaurant calling itself a diner, you may be thinking, "been there, done that." Well, this "diner" is different. Here the emphasis is on giving a modern twist to old-time comfort food favorites. The decor is part old diner—chrome-edged tables, booths along the curved walls, and plates and cups that look at least 50 years old—but there's an upscale feeling, too. A closer look at the

route 66 REVISITED: REDISCOVERING NEW MEXICO'S STRETCH OF THE MOTHER ROAD

You know how the song goes: "Get your kicks on Route 66." The highway that once stretched from Chicago to California was hailed as the road to freedom. During the Great Depression, it was the way west for farmers escaping Dust Bowl poverty, and if you found yourself in a rut in the late 1940s and 1950s, all you had to do was hop in the car and head west on Route 66.

Of course, the road existed long before it gained such widespread fascination. Built in the late 1920s and paved in 1937, it was the lifeblood of communities in eight states. Nowadays, however, US 66 is as elusive as the fantasies that once carried hundreds of thousands west in search of a better life. Replaced by other roads, covered up by interstates (mostly I-40), and just plain out of use, Route 66 still exists in New Mexico, but you'll have to do a little searching and take some extra time to find it.

Motorists driving west from Texas might be able to find a gravel stretch of the original highway running from Glenrio to San Jon. After San Jon, you can actually enjoy some paved sections of vintage 66, including the main drags in both Tucumcari and Santa Rosa. In Albuquerque, US 66 follows Central Avenue for 18 miles, from the state fairgrounds, past what's left of some original 1930s motels and the historic Nob Hill district, on west through downtown.

You can also pick up old Route 66 in Grants, along the 6-mile Santa Fe Avenue. In Gallup, a 9-mile segment of US 66 is lined with restaurants and hotels reminiscent of the city's days as a Western film capital from 1929 to 1964.

For more information about Route 66, check out **www.historic66.com** and **www.national66.org**.

menu shows off the kitchen's innovative side. What is called the "Standard Scramble," for example, is scrambled eggs all right, but with spinach, tomato, green chile, and white cheddar. The meatloaf is bacon-wrapped, with smashed potatoes and red wine gravy. Curious about the building, with its garage doors and interior red brick walls? In the late 1930s, when Central Avenue was still vintage Route 66, this was a Texaco service station. There's a full bar and daily happy hour from 4 to 6pm.

320 Central Ave. SE. www.standarddiner.com. ✆ **505/243-1440.** Main courses breakfast $8–$15, lunch and dinner $9–$25. Sun–Thurs 8am–9pm, Fri–Sat 8am–10pm.

Texas Land & Cattle ★★ AMERICAN/MEXICAN This moderately priced steakhouse is the only New Mexico location of a small Texas-based operation that prides itself on its genuine Texas food. The dining room looks like a typical steakhouse, with lots of wood and stone, including a handsome stone fireplace sporting the head of a Texas longhorn. Although this will probably not be the very best steak you have ever eaten, the beef is good and a good value. For dinner, we suggest the house specialty smoked sirloin, or have the sirloin without smoke. Also good is the hickory-smoked half-chicken, or for those who want some spice in their lives, the ranchero steak and enchiladas—a seared skirt steak with cheese and onion enchiladas and red chile sauce. For lunch there are burgers, several sandwiches and salads, smaller versions of the dinner steaks, and tacos. There's a full bar, and good drink and appetizer specials during happy hour, which runs from 2 to 6pm Monday through Wednesday and Friday, plus all day Thursday.

4949 Pan American West Fwy. NE (I-25 exit 229, take frontage road south). www. texaslandand cattle.com. ℂ **505/343-9800.** Main courses lunch $10–$14, dinner $10–$32. Sun–Thurs 11am–10pm, Fri–Sat 11am–11pm.

Trombino's Bistro Italiano ★★★ ITALIAN   Since 1979 the Trombino family has been serving some of the best genuine Italian food in Albuquerque, prepared from scratch, at very reasonable prices. The dining room and bar have rustic Italian decor, what we might call colorful, comfortable, and casually elegant, and maybe just a bit over the top. The menu, much of it from old family recipes, ranges from Italian standards such as veal Parmigianino, lasagna, and three-cheese ravioli to specialties such as Shrimp Fra Diavolo— brandied shrimp tossed with a hot, spicy fire-roasted tomato sauce, served over pasta marinara. You can also create your own main course: Choose one of six types of pasta and combine it with one of 11 sauces, ranging from the Trombino family's own marinara sauce to clams in white wine and garlic, or a basic tomato meat sauce. Especially popular is the house-made Italian sausage, either spicy or mild, grilled and topped with roasted peppers and onions. Steaks and pork chops are also served, and the tiramisu cake is extra special.

5415 Academy Rd. NE. www.bistroitaliano.com. ℂ **505/821-5974.** Main courses $11– $27. Mon–Thurs 4–10pm, Fri 4–10:30pm, Sat 3–10:30pm, Sun 3–9pm. Closed Thanksgiving, Christmas, and Super Bowl Sunday.

INEXPENSIVE

Duran Central Pharmacy ★★★ NEW MEXICAN   Those old enough to remember going to the local drugstore to sit at a counter for a sandwich or an ice cream soda will feel right at home at Duran's. A genuine old-time drugstore, with plenty of stuff to browse through (check out the special occasion and note cards and the rather strange religious icons), this busy locals' favorite also offers some of the best genuine northern New Mexico food you'll find in Albuquerque, and at bargain prices. The somewhat noisy restaurant section is in the back of the store, with stainless-steel tables and diner-style orange vinyl chairs. There are also stools along a long curved counter overlooking the open cooking area, and an outdoor covered patio. You'll find all the usual suspects here—tacos, burritos, enchiladas, and of course, green chile cheeseburgers—but our favorites are the Frito pie (Fritos topped with beans, cheese, lettuce, tomatoes, and chile sauce) and the turkey and jack cheese wrap, in a tortilla with enough green chile to set your head on fire. Duran's serves seriously hot chile, so ask for recommendations before ordering, or request that the chile be served on the side.

1815 Central Ave. NW. www.durancentralpharmacy.com. ℂ **505/247-4141.** Menu items $7–$12. Mon–Fri 9am–6:30pm, Sat–Sun 9am–2pm. Longer hours at pharmacy and store.

Mario's Pizzeria & Ristorante ★ ITALIAN   Mario's reminds us of the Italian restaurants of our youth in New York and New Jersey, and it's no

family-friendly RESTAURANTS

Mario's Pizzeria & Ristorante (p. 191) There's a lot of people-watching to be done here, and what kid doesn't like pizza?

Range Café (p. 189) The fun and funky decor and ice cream specialties make this a good spot for kids.

Rex's Hamburgers (p. 192) Fast food is fun, the burgers are good, and the walls are covered with fascinating posters and photos. It's also a popular spot for kids' birthday parties.

Standard Diner (p. 189) Set in a renovated 1938 Texaco station, this upscale diner serves mac and cheese and other Route 66 favorites for the young and young at heart.

66 Diner (p. 193) A full range of burgers and treats such as root beer floats and hot fudge sundaes will make any youngster happy.

wonder, since the Burgarello family, immigrants from Sicily, opened their first restaurant in Queens, New York, in 1965. The family moved to Albuquerque in 1972, and the rest, as they say, is history. This is not "fine dining," whatever that is, but well-prepared everyday Italian food, in this case using Mama Ann's made-from-scratch old family recipes. The unpretentious dining room is designed to resemble an Italian villa, with plaster walls and half-moon windows, decorated with posters, photos, and some old menus. The menu features practically all the Italian standards, from spaghetti to lasagna to veal parmigiana. There are also calzones, Italian subs, and sandwiches (including a French dip!), and of course, pizza. We especially like the lasagna and pizza, but we haven't discovered anything we wouldn't recommend in the years we've been coming here. *Note:* The lunch and dinner is the same, including portions, but dinner prices, from 3pm, are slightly higher. Beer and wine is available. This is the original Mario's, but there are also Mario's, with the identical menu, at 11500 Menaul Blvd. NE (*C* **505/294-8999**), 5700 4th St. NW (*C* **505/344-4700**), and 7501 Paseo del Norte NE (*C* **505/797-1800**).

2401 San Pedro Blvd. NE www.mariospizzaabq.com. *C* **505/883-4414.** Main courses $9–$16, pizzas from $12. Sun–Thurs 11am–9:30pm, Fri–Sat 11am–10pm.

Rex's Hamburgers ★★★ AMERICAN/NEW MEXICAN   Thinking of stopping at one of the national fast-food chains for a burger and fries? Forget it. Instead, head to Rex's, hidden in a little shopping center along busy Montgomery Boulevard, for better burgers, better fries, and great shakes and malts. Here you order at the counter, go find a booth or table, and they deliver your food, very quickly. The dining room is simply decorated diner-style, with some interesting signs, photos, and posters, including Marilyn, of course. Chairs and booth seating are upholstered, and the tabletops are tile, a nice touch. In addition to various burgers—we usually get the green chile cheeseburger—there are hot dogs, fish and steak sandwiches, several salads, burritos, and tacos. You can order a la carte or get a platter, which includes your entree plus fries, one onion ring, and applesauce. There are also full dinners (steak, chicken, fish, and shrimp) that include everything on the platter plus a soft drink. The fresh lemonade is good, and we especially like the malts. No alcohol is served. There's an outdoor patio overlooking the parking lot where your dog is welcome.

5555 Montgomery Blvd. NE. © **505/837-2827.** Main courses $3.05–$11 (most items $4–$6). Daily 8am–9pm.

66 Diner ★★ AMERICAN   This somewhat hokey 1950s-style diner didn't exist during the glory days of Route 66, but it certainly does a good job of capturing the spirit of those times, or at least capturing our rose-colored recollections of that era. There are photos of Elvis and Marilyn, plenty of neon and chrome, and even the servers dress the part. The food is exactly what you would expect—good burgers, sandwiches, meals such as grilled liver and onions or meatloaf with mashed potatoes and gravy, and green chile chicken enchiladas. There are daily blue plate specials, including chicken pot pie on Tuesdays and fried catfish on Fridays, and an old-fashioned soda fountain creates wonderful malts and milkshakes. Breakfasts—all the usual American items—are served Saturdays and Sundays only, 8am to noon. No alcohol is served.

1405 Central Ave. NE. www.66diner.com. © **505/247-1421.** Main courses $6–$14. Mon–Thurs 11am–10pm, Fri 11am–11pm, Sat 8am–11pm, Sun 8am–10pm.

EXPLORING ALBUQUERQUE

A lbuquerque is all too often overshadowed by Santa Fe and Taos, two historic towns with enormous tourist appeal, and it really isn't fair. Yes, Albuquerque also has its Spanish Colonial plaza and historic Old Town area, but it also seems to live more in the 21st century, with a diverse and dynamic selection of museums, an impressive array of urban green spaces, and a large state university adding more museums, performing arts, and spectator sports into the mix. (Frankly, if you're traveling with kids, they may enjoy Albuquerque's family-friendly sights more than artsy Santa Fe and Taos.) And because lodging and dining costs are more reasonable here in the big city, it can be a better base for excursions into northern New Mexico's fascinating desert landscapes.

WHAT TO SEE & DO IN ALBUQUERQUE

Albuquerque's original town site, known today as Old Town, is the central point of interest for visitors. Here, grouped around the plaza, are the venerable Church of San Felipe de Neri and numerous restaurants, art galleries, and crafts shops. Several important museums are close by, and within a few blocks you'll find BioPark, with its excellent aquarium, botanic garden, zoo, and beach. (Yes, a beach in the desert.) But don't get stuck in Old Town. Elsewhere, you'll find the Sandia Peak Tramway, the Balloon Museum, and a number of natural attractions.

The Top Attractions

Albuquerque Museum ★★　Visit the "Only in Albuquerque" history gallery to get a fresh look at the city's history in this fine modern museum on the edge of Old Town. It's interactive and fun, a great introduction to the cultural history of New Mexico. Exhibits tell the city's story from pre-written history up to now, plus virtual reality storybooks and theaters, and the chance to electronically send a Route 66 postcard to someone and even create your own coat of arms. Don't miss the art portion of this museum, either: The permanent exhibit in the East Gallery highlights significant works

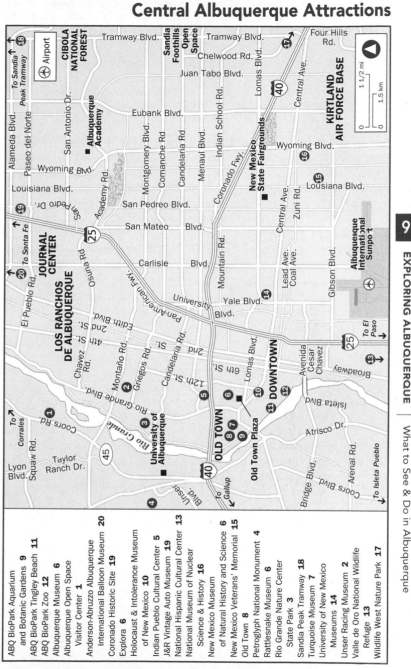

Tramway Blvd.
Tramway Blvd.
Four Hills Rd.
Chelwood Rd.
Juan Tabo Blvd.
Eubank Blvd.
Montgomery Blvd.
Comanche Rd.
Candelaria Rd.
Menaul Blvd.
Indian School Rd.
Lomas Blvd.
Central Ave.
Wyoming Blvd.
San Pedreo Blvd.
San Mateo   Blvd.
Carlisle   Blvd.
Mountain Rd.
University   Blvd.
Yale Blvd.
Lead Ave.
Coal Ave.
Gibson Blvd.
Zuni Rd.
Central Ave.
Lousiana Blvd.
Wyoming Blvd.
Alameda Blvd.
Paseo del Norte
Wyoming Blvd.
Louisiana Blvd.
San Antonio Dr.
San Pedro Dr.
Academy Rd.
Osuna Rd.
El Pueblo Rd.
2nd St.
4th St.
Edith Blvd.
Pan-American Fwy.
Coronado Fwy.
Montaño Rd.
Griegos Rd.
Candelaria Rd.
2nd St.
12th St.
6th St.
Lomas Blvd.
Avenida Cesar Chavez
Isleta Blvd.
Broadway
Atrisco Dr.
Bridge Blvd.
Arenal Rd.
Coors Blvd.
Chavez Rd.
Rio Grande Blvd.
Coors Rd.
Lyon Blvd.
Squaw Rd.
Taylor Ranch Dr.
Unser Blvd.
Rio Grande

CIBOLA NATIONAL FOREST
Sandia Foothills Open Space
KIRTLAND AIR FORCE BASE
Albuquerque Academy
JOURNAL CENTER
LOS RANCHOS DE ALBUQUERQUE
University of Albuquerque
OLD TOWN
Old Town Plaza
DOWNTOWN
New Mexico State Fairgrounds
Albuquerque International Sunport

To Sandia
To Sandia Peak Tramway
Airport
To Santa Fe
To El Paso
To Corrales
To Gallup
To Isleta Pueblo

40 40 25 25 45 17

1 1/2 mi
1.5 km

ABQ BioPark Aquarium and Botanic Gardens **9**
ABQ BioPark Tingley Beach **11**
ABQ BioPark Zoo **12**
Albuquerque Museum **6**
Albuquerque Open Space Visitor Center **1**
Anderson-Abruzzo Albuquerque International Balloon Museum **20**
Coronado Historic Site **19**
Explora **6**
Holocaust & Intolerance Museum of New Mexico **10**
Indian Pueblo Cultural Center **5**
J&R Vintage Auto Museum **19**
National Hispanic Cultural Center **13**
National Museum of Nuclear Science & History **16**
New Mexico Museum of Natural History and Science **6**
New Mexico Veterans' Memorial **15**
Old Town **8**
Petroglyph National Monument **4**
Rattlesnake Museum **6**
Rio Grande Nature Center State Park **3**
Sandia Peak Tramway **18**
Turquoise Museum **7**
University of New Mexico Museums **14**
Unser Racing Museum **2**
Valle de Oro National Wildlife Refuge **13**
Wildlife West Nature Park **17**

from the late–19th century to today, many of them by New Mexico artists. In addition, there are wonderful changing exhibits, sometimes with an unusual focus. Summer brings an artist-in-residence, who installs a temporary show in the museum's lobby.

2000 Mountain Rd. NW. www.cabq.gov/museum. ℂ **505/243-7255.** Adults $4, seniors 65 and up $2, children ages 4–12 $1. Free admission 1st Wed of the month, 2–5pm Sat, and 9am–1pm Sun. Fees for special exhibits and events may apply. Docent tours at 2pm, other times by pre-arrangement. Old Town walking tours 11am daily Mar–mid-Dec, Tues–Sun 9am–5pm. Closed major holidays.

Anderson-Abruzzo Albuquerque International Balloon Museum ★★

Fun and fascinating, entertaining and educational, all at once. A natural favorite for kids—what's not to love about hands-on activities, multimedia technology, and the balloon flight simulator?—the Balloon Museum explores the history of ballooning, from the first flight in France in 1783 (a rooster, sheep, and duck were the passengers, to see if they could survive the trip) to the present. The sprawling museum covers all aspects of ballooning, including the largest lighter-than-air vehicles—dirigibles, which were filled with hydrogen or helium for lift and used gasoline engines to push them forward. One of the scariest uses of balloons was during World War II, when Japanese children built them, and the government added bombs and launched them into the jet stream, which flowed toward North America. Of the 10,000 launched, about 1,000 made it to land in North America. Additional exhibits show crossings of the Atlantic and Pacific oceans, the first around-the-world flight, and the beginning of aerial photography. The museum is named for Albuquerque balloonists Maxie Anderson and Ben Abruzzo, who, with Larry Newman, completed the first manned crossing of the Atlantic Ocean in 1978.

9201 Balloon Museum Dr. NE (from I-25 exit 233 for Alameda Blvd., west to Balloon Museum Dr.). www.cabq.gov/balloon.com. ℂ **505/768-6020.** Adults $4, seniors 65 and up $2, children ages 4–12 $1, free for children 3 and under. Tues–Sun 9am–5pm. Closed New Year's Day, Thanksgiving, Christmas, and some other city holidays.

Indian Pueblo Cultural Center ★★

Owned and operated by the 19 pueblos of New Mexico, this museum has a stated purpose of perpetuating their culture and advancing understanding by presenting the Pueblo people's accomplishments and evolving history. It is an excellent place to begin your exploration of Puebloan cultural history. Start by wandering among the informational exhibits and contemporary arts and crafts shows on the ground floor, then head downstairs to view the history and culture of these peoples, from prehistory to the present. Throughout the year, Native American dancers perform in an outdoor arena surrounded by original murals, generally on weekends (at noon in winter, at 11am and 2pm in spring and summer, more frequently in fall). During Balloon Fiesta, there is a full daily schedule of dancing and music; check the website about a week ahead if you're planning a trip then. A large shop on the ground floor offers fine pottery, rugs, sculptures, fetishes, baskets, and jewelry, among other things. There's also a very

A GREAT DEAL for museum lovers

If you're a fan of museums and historic sites, and especially if you'll be touring other areas of the state, pick up a **New Mexico CulturePass.** It's good at some 14 museums and historic sites across the state. Cost is $25 per person and entitles the bearer to one visit at each of the properties in a 12-month period. You can buy the CulturePass online at www.new mexicoculture.org or at any of the participating museums and historic sites.

Sites in the Albuquerque area are the **National Hispanic Cultural Center** (see below), the **New Mexico Museum of Natural History and Science** (p. 205), and the **Coronado Historic Site** (see p. 203).

Sites included in the Santa Fe area are the **New Mexico History Museum, New Mexico Museum of Art,** and the **Palace of Governors**, and the **Museum of International Folk Art and the Museum of Indian Arts and Culture**.

Other sites included in the pass are the **New Mexico Museum of Space History** in Alamogordo, the **New Mexico Farm and Ranch Heritage Museum** in Las Cruces, and five other historic parks: **Bosque Redondo Memorial/Fort Sumner Historic Site, El Camino Real Historic Trail Site, Fort Selden Historic Site, Jemez Historic Site** (see p. 225), and **Lincoln Historic Site.**

9

EXPLORING ALBUQUERQUE | What to See & Do in Albuquerque

nice **cafe,** open from 8am to 8:30pm Monday through Thursday, 8am to 9pm Friday and Saturday, and 8am to 4 pm Sunday.

2401 12th St. NW. www.indianpueblo.org. © **866/855-7902** or 505/843-7270. Adults $6, students $3, free for children 4 and under. Daily 9am–5pm. Closed New Year's Day, July 4, Labor Day, Thanksgiving, and Christmas.

National Hispanic Cultural Center ★★ Take a rich cultural journey through hundreds of years of Hispanic history world-wide in this fine museum located in the historic Barelas neighborhood on the Camino Real. It explores Hispanic arts and lifestyles with visual arts, drama, music, dance, and other programs. There's an intriguing 4,000-square-foot concave fresco depicting thousands of years of Hispanic and pre-Hispanic history from the Iberian Peninsula to the Americas. There's a circulating exhibit entitled *"¡Aqui Estamos!"* ("Here It Is!"), showing works taken from the center's permanent collection, including those from the United States, Latin America, Spain, and other regions of Spanish emigration. **M'Tucci's Cocina Restaurant** serves an appealing combination of Spanish, Italian, and northern New Mexico cuisine Tuesday through Saturday from 4 to 10pm, with prices from $14 to $32.

1701 4th St. SW (corner of 4th St. and Av. Cesar Chavez). www.nhccnm.org. © **505/246-2261.** Adults $3, free for children under 16, Sun free for all ages. Free admission with New Mexico CulturePass (see box above). Tues–Sun 10am–5pm. Closed New Year's Day, Memorial Day, Labor Day, and Christmas.

Old Town ★★★ This plaza was once the heart of town, with mercantile and grocery stores, government offices, and businesses to serve the needs of the public. The importance of Old Town as Albuquerque's commercial center declined after 1880, when the railroad came through 1¼ miles east, and businesses relocated to be closer to the trains. The area fell into disrepair until the 1930s and 1940s, when artisans and other shop owners rediscovered it and the tourism industry burgeoned. Some 150 shops, boutiques, galleries, and studios comprise Old Town today. Its central grassy square with wrought-iron and adobe benches set under old cottonwood trees is a great place for people-watching.

On the north side of the plaza, you can see where the first building was erected when Albuquerque was established in 1706, the **Church of San Felipe de Neri** ★★ (sanfelipedeneri.org). The original church collapsed in 1782 after a particularly wet season, and the present church was erected the next year. Its 5-foot-thick adobe walls have withstood the years through constant maintenance and occasional renovation. Inside, the plaster walls are off-white above light blue wainscoting, with deep window enclosures strikingly painted in a geometric motif. Oak pews rest on the brick floor (not original) of the sanctuary, whose walls are lined with large paintings of the Stations of the Cross. This is a simple house of worship that has been in almost continuous use for numerous generations of Albuquerque residents. The church's gift shop, located in the Sister Blandina Convent and Chapel to the west of the church, is filled with religious art used in the life and liturgy of the parish, including a charming assortment of angels and lovely crosses at reasonable prices, including many of brightly painted and glazed terra cotta.

Around the plaza, and a block or two in all directions around it, you can find food and drink from snacks to fine dining, galleries offering fine art and jewelry, and of course, the inevitable souvenir shops, plus some fun clothing boutiques. An excellent **Old Town historic walking tour** originates at the Albuquerque Museum (see above) at 11am daily March through mid-December.

North of Central Ave. and east of Rio Grande Blvd. NW. Old Town Visitor Center: 303 Romero St. NW (across from San Felipe de Neri). www.albuquerqueoldtown.com. ⓒ **505/243-3215.** Visitor Center daily 10am–4:30pm, open until 6pm in summer.

Sandia Peak Tramway ★★   Not for those with vertigo, this fun trip up the face of the Sandias in a metal box hanging from a cable presents wonderful views of the city and out to everywhere and nowhere in particular. For a panoramic view, it can't be beaten. The Sandia Peak Tram is a "jigback": as one car approaches the top, the other nears the bottom. The two pass halfway through the trip, in the midst of a 1½-mile "clear span" of unsupported cable between the second tower and the upper terminal. Several hiking trails are available on Sandia Peak, but may not be suitable for children. Call the Sandia Ranger station for information (ⓒ **505/281-3304**). If you're riding up in the late afternoon, plan to dine at **High Finance** restaurant (p. 186) and watch the sunset—it's an unsurpassed experience. Special tram rates apply with dinner reservations. Be aware that certain weather conditions, such as high winds, can cause the tram to be shut down.

10 Tramway Loop NE (I-25 exit 234 or I-40 exit 167). www.sandiapeak.com. ⓒ **505/856-7325.** Adults $20, seniors 62 and up and ages 13–20 $17, children ages 5–12 $12, free for children under 5. Memorial Day–Labor Day and Balloon Fiesta, daily 9am–9pm; rest of year Wed–Mon 9am–8pm, Tues 5–8pm. Regular maintenance closures in April and November; call or visit website for details. Parking $1 daily.

Unser Racing Museum ★★★   This fascinating museum is a must-see for all auto-racing fans. Created by the Unser family, New Mexico's first family of auto racing, it pays homage to the family's top race car drivers. But it isn't simply an "aren't we great" opportunity to show off, it's an honest and well-done history of auto racing throughout the Unsers' long career. (Anyone who knows anything about auto racing knows that the Unser family is a large part of auto racing in America, with multiple wins at the Indy 500, Pikes Peak Race, and other venues.) The museum includes numerous race cars and motorcycles, including some historic ones from racing's early days. There are interactive kiosks and videos, a simulator to let you get the feel of racing, and some great car art. Optional short guided tours of the main museum are included in the admission price. Main museum, you say? Yes. After the museum was built, it turned out that there wasn't room for all the cars, trophies, and other racing memorabilia, so a second building was constructed. It contains more race cars and such, including Al Unser Sr.'s personal collection of classic cars.

1776 Montano Rd. NW. www.unserracingmuseum.com ℗ **505/341 1776.** Adults $10, seniors 60 and up and military $6, free for ages 15 and under. Daily 10am–4pm. Closed New Year's Day, Easter, Thanksgiving, and Christmas.

ABQ BioPark

This city park complex is our favorite outdoor and nature experience in Albuquerque, where you could easily spend an entire afternoon or day. It combines a fine aquarium, excellent botanic gardens, and the best zoo in the state, with a train connecting all three, as well as fishing and pedal-boat lakes and walking and fitness trails.

BioPark Aquarium and Botanic Gardens ★★   At the Aquarium you can follow a drop of water from the beginning of the Rio Grande in the Colorado mountains to the Gulf Coast, where it dumps into the Pacific Ocean, and get to know sea creatures from around the world. There's a 280,000-gallon shark tank, river otters and jellyfish, a colorful coral-reef exhibit, and an exhibit of a dramatic encounter between a shark and a ray. The Botanic Gardens offer a peaceful stroll among fragrant flowers as you wander through gardens en route to a 10,000-square-foot conservatory, with separate sections for desert plants and Mediterranean flora. Heritage Farm is a recreation of a 1930s Rio Grande Valley farm with corrals, a vineyard, orchard, Navajo churro sheep, horses, cattle, and goats. The high desert rose garden shows off native roses, and the Sasebo Japanese Garden, with a koi pond, bell tower, and tiered waterfall, combines aspects of a traditional Japanese garden with New Mexico influences. If you're visiting with children, a stop in the Children's Fantasy Garden is a must, where they can walk among giant vegetables, feel themselves getting smaller as they step into a rabbit hole, and learn about plants through various interactive displays. In warmer months the Butterfly Pavilion fills with the colors of several hundred North American butterflies.

2601 Central Ave. NW. www.cabq.gov/biopark. ℗ **505/768-2000.** Adults $12.50 ($20 for combo ticket with zoo and trains), seniors 65 and over $5.50 ($10 for combo ticket), children ages 3–12 $4 ($6 for combo ticket), free for children under 3. Daily 9am–5pm; June–Aug Sat–Sun and holidays open until 6pm. Ticket sales stop 30 min. before closing. Closed New Year's Day, Thanksgiving, and Christmas.

BioPark Tingley Beach ★ Anglers, pedal-boaters, and those just wanting to stretch their legs will find the ponds at Tingley Beach a refreshing break from the city. Anglers 12 and older must have a New Mexico fishing license, but other than that there is no charge for fishing. The ponds are stocked with trout and catfish. Pedal boats are available to rent at the Central Pond (the largest pond) in summer at $10 per half-hour or $14 for a full hour. The boats seat two to four people; fishing is not permitted from the boats. There are also walking paths and a fitness course. Dogs are welcome, but must be leashed and you need to clean up after them.

1800 Tingley Dr. SW. (from Rio Grande Blvd., head west on Central Ave. to Tingley Dr., then turn south). www.cabq.gov/biopark. © **505/768-2000.** Free admission. Daily sunrise–sunset. Closed New Year's Day, Thanksgiving, and Christmas.

BioPark Trains ★ There are two narrow-gauge trains at the BioPark. The **Rio Line** provides transportation between the aquarium/botanic gardens and the zoo over a 1.5-mile route along the Rio Grande, and the **Thunderbird Express** offers a 20-minute scenic loop through the zoo grounds. Trains are wheelchair-accessible. Strollers are permitted on the Rio Line but not on the Thunderbird Express, although a secure storage area is available at the Thunderbird Express station. Trains do not run on Christmas Eve. *Note:* If you purchase a combo ticket for the Biological Park and Rio Grande Zoo, use of the trains is included.

www.cabq.gov/biopark. Rio Line tickets available only with combo ticket to Aquarium/ Botanic Gardens/Zoo. Thunderbird Express loop for zoo visitors: Adults $3, children age 3–12 $2, free for children under 2. Trains usually operate Tues–Sun 10:15am–3:45pm.

BioPark Zoo ★★★ Some 250 species—about 1,000 animals in all—call this zoo home, including two dragons. Sunny, a 10-foot-long, 155-pound Komodo dragon, arrived in late 2015 in hopes that he and Nancy, the zoo's female Komodo dragon, would hit it off and there will soon be baby Komodo dragons scampering about. (Natives of Indonesia, Komodo dragons are the largest monitor lizards in the world and are listed as a threatened species.) Other major exhibits include polar bears, giraffes, sea lions (with underwater viewing), the cat walk, the bird show, and ape country, with gorillas and orangutans. The zoo has an especially fine collection of elephants, koalas, polar bears, reptiles, and native southwestern species; open-moat exhibits with animals in naturalized habitats give you a feel for what the animals' lives are like in the wild. Check out the various feeding times when you arrive so you can see the animals chowing down.

903 10th St. SW. www.cabq.gov/biopark/zoo. © **505/768-2000.** Adults $12.50 ($20 for combo ticket with aquarium, botanic gardens, and trains), seniors 65 and over $5.50 ($10 for combo ticket), children ages 3–12 $4 ($6 for combo ticket), free for children under 3. Daily 9am–5pm; June–Aug Sat–Sun and holidays open until 6pm. Ticket sales stop 30 min. before closing. Closed New Year's Day, Thanksgiving, and Christmas.

Other Museums

Holocaust & Intolerance Museum of New Mexico ★★ This is not a fun museum, but it is an important one that deserves a bit of your time when you're in Albuquerque. Its purpose is to fight hate and intolerance through education, and it does this through historic photos, documents, and artifacts. The photos can be shocking, and the artifacts, such as the devices used by the Nazis in World War II, are sobering. On a more positive note, there are also exhibits depicting how people and even governments have put themselves in mortal danger to help victims escape, such as Christians who hid Jewish children from the Nazis. Many of the museum's exhibits are about the Holocaust, but there are also displays depicting the persecution of American Indians, slavery in America, and genocides in Armenia, Greece, and Rwanda.

616 Central Ave. SW. www.nmholocaustmuseum.org. ℂ **505/247-0606.** Admission free; donations welcome. Tues–Sat 11am–3:30pm. Closed New Year's Day, Easter, Thanksgiving, and Christmas.

J&R Vintage Auto Museum ★★ They don't make 'em like they used to. Today's cars and trucks may be safer, more comfortable, less polluting, and more fuel efficient than those from the past, but they're boring to look at— especially compared to the beautiful cars and trucks of the golden age of automobiles, as displayed at this museum in Rio Rancho, a short drive from Albuquerque. You'll see more than 60 vehicles, some more than 100 years old. Many of the cars are for sale—you did remember to bring some extra spending money, didn't you?—so the collection changes, but you'll always see a variety of fine classics, from the exotic cars driven by movie stars of the 1930s to the muscle cars of the 1960s. The collection includes a lot of Fords from the 1920s and '30s (the favorites of museum founder Gab Joiner), plus vehicles from the very beginning of the 20th century with lots of brass and wooden wheels. You'll likely see a Ford Model A V-8 sedan or two, supposedly the favorite getaway car of outlaws Bonnie and Clyde. There's a well-stocked auto-related gift shop and large windows that provide a good view of the restoration shop.

3642 NM 528, Rio Rancho (I-25 exit 242, south on NM 528, then east onto Montoya St., turn left onto Christopher Way then right onto Gabby Lane). www.jrvintageautos.com. ℂ **888/298-1885** or 505/867-2881. Adults $6, seniors 55 and up $5, children ages 6–12 $3, free for ages 5 and under. Mon–Sat 10am–5pm. Closed New Year's Day, Easter, Thanksgiving, and Christmas.

National Museum of Nuclear Science & History ★★ Second only to the Bradbury Science Museum in Los Alamos (p. 112), this museum challenges the visitor to learn, imagine, think, and then draw his or her own conclusions. It describes the early research into nuclear science, then tracks it through weapons development to the peaceful uses of the technology today. Kids will love Little Albert's Lab, where they can explore hands-on science activities. Don't miss the planes, missiles, and atomic cannon spread over 9 acres in the outdoor Heritage Park.

601 Eubank SE (at Southern). www.nuclearmuseum.com. ℂ **505/245-2137.** Adults $12, ages 6–17 and 60 and up $10, veterans $8, active military and dependents $7, free for

children 5 and under. Children under 12 not admitted without adult. Daily 9am–5pm. Closed New Year's Day, Easter, Thanksgiving, and Christmas.

Turquoise Museum ★   Displaying what's said to be the world's largest collection of turquoise, amassed from 60 mines around the world, this fascinating museum can be visited only on a 90-minute guided tour. Turquoise is the passion of the Lowrys, father and son, whose collection this is. In addition to a whole lot of turquoise in all manner of settings, you'll get to see a lapidary demonstration. Exhibits explain the blue stone's geology, history, and mythology; there are maps showing mine locations from Egypt to Kingman, Arizona; and you can learn how to determine the quality of the turquoise you're considering buying.

2107 Central Ave. NW just west of Rio Grande Blvd. www.turquoisemuseum.com. © **505/247-8650.** Adults $10; seniors 60 and up, military, and children ages 7–12 $8; free for children 6 and under. Tours run Mon–Sat at 11am and 2pm. Reservations recommended in summer.

University of New Mexico Museums   On the 70-acre campus of New Mexico's flagship university, about 2 miles east of downtown Albuquerque, there are four campus museums, all with free admission, built in modified Pueblo-style architecture. In the Center for the Arts complex off Redondo Drive NE, the **University of New Mexico Art Museum ★★** (1700 Lomas Blvd. NE, © **505/277-4001**) has especially strong collections of prints and rare and printed books, spanning the history of the graphic arts from 1493 to the present, and a photography collection with some 10,000 photographs by over 1,000 different photographers spanning the entire history of the medium. In painting and sculpture, the museum owns many works of modern and contemporary American art as well as historic European and Spanish Colonial paintings, *retablos*, and polychrome wood sculpture, plus African sculpture. A number of noted New Mexican artists are represented, including Georgia O'Keeffe, Richard Diebenkorn, and Agnes Martin. It's open Tuesday to Friday 10am to 4pm, Saturday 10am to 8pm. Beside the main UNM library, the **Maxwell Museum of Anthropology ★★** (1 University Blvd. NE on Redondo W. Dr.; © **505/277-4405**) is one of the nation's finest anthropology museums, with a number of intriguing changing exhibitions, as well as two permanent exhibits in the Main Gallery: "People of the Southwest," which delves into the history of the area from 10,000 years ago into the 16th century, and "Ancestors," which looks at human evolution. The Maxwell is open Tuesday to Saturday 10am to 4pm. About midway between these two museums, in Northrup Hall (200 Yale Blvd. E.) are two smaller museums. The **Geology Museum ★** (© **505/277-4204**) has some fascinating displays of minerals, rocks, and fossils, many of them incredible works of art with nature as the artist, created over the span of eons. It's open 8:30am to noon and 1 to 4:30pm, Monday to Friday. The highlight of the **Meteorite Museum ★** (© **505/277-1644**) is a 1-ton piece of the stony meteorite that fell in Kansas in 1948. The Meteorite Museum is currently open by appointment only; call © **505/277-2747** to schedule a visit.

A snow-free SNOWMAN?

When one lives in the desert where not much snow falls, how can you build a snowman? One must use one's ingenuity. And that's just what the Albuquerque Metropolitan Arroyo Flood Control Authority, or AMAFCA, does. After clearing seemingly millions of tumbleweeds from arroyos every fall, where they can block drains and cause flooding, the AMAFCA a number of years ago decided to make something with them: It built a snowman. Now it's an Albuquerque tradition, and when the 15-to-20-foot tall fellow appears on I-40 just east of the University exit, people know the holiday season has officially begun. If you're here during the month of December, be sure to drive by there to see a true Southwest "Snowman."

University of New Mexico, 1 University Hill NE north of Central Ave. www.unm.edu. ℗ **505/277-0111.** Free admission to all museums. Parking garage east of the Center for the Arts at Redondo Dr. and Stanford Dr plus limited metered parking along Redondo Dr. Museums closed on major holidays.

Historic & Cultural Attractions

Coronado Historic Site ★★　When Spanish explorer Francisco Vásquez de Coronado traveled through this region in 1540–41, searching for the Seven Cities of Cíbola, he wintered at one of about a dozen Indian villages on the west bank of the Rio Grande, displacing the ancestral Puebloans (called Tiwa) who had lived here since the early 1300s. Coronado's forces also stole their food. In 1541, a short but bloody conflict erupted between the two groups that left hundreds of Tiwas dead and two of the villages destroyed. Here at Kuaua (Tiwa Indian language for "evergreen"), a multistoried building with over 1,200 small rooms was excavated in the 1930s as a Works Progress Administration project. Although the actual ruins remain buried for their protection, their outline has been created in adobe mud to show what this village would have looked like. In addition, a kiva has been reconstructed so that visitors can descend a ladder into the enclosed space, once the site of sacred rites. Unique multicolored murals, depicting human and animal forms, were found on successive layers of wall plaster in this and other kivas here, and some of those murals have been replicated. Some of the original murals are displayed in the site's museum. *Note:* Photography is not permitted inside the kiva or of the murals in the museum. The site, located along the Rio Grande just north of Albuquerque, also has splendid views of the Sandia Mountains, nature trails, and a birding checklist listing the 150 species that are seen here.

Kuaua Rd., Bernalillo. (I-25 exit 242, then 1.5 miles west on NM 550). www.nmhistoricsites.org. ℗ **505/867-5351.** Adults $3, free for children 16 and under. Free admission with New Mexico CulturePass (see p. 197). Wed–Mon 8:30am–5pm. Closed New Year's Day, Easter, Thanksgiving, and Christmas.

New Mexico Veterans' Memorial ★★　Covering 25 acres, the New Mexico Veterans' Memorial park honors the men and women who have served the United States, and New Mexico even before it became a state. The

TAKING HOME A southwest KITCHEN

If the unique and spicy New Mexican cuisine has taken over your taste buds, you might consider taking a cooking class with Jane Butel, a leading Southwest cooking authority, author of 19 cookbooks, and host of the national TV show *Jane Butel's Southwestern Kitchen*. Her **Jane Butel Cooking School ★,** 138 Armijo Court, Corrales (www.janebutel cooking.com; © **505/243-2622**) offers both weekend and week-long classes. In both you'll be treated to Jane's review of the history of the cuisine and its major ingredients, plus hints and techniques for success. Students cook in small groups, most often 2 or 3 people, with guidance provided by Jane and her staff. The week-long sessions allow ample time to explore native breads and main dishes, appetizers, and desserts. Call or visit Jane's website for current schedules and fees.

park provides places for reflection as well as events on special days such as Veterans Day and Memorial Day. As you enter the grounds you pass through the Boulevard of Flags, the American flag plus flags representing the six U.S. military services and the POW/MIA flag. There are about three dozen monuments to various aspects of the military and those who served, from the first encounters between the Spanish and American Indians through more current conflicts including the Gulf War and the War on Terror. There are monuments to the Merchant Marines, the Navajo Code Talkers, women in the military, and the Buffalo Soldiers, as well as monuments depicting the stages in a soldier's life: The Call, The Battle, The Fallen Friend, and finally, The Homecoming. The museum has exhibits about veterans. Tours of the facilities are available by appointment.

1100 Louisiana Blvd. SE. www.nmvetsmemorial.org. © **505/256-2042.** Admission free. Grounds open daily 6am–10pm, visitor center and museum open daily 9am–3pm. Closed New Year's Day and Christmas.

Petroglyph National Monument ★★   These lava flows were once a hunting and gathering area for prehistoric American Indians, who left a chronicle of their beliefs etched on the dark basalt boulders. Some 25,000 petroglyphs provide a nice outdoor adventure after a morning in a museum. Stop first at the visitor center to get a map and check out the interactive exhibits. From the visitor center, drive north to the **Boca Negra** area, which has an incredible array of images easily seen along three short trails. The Mesa Point Trail (30 min.) climbs quickly up the side of a hill, and offers many petroglyph sightings including four-pointed stars, handprints, and a human-like mask that seems to look in two directions at once. From the top of the escarpment you can see the Sandia Mountains to the east and the volcanic cones that formed this escarpment to the west. The two other trails here are easy, with an excellent petroglyph of a macaw easily found along the—you guessed it—Macaw Trail. Returning south past the visitor center, you'll reach **Rinconada Canyon,** where you can hike at least part of the Rinconada Trail, following a path created by wildlife and used by Spanish sheepherders. Along here you'll see older images including roadrunners and lizards, handprints, and human and god-like figures, plus more recent images of livestock brands, crosses, and sheep left by Spanish settlers. The park also has picnic areas, drinking water, and restrooms.

6001 Unser Blvd. NW (3 miles north of I-40 at Unser and Western Trail). www.nps.gov/petr. (C) **505/899-0205.** Admission is free; parking at Boca Negra Canyon $1 per vehicle weekdays, $2 weekends. Visitor Center and Boca Negra area open daily 8am–5pm. Closed New Year's Day, Thanksgiving, and Christmas.

Especially for Kids

Explora ★★ Part science center, part children's museum, part grandma's attic and grandpa's garage, part lab, and part neighborhood full of interesting and friendly people, Explora is a new kind of learning place. It provides real experiences with real things in exhibits that foster thoughtful activity in visitors of all ages. It's filled with small spaces of mostly tabletop exhibits with hand-sized parts made for manipulating, where you can experience and explore the properties of bubbles; create your own sea creature, releasing it into the digital sea; play with the properties of air, water, light, sound, and gravity; and much, much more. Little kids love the arts and crafts workshop where they can make something, with recycled materials of course, to take home. You can spend anywhere from an hour to all day here.

1701 Mountain Rd. NW. www.explora.us. (C) **505/224-8300.** Adults $8; students, military, and seniors 65 and up $5, children ages 1–11 $4. Mon–Sat 10am–6pm, Sun noon–6pm.

New Mexico Museum of Natural History and Science ★★ Take a walk through time here, beginning some 12 billion years ago with the

---

IN SEARCH OF adrenaline rushes

For a seriously fun and exciting time, though not on the scale of Disneyland, take the kids to **Cliff's Amusement Park ★,** 4800 Osuna Rd. NE (www.cliffs amusementpark.com; (C) **505/881-9373**). This park has rides that'll thrill every adrenaline junkie. The Cliff Hanger zips 120 feet in the air, then drops like a rock; the SideWinder spins and swings 80 feet up, around, and over; and the Fireball is an 80-foot high looping ride that flips upside-down and back around 13 times a minute. For those with less desire for such thrills, there's the carousel, bumper cars, and a pretty train you can ride around the park. There are height limitations on many of the rides, and it's fully open only in summer, weekends in May

and September, with special holiday programs in December. Ride passes start at $27.95 per person.

The **Hinkle Family Fun Center ★** offers a different kind of fun: an eighth-mile (220-yard) go-cart track, bumper boats, a couple of miniature golf courses, plus two state-of-the-art game rooms with redemption, merchandise, and arcade games. It's located at 12931 Indian School Rd. NE (www.hinklefamily funcenter.com; (C) **505/299-3100**) in the foothills just west of Tramway Blvd. It's open year-round except Thanksgiving and Christmas. Prices for activities vary; most charge $8 per person. Unlimited daily pass is $33 per person.

formation of the universe and moving right on up to now. Stop for a visit with the early dinosaurs of the Triassic era and the giants of the Jurassic age. See what New Mexico looked like some 75 million years ago when it was covered by an inland sea, followed by the volcanoes that raged here as recently as 1.8 million years ago. FossilWorks gives visitors a chance to observe the painstaking process of excavating the ancient bones on display. Ride the Evolator, a simulated time-travel machine that moves and rumbles, taking you through 38 million years of history. Don't miss the planetarium, or the DynaTheater, with its 2D/3D digital 4K dual projection system, five-story-high screen, and surround sound—seeing (and hearing) is believing. The NatureWorks Discovery Store completes your visit with a wide offering of educational, unique, and fun items. There's also a **cafe** where you can get breakfast or lunch, or just a quick snack to tide you over.

1801 Mountain Rd. NW. www.nmnaturalhistory.org. © **505/841-2800.** Adults $7, seniors 60 and up $6, children ages 3–12 $4, free for children 2 and under. Additional costs for DynaTheater ($10 adults, $8 seniors, $6 children); Planetarium and Virtual Voyages (prices in the $7 range for adults and $4 range for children). Discount ticket combinations available. Free admission with New Mexico CulturePass (see p. 197). Daily 9am–5pm. Closed New Year's Day, Thanksgiving, and Christmas.

Rattlesnake Museum ★   Danger! Look but don't touch! Well, you can't touch the rattlesnakes because they're behind glass, although that's just as much for their protection as for yours at this facility that bills itself as an animal conservation museum. Fairly small, the museum is packed with some 30 species of rattlesnakes—what it claims is the largest collection of different species of live rattlesnakes in the world—each housed in its appropriate habitat with signs telling you about it. There are also other creepy-crawly creatures, including horned lizards and Gila monsters. There's a short film on rattlesnakes, and exhibits of rattlesnake memorabilia including American Indian pottery with designs depicting rattlesnakes and a poster for the 1944 film *Cobra Woman*.

202 San Felipe St. NW. www.rattlesnakes.com. © **505/242-6569.** Adults $5, seniors 60 and up and military $4, children ages 3–12 $3. Mon–Sat 10am–6pm, Sun 1–5pm. Closed New Year's Day, Easter, Thanksgiving, and Christmas.

Parks, Gardens & Zoos

Rio Grande Nature Center State Park ★★★   Located on the east bank of the Rio Grande, this delightful oasis just a few miles from Old Town is an excellent place for bird-watchers, hikers, and anyone just wanting a break from the bustle of the city. The park is in what is called a *bosque*, a Spanish word for forest that in New Mexico is often used to describe the wetlands along rivers, particularly along the Rio Grande. The nature center covers some 270 acres of woods and meadows, with native grasses, wildflowers, willows, Russian olives, and cottonwoods. It also has a 3-acre pond, which helps attract more than 260 species of birds. The Rio Grande Flyway, an important migratory route for many birds, is an excellent place to see sandhill cranes, Canadian geese, and quail. The interpretive River Loop and Bosque Loop trails

ALBUQUERQUE open space

Realizing that its residents like to get outside, the city of Albuquerque initiated an open space program that is considered one of the most ambitious in the country. It began buying land in the 1960s for as little as $2.50 an acre, and today has nearly 30,000 acres, including lands inside city limits as well as nearby. These protected lands include one of the world's largest riverside cottonwood forests and a major winter home for sandhill cranes. Throughout the open space lands are opportunities for hiking, biking, birding, and photography.

Among recommended areas in the system are the **Elena Gallegos Picnic Area and Albert G. Simms Park** on the east side of the city. There are magnificent views of the Sandia Mountains, covered picnic tables, and a variety of multi-use trails including the Cottonwood Springs Trail, a wheelchair-accessible trail featuring interpretative artwork and a wildlife blind that overlooks a wetland.

The **Rio Grande Valley State Park,** along the Rio Grande south of I-40, includes 4,300 acres of riverside forest, known locally as the *bosque* (Spanish for forest). This park has picnic areas and multi-use trails, including the scenic and shady Rio Bravo Nature Trail.

Your first stop should be the **Open Space Visitor Center** (6500 Coors Blvd., at the end of Bosque Meadows Rd., www.cabq.gov/openspace, ✆ 505/897-8831), where you can get detailed information on trails, birding checklists, and other aspects of the system. The visitor center is open Tuesday to Sunday, 9am to 5pm. Some trails leave from the visitor center, and it also has exhibits. Be sure to pick up the free brochure on the *"Arbol de la Vida"* ("The Tree of Life") and then head just outside the center to this chainsaw-carved tree trunk and see how many of the 25 animals carved into the wood you can find.

meander through the bosque, and the paved Paseo del Bosque Trail runs along a flood-control ditch between the visitor center and river, and is open to bicycles. The visitor center has self-guided exhibits as well as photo exhibits, a library, a small nature store, and a children's resource room.

2901 Candelaria Rd. NW. www.nmparks.com. ✆ **505/344-7240.** Admission $5 per vehicle. No credit cards. Daily 10am–5pm; store Mon–Fri 11am–3pm, Sat–Sun 10am–4pm. Closed New Year's Day, Thanksgiving, and Christmas.

Valle de Oro National Wildlife Refuge ★ This work in progress, currently being developed by the U.S. Fish & Wildlife Service, covers 570 acres of land along the east bank of the Rio Grande. It offers stunning views of the Sandia Mountains, Vulcan volcano tubes, and the lush Rio Grande Bosque. As of this writing, the refuge continues to be a working alfalfa farm, but it also offers opportunities for bird-watching, especially cranes (in winter), geese, ground-nesting birds, and various wading birds. Additional wildlife viewing opportunities are expected as native habitats are restored, and nature trails, a visitor center, and interpretative programs are planned.

5 miles south of downtown Albuquerque (I-25 exit 220, Rio Bravo Blvd., west on Rio Bravo, then south on 2nd St.). www.fws.gov/refuge/valle_de_oro. ✆ **505/248-6667.** Admission free. Daily 8am–5pm.

Wildlife West Nature Park ★★ They can't go home, but you're invited to visit them here at this rescued wildlife zoo about 20 minutes east of Albuquerque. A project of the non-profit New Mexico Wildlife Association, all the wildlife at this nature park has been injured, orphaned, or for some other reason cannot be released back into the wild. There are 25 species of New Mexico wildlife represented, including cougars, wolves, raccoons, deer, bear, elk, pronghorn, javelina, and hawks, along with native plants, at this 122-acre park and environmental education center. There's a raptor viewing area and a half-mile birding walk. A variety of festivals, classes, and other events are held (call or check the website for the current schedule), and Saturday evenings from mid-June through Labor Day weekend the center has a chuckwagon supper and western show ($25 adults, $12 children 5 to 11, and free for kids under 5).

87 N. Frontage Rd., Edgewood (I-40 exit 187, head west on North Frontage Rd.). www.wildlifewest.org. © **877/981-9453** or 505-281-7655. Adults $9, seniors 60 and up $7, students (including college students) $5, children under 5 free. Mid-Mar–Oct daily 10am–6pm, Nov–mid-Mar daily noon–4pm. Closed New Year's Day, Thanksgiving, and Christmas.

Organized Tours

ABQ Trolley Company ★ A great way to get acquainted with the city, the Best of ABQ open-air trolley tour takes visitors on an 85-minute, 18-mile jaunt, starting in Old Town and winding through the most interesting parts of the city. You'll see filming locations for major movies and TV shows (including the series *Breaking Bad*), historic Route 66, a beach, the zoo, and even a spaceship. *Note:* This is not a hop-on hop-off service, but a tour where you stay onboard for its duration. Well-behaved pets are welcome.

Departs from Hotel Albuquerque at Old Town, 800 Rio Grande Blvd. NW (free parking for trolley riders at hotel). www.abqtrolley.com. © **505/240-8000.** Adults $25, children 12 and under $15. Operates 2–4 times daily Tues–Sun Apr–Oct. Check website for exact times.

SPORTS & RECREATION

With sunny skies and pleasant temperatures almost year-round, the Albuquerque area is a delightful locale for outdoor activities, from hiking and biking to fishing and bird-watching. Just remember that summer temperatures can sometimes be scorching and winter winds can produce biting wind chills. Also, especially in summer, be sure to carry drinking water on any outdoor excursion, and drink it. It's dry out there!

Ballooning

Visitors have a choice of several hot-air balloon operators; rates start at about $199 per person per hour. Contact **Rainbow Ryders** ★ (www.rainbowryders.com; © **800/725-2477** or 505/823-1111) or **World Balloon Corporation** ★ (www.worldballoon.com; © **505/293-6800**). If you'd rather just watch, go to

ALOFT OVER albuquerque

From a distance it looks like a kids' birthday party gone wild, but up close it's fantastic, a seemingly endless explosion of colorful hot-air balloons literally filling the skies, accompanied by the deafening sound of the balloons' propane heaters. The **Albuquerque International Balloon Fiesta,** begun in 1972 when 13 balloons launched from a parking lot, now includes almost 600 balloons launching from the event's own Balloon Fiesta Park in early October, with nine days of events. Most exciting are the mass ascensions at 7am most mornings (weather permitting), but there are also races and flying competitions, dawn patrol shows, chainsaw carving contests, and morning and evening glows, when the balloons come alive in the darkness with light from the propane heaters shining through the balloon fabric.

You can see the balloons from anywhere in the city (that's free), but the best close-up views are from **Balloon Fiesta Park,** which charges $8 per person 13 and older, per session; 12 and under free. A session is either a morning or afternoon/evening. There are also parking fees, and five-pack tickets ($35) and various other packages. Crowds for some of the events exceed 100,000 people, so you'll want to get to the park between 4 and 4:30am for the morning events. The park is located north of Alameda Boulevard, 1 mile west of I-25, on the north side of the city.

If you want to take to the skies yourself during the fiesta, contact **Rainbow Ryders,** the fiesta's official balloon ride concessionaire (see "Ballooning," above). For additional information see www.balloonfiesta.com or call ℭ **888/422-7277** or 505/821-1000.

the annual **Albuquerque International Balloon Fiesta ★★★**, which is held the first through second weekends of October (see above).

Biking

With some 400 miles of bike paths and trails, Albuquerque is a major bicycling hub in the summer, for both road racers and mountain bikers. A great place to mountain bike is **Sandia Peak ★★** (www.sandiapeak.com; ℭ **505/242-9133**) in Cíbola National Forest. You can't take your bike on the tram, but the ski area's chairlift no. 1 is available for uphill or downhill transportation with a bike. The lift runs weekends from July through Labor Day and daily during the Balloon Fiesta; tickets cost $8 one-way and $10 roundtrip. You can rent a bike for $48, which includes a helmet and one lift trip. Helmets are mandatory. Bike trail maps are available; the clearly marked trails range from easy to very difficult.

Down in the valley, there's a **bosque trail ★** that runs along the Rio Grande, accessed through the Rio Grande Nature Center (see p. 206). To the east, the **Foothills Trail ★★** runs along the base of the mountains. It's a fun, 7-mile-long trail with stupendous views. Access it by driving east from downtown on Montgomery Boulevard, past the intersection with Tramway Boulevard. Go left on Glenwood Hills Drive and head north about a half-mile before turning right onto a short road that leads to the Embudito trail head.

Northeast Cyclery ★, 8305 Menaul Blvd. NE, just west of Wyoming Boulevard (℗ **505/299-1210**), rents bikes at the rate of $25 per day for front-suspension mountain bikes and $35 per day for road bikes. Multiday discounts are available. Unfortunately, the shop doesn't rent children's bikes. Rentals come with helmets.

Bird-Watching

The Rio Grande is the fourth-longest river on the continent and the basis for the **Rio Grande Flyway,** one of North America's most important flyways for migratory waterfowl and other birds. The river flows through the heart of Albuquerque, and the city area has an abundance of local, state, and federally protected land that supports wildlife and serves as ideal habitat for nesting and migratory birds. **Albuquerque Open Space** (p. 207) offers several excellent bird-watching spots around the city, and its visitor center has a bird checklist that indicates what time of year each species has been sighted. Another place to check out is the **Rio Grande Nature Center State Park** (p. 206). And if you're here from November through March, head south to **Bosque del Apache National Wildlife Refuge** (p. 221), where vast numbers of many bird species winter.

> ### Where's the Nearest Tennis Court or Hiking Trail?
>
> The **Albuquerque Parks & Recreation Department** (www.cabq.gov/parksandrecreation; ℗ **505/768-5300**) has maps and lists of places for many outdoor activities: bicycle and hiking trails, golf courses, tennis courts, swimming pools, skate parks, a rock-climbing wall, and skiing and snowboarding.

Golf

There are quite a few public courses in the Albuquerque area. The **Championship Golf Course at the University of New Mexico** ★★★, 3601 University Blvd. SE (www.unmgolf.com; ℗ **505/277-4546**), is one of the best in the Southwest. Check with the city's Parks and Recreation Department (see box above) for a complete list of public courses. See also "Golf on the Santa Fe Trail," below).

Hiking

The 1½-million-acre **Cíbola National Forest** (www.fs.usda.gov/Cibola) offers ample hiking opportunities. Within town, the best hike is the **Embudito Trail** ★, which heads up into the foothills, with spectacular views down across Albuquerque. The 5.5-mile one-way hike is moderate to difficult. Allow 1 to 8 hours, depending on how far you want to go. Access it by driving east from downtown on Montgomery Boulevard past the intersection with Tramway Boulevard. Go left on Glenwood Hills Drive and head north about a half-mile before turning right onto a short road that leads to the trail head. The premier Sandia Mountain hike is **La Luz Trail** ★★, a very strenuous journey from the Sandia foothills to the top of the Crest. It's a 15-mile round-trip jaunt, but it's half that if you take the Sandia Peak Tramway (p. 198) either

Those golfers traveling through Albuquerque and northward will appreciate the eight world-class courses that have teamed together to offer customized golf packages. **Golf on the Santa Fe Trail** ★ (www.santafetrailgolf.com; ℂ **866/465-3660**) includes such prestigious courses as the **Santa Ana Pueblo Course** ★★, just north of Albuquerque in Bernalillo (I-25 exit 242, 2 miles west), and the **Black Mesa Golf Club** ★, north of Santa Fe at Santa Clara Pueblo, one of the state's premier golf settings since opening in 2003. For the other courses involved, visit the website.

up or down. Allow a full day for this hike. The trail head is off Tramway Boulevard and Forest Service Road 333.

Horseback Riding

Want to see the area from the back of a horse? Call the **Stables at Tamaya** ★ at the Hyatt Regency Tamaya Resort and Spa, 1300 Tuyuna Trail, Santa Ana Pueblo (www.tamaya.hyatt.com; ℂ **505/771-6060**). A 2-hour trail ride costs $75 per person; for children ages 4 through 8, you can do a "leadaround" (a handler guides the horse and young rider around the stable's corral) for $35. More than half the horses here are rescue animals. The resort is about 15 miles north of Albuquerque in Bernalillo (I-25 exit 242, west on US 550 and turn right just past the casino).

Skiing

The **Sandia Peak Ski Area** ★ is a good place for family skiing, with plenty of beginner and intermediate runs. (If you're looking for more challenge or more variety, head north to Taos.) The ski area has twin base-to-summit chairlifts to its upper slopes at 10,350 feet. The trails are rated as 35% beginner, 55% intermediate, and 10% advanced; there's a day lodge and ski-rental shop at the base. Four chairs whisk skiers to the top, with a fifth chair about halfway up the slopes; and two Pomas service the beginner slopes. All-day lift tickets are $55 for adults, $45 for ages 13 to 20, and $40 for children ages 6 to 12 and seniors 62 to 71; free for seniors 72 or over and for children less than 46 inches tall in ski boots. Rental packages are available. The season runs mid-December to mid-March. Contact the ski area, 10 Tramway Loop NE (www.sandiapeak.com; ℂ **505/242-9052**), for more information, or call the hotline for a snow report (ℂ **505/857-8977**).

Cross-country skiers can enjoy the trails of the Sandia Wilderness from the ski area, or they can go an hour north to the remote Jemez Wilderness and its hot springs.

Tennis

Albuquerque has 29 public parks with tennis courts. Check with the city's Parks and Recreation Department (p. 210) for a complete list to determine which is closest to your hotel.

9

EXPLORING ALBUQUERQUE

Sports & Recreation

GETTING PAMPERED: the spa scene

If you're looking to get pampered, you have a few options. **Mark Pardo Salon & Spa ★** (*C* 505/298-2983 all locations) offers treatments at four locations: 1100 Juan Tabo Blvd. NE; 8001 Wyoming Blvd. NE at Paseo del Norte; Nob Hill area at 3500 Central Ave. SE; and Cottonwood Mall, 10420 Coors Bypass NW.

Albuquerque's top two luxurious spa experiences are at the **Hyatt Regency Tamaya Resort & Spa ★★** at Santa Ana Pueblo (www.tamaya.hyatt.com; *C* 505/867-1234), and the **Sandia Resort & Casino ★,** 30 Rainbow Rd. NE (www.sandiacasino.com; *C* 800/526-9366 or 505/796-7500). Each offers a broad array of treatments, as well as a sauna and a steam room, in refined atmospheres. The Tamaya is 15 minutes north of Albuquerque in Bernalillo, while the Sandia is on the north end of town, off Tramway Road.

9 SPECTATOR SPORTS

Auto Racing

The **Sandia Speedway ★★** (www.racesandia.com; *C* 505/400-0611) attracts fans of fast cars, with races scheduled most Saturdays from April through mid-October. Tracks include ½- and ¼-mile paved ovals, a high banked ⅜-mile dirt oval, and a 1.7-mile road course. It's about 4 miles west of I-40, exit 149.

Baseball

The **Albuquerque Isotopes ★★** (www.albuquerquebaseball.com; *C* 505/924-2255) are part of the Pacific Coast League, and when home, play in Isotopes Park on the UNM South Campus. Isotopes Park is on the northeast corner of Avenida Cesar Chavez and University Boulevard. Take I-25 south to exit 223 and go east to University.

Basketball

The University of New Mexico team, **the Lobos ★** (www.golobos.com; *C* 505/925-5626), plays an average of 16 home games from late November to early March. Capacity crowds cheer the team at the 17,000-seat University Arena (fondly called "the Pit") on the southwest corner of Avenida Cesar Chavez and University Boulevard. Take I-25 south to exit 223 and go east to University.

Football

The **UNM Lobos ★** football team plays a September-to-November season—usually with five home games—at the 30,000-seat UNM Stadium, on the southeast corner of Avenida Cesar Chavez and University Boulevard, opposite both the Albuquerque Sports Stadium and the University Arena at University and Stadium boulevards. Take I-25 south to exit 223 and go east to University. For tickets and information, call *C* 505/925-5626 (www.golobos.com).

Horse Racing

The **Downs at Albuquerque Racetrack and Casino ★** (www.abqdowns. com; © **505/266-5555** for post times) is on the northeast corner of Central Avenue and Louisiana Boulevard. Racing and betting—on thoroughbreds and quarter horses—take place mid-August through mid-November. The Downs has a glass-enclosed grandstand and exclusive club seating. General admission is free; parking is free if you enter off Central. Simulcast racing occurs daily year-round, except Christmas. The casino offers almost 700 slot machines plus an electronic pit area of table games including craps, roulette, and blackjack.

ALBUQUERQUE SHOPPING

Many New Mexicans think of Albuquerque as one big shopping center, and come here to stock up on basics, building materials, and appliances. What? You didn't come to New Mexico to buy a refrigerator? Well, although Albuquerque can't really compete with Santa Fe and Taos as far as art galleries and fancy shops, the city does have its share of interesting places to leave some coin, and there's a good chance you'll find something you just have to take home with you. As a bonus, it will probably be cheaper here than in Santa Fe or Taos; plus the sales tax is about 1% lower in Albuquerque than either Santa Fe or Taos. By far, the most galleries and top-quality shops are in Old Town; others are spread around the city, and don't forget the museum shops.

Twice a month, usually the first Friday and third Saturday, the **Albuquerque Art Business Association** (www.artscrawlabq.org; © **505/244-0362**) sponsors an **ArtsCrawl ★★** to dozens of galleries and studios. It's a great way to meet the artists.

The state's best shopping mall is **Coronado Center ★★,** 6600 Menaul Blvd. NE (www.coronadocenter.com; © **505/881-2700**), with more than 125 stores including Macy's, Sears, Godiva Chocolatier, Bath & Body Works, Dick's Sporting Goods, and Barnes & Noble Bookstore. Smaller but slightly more upscale is **ABQ Uptown ★,** at Louisiana Blvd. NE and Indian School Rd. NE (www.abquptown.com; © **505/792-1929**), where you'll find Williams-Sonoma, Pottery Barn, Ann Taylor, J. Crew, Eddie Bauer, and The North Face.

Arts & Crafts

Albuquerque Photographers' Gallery ★★   This fine art photography gallery specializes in unique images of the American West. 303 Romero St. NW. www.abqphotographersgallery.com. © **505/244-9195.**

Amapola Gallery ★   Dozens of New Mexico artists and craftspeople sell their work at this artists'-owned gallery established in 1980. 205 Romero St. NW. www.amapolagallery.com. © **505/242-4311.**

Bien Mur Indian Market ★★★   Billing itself as the largest retail arts and crafts store in the Southwest, this market, owned and operated by Sandia

Pueblo, has been in operation since 1975. It offers top-quality, genuine American Indian arts and crafts, including Navajo, Hopi, Zuni, and Santo Domingo jewelry; Zuni fetishes; Navajo rugs; Pueblo pottery; storytellers; sand paintings; and even war bonnets. I-25 at Tramway Rd. NE, next to the Bien Mur Travel Center. www.sandiapueblo.nsn.us/bien-mur-indian-market. ℂ **800/365-5400** or 505/821-5400.

Gallery at 400 ★   An artists' collective, this gallery sells paintings, pottery, jewelry, and cards by New Mexico artists. 400 Romero St. NW, Ste. 5. www.galleryat400.com. ℂ **505/243-1005.**

La Casita de Kaleidoscopes ★   Over 50 kaleidoscope artists produce these interactive works, blending art, craft, and science. 400 B San Felipe St. NW. www.casitascopes.com. ℂ **505/247-4242.**

Mariposa Gallery ★★   This fun gallery has been selling contemporary crafts and jewelry since 1974, including ceramics, paintings, mixed media, and wood. Look for the colorfully painted model cars by Albuquerque area resident Lou Baudoin. 3500 Central Ave. SE. www.mariposa-gallery.com. ℂ **505/268-6828.**

Skip Maisel's ★★   An enormous selection of American Indian jewelry and crafts is displayed at this Albuquerque landmark. There's plenty of Navajo turquoise and silver jewelry, of course, plus Hopi, Santo Domingo, and Zuni jewelry; and this is one of the best places to come for genuine Hopi kachinas. Don't miss seeing the murals painted by Indian artists in the 1930s. 510 Central Ave. SW. www.skipmaisels.com. ℂ **505/242-6526.**

Tanner Chaney Gallery ★★   For authentic and unique historic and contemporary American Indian jewelry, including old pawn jewelry, this is the place to come. It also sells pueblo pottery, Zapotec rugs, and other handmade crafts. 323 Romero St. NW. www.tannerchaney.com. ℂ **800/444-2242** or 505/247-2242.

Books

Barnes & Noble ★   There are two Barnes & Noble bookstores in Albuquerque, both with everything readable you might want. Each also has a large children's book section, weekly children's story time, and a coffee shop. At the Coronado Center, 6600 Menaul Blvd. NE. www.barnesandnoble.com. ℂ **505/883-8200.** 3701 Ellison Dr. NW, North of Cottonwood Mall. www.barnesandnoble.com. ℂ **505/792-4234.**

Bookworks ★   A good place to come for books on the Southwest, this store is also a good spot to meet authors, with numerous author events. Bookworks also has special children's events such as storytelling, and sells both new and used books. 4022 Rio Grande Blvd. NW. www.bkwrks.com. ℂ **505/344-8139.**

Page One ★★   Locally owned and operated since 1981, Page One is likely to have whatever book you're looking for, including out-of-print and rare books. It also has a popular children's story reading program. Mountain Run Shopping Center, 5850 Eubank Blvd. NE. www.page1book.com. ℂ **505/294-2026.**

A TASTE OF THE grape

In addition to New Mexico's many enchanting sights, wineries abound across the state, providing an excellent way to taste some of the 400-year-old growing tradition. Call or check websites to find out their wine-tasting hours. The top Albuquerque area wineries are **Casa Rondeña Winery** ★★, 733 Chavez Rd., Los Ranchos de Albuquerque (www.casarondena.com; ☎ **800/706-1699** or 505/344-5911), and **Gruet Winery** ★★★, 8400 Pan-American Fwy. NE (www.gruetwinery.com; ☎ **888/857-9463** or 505/821-0055). For additional information on New Mexico's wineries, check the New Mexico Winegrowers Association website: **www.nmwine.com**.

Food

The Candy Lady ★★   Practically every type of candy you've ever heard of, and a few you haven't heard of, are prepared fresh by The Candy Lady. Here you'll find truffles, caramels, peanut butter crunch, hard rock candy, fudge, and special New Mexico flavors such as chocolate red chile and pecan nut clusters, made with New Mexico pecans clustered in milk, white, or dark chocolate. You can also order a custom cake. 424 San Felipe St. NW. www.thecandylady.com. ☎ **800/214-7731** or 505/243-6239.

Gifts/Souvenirs

The Christmas Shop ★★   Want to have a New Mexico Christmas when you get home? This shop offers excellent holiday items by southwestern artists and crafts workers, including American Indian tree ornaments and handmade nativities. You can also get chile pepper tree lights, Mexican ornaments, and southwestern-design tin cookie cutters, ranging from chile peppers to geckos. 400 Romero St. NW (behind the church). www.christmasinoldtown.com. ☎ **505/843-6744.**

Old Town Emporium ★   From T-shirts to jewelry, Christmas ornaments to Route 66 souvenirs, you'll find it all at this gift and souvenir shop. And it's not all tacky souvenirs, either. The shop sells handmade pottery from Acoma, San Juan, and Isleta pueblos, and other quality crafts. 204 San Felipe St. NW. www.old-town-emporium.com. ☎ **505/842-8102.**

Wearables

Old Town Hat Shop ★★   From berets to baseball caps to every possible type of fedora and cowboy hat, this is where to shop in Albuquerque if you want to protect your head from the New Mexico sun, or just to make a fashion statement. All the major brands are offered, and especially fun are some of the vintage-style hats for both men and women. The shop also sells belts, scarves, and purses. 205-C San Felipe St. NW. www.oldtownhats.com. ☎ **505/242-4019.**

Wild Moon Boutique ★★   Are you a wild woman? Then this is your clothing shop. From traditional to chic, mild to wild, this is the place to find your inner wild woman and dress her up in colorful clothing from around the world, or perhaps created by a skilled local artisan using natural fibers. There are dresses, pants and skirt sets, separates, boots, accessories, and Indian jewelry. 326½ San Felipe St. NW. wildmoonboutique.com. © **505/247-2475.**

ALBUQUERQUE AFTER DARK

In this city of half a million people, most of them apparently go to bed early and don't go out much at night, as there aren't as many performing-arts groups and venues or other nightlife as in Santa Fe or even Taos. However, what there is, is choice.

Complete information on all major cultural events can be obtained from the **Albuquerque Convention and Visitors Bureau** (www.itsatrip.org; © **800/ 284-2282**), and current listings and a weekend arts calendar can be found in Friday's *Albuquerque Journal* (www.abqjournal.com).

Tickets for nearly all major entertainment and sporting events can be obtained from **Ticketmaster,** 4004 Carlisle Blvd. NE (www.ticketmaster.com; © **800/ 745-3000**). Discount tickets are sometimes available for midweek and matinee performances; check with individual theater or concert hall box offices.

The Performing Arts

Albuquerque Little Theatre ★★★ The Albuquerque Little Theatre has been offering a variety of productions ranging from comedies to dramas to musicals since 1930. Seven plays are presented here over the course of the year. Located across from Old Town, the theater offers plenty of free parking. 224 San Pasquale Ave. SW (I-40 exit 157A). www.albuquerquelittletheatre.org. © **505/242-4750.** General admission $24.

KiMo Theatre ★★ In September 1927, the KiMo, a Pueblo Deco picture palace, opened. Pueblo Deco was a flamboyant, short-lived architectural style that used Pueblo Indian motifs in an Art Deco style, and the elaborate corbels and mosaic tile work here are astonishing. The KiMo offers a variety of entertainment, including film, theater, and musical performances. 423 Central Ave. NW at 5th St. www.cabq.gov/culturalservices/kimo. © **505/768-3544.** Tickets prices vary by production.

Musical Theatre Southwest ★ This theater presents five Broadway musicals and several smaller productions throughout the year. Most productions are staged for three consecutive weekends, including some Sunday matinees. The black box theater seats 100. 6320 Domingo Rd. NE, just north of Central and west of the state fairgrounds. www.musicaltheatresw.com. © **505/265-9119.** Tickets $25–$35.

New Mexico Ballet Company ★ Founded in 1972, the state's oldest ballet company holds most of its performances at Popejoy Hall. Typically there's a fall production, such as *Dracula,* a holiday one such as *The Nutcracker* or *A Christmas Carol,* and a contemporary spring production. 4200 Wyoming Blvd. NE, Ste. B2. www.newmexicoballet.org. © **505/292-4245.** Tickets $15–$40, depending on performance and venue.

South Broadway Cultural Center ★★ An architectural and artistic jewel, South Broadway Cultural Center features a 300-seat theater, an art gallery, a large community meeting and event room, and a library. The John Lewis Theater offers a wide variety of live entertainment throughout the year. 1025 Broadway Blvd. SE. www.cabq.gov/culturalservices/south-broadway-cultural-center. ℭ **505/848-1320.** Tickets prices vary.

University of New Mexico Fine Arts Department ★★ The university has an excellent fine arts department, with programs in theater, dance, and music. Wonderful recitals, performances, and large-scale productions are offered during the school year. Most performances take place in the Center for the Arts, which houses Popejoy Hall (ℭ **505/277-3824**), Keller Hall (ℭ **505/277-4569**), and Rodey Theatre. The Center for the Arts is located on Redondo Drive just north of Central Avenue between the Yale and Stanford entrances. Some dance productions are presented in the Elizabeth Waters Center for Dance in Carlisle Gym. Call the dance office for information: ℭ **505/277-3660.** 1 University Hill NE, north of Central Ave. www.unm.edu ℭ **505/277-0111.**

Vortex Theatre ★ This black-box theater has been a pioneering venue for classic, contemporary, and cutting-edge productions since 1976. It has offered Tennessee Williams' *The Glass Menagerie*, Rudolfo Anaya's *Bless Me, Ultima*, several Shakespeare plays, and *The Underpants* by Steve Martin, among many others. Performances take place on Friday and Saturday evenings, with a matinee on Sunday. 2900 Carlisle Blvd. NE, just south of Candelaria Rd. www.vortexabq.org. ℭ **505/247-8600.** Adults $22, students $15.

The Bar Scene

Despite the fact that Albuquerque is a bigger city than Santa Fe, Santa Fe has a much more active nightlife, and a much more stable one, too. It seems that every time we go back to an old favorite in Albuquerque, it's gone. Fortunately there are still some old reliable bars and clubs left, and a few relatively new ones that are fun. In addition, a lot of the hotels and restaurants here have good bars, some with live entertainment. Entertainment schedules vary, and cover charges for entertainment usually range from nothing to $10, with an occasional special performance charging more. Check websites or call to see what's happening.

Billy's Long Bar ★ Serious beer drinkers will like this spot, which has about the best selection of beers on tap in New Mexico. The brick walls are plastered with beer signs, and there are numerous TVs and several pool tables. 4800 San Mateo Blvd. NE. ℭ **505/889-0573.**

The Cooperage ★ Ready for some salsa music? The Cooperage has live entertainment most weekends, with salsa every Saturday evening. 7220 Lomas Blvd. NE. www.cooperageabq.com. ℭ **505/255-1657.**

The Dirty Bourbon Dance Hall & Saloon ★★ For some serious two-steppin', head to this lively spot, which boasts two 53-foot bars and a 1,300-square-foot dance floor. It has frequent live music, line dancing lessons, pool tables, and events such as the "ugly sweater party." 9800 Montgomery Blvd. NE. www.thedirtybourbon.com. ℭ **505/296-2726.**

HITTING THE casinos

If you'd like to include a little gambling in your visit to Albuquerque, or maybe see some big-name entertainers, the best spot is the expansive **Sandia Resort & Casino** ★★, north of I-25 and a quarter-mile east on Tramway Boulevard (www.sandiacasino.com; ℂ **800/526-9366** or 505/796-7500). The huge complex sits on Sandia Pueblo land and has outstanding views of the Sandia Mountains. Built in pueblo architectural style, the casino has more than 2,300 slot machines and numerous table games, including blackjack, roulette, and craps, and New Mexico's largest non-smoking poker room. There's a 4,000-seat outdoor amphitheater, a large indoor ballroom, three restaurants, and a lounge, where there's nightly DJ or live entertainment. Sandia also brings in top musical acts such as ZZ Top, Alabama, James Taylor, and Ringo Starr.

Just south of town, the **Isleta Resort & Casino** ★, 11000 Broadway SE, at I-25 exit 215 (www.isleta.com; ℂ **505/724-3800**), has over 1,800 slot machines and more than two dozen table games in a luxurious casino with a full-service restaurant and bar, and occasional live entertainment.

Ibiza ★   This rooftop hotspot offers great city views, a broad patio, and live or recorded music. Hotel Andaluz, 125 2nd St. NW. www.hotelandaluz.com. ℂ **505/243-9090.**

Kelly's Brew Pub ★★   Near the University of New Mexico, you'll find this brewpub in a renovated car dealership and service station from the late 1930s, a heritage that inspired its gas station decor. Kelly's offers its own excellent craft beers—about 20 in all—plus some "guest" brews and good pub fare. It has 12 TVs tuned to whatever games are being played. 3222 Central Ave. SE. www.kellysbrewpub.com. ℂ **505/262-2739.**

Nob Hill Bar & Grill ★   As the name suggests, this plush nightspot is where the highbrows like to hang out and enjoy the large selection of beers, tequilas, and whiskeys. 3128 Central Ave. SE. www.upscalejoint.com. ℂ **505/266-4455.**

O'Niell's Pub ★   Another good bar near UNM, O'Niell's has live music on Sundays. There's another O'Niell's at 3301 Juan Tabo Blvd. NE (ℂ **505/293-1122**). 4310 Central Ave. SE. www.oniells.com. ℂ **505/255-6782.**

QBar Lounge ★★   You'll find a sophisticated and relaxing atmosphere here, with dancing, a piano lounge, excellent drinks, and a lot of plush furnishings. In Hotel Albuquerque at Old Town, 800 Rio Grande Blvd. NW. www.hotelabq.com. ℂ **505/225-5928.**

EXCURSIONS FROM ALBUQUERQUE

With bargain lodging rates and interstate highways heading in all four directions of the compass, Albuquerque is an excellent base for exploring New Mexico. The following trips can be done in one or two days, and will take you

0   40 mi

0   40 km

Taos

■ Picuris Pueblo

550

84   285   68

Española

Cuba

Los Alamos

25

Jemez Pueblo ■ Jemez
                Springs

Santa Fe

4

84 ■ Pecos
        National
        Historic Park Las Vegas

Cerrillos
Madrid

Bernalillo

Grants

14

84   Pecos River

Rio Rancho   Golden —Turquoise Trail

40   **ALBUQUERQUE** Cedar Crest

40

Moriarty   Santa Rosa

■ Isleta
  Pueblo   337

ALAMO
NAVAJO
RESERVATION

337

7

60   6   Mountainair

25

5

60

Socorro

4   380

54

Acoma Pueblo **3**

Bosque del Apache National
   Wildlife Refuge **4**

Chaco Culture National
   Historic Park **1**

Jemez Historic Site **2**

Salinas National Monument:
   Abo **6**

Salinas National Monument:
   Gran Quivera **5**

Salinas National Monument:
   Quarai **7**

through old mining towns, to one of the premier bird-watching areas of the West, to ancient sites once occupied by ancestral Puebloan people and Spanish conquistadors, and to a bustling handsome Indian Pueblo that may be the longest continuously occupied community in North America.

The Turquoise Trail

Known as "the Turquoise Trail," NM 14 begins about 16 miles east of downtown Albuquerque, at I-40's Cedar Crest exit, and winds some 46 miles to Santa Fe along the east side of the Sandia Mountains. The route takes you to the revived ghost towns of Golden, Madrid, and Cerrillos, where gold, silver, coal, and turquoise were once mined in great quantities. Modern-day settlers, mostly artists and craftspeople, have brought a renewed frontier spirit to the old mining towns.

As you start along the Turquoise Trail, you may want to turn left onto Sandia Crest Road and drive about 5 minutes to the **Tinkertown Museum ★**, 121 Sandia Crest Rd. (www.tinkertown.com; ✆ **505/281-5233**). Created by the late folk artist Ross Ward and now run by his family, it is primarily a miniatures museum, featuring an animated mining town and three-ring circus, odd collections of Western Americana, and plenty of silliness. The building's walls are constructed of 50,000 glass bottles. It's open daily from late March through October from 9am to 6pm. Admission costs $3.50 for adults, $3 for seniors 62 and up, $1 for children 4 to 16, and free for kids under 4.

Approximately 10 miles north of the Sandia Park junction on NM, you come to the ghost town of **Golden,** first settled in 1839. Its sagging houses, with their missing boards and the wind whistling through the broken eaves, make it a purist's ghost town. There's a general store widely known for its large selection of well-priced jewelry, and across the street, a bottle seller's "glass garden." Be sure to slow down and look for the village church, a great photo opportunity, on the east side of the road. Nearby are the ruins of a pueblo called **Paako,** abandoned around 1670.

Madrid (pronounced "*Mah*-drid") is about 12 miles north of Golden. This town and neighboring Cerrillos were in a fabled turquoise-mining area dating back to prehistory. Gold and silver mines followed, and when they faltered, there was coal. These towns supplied fuel for the locomotives of the Santa Fe Railroad until the 1950s, when the railroad converted to diesel. Madrid used to produce 100,000 tons of coal a year and was a true "company town," but the mine closed in 1956. Today, Madrid is a funky village of artists and crafts-people seemingly stuck in the 1960s hippie era, with numerous galleries and crafts stores. The best way to see Madrid is to park somewhere along the road and walk up one side and down the other. It's only about a mile long, so it doesn't take too long unless you spend a lot of time in the shops. However, beware: Madrid residents don't believe in leashing or constraining their dogs, so wandering dogs are everywhere. The **Old Coal Mine Museum ★** (© 505/438-3780) invites visitors to explore a mine that operated from 1835 until 1956. There's a 1901 steam locomotive, machinist shop, dusty offices, and other mining memorabilia. It's open daily in summer; admission costs $5 for adults, $3 for seniors and children. Next door, the **Mine Shaft Tavern ★** (www.themineshafttavern.com; © 505/473-0743) offers a variety of burgers, sandwiches, and grilled pizza, mostly in the $10 to $15 range, plus full dinners starting at $18. This lively place has a full bar and frequently has live music. Hours vary, so either call ahead or just stop by to see if the museum and tavern are open.

Cerrillos, about 3 miles north of Madrid, is an enchanting village of dirt roads that sprawls along Galisteo Creek. It appears to have changed very little since it was founded during a lead strike in 1879, although some renovations were underway in 2015. However, the whole place, including the saloon, still looks very much like an Old West movie set. The top attraction here is **Casa Grande Trading Post ★★,** 17 Waldo St. (www.casagrandetradingpost.com; © 505/438-3008), a sprawling shop crammed with jewelry (especially tur-quoise jewelry), New Mexico minerals including locally mined raw turquoise stones, old bottles and glass insulators, and other western memorabilia. This rambling 28-room adobe is also the home of the **Cerrillos Turquoise Mining**

Museum ★, full of tools and other artifacts from the region's mining era, and a **petting zoo ★** with llamas, goats, and chickens. The complex is open daily 9am to 5pm. Admission to the museum costs $2, as does a sack of food for the petting zoo.

Just north of the village of Cerrillos is **Cerrillos Hills State Park ★★,** 37 Main St., southwest of the railroad crossing (nmparks.com; ✆ **505/474-0196**). This day-use park has 5 miles of trails leading past historic mines to scenic overlooks of the Sandia, Ortiz, Jemez, and Sangre de Cristo mountain ranges. Trails are open to hikers, mountain bikers, and horseback riders. The park is open daily during daylight hours and the visitor center is open daily 2 to 4pm. Admission costs $5 per vehicle, payable at the visitor center or at the self-pay station if the center's closed. There's a rack near the door to the visitor center that's usually stocked with trail maps, a list of guided hikes, and other special events in the park, plus a handout with a map of Cerrillos and history of the village.

From Cerrillos it's a scenic 15-mile drive to the intersection of I-25 and Cerrillos Road in Santa Fe.

Bosque del Apache National Wildlife Refuge ★★

About 90 miles south of Albuquerque via I-25, Bosque del Apache—the name is Spanish for "woods of the Apaches," so named by Spanish settlers who saw that Apache Indians frequently camped here—is known as a haven for migratory waterfowl, including sandhill cranes, snow geese, and a variety of ducks. At the northern edge of the Chihuahuan desert, this 57,000-acre preserve's riparian habitat, a mix of marshlands, meadows, agricultural fields, and old-growth cottonwood forests lining the Rio Grande, attracts more than 340 species of birds.

If you're here between November and March, the experience is thrilling, not only because of the variety of birds but also for the sheer numbers of them. Huge clouds of thousands of snow geese and sandhill cranes take flight at dawn and dusk, the air filling with the sounds of their calls and flapping wings. There are also plenty of raptors, including numerous red-tailed hawks and northern harriers (or marsh hawks), Cooper's hawks and kestrels, and even some bald and golden eagles.

Sandhill cranes usually begin to make their annual appearance in late September or early October, with late December and January being the peak time to see these spectacular birds. Other birds are year-round residents, including red-winged blackbirds, Gambel's quail, American coots, western meadowlarks, American kestrels, ring-necked pheasants, and wild turkeys. There are several dozen species of mammals at the refuge. You'll quite likely see coyotes (probably in search of a snow goose dinner), and possibly mule deer and elk.

A good first stop is the **visitor center,** where you can examine the exhibits, pick up a free refuge newspaper, rent binoculars if you neglected to bring your own, check on recent bird and wildlife sightings, and if you're there from late

November through February, sign up for a free guided tour. Tours are Saturdays, Sundays, and some Fridays, and take from 1 to 3 hours.

A 12-mile **self-guided auto tour** loop allows you to explore the refuge (get a map at the visitor center). You will often get closer to the birds and animals by staying in your vehicle, which acts as a blind, but there are some observation decks along the route, and a boardwalk into a marshy area helps you see waterfowl and some mammals up close. There are also about a half-dozen **walking trails,** described in the refuge newspaper, ranging from less than a mile to almost 10 miles. Early and late in the day are usually the best times to see the birds and other wildlife.

The refuge grounds are open daily a half-hour before sunrise to a half-hour after sunset. From September through May the visitor center is open daily 8am to 4pm; from June through August it's open the same hours but closed Tuesdays and Wednesdays. Admission costs $5 per vehicle. For information, see www.fws.gov/refuge/bosque_del_apache or call ☏ 575/835-1828. The refuge is located 18 miles south of Socorro; from Albuquerque, go south on I-25 to exit 139, at the small village of San Antonio, and then follow signs south on US 380 and NM 1 to the refuge.

Because you'll probably want to be in the refuge at sunrise, you may want to find overnight lodging in Socorro, which has a variety of chain motels and a few bed and breakfasts. See **www.visitsocorro.com**.

Acoma Pueblo ★

This "Sky City," a walled adobe village perched high atop a sheer rock mesa 365 feet above the valley floor, is believed to have been inhabited at least since the 11th century—the longest continuously occupied community in North America (native legend claims that it has been inhabited since before the time of Christ). The name "acoma" in local dialect means "the place that always was." To reach Acoma from Albuquerque, drive west on I-40 approximately 52 miles to the Acoma–Sky City exit (exit 102), then travel about 15 miles southwest, following signs.

Visitors aren't allowed to wander around Acoma Pueblo on their own—you can only see the pueblo on 90-minute guided tours ($23 for adults; $20 for college students, military, and seniors 60 and up; $15 for children 6 to 17; and free for children 5 and under). Tours run daily March to November, but only on Saturdays and Sundays the rest of the year. You can bring a still camera ($13 fee) but no video cameras or sound recording equipment, and you're forbidden to take photos of the cemetery or

Home, Home on the Mesa

Officially, the Keresan-speaking Acoma (*Ack*-oo-mah) Pueblo boasts some 6,000 inhabitants, but in fact only a small number still reside year-round on the 70-acre mesa top. The rest come only for ceremonies and other events. The Pueblo is still of vital importance to the tribe, however—not least because the Pueblo people make a fair bit of their living from visitors coming to see their ancient "sky city."

inside the mission church; no cameras are allowed on feast days or during Christmas events. Visitors to the pueblo should not wear what tribal officials consider "revealing clothing."

Start your tour at the **Sky City Cultural Center and Haak'u Museum,** (www.acomaskycity.org; © **800/747-0181**), which gives a good look into the Acoma culture, and peruse the gallery, which showcases pottery, textiles, baskets, and other art from the tribe (as well as offering art and crafts for sale). You can have a meal at the **Yaak'a Café.** Then board the **tour bus,** which climbs through a rock garden of 50-foot sandstone monoliths and past precipitously dangling outhouses to the mesa's summit. There's no running water or electricity in this medieval-looking village; a small reservoir collects rainwater for most purposes, but drinking water has to be transported up from below. Wood-hole ladders and mica windows are prevalent among the 300 or so adobe structures. The most striking feature of the mesa-top village, however, is the **San Esteban del Rey Mission,** an impressively large adobe church with two bell towers, which was built by Franciscan friars in the early 1600s — making it the oldest surviving European church in New Mexico. Inside you'll find many examples of Spanish Colonial art. Both the pueblo and the mission church have been denoted National Historic Landmarks.

As you tour the village, you'll have many opportunities to buy pueblo crafts, especially their distinctive thin-walled white pottery with polychrome designs. Pottery is expensive here, but you're not going to find it any cheaper anywhere else, and you'll be guaranteed that it's authentic if you buy it directly from the craftsperson. Along the way, be sure to sample some Indian fry bread topped with honey.

The annual **San Esteban del Rey feast day** is September 2, when the pueblo's patron saint is honored with an 8am Mass, a procession, a harvest dance, and an arts-and-crafts fair, which includes homemade games of chance and food stalls. A tribal Officers' Feast is held annually in February, and Christmas festivities run from December 24 to 28. Guided tours do not operate on the mesa during feast days. Note that the pueblo is closed to visitors on Easter weekend (some years), June 24 and 29, July 9 to 14, the first or second weekend in October, and the first Saturday in December. It's best to call ahead to make sure the tour is available when you're visiting.

Acoma Pueblo also operates **Sky City Casino Hotel** (I-40 exit 102; www.skycity.com; © **888/759-2489**), open daily 24 hours, with more than 600 slot machines, table games, live bingo, and live music most weekends.

Salinas Pueblo Missions National Monument ★★

This national monument, about 80 miles south-southeast of Albuquerque, consists of three separate sites that preserve the ruins of three large American Indian pueblos, along with some of the best remaining 17th-century Franciscan mission churches in the United States. Each site offers a slightly different perspective on the history of the area, but all three explain the conflict of cultures that occurred between the Pueblo people and the Spanish colonists who arrived in the 1700s. Collectively, these pueblos are now known as **the Salinas**—the Spanish word for salt—which was abundant in the area and an important trade good.

Abó, Gran Quivira (also called Las Humanas), and Quarai were constructed by people of the ancestral Puebloan and Mogollon cultures beginning in the 1300s. The pueblos traded with the Plains tribes to the east and the Rio Grande pueblos to the west and north, and they were thriving communities when Spanish conquistadors first saw them in the late 1500s. One of Spain's goals in exploring the new world was economic—the search for gold and other riches—but converting the local people to Christianity was almost equally important. The Franciscan missionaries were partly successful in their conversion efforts, but along with religion they also brought European diseases, to which the Indians had little immunity.

The Pueblo people practiced a religion in which Kachina dances and other rituals were intended to take the people's prayers to the gods in hopes of ensuring sufficient rain, good harvests and hunting, and overall universal harmony. The missionaries considered the Indians' religion to be idolatry, and tried to prevent the Pueblo people from practicing their Kachina dances and other rituals. At first the Pueblo religious leaders thought they could incorporate this new Christian god into their rituals, but after some of the Franciscans destroyed kivas and Kachina masks, it became obvious that there could be no middle ground. Adding to the animosity of the Pueblo people was that some Spanish colonists were allowed to demand tribute from the Indians, often in the form of grain or cloth.

In the 1660s and 1670s, drought and the resulting famine (along with European diseases) decimated the Pueblo people. The remaining residents abandoned their villages in the 1670s, mostly joining other pueblos. Then in 1680 the pueblos to the north revolted against the Spanish (see "The Great Pueblo Revolt," p. 108), driving them back into Mexico, where they stayed until the reconquest of New Mexico in 1692.

Start your visit at the national monument **visitor center** in the community of Mountainair, on US 60, 1 block west of the intersection of US 60 and NM 55 (corner of Ripley Street and Broadway; www.nps.gov/sapu; ✆ **505/847-2585;** open daily 8am–5pm). The visitor center has exhibits on all three pueblos and the missions, and will give you a self-guided tour pamphlet. Then head out to the individual sites, where you'll find the ruins that can be seen on short, easy paths.

At **Abó** (✆ **505/847-2400;** 9 miles west of the visitor center on US 60 and ½ mile on NM 513), a paved quarter-mile trail leads to the towering walls of San Gregorio de Abó church, and continues for another half-mile among unexcavated ruins, with a number of visible walls, from the Abó Pueblo.

At **Gran Quivira** (✆ **505/847-2770;** 26 miles south of the visitor center on NM 55), a half-mile gravel trail winds among the ruins of two churches—the Mission of San Buenaventura and the Church of San Isidro—plus the excavated and stabilized ruins of the Pueblo de Las Humanas, the largest of the

Salinas pueblos. Also at the Gran Quivira site you can see a video on the excavation of a section of the pueblo.

Quarai (© 505/847-2290; 8 miles north of the visitor center on NM 55 and 1 mile west) has the most impressive mission—the Nuestra Senora de la Purísima Concepción de Cuarac Church—where a half-mile gravel loop trail leads from the contact station/museum into the church and past some partially excavated pueblo ruins. An easy side trip off the main trail takes you onto the 1-mile round-trip Spanish Corral Trail, which follows a hillside to the remains of what historians believe was a pen for sheep used by Hispanic settlers in the 19th century. Also from this trail are views east into the Estancia Valley and its salt lakes, where, since prehistoric times, people mined salt. Of the more than 100 species of **birds** that frequent the three units of Salinas Pueblo Missions National Monument, the most variety, and an especially colorful assortment, are in the riparian area along the Spanish Corral Trail at Quarai. Some species, such as Say's phoebes, nest in the ruins themselves. Watch for mourning doves, cliff swallows, northern mockingbirds, violet green swallows, and red-tailed hawks.

The three pueblos are open daily 9am–6pm (closing at 5pm mid-Sept through mid-May). The visitor center and sites are closed New Year's Day, Thanksgiving, and Christmas.

Jemez Historic Site ★★

Some of the best preserved prehistoric and historic ruins in New Mexico are at **Jemez Historic Site** (18160 NM 4, www.nmhistoricsites.org; © 505/829-3530), where you'll see the ruins of a 500-year old Indian village once occupied by the ancestors of today's Jemez Pueblo people, and the massive San José de los Jemez Church, built in the early 1620s. It's about 60 miles north of Albuquerque; from Albuquerque, take NM 550 (NM 44) to NM 4 and then continue north on NM 4 for about 18 miles to Jemez Springs.

Start at the **museum,** which tells the tale of Giusewa, "place of boiling waters," the original Indian name for the area from the many hot springs found there. Then take the quarter-mile-long **interpretive trail** through the impressive ruins of the pueblo and the mission church, with its massive stone walls built at about the same time the Pilgrims landed at Plymouth Rock. Small plaques along the trail tell the story, juxtaposing the first impressions of the missionaries against the reality of Jemez life. The missionaries saw the Jemez people as barbaric and set out to civilize them—a process which also (conveniently) included forcing them to haul river stones to the site to erect 6-foot-thick walls for their mission. The church was abandoned less than 20 years after it was built, and the Jemez people abandoned their pueblo about 40 years later, during the Pueblo Revolt (see p. 108). Excavations in the early–20th century, however, unearthed this massive complex, which you'll enter through a broad doorway to a room that once held elaborate fresco paintings, with a giant bell tower.

Admission to the site costs $3 for adults and is free for children 16 and under; it's free if you have a New Mexico CulturePass (see p. 197). The site

Historic Culture with a Hint of Honey

The nearby **Jemez Pueblo** does not welcome visitors except on selected days. However, visitors can get a taste of the Jemez culture at the **Walatowa Visitor Center,** on NM 4, 8 miles north of the junction with US 550 (www.jemez pueblo.com; ℂ **575/834-7235**). A museum presents the history of the Jemez people and displays pottery and drums. A gift shop sells works by Jemez artists and other items. While in the area, you may encounter Jemez people sitting under *ramadas* (thatch-roofed lean-tos) and selling home-baked bread, cookies, and pies. If you're lucky, they may also be making fry bread, which you can smother with honey for one of New Mexico's more delectable treats. The visitor center is open daily 8am to 5pm in summer and 10am to 4pm Wednesday to Sunday the rest of the year.

is open Wednesday through Sunday 8:30am–5pm; it's closed New Year's Day, Thanksgiving, and Christmas.

Chaco Culture National Historical Park ★★★

A combination of a stunning setting and well-preserved ruins makes the long drive to **Chaco Culture National Historic Park,** about 150 miles northwest of Albuquerque in the middle of nowhere, worth the trip. A trip to Chaco is a journey to another time and place, to the prehistoric world of a people who dominated the Four Corners area (where the states of New Mexico, Colorado, Arizona, and Utah meet today) more than 1,000 years ago. This remote park offers not just another ruin, but a feeling for the immensity of what we now call the Chacoan culture, a link with a distant past that provides an awe-inspiring look into the very center of a remarkable civilization.

No matter which route you take into this national historic park, often referred to simply as Chaco Canyon, you drive in on a dusty road. But that's only if you're lucky—with a bit of rain the road turns to mud. When you finally arrive, you walk through stark desert country that seems perhaps ill-suited as a center of culture. But centuries ago, the ancestral Puebloans built a complex culture here, the ruins of which remain, a tantalizing glimpse of a mysterious and long-ago past.

Begin at the **visitor center** (www.nps.gov/chcu; ℂ **505/786-7014**), which has background exhibits on the Chacoan culture and construction of this pre-historic city, plus artifacts discovered here during excavations. A video program tells about the ancestral Puebloans. Trail maps are available, ranger programs take place daily, and rangers also lead guided hikes and walks. The visitor center is open daily from 8am to 5pm; closed New Year's Day, Thanksgiving, and Christmas. Trails are open from 7am to sunset.

Una Vida, a short walk from the visitor center, was one of the first of the Chacoan buildings to be constructed and has been only partially excavated. Considered a "great house," it had 150 rooms and 5 kivas, including a Great Kiva. A walking trail leads on from Una Vida to several petroglyph sites; it's

chaco canyon: A WINDOW ON THE PAST

Despite the harsh and unforgiving desert climate, the ancestral Puebloan people successfully farmed these lowlands. Some 1,200 years ago, they launched an ambitious building project here. Instead of simply starting with a few small rooms and adding more as the need arose, as was usual at the time, the Chacoans constructed massive stone buildings of multiple stories. More significant, though, is that these buildings show evidence of skillful planning. Obviously, a central government was in charge. Within a century, six large pre-planned public buildings, or "great houses," were underway. New communities, each consisting of a large central building surrounded by smaller villages, sprang up; and established villages followed the trend by adding large public and ceremonial buildings.

Eventually there were more than 150 such communities, most of them closely tied to Chaco by an extensive system of roads. You can't see them from the ground, but get up in a plane and you can see evidence of hundreds of miles of roads connecting the outlying settlements with the large buildings at Chaco. These communities appear to have been established along the roads at precise intervals, one day's travel apart. Not simply trails worn into the stone by foot travel, these were carefully engineered

roadways 30 feet wide, with a low wall of rock to contain the fill. Where the road went over flat rock, walls were erected along the edges.

By A.D. 1000, Chaco had become the center of commerce, ceremony, and culture for the area, with as many as 5,000 people living in some 400 settlements. Artifacts found at Chaco, including shell necklaces, turquoise, copper bells, and the remains of Mexican parrots, indicate that their trade routes stretched from the California coast to Texas, and south into Mexico.

The decline and abandonment of Chaco in the 12th century coincided with a drought in the area, although archeologists are not certain that this was the only or even the major reason that the site was eventually abandoned. Some argue that an influx of outsiders may have brought new rituals to the region, causing a schism among tribal members. A somewhat controversial theory maintains that cannibalism existed at Chaco, practiced either by the ancestral Puebloans themselves or by invaders, such as the Toltecs of Mexico. Even though archeologists do not agree on why Chaco Canyon was abandoned, they generally concur that the Chacoans' descendants live among today's Pueblo people.

about 1 mile round-trip, returning to the visitor center, with some rocky or steep sections.

A paved **9-mile one-way loop road** winds from the visitor center through Chaco Canyon, providing access to short walking trails that lead into Chaco's major sites (most trails are about half a mile round-trip; a few have some steep sections, but they're otherwise easy walking). Along that road, one must-see for every Chaco visitor is impressive **Pueblo Bonito** (Spanish for Beautiful Town), which is believed to have been the largest structure in the Chacoan system, as well as the largest prehistoric dwelling ever excavated in the Southwest. Covering more than 3 acres, it contains about 800 rooms surrounding two plazas, in which there were over two dozen kivas. Other ruin sites accessible directly from the loop road include **Chetro Ketl,** which had about 500 rooms, 16 kivas, and an impressive enclosed plaza. **Pueblo del Arroyo** was a four-story, D-shaped structure with about 280 rooms and 20 kivas. Another of Chaco's "great houses," **Hungo Pavi** contained about 150 rooms and rose up three stories in places. The largest Great Kiva in the park, **Casa Rinconada,** was astronomically aligned to the four compass points and the summer solstice, which suggests it may have been a center for the community at large, used for major religious observances.

The park also has four longer **backcountry trails,** ranging from 3 to 7 miles, which lead to additional archeological sites. Backcountry permits must be obtained (free) at the visitor center. Wear good hiking boots and take drinking water (the visitor center is the only place in the park where you can buy drinking water). There is a surprising amount of **wildlife** at Chaco, considering its harsh landscape. You are quite likely to see white-tailed antelope squirrels, and also watch for collared lizards, desert cottontails, black-tailed jackrabbits, prairie dogs, gray foxes, deer, coyotes, and even bobcats. Birds seen here include western meadowlarks, mountain chickadees, western bluebirds, white-crowned sparrows, canyon towhees, scaled quail, rock and canyon wrens, and golden eagles. You'll want to avoid the rattlesnakes.

Gallo Campground, inside the park about 1 mile from the visitor center, has 49 campsites (14 for tents only) with picnic tables and fire grates (bring your own wood or charcoal). Central flush toilets are available in warmer weather; in cold weather, only portable toilets are available. Water in the campground is not potable; the visitor center is the only place in the park to obtain drinking water. There are no showers or RV hookups, but there is a dump station. The campground cannot accommodate trailers and motor homes over 35 feet long. Camping costs $15 per night; reservations can be made at least three days in advance at www.recreation.gov; ✆ **877/444-6777.**

To get to Chaco from Albuquerque, take I-25 north to Bernalillo, then US 550 northwest 112 miles. Turn off US 550 onto CR 7900 and follow signs for about 21 miles to the park entrance. This route includes 8 miles of paved road (County Road 7900) and 13 miles of rough dirt road (County Road 7950). Call the park office (✆ **505/786-7014**) to inquire about road conditions. Park admission is $16 per car, truck, or RV, and $12 per motorcycle, for up to seven days (2016); $20 per car, truck, or RV, and $15 per motorcycle, for up to seven days (2017).

The closest motels and restaurants are 1½ hours away in several directions, so unless you camp in the park, you'll be doing some traveling. Along the route from Albuquerque, the quiet little town of **Cuba** on US 550 will be your last chance to get a bed and a meal before arriving at Chaco, 69 miles away. Cuba has several mom-and-pop motels, two bed and breakfasts, several commercial campgrounds, a half-dozen or so restaurants, plus some small grocery stores. See www.cubanm.org or call ✆ **575/289-3808.**

PLANNING YOUR TRIP TO NORTHERN NEW MEXICO

A trip to northern New Mexico may affect your attitude. You may return home and find that your responses to the world are different than they used to be. (That is, if you return at all—you wouldn't be the first person to vacation in northern New Mexico, fall in love with it, and move here!) In fact, in many ways northern New Mexico is not simply a destination, but a state of mind, and it can be very addictive. The pace here is slow and the objectives are less obvious than in most places. As some transplants to the area report, once they've lived here for five years or so, they're not fit to go back to the real world.

Travelers often think that because this is the desert, it should have saguaro cactus and always be warm. Think again. Much of northern New Mexico lies upward of 5,000 feet in elevation, which means that four full seasons act upon the land. So, when you're planning your trip, be sure to take a look at the "When to Go" section below so you will be prepared.

That said, preparation is simple. Even though many people mistake New Mexico for our neighboring country to the south, traveling here is much like going anywhere in the U.S. You can drink the water and eat all the food you care to eat, being mindful of your tolerance for the heat of our chile. The sun at these elevations can also be scorching, so come with a hat, plenty of sunscreen, and sunglasses with good UV protection. In fact, the elements here may present the greatest challenge, so be sure to review "Fast Facts: Health Concerns" (p. 237).

Another point to be aware of is the distance between cities. It's easiest to drive your own vehicle, so you can go where you want when you want. There are few enjoyments as great as driving in the sparkling light through unpretentious farming villages, past ancient ruins, around plazas, and over mountain passes. However, public transportation can be useful in some places, such as downtown Santa Fe, where parking can be a total frustration.

As with any trip, a little preparation is essential. This chapter provides a variety of planning tools, including information on when to go and how to get there.

WHEN TO GO

Forget any preconceptions you may have about the New Mexico "desert." The high desert climate of this part of the world is generally dry, but not always warm. Santa Fe and Taos, at 7,000 feet above sea level, have **midsummer** highs in the 90s (30s Celsius) and lows in the 50s (teens Celsius). This tends to be the busiest time of year in New Mexico, when most cultural activities are in full swing and prices and temperatures rise. You'll want to make hotel reservations well in advance, and avoid areas that have major events, such as fiestas and hot-air balloon rallies, unless you have a great desire to participate in them.

Spring and fall are some of New Mexico's most pleasant seasons, with highs in the 60s (teens Celsius), and lows in the 30s (as low as –1°C). Spring can be quite windy, but the skiing is often still excellent, with sunny days and the season's accumulated deep snow. Fall is a particularly big draw because the aspens turn scenically golden in the mountains.

Winter can be delightful in northern New Mexico, when typical daytime temperatures are in the low 40s (single digits Celsius), and overnight lows are in the teens (–7°C and below). The snowy days here are some of the prettiest you'll ever see, and during a good snow year (more than 300 inches at Taos Ski Valley), skiers can't get in enough slope time. However, during holidays, the ski areas can be jammed.

During all the seasons, temperatures in Albuquerque, at 5,300 feet, often run about 10° warmer than elsewhere in the northern region, and snow often melts by noon.

Average Temperatures (High/Low) & Annual Rainfall (In.)

		JAN	APR	JULY	OCT	RAINFALL
Albuquerque	Temp (°F)	46/21	70/38	92/64	74/45	8.5
	Temp (°C)	8/–6	21/3	33/18	22/7	
Santa Fe	Temp (°F)	47/18	64/33	85/56	67/38	11.4
	Temp (°C)	8/–8	18/1	29/13	19/3	
Taos	Temp (°F)	40/10	64/29	87/50	75/32	12.0
	Temp (°C)	4/–12	18/–2	31/10	24/0	

Northern New Mexico Calendar of Events

A good resource for events is **www.newmexico.org/events.** Here are some favorites.

JANUARY

Winter Wine Festival, Taos and Taos Ski Valley. Wine seminars, wine dinners, wine tastings—quite simply 4 days of everything wine, featuring several local restaurants and more than 40 national wineries. www.taos winterwinefest.com. ℂ **505/438-8060.** Last weekend in January.

APRIL

Gathering of Nations Powwow, University Football Stadium, Albuquerque. North America's largest powwow and American Indian competition in singing and dancing. Plus arts and crafts, native food, and music. www.gatheringofnations.com. ℂ **505/836-2810.** Late April.

JUNE

Taos School of Music, Taos and Taos Ski Valley. This 8-week "school" (see p. 163) has been performing stupendous chamber music for more than 50 years. Thirteen concerts and three seminars take place over the course of the program. www.taosschoolof music.com. ✆ **575/776-2388.** Mid-June to mid-August.

New Mexico Arts and Crafts Fair. A tradition since 1962, this juried show offers work from more than 200 New Mexico artisans and craftspeople. There's lots to see, with demonstrations, a youth art exhibit, and a silent auction. The fair is held at Expo New Mexico at the state fairgrounds in Albuquerque. Admission starts at $7. www.nmartsand craftsfair.org. ✆ **505/884-9043.** Last full weekend in June.

JULY

Taos Pueblo Powwow. Powwow is a gathering of tribal nations in friendship. There's competition in traditional and contemporary dances, plus arts and crafts, and food booths. www.taospueblopowwow.com. ✆ **575/758-1028.** Second weekend in July.

Taos Fiestas de Santiago y Santa Ana. The celebration begins with a Friday-night Mass at Our Lady of Guadalupe Church behind Taos Plaza, where the fiesta queen is crowned. During the weekend, there are candlelight processions, special Masses, music, dancing, parades, crafts, and food booths. Taos Plaza hosts many events; most are free. www.fiestasdetaos.com. ✆ **800/732-8267.** Third weekend in July.

Santa Fe Opera. Seven miles north of Santa Fe. For some 40 years, opera lovers have been coming here to enjoy superb opera in a spectacular setting. Five operas are presented in repertory. www.santafeopera.org. ✆ **800/280-4654.** July and August.

Spanish Market. Santa Fe Plaza. More than 500 traditional and contemporary Hispanic artists from New Mexico and southern Colorado exhibit and sell their work in this lively community event, with demonstrations, traditional Hispanic music, dance, and food.

www.spanishcolonial.org. ✆ **505/982-2226.** Last full weekend in July.

AUGUST

Indian Market. Santa Fe Plaza. The largest and most prestigious intertribal fine art market in the world brings more than 1,000 artisans together to display their baskets and blankets, jewelry, pottery, woodcarvings, rugs, sand paintings, and sculptures. Watch the spectacular costumed tribal dancing and crafts demonstrations. The market is free, but hotels are booked months in advance. Produced by the **Southwestern Association for Indian Arts.** www.swaia.org. ✆ **505/983-5220.** Third weekend in August.

Music from Angel Fire. World-class musicians gather in Angel Fire and nearby communities to perform classical music. See p. 163. www.musicfromangelfire.org. ✆ **888/377-3300.** Mid-August to early September.

SEPTEMBER

Las Fiestas de Santa Fe. An exuberant combination of spirit, history, and general merrymaking, Las Fiestas are billed as the oldest community celebration in the United States. The first fiesta was celebrated in 1712, 20 years after the resettlement of New Mexico by Spanish conquistadors in 1692. Included are Masses, a parade for children and their pets, an historical/hysterical parade, mariachi concerts, dances, food, and arts. **Zozobra** (www.burnzozobra.com), "Old Man Gloom," a 50-foot-tall effigy made of wood, canvas, and paper, is burned at dusk on Thursday. www.santafefiesta.org. ✆ **505/204-1598.** Labor Day weekend.

New Mexico State Fair and Rodeo. One of America's top state fairs, it features a nationally acclaimed rodeo, entertainment by top country artists, livestock shows, arts and crafts, a fun midway carnival, and more. Get advance tickets online or by phone. Expo New Mexico in Albuquerque. www.exponm.com. ✆ **505/222-9700.** Two weeks in early September.

Taos Fall Arts Festival. Highlights include arts and crafts exhibitions and competitions, studio tours, gallery openings, lectures, concerts, dances, and plays. Simultaneous events include the **Taos Trade Fair** at La

Hacienda de los Martinez (www.taoshistoric museums.org), the **Wool Festival** (www.taos woolfestival.org) in Kit Carson Park, and **San Geronimo Day** at Taos Pueblo (www. taospueblo.com). www.taosfallarts.com. Mid-September to the first week in October.

OCTOBER

Albuquerque International Balloon Fiesta. The skies are alive with the colors of balloons at this 9-day festival (see p. 209). Some 600 balloons rise over the city in the largest balloon rally in the world. There are races and contests, mass ascensions at sunrise, "balloon glows" in the evening, balloon rides for those desiring a little lift, and various other special events. Balloon Fiesta Park (at I-25 and Alameda NE) on the north side of Albuquerque. www.balloonfiesta.com. ℂ **505/821-1000**. First full week in October.

Taos Mountain Balloon Rally, Taos. Anywhere from 35 to 50 vibrantly colored balloons soar above the Taos Valley in early morning and at dusk on Saturday for a "balloon glow." There is usually a tethered balloon ride for kids. www.taosballoonrally.com. ℂ **575/758-9210**. Last full weekend in October.

NOVEMBER

Festival of the Cranes. Bosque del Apache National Wildlife Refuge, 77 miles south of Albuquerque via I-25. Migratory birds, especially sandhill cranes, winter here, and this is the time they are arriving. People come from all over the world to see them, and take advantage of the numerous photography, art, and ecology workshops. www.friends ofthebosque.org. ℂ **575/835-1828**. Mid-November.

GETTING THERE & AROUND
Getting to Northern New Mexico
BY PLANE

The gateway to Santa Fe, Taos, Albuquerque, and other northern New Mexico communities is the **Albuquerque International Sunport** (ABQ; www.cabq. gov/airport; ℂ **505/244-7700** for the administrative offices). For airlines that fly into Albuquerque, see "Fast Facts: Airline Websites" (p. 236).

Santa Fe is only about 58 miles northeast of Albuquerque via I-25, so many visitors to Santa Fe fly into Albuquerque. Though it's a bit more costly, visitors can also fly into the **Santa Fe Municipal Airport** (SAF; www.santafenm. gov/airport; ℂ **505/955-2903**), where there is non-stop service from Dallas/ Fort Worth and seasonally from Los Angeles with **American Airlines,** and non-stop service from Denver with **United Airlines.**

Once you land at the airport you'll need to either rent a car (see p. 233) or use a shuttle service to get anywhere. Many Albuquerque hotels have courtesy vans to meet their guests and take them to their respective destinations. In addition, **Sunport Shuttle** (www.sunportshuttle.com; ℂ **505/883-4966**) in Albuquerque runs vans to and from city hotels. Limousine service is available from **American Limousine** (ℂ **505/877-7576**) and **Carey Southwest Limousine** (ℂ **505/766-5466**).

If you're heading directly to Santa Fe, you can take a shuttle from the Albuquerque airport, at a cost of about $25 to $30 one-way. Book a ride on the **Sandia Shuttle Express** (www.sandiashuttle.com; ℂ **888/775-5696** or 505/474-5696), which makes the 70-minute run between the Albuquerque airport and various Santa Fe hotels 10 times daily each way (from Albuquerque to Santa Fe, 8:45am–10:45pm; from Santa Fe to Albuquerque, 5am–7pm). Reservations are required, ideally 48 hours in advance. It's also possible to get to Santa Fe on the **New Mexico Rail Runner Express** train (www.nmrail runner.com; © **866/795-7245** or 505/245-7245), with connecting buses from the Albuquerque airport to the train.

If you fly into the Santa Fe airport, **RoadRunner Shuttle & Charter** (www. roadrunnershuttleandcharter.com; © **505/424-3367**) will meet your flight and take you where you want to go.

Taos Ski Valley (www.skitaos.org; © **575/776-2291**) also offers year-round shuttle service linking the ski area to the Santa Fe ($50 one-way) and Albuquerque ($67 one-way) airports, with a stop in the town of Taos as well.

BY CAR

Albuquerque is at the crossroads of two major interstate highways. I-40 runs from Wilmington, North Carolina (1,870 miles east), to Barstow, California (580 miles west). I-25 extends from Buffalo, Wyoming (850 miles north), to El Paso, Texas (265 miles south), skimming past Santa Fe's southern city limits. To reach Taos, you have to leave I-25 at Santa Fe and travel north 74 miles via U.S. 84/285 and N.M. 68; or exit I-25 9 miles south of Raton and proceed 100 miles west on US 64.

BY TRAIN

Amtrak (www.amtrak.com; © **800/872-7245**) passes through northern New Mexico. The *Southwest Chief,* which runs between Chicago and Los Angeles, stops once eastbound and once westbound in Gallup, Albuquerque, Lamy (for Santa Fe), Las Vegas, and Raton. The Albuquerque train station is in the center of downtown, with easy access to hotels. A spur runs on a limited schedule from Lamy, approximately 20 miles to downtown Santa Fe, within walking distance to the plaza. A photo ID is required to ride Amtrak trains. Amtrak offers a **USA Rail Pass,** good for 15, 30, or 45 days of travel (each with a limited number of segments, or stops). Reservations are necessary and should be made as early as possible.

Northern New Mexico also has local rail transport with the **New Mexico Rail Runner Express** (www.nmrailrunner.com; © **866/795-7245** or 505/245-7245). Trains run daily from various points in Albuquerque to various ones in Santa Fe, with connecting buses to the Albuquerque International Sunport and to Taos.

BY BUS

Greyhound (www.greyhound.com; © **800/231-2222**) is the sole nationwide bus line, with a **depot** in Albuquerque at 100 1st St. SW. Its buses no longer run to Santa Fe or to Taos.

Getting Around
BY CAR

The most convenient, and scenic, way to get around northern New Mexico is by private vehicle. Auto and RV rentals are widely available for those who arrive without their own transportation, either at the Albuquerque airport or at locations around each city. International visitors should note that insurance and taxes are almost never included in quoted rental-car rates in the U.S. Be sure to ask your rental agency about additional fees for these. They can add a significant cost to your car rental.

Drivers who need wheelchair-accessible transportation should call **Wheelchair Getaways of New Mexico,** 1015 Tramway Lane NE, Albuquerque (www.wheelchairgetaways.com; ℭ **800/408-2626** or 505/247-2626); the company rents vans by the day, week, or month.

If you're visiting from abroad and plan to rent a car in the United States, keep in mind that although foreign driver's licenses are usually recognized in the U.S., you may want to consider obtaining an international driver's license. Check with the agency that issues your local driver's license for the proper procedure and the required documents for driving outside your home country.

Note that American Indian reservations enjoy a measure of self-rule, and therefore they can legally enforce certain designated laws. For instance, on the Navajo reservation, it is forbidden to transport alcoholic beverages or leave established roadways. If you are caught breaking reservation laws, you are subject to reservation punishment—often stiff fines and, in some instances, detainment.

BY TRAIN

New Mexico Rail Runner Express (www.nmrailrunner.com; ℭ **866/795-7245**) runs daily from various points in Albuquerque to various ones in Santa Fe, with connecting buses to the Albuquerque International Sunport and to Taos. **Amtrak** (www.amtrak.com; ℭ **800/872-7245**) also provides limited service between Gallup, Albuquerque, Lamy (for Santa Fe), Las Vegas, and Raton, with a spur train from the Lamy station into downtown Santa Fe.

BY BUS & SHUTTLE

Although Greyhound maintains a station in Albuquerque (see above), it no longer runs between northern New Mexico cities. There is no regularly scheduled shuttle service between central Albuquerque and Santa Fe, but see connections from the Albuquerque International Sunport (p. 232). Shuttle service between Albuquerque and Taos runs $50 to $60 one-way from **Twin Hearts Express & Transportation** (www.ridetwinheartsexpress.com; ℭ **800/654-9456** or 575/751-1201).

SPECIAL-INTEREST & ESCORTED TRIPS

Academic & Cultural Trips

Those who like a scholarly bent to their vacations can hook up with **Southwest Seminars** (www.southwestseminars.org; ℭ **505/466-2775**) and their "Travels with a Scholar" program. This Santa Fe organization offers tours around the

Southwest, led by museum directors, historians, geologists, archaeologists, anthropologists, and authors. These tours are often to sites that are not open to the general public, such as archaeological sites, petroglyph panels, volcanic calderas, contemporary Indian pueblos, and native artists' homes and studios. *Note:* Mondays at 6pm, lectures are given by regional scholars on a variety of topics.

Bike Tours

Bicycle Adventures (www.bicycleadventures.com; © **800/443-6060** or 425/250-5540) offers tours to northern New Mexico. Riders get to experience some of the region's loveliest routes, such as the High Road to Taos and the Enchanted Circle. Participants visit major sights, such as Santa Fe's Canyon Road and Taos Pueblo, and can even opt for a river trip. In business for over two decades, this company knows how to put together a good tour.

Food Trips

Learn to cook meals in the spicy New Mexico tradition at the **Jane Butel Cooking School** (www.janebutelcooking.com; © **800/473-8226** or 505/243-2622; see p. 204). There are weeklong and weekend packages with a hotel stay and full-participation classes. Classes are generally held in noted chef and television personality Jane Butel's home kitchen in Corrales, a village along the Rio Grande on the edge of Albuquerque.

Outdoor Adventures

If you're looking for an active adventure with some relaxation thrown in, one excellent operator is **Santa Fe Mountain Adventures** (www.santafemountain adventures.com; © **800/965-4010** or 505/988-4000; see p. 91), which combines outdoor adventures, such as hiking and river running, with cultural activities, such as visits to pueblos or museums, with more relaxing ones, such as spa treatments and meditation practices. The business is eco-conscious.

Photography & Art Trips

Some of the world's most outstanding photographers convene in Santa Fe at various times during the year for the **Santa Fe Workshops,** at a delightful campus in the hills on the east side of town (www.santafeworkshops.com; © **505/983-1400**). Most courses last a week. Food and lodging packages are available.

If you'd like to pursue an artistic adventure, check out the weeklong classes in such media as painting, Native American pottery making, and weaving offered by **Taos Art School** (www.taosartschool.org; © **505/758-0350;** see p. 149). Open since 1989, the school is a virtual campus in which classes go where they need to be. For instance, a painting class on Georgia O'Keeffe is held in Abiquiu and a Pueblo pottery class at Taos Pueblo. Classes are limited to 12 people; fees vary from class to class and include lodging and meals.

[FastFACTS] NORTHERN NEW MEXICO

Airline Websites The airlines currently servicing Albuquerque are **Alaska Airlines** (www.alaskaair.com), **American Airlines** (www.aa.com), **Delta Air Lines** (www.delta.com), **Jet-Blue Airways** (www.jetblue.com), **Southwest Airlines** (www.southwest.com), and **United Airlines** (www.united.com).

Area Codes The telephone area code for the Albuquerque and Santa Fe areas is **505.** Taos' area code is **575.**

ATM Networks As in most U.S. destinations, you'll find Automatic Teller Machines practically everywhere in the cities of northern New Mexico. However, in the small mountain towns, they may be more difficult to locate. Usually someone in a store or other business can direct you. ATMs are linked to a network that most likely includes your bank at home. **Cirrus** (www.mastercard.com; ✆ **800/424-7787**) and **PLUS** (www.visa.com; ✆ **800/843-7587**) are the two most popular networks in the United States and in this region.

Business Hours
Offices and general merchandise and grocery **stores** are usually open Monday to Friday 9am to 5pm, with larger stores also open Friday night, Saturday, and Sunday. However, in tourist areas such as Santa Fe and Taos, many art galleries and

gift shops open at 10am. Most **banks** are open Monday to Friday 9am to 5pm, and sometimes until 6pm Friday. Some may also be open Saturday morning. Most branches have ATMs available 24 hours.

Disabled Travelers
Throughout New Mexico, measures have been taken to provide access for travelers with disabilities. Hotels will often have several rooms that comply with the Americans with Disabilities Act (ADA), and many bed-and-breakfasts have made one or more of their rooms completely wheelchair accessible. Most restaurants have at least two marked accessible parking spaces. Some historic properties, however, including museums and historic sites, may not be able to accommodate those with disabilities, so if this is an issue for you, we suggest you call the site before visiting to check on its accessibility.

Doctors See "Fast Facts" in each city's "Essentials" section for information on the nearest urgent care facility and other medical contacts.

Drinking Laws The legal age for purchase and consumption of alcoholic beverages is 21; proof of age is required and often requested at bars, nightclubs, restaurants, and retail outlets, so it's always a

good idea to bring ID when you go out.

Bars may remain open until 2am Monday to Saturday and until midnight on Sunday. Wine, beer, and spirits are sold at licensed supermarkets and liquor stores, but there are no package sales on election days until after 7pm and on Sundays before noon. It is illegal to transport liquor through most American Indian reservations.

It is illegal to carry open containers of alcohol in your car or in any public area that isn't zoned for alcohol consumption.

Driving Laws Unless otherwise posted, the speed limit on interstate highways in New Mexico is 75 mph; on most other two-lane open roads it's 50 to 65 mph. The minimum age for drivers is 16. Seat belts or approved child restraint seats are required for all drivers and passengers. Motorcyclists under 18 must wear helmets.

Electricity Like Canada, the United States uses 110 to 120 volts AC (60 cycles), compared to 220 to 240 volts AC (50 cycles) in most of Europe, Australia, and New Zealand. Downward converters that change 220 to 240 volts to 110 to 120 volts are difficult to find in the United States, so bring one with you.

Embassies & Consulates All embassies are in

the nation's capital, Washington, D.C. Some consulates are in major U.S. cities, and most nations have a mission to the United Nations in New York City. If your country isn't listed below, check **www. embassy.org/embassies.**

The embassy of **Australia** is at 1601 Massachusetts Ave. NW, Washington, DC 20036 (www.usa.embassy. gov.au; ✆ **202/797-3000**). Consulates are in Honolulu, Houston, Los Angeles, New York, and San Francisco.

The embassy of **Canada** is at 501 Pennsylvania Ave. NW, Washington, DC 20001 (www.canadianembassy.org; ✆ **202/682-1740**). Other Canadian consulates are in Buffalo (New York), Detroit, Los Angeles, New York, and Seattle.

The embassy of **Ireland** is at 2234 Massachusetts Ave. NW, Washington, DC 20008 (www.embassyofireland.org; ✆ **202/462-3939**). Irish consulates are in Boston, Chicago, New York, San Francisco, and other cities. See the website for a complete listing.

The embassy of **New Zealand** is at 37 Observatory Circle NW, Washington, DC 20008 (www.nzembassy. com; (✆ **202/328-4800**). New Zealand consulates are in Los Angeles, Salt Lake City, San Francisco, and Seattle.

The embassy of the **United Kingdom** is at 3100 Massachusetts Ave. NW, Washington, DC 20008 (www.ukinusa.fco.gov.uk; ✆ **202/588-6500**). Other British consulates are in Atlanta, Boston, Chicago, Cleveland, Houston, Los Angeles, New York, San Francisco, and Seattle.

Emergencies In case of emergency, dial ✆ **911.**

Family Travel You may find family travel in northern New Mexico a bit different from what you're accustomed to. The state doesn't have huge Disney-like attractions, but it does have colossal mountains, vast mesas, an immensely deep gorge, and several-hundred-year-old Indian dwellings, to name just some of the outdoor attractions. Then there are the cultural offerings: history and art, museums and craft shows, musical performances ranging from classical to rock, opera to bluegrass, and everything in between.

Many of the hotels and resorts listed in this book have inviting pools to laze around in or on-site activities planned especially for kids. Wherever you wander, northern New Mexico will definitely give your children a new perspective on the United States by exposing them to ancient ruins, southwestern cuisine, and Hispanic and American Indian cultures that they may not experience elsewhere.

The Santa Fe quarterly *Tumbleweeds* (www.sftumbleweeds.com; ✆ **505/984-3171**) offers useful articles on family-oriented subjects in the Santa Fe area, as well as a quarterly day-by-day calendar of family events and a seasonal directory of children's classes, camps, and programs. It's available free in locations all over Santa Fe.

Health Concerns One thing that sets New Mexico apart from most other states is its elevation. Santa Fe and Taos are about 7,000 feet above sea level; Albuquerque is more than 5,000 feet above sea level. The reduced oxygen and low humidity can yield some unique problems, and the desert environment can also present some challenges. Those with heart or respiratory problems should consult their doctors before planning a trip to higher elevations. If you're in generally good health, you don't need to take any special precautions, but it's advisable to ease into high elevations by changing altitude gradually. Stay in Albuquerque for a few days before venturing to Santa Fe and Taos. Also, get plenty of rest, avoid large meals, and drink plenty of nonalcoholic fluids, especially water.

One of the most common ailments in northern New Mexico, especially in the mountains above Santa Fe and Taos, is **acute mountain sickness,** the mildest and most common form of high altitude sickness. Rather similar to a hangover, it causes headache, nausea, and fatigue, and can usually be treated by taking aspirin, resting, and drinking lots of water. However, if the condition persists or worsens, it could be serious. You should see a doctor—there are urgent care centers in

Santa Fe, Taos, and Albuquerque—and you will most likely be told to go to a lower altitude.

Other dangers of higher elevations include hypothermia and sun exposure, and these should be taken seriously. To avoid dehydration, drink water as often as possible.

Limit your exposure to the sun, especially between 11am and 2pm. Liberally apply sunscreen with a high protection factor, and wear a wide-brimmed hat and sunglasses with good UV protection.

Holidays Banks, government offices, post offices, and many stores, restaurants, and some museums are closed on the following legal national holidays: January 1 (New Year's Day), the third Monday in January (Martin Luther King, Jr., Day), the third Monday in February (Presidents' Day), the last Monday in May (Memorial Day), July 4 (Independence Day), the first Monday in September (Labor Day), the second Monday in October (Columbus Day), November 11 (Veterans' Day/Armistice Day), the fourth Thursday in November (Thanksgiving Day), and December 25 (Christmas). The Tuesday after the first Monday in November is often Election Day, a federal government holiday in presidential-election years (held every 4 years, and next in 2016).

Insurance Because of the high cost of travel, travel insurance is always a good idea. If you find that option costly, consider that in this region it is unlikely that your trip will be canceled because of major weather problems or other factors, so you may consider travel insurance unnecessary. For information on traveler's insurance, trip cancellation insurance, and medical insurance while traveling, please visit www.frommers.com/tips.

Internet Access/Wi-Fi Wi-Fi and traditional Internet access are widely available in the cities in the region. Most hotels and commercial campgrounds now offer free Wi-Fi, as do all the municipal libraries, and all cities in the region have cafes with wireless access.

Legal Aid If you are pulled over for a minor traffic infraction (such as speeding), never attempt to pay the fine directly to a police officer; this could be construed as attempted bribery, a much more serious crime. Pay fines by mail, or directly into the hands of the clerk of the court. If accused of a more serious offense, say and do nothing before consulting a lawyer. Here the burden is on the state to prove a person's guilt beyond a reasonable doubt, and everyone has the right to remain silent, whether he or she is suspected of a crime or actually arrested. Once arrested, a person can make one telephone call to a party of his or her choice. The international visitor should call his or her embassy or consulate (see above).

LGBT Travel New Mexico is a pretty gay-friendly place in general—only occasionally might someone look askance. The state's best resource for gay, lesbian, bisexual, and transgender visitors is **Pride Guide New Mexico** (www.gogaynewmexico.com). The guide and website offer information about LGBT-friendly areas and community information, and will be an aid in planning your visit.

Mail At press time, domestic postage rates were 49¢ for a letter and 35¢ for a standard-size postcard. For international mail, a first-class letter of up to 1 ounce costs $1.20. See "Fast Facts" in each city's "Essentials" section for post office locations, or go to **www.usps.com** or call ℂ **800/275-8777.** If you aren't sure what your address will be in the United States, mail can be sent to you, in your name, c/o General Delivery at the main post office of the city or region where you expect to be. The addressee must pick up mail in person and must produce proof of identity (driver's license, passport, etc.).

Mobile Phones Cellphones from practically all major networks will work fine in Santa Fe, Taos, and Albuquerque, and along most sections of I-25 and I-40, but service is spotty in rural areas. As of this writing there is no statewide ban on using handheld phones while driving, but there are local laws prohibiting it in Albuquerque, Santa Fe, Las

Cruces, Gallup, Taos, and Española. There is a statewide ban on typing on handheld mobile devices and the use of websites while driving.

Road Conditions For statewide road and driving conditions, call the state **Road Advisory Hotline** at **511** or 800/432-4269, or see www.nmroads.com.

Safety Although the frequently visited tourist areas are generally safe, northern New Mexico is not on the whole a safe place to be. Santa Fe, Albuquerque, and Taos all have higher crime rates than the rest of the state and considerably higher than the national average. When walking city streets, guard your purse carefully; there are many bag-grab thefts, particularly during the summer tourist months. Also, be as aware of your surroundings as you would in any other cities.

Senior Travel Publications offering travel resources and discounts for seniors include the Albuquerque-based monthly tabloid *Prime Time* (www.ptpubco.com; ⓒ **505/ 880-0470**), by North American Mature Publishers Association (www.mature publisher.com), offering a variety of articles aimed at those 50 years and older.

Smoking Smoking in indoor public places, including restaurants and nightclubs, is illegal in New Mexico. Some hotels offer a limited number of rooms that allow smoking, though

the number of these is dwindling.

Taxes The United States has no value-added tax (VAT) or other indirect tax at the national level. Every state, county, and city may levy its own local tax on all purchases, including hotel and restaurant checks and airline tickets. These taxes will not appear on price tags. In Albuquerque the sales tax on goods and services is 7.185%, in Santa Fe 8.3125%, and in Taos 7.125%. But outside city limits it changes, and it is subject to change frequently. Lodging tax totals about 15% in all three cities.

Time New Mexico is on **Mountain Standard Time,** 1 hour ahead of the West Coast and 2 hours behind the East Coast. When it's 10am in Santa Fe, it's noon in New York, 11am in Chicago, and 9am in San Francisco.

Daylight Saving Time (summer time) is in effect from 1am on the second Sunday in March to 1am on the first Sunday in November, except in most of Arizona, Hawaii, the U.S. Virgin Islands, and Puerto Rico. One exception is that the Navajo Nation, which is partly in Arizona, does recognize Daylight Saving Time. Daylight Saving Time moves the clock 1 hour ahead of standard time.

Tipping In hotels, tip **bellhops** at least $1 per bag ($2 to $3 if you have a lot of luggage) and tip the **chamber staff** $1 to $2 per day (more if you've left a big mess for him or her to

clean up). Tip the **doorman** or **concierge** only if he or she has provided you with some specific service (for example, calling a cab for you or obtaining difficult-to-get theater tickets). Tip the **valet-parking attendant** $1 every time you get your car. In restaurants, bars, and nightclubs, tip **service staff** and **bartenders** 15% to 20% of the check, and tip **checkroom attendants** $1 per garment. As for other service personnel, tip **cab drivers** 15% of the fare, tip **skycaps** at airports at least $1 per bag ($2 to $3 if you have a lot of luggage), and tip **hairdressers** and **barbers** 15% to 20%.

Visitor Information Numerous agencies can assist you with planning your trip. The best place to start is the state website at **www.newmexico.org** or call the office at ⓒ **505/ 827-7336.** Santa Fe, Taos, and Albuquerque each have their own information services for visitors (see the "Orientation" sections in chapters 4, 6, and 8, respectively).

Weather Northern New Mexico's weather is fickle. You don't like the clouds? Wait a few minutes and they'll be gone. Or maybe it will start hailing (even in summer) and the temperature will plummet. So make sure to take jackets, sweaters, and hats when going out on hikes, and keep them handy in your vehicle while driving. For weather reports, see www.weather. gov, www.weather.com, or www.wunderground.com.

Index

See also Accommodations and Restaurant indexes, below.

General Index

Restaurants